The Architecture Handbook for Milvus Vector Database

Design and implement high-performance vector search systems with Milvus

Yudong Cai
Jeremy Zhu
Xuan Yang
Bang Fu

<packt>

The Architecture Handbook for Milvus Vector Database

This book was written by Yudong Cai, Xuan Yang, Jeremy Zhu, and Bang Fu. Generative AI tools were used only to assist with ideation, phrasing, and diagram drafts, and all technical content and code were created, verified, and tested by the author and Packt's editorial team. Packt does not accept AI-generated content that replaces expert authorship.

Portfolio Director: Gebin George
Relationship Lead: Gebin George/Sonia Chauhan
Project Manager: Prajakta Naik
Content Engineer: Aditi Chatterjee
Technical Editor: Rahul Limbachiya
Indexer: Manju Arasan
Proofreader: Aditi Chatterjee
Production Designer: Ponraj Dhandapani
Growth Lead: Nimisha Dua

First published: March 2026
Production reference: 1270326

Published by Packt Publishing Ltd.
Grosvenor House
11 St Paul's Square
Birmingham
B3 1RB, UK.

ISBN 978-1-83588-170-5
`www.packtpub.com`

I would like to dedicate this book to my wife, Chai Lei, and my daughter, Cai Chaifei, who are the most important people in my life. They have brought me endless joy and strength, and without their support, this book would not have been possible.

I also wish to dedicate this work to Starlord Xie, CEO of Zilliz, who gave me the opportunity to join Zilliz and collaborate with the team to build the remarkable Milvus project.

– Cai Yudong

I would like to dedicate this book to my husband, Tailang Li, whose unwavering support and encouragement made this journey possible. His patience and belief in me gave me the strength to see this work through to completion.

– Xuan Yang

Contributors

About the authors

Yudong Cai is a senior software engineer with over 20 years of experience in large-scale system development. As one of the founding members of the Milvus project, he helped build Milvus from the ground up and has been involved in the development and iteration of every version since its initial open-source release. His key contributions include delivering the first production-grade Range Search implementation, as well as the refactoring of the entire Milvus configuration system, alongside the design and implementation of numerous other critical features. He is also the original developer and key maintainer of Knowhere, Milvus' core vector computation engine, where he designed its architecture to support multiple hardware acceleration frameworks and a wide range of vector search algorithms.

Jeremy Zhu is a quality assurance engineer at Zilliz, focused on ensuring the robustness and high performance of the Milvus vector database. His core responsibilities include designing comprehensive test cases, developing automated system test pipelines for diverse scenarios, and executing rigorous stress, recovery, and performance testing. Jeremy possesses deep expertise in chaos engineering, distributed systems testing, and test automation frameworks, playing a key role in maintaining Milvus' high-quality standards.

Xuan Yang is a senior software engineer at Zilliz in China, passionate about designing high-performance, scalable distributed database systems. As a core Milvus contributor, she architected the DataNode module, implemented the compaction process, and led the L0 segment design. She is the primary maintainer of PyMilvus, the official Python SDK, and VectorDBBench, an open-source benchmarking framework for vector databases. She cares deeply about system stability and performance and is always eager to collaborate with the community to push the boundaries of large-scale AI and vector data infrastructure.

Bang Fu is a senior software engineer at Zilliz. With extensive experience in both Go and Python, he has actively contributed to the development of several key features for Milvus, including permission verification, request interception, incremental synchronization, and serverless metering functionalities. He is also interested in AI technology and led the development of the GPTCache project, which focuses on caching LLM responses to improve speed and reduce costs. In addition, he has participated in the development of the DeepSearcher project.

About the reviewers

Anwar Hermuche is a senior AI engineer and founder of DascIA, with six years of experience in Data and AI solutions. He is dedicated to the mission of democratizing AI education, believing in technology as a robust, ethical, and accessible production infrastructure to transform the global ecosystem.

Andrew Zhu is a software engineer and AI enthusiast with deep expertise in vector databases, machine learning systems, and distributed computing. With over a decade of experience in technology development, Andrew brings practical insights from both industry applications and research implementations.

Currently based in the Seattle area, Andrew works extensively with modern AI infrastructure, including Milvus for scalable similarity search. His background includes hands-on experience building **retrieval-augmented generation** (**RAG**) systems, implementing **approximate nearest neighbor** (**ANN**) algorithms, and optimizing vector database performance at scale. When he's not working with vector databases, Andrew contributes to open-source projects, experiments with LLM applications, and helps mentor others entering the AI engineering field.

Priyanka Mohekar is an AI engineer specializing in generative AI, RAG, and data engineering. She builds scalable, enterprise-grade AI systems using LLMs, agentic frameworks, and modern data platforms. With experience in designing end-to-end data pipelines and intelligent automation solutions, she is passionate about solving real-world problems through AI. Priyanka also actively shares her knowledge through mentoring and content creation, aiming to make advanced AI concepts more accessible and impactful.

Hitesh Chaudhari is an AI/ML engineer specializing in generative AI, large-scale vector search, and distributed AI systems. He has deep expertise in Milvus, including cluster deployment, indexing strategies, and performance optimization for high-scale RAG pipelines. His work spans multi-agent LLM systems, hybrid search, embeddings, and production-grade AI architectures. He focuses on building scalable, low-latency, and fault-tolerant AI systems and provides enterprise AI consulting to design and deploy cutting-edge AI platforms.

Subscribe for a free eBook

New frameworks, evolving architectures, research drops, production breakdowns—*AI_Distilled* filters the noise into a weekly briefing for engineers and researchers working hands-on with LLMs and GenAI systems. Subscribe now and receive a free eBook, along with weekly insights that help you stay focused and informed.

Subscribe at `https://packt.link/8Oz6Y` or scan the QR code below.

Table of Contents

Part 3: Vector Computing Engine, Indexing, and Advanced Query Mechanisms

Chapter 13: Stability and Reliability Evaluation for the Milvus Vector Database 283

Chapter 14: Scalability Evaluation for the Milvus Vector Database 317

Chapter 15: Getting Started with Milvus Performance Tuning 349

Chapter 16: Implementing Multi-Tenancy in Milvus 393

Chapter 17: How Milvus Works in AI 419

Preface

The rapid deployment of **large language model** (**LLM**) technologies has made the storage, retrieval, and management of unstructured data a core pain point for AI applications, as traditional databases struggle to adapt to the processing demands of massive high-dimensional vectors. As a benchmark open-source vector database, Milvus has earned high recognition from the global tech community for its exceptional scalability and stability, with in-depth collaboration from industry giants including Apple and Nvidia. It has firmly established itself as the preferred foundation for building large-scale AI engineering systems. Written by the core contributors of the Milvus project, this handbook shares the essence of its underlying design and engineering best practices without reservation, guiding you to fully master the processing of large-scale high-dimensional vector data.

This book follows a scientific progression: ***Fundamentals*** → ***Hands-on practice*** → ***Core principles*** → ***Performance tuning*** → ***Real-world deployment***, systematically unpacking Milvus' full technology stack. It opens with detailed explanations of Milvus basic concepts, multi-mode deployment, and interactive operations to help beginners get started quickly. The middle chapters dive into core principles such as the data model, layered architecture, data read/write workflows, the Knowhere vector engine, and index selection, while uncovering the underlying logic of background compaction, garbage collection, and complex search processing. Later chapters focus on critical production-grade capabilities, including system configuration, log monitoring, stability and reliability evaluation, scalability testing, performance tuning, and multi-tenancy isolation, with hands-on verification using dedicated testing tools. The book also details Milvus' integration with frameworks like LangChain, covering mainstream AI scenarios such as **retrieval-augmented generation** (**RAG**) and image retrieval. Finally, it distills engineering experience through real-world cases to comprehensively enhance your vector database practical skills.

After finishing this book, you will not only thoroughly understand Milvus' internal operating mechanisms and proficiently handle system operation, performance optimization, and troubleshooting, but also seamlessly integrate it into AI engineering systems. You will be able to build stable, efficient, and scalable vector search applications to confidently tackle challenges across various enterprise-level scenarios.

Who this book is for

This book is designed for developers and engineers who want to systematically master Milvus and vector database technologies. It is especially suitable for database engineers, backend developers, AI infrastructure engineers, system architects, DevOps, and **Site Reliability Engineering** (**SREs**), as well as engineers building vector search and RAG systems.

Readers should have basic knowledge of database concepts and proficiency in at least one programming language (Python, C++, or Go). Familiarity with distributed systems, Docker, and Kubernetes will help you learn more efficiently. Whether you are new to vector databases or an experienced engineer looking to dive into Milvus internals and performance tuning, this book provides practical and in-depth guidance.

What this book covers

Chapter 1, Introduction to Milvus, introduces vector databases and Milvus, explaining the limitations of traditional databases for unstructured data and Milvus' core value. It uses practical cases to build foundational knowledge of vector search and Milvus' key advantages.

Chapter 2, Deploying Milvus in Multiple Ways, covers common Milvus deployment methods (Docker, Docker Compose, Kubernetes Operator, Helm Chart), comparing their pros and suitable scenarios, with hands-on guides for each approach.

Chapter 3, Interacting with Milvus, walks through Milvus core concepts (collections, schemas, fields, indexes) and basic workflows, demonstrating interactions via Python SDK and lightweight REST APIs.

Chapter 4, Configuring the Milvus System, delves into Milvus dependency services, startup configurations, core system settings, and log monitoring for operational stability and performance tuning.

Chapter 5, Understanding the Milvus Data Model and Architecture, explores Milvus' scalable design, including its data model, layered architecture, and the message queue that underpins streaming data processing.

Chapter 6, Data Modification and Maintenance in Milvus, focuses on the data write path, explaining the segment as the core data unit, its lifecycle, and the full journey of DML requests (insert/delete/upsert) inside Milvus.

Chapter 7, Reading Data in Milvus, explains Milvus' read-write separation architecture, detailing the Scatter-Gather query pattern, data loading, load balancing, and how deletions are handled to ensure consistency.

Chapter 8, Compaction and Garbage Collection, introduces compaction and garbage collection (GC), which are the two critical background processes that clean fragmented data, free storage, and maintain Milvus' long-term performance.

Chapter 9, Exploring Milvus' Vector Engine, dives into Knowhere, Milvus' core vector engine, covering its architecture, core functionalities, and unique advantages in high-dimensional vector search.

Chapter 10, How to Select a Vector Index, reveals the general principles of vector indexing, guiding readers to choose appropriate index types and parameters to balance query efficiency, accuracy, and performance.

Chapter 11, Handling Complicated Search Requests, explores advanced search processing in Milvus, including attribute filtering, soft deletion via BITSET, and SIMD acceleration for distance calculation.

Chapter 12, Getting Started with Milvus Performance Benchmarking, teaches how to measure Milvus performance using metrics and tools like VectorDBBench, identifying key factors that impact search speed and throughput.

Chapter 13, Stability and Reliability Evaluation for the Milvus Vector Database, provides a practical guide to Milvus reliability testing, including Kubernetes-based environment setup, load testing, and failure simulation with recovery verification.

Chapter 14, Scalability Evaluation for the Milvus Vector Database, covers Milvus' vertical and horizontal scaling strategies, with hands-on labs to demonstrate scaling a Milvus cluster on Kubernetes for growing data and workloads.

Chapter 15, Getting Started with Milvus Performance Tuning, explores practical optimization techniques to balance search speed, ingestion throughput, and load capacity, which are the three pillars of vector database performance.

Chapter 16, Implementing Multi-Tenancy in Milvus, compares four multi-tenancy strategies (database-level, collection-level, partition-based, resource groups) and provides a decision framework for choosing the right isolation approach.

Chapter 17, How Milvus Works in AI, illustrates Milvus' role in AI applications, especially RAG, and extends to use cases like autonomous driving, biomedicine, and financial risk control.

Appendix explains **K-nearest neighbors search** (**KNNS**) and **approximate nearest neighbors search** (**ANNS**), with deep dives into ANNS-based algorithms for beginners.

To get the most out of this book

Readers should have a basic understanding of Python programming, familiarity with machine learning concepts, and a basic understanding of large language models. This book assumes readers have some experience with AI development environments and are comfortable working with APIs. Readers should have foundational knowledge of databases and basic Python programming skills, since hands-on SDK operations are featured throughout the book.

This book also assumes readers are familiar with container tools, such as Docker, and orchestration tools, such as Kubernetes. Experience with distributed systems is a plus.

No prior in-depth expertise in vector databases is required.

Software/hardware covered in the book	Operating system requirements
VSCode	MacOS or Linux
Python 3.x	MacOS or Linux
Docker	MacOS or Linux
K8s	MacOS or Linux

You will need access to a Python development environment. A machine with at least 8 GB of RAM is recommended for running the more complex examples.

If you are using the digital version of this book, we advise you to type the code yourself or access the code from the book's GitHub repository (a link is available in the next section). Doing so will help you avoid any potential errors related to the copying and pasting of code.

Download the example code files

The code bundle for the book is hosted on GitHub at `https://github.com/PacktPublishing/The-Architecture-Handbook-for-Milvus-Vector-Database`. We also have other code bundles from our rich catalog of books and videos available at `https://github.com/PacktPublishing`. Check them out!

Disclaimer on images

Some images in this title are presented for contextual purposes, and the readability of the graphic is not crucial to the discussion. Please refer to our free graphic bundle to download the images.

Download the color images

We also provide a PDF file that has color images of the screenshots/diagrams used in this book. You can download it here: `https://packt.link/gbp/9781835881705`.

Conventions used

There are a number of text conventions used throughout this book.

`CodeInText`: Indicates code words in text, database table names, folder names, filenames, file extensions, pathnames, dummy URLs, user input, and Twitter handles. For example: "Create a comprehensive soak test script `milvus_soak_test.py`:"

A block of code is set as follows:

```
# Basic similarity search - most common operation
client.search(
    collection_name="ecommerce_products",
    data=[search_vector],
    anns_field="embedding",
    search_params={"metric_type": "COSINE"},
    limit=10
)
```

Any command-line input or output is written as follows:

```
pip install vectordb-bench==1.0.11
```

Bold: Indicates a new term, an important word, or words that you see on the screen. For instance, words in menus or dialog boxes appear in the text like this. For example: "For load testing Milvus, we'll use **Locust**, an open-source load testing tool based on Python."

> Note
>
> ***Warnings*** or important notes appear like this.

> Tip
>
> Tips and tricks appear like this.

Get in touch

Feedback from our readers is always welcome.

General feedback: If you have questions about any aspect of this book or have any general feedback, please email us at `customercare@packt.com` and mention the book's title in the subject of your message.

Errata: Although we have taken every care to ensure the accuracy of our content, mistakes do happen. If you have found a mistake in this book, we would be grateful if you reported this to us. Please visit `http://www.packt.com/submit-errata`, click **Submit Errata**, and fill in the form.

Piracy: If you come across any illegal copies of our works in any form on the internet, we would be grateful if you would provide us with the location address or website name. Please contact us at `copyright@packt.com` with a link to the material.

If you are interested in becoming an author: If there is a topic that you have expertise in and you are interested in either writing or contributing to a book, please visit `http://authors.packt.com/`.

Free benefits with your book

This book comes with free benefits to support your learning. Activate them now for instant access (see the "*How to Unlock*" section for instructions).

Here's a quick overview of what you can instantly unlock with your purchase:

How to Unlock

Scan the QR code (or go to `packtpub.com/unlock`). Search for this book by name, confirm the edition, and then follow the steps on the page.

UNLOCK NOW

Note: Keep your invoice handy. Purchases made directly from Packt don't require one.

Share your thoughts

Once you've read *The Architecture Handbook for Milvus Vector Database*, we'd love to hear your thoughts! Scan the QR code below to go straight to the Amazon review page for this book and share your feedback.

https://packt.link/r/1835881718

Your review is important to us and the tech community and will help us make sure we're delivering excellent quality content.

Join our Discord and Reddit Space

You're not the only one navigating fragmented tools, constant updates, and unclear best practices. Join a growing community of professionals exchanging insights that don't make it into documentation.

Join our Discord at `https://packt.link/z8ivB` or scan the QR code below:	Follow us on Reddit at `https://packt.link/0rExL` or scan the QR code below:

Part 1

Getting Started with Milvus

Part 1 lays the groundwork for mastering Milvus, starting with a foundational introduction to vector databases and the core value of Milvus amid unstructured data challenges. It walks readers through practical, step-by-step guidance on multi-mode deployment methods, basic SDK-driven interactions with Milvus, and essential system configuration. Geared toward beginners, this part ensures you can quickly set up a usable Milvus environment, grasp core operating concepts, and lay a solid hands-on foundation for subsequent in-depth learning.

This part contains the following chapters:

- *Chapter 1, Introduction to Milvus*
- *Chapter 2, Deploying Milvus in Multiple Ways*
- *Chapter 3, Interacting with Milvus*
- *Chapter 4, Configuring the Milvus System*

1

Introduction to Milvus

Databases serve as a fundamental infrastructure in enterprises for managing business data. With the rapid development of large models over the past two years, more and more developers and businesses are leveraging large model technologies to optimize, enhance, or initiate new operations. The data generated in this process, known as **unstructured data**, has seen an increasing demand for management, leading to heightened requirements for database systems across various aspects. Traditional databases can no longer meet the data management needs in such scenarios, where the focus shifts away from **Atomicity, Consistency, Isolation, and Durability** (**ACID**), the four key characteristics of relational databases, to their ability to function reliably under large data volumes and high concurrency. This is the very impetus for the emergence of the **Milvus vector database**.

Throughout this book, we will discover a new type of database – vector databases. As the world's most popular and powerful vector database, Milvus will be the focus of our learning, covering its basic introduction, how to create and set up a database in Milvus, and build simple RAG applications with Milvus, followed by a deep dive into Milvus architecture, indexing strategies, deployment modes, and how to scale applications using Milvus.

But to begin our journey in this chapter, we will first focus on what vector databases are, several advantages they offer, and how they help us deal with unstructured data. We will finally introduce you to the Milvus vector database to get started.

Here, we will discuss the following topics:

- Understanding a vector database
- Introducing Milvus

> Note
>
> **Your purchase includes a free PDF copy + exclusive extras**
>
> Your purchase includes a DRM-free PDF copy of this book, a 7-day trial to the Packt+ library (no credit card required), and additional exclusive extras. See the *Free benefits with your book* section in the *Preface* to unlock them instantly and maximize your learning.

Technical requirements

The practical case studies covered in this chapter require very basic tools that are free of charge, including the following:

- **Google Colab**: It's a free cloud-based Jupyter notebook environment that allows you to write and execute Python code in your browser.
- **VS Code**: Used as the code editor. We recommend using the latest stable release of VS Code for the best experience and to benefit from the most recent features and bug fixes. You can download it from the official website: `https://code.visualstudio.com/download`.
- **Docker**: Simplifies the installation of the code runtime environment and is easy to use. For this book, we recommend using the latest stable version of Docker Desktop, as it provides a comprehensive and user-friendly environment for running containers on Windows, macOS, and Linux. You can download Docker Desktop from the official Docker website: `https://www.docker.com/products/docker-desktop/`.
- The code used in this chapter can be found in our GitHub repository: `https://github.com/PacktPublishing/The-Architecture-Handbook-for-Milvus-Vector-Database`

> Note
>
> The code examples in this chapter can be run using either Google Colab or a local Python Notebook environment. We highly recommend Google Colab, as it enables you to practice the chapter content more efficiently while providing a more enjoyable and engaging learning experience.

Understanding a vector database

If you are a beginner to the magical world of vector databases, don't worry, we will introduce it step by step in this section. Some basic computer science knowledge is enough. If you are familiar with vector databases, you can skip this section. The core points of discussion here will be types of **databases**, **unstructured data**, exploring the **encoding process,** and **similarity search algorithms**.

Let's get started.

Types of databases

Databases are a familiar concept to most people; in simple terms, they are systems designed for storing and retrieving data. Databases are generally categorized into two types: **relational databases** and **non-relational databases** (commonly referred to as NoSQL). A key distinction lies in their approach to data consistency. Relational databases are designed to strictly adhere to the ACID properties, which ensure reliable transaction processing.

Non-relational databases, on the other hand, often prioritize scalability and performance over strict ACID compliance. While many NoSQL databases do not guarantee full ACID properties across all operations, it's worth noting that ACID properties can still be achieved in specific scenarios or contexts within some non-relational databases, depending on their design and the particular use case. This trade-off allows NoSQL databases to offer greater flexibility and horizontal scaling for handling large volumes of diverse data.

Common relational databases include MySQL, Oracle, and Microsoft SQL Server, while popular non-relational databases include MongoDB, Cassandra, and Redis.

The core function of a database is **data management**, as data represents a form of virtual wealth for every enterprise, particularly user data. This data needs to be added or updated as necessary while ensuring it is not lost or subject to leakage or tampering. The information managed daily is often represented in fixed formats, such as user information, which may include usernames, ages, occupations, and addresses. However, in real life, there exists a significant amount of information that cannot be organized in fixed formats, such as documents, images, videos, and audio files. This latter category constitutes the core of our lives, as the former mostly consists of raw information processed by individuals or enterprises, retaining only the data relevant to their applications.

Most often, you will have to deal with unstructured data that comes in a variety of forms and formats. Let's understand how to work with this data and associated challenges.

Unstructured data

Unstructured data refers to types of information such as documents, images, videos, and audio. Compared to simple text, managing unstructured data presents greater challenges. The first challenge is storage; this type of information needs to be encoded before being stored on media such as disks or CDs. When retrieving the data, it must be decoded so that the computer can display it according to specific rules.

Different scenarios require various storage methods. For example, when an individual takes personal photos, the clarity requirement may not be high. In contrast, movies demand very high clarity. Beyond storage, retrieving this type of information is also a significant challenge. Regardless of the text retrieval method employed, the process ultimately involves letter matching. However, dealing with unstructured data can be quite difficult.

Consider this example: there are 100 images, and a person has viewed all of them and clearly remembers their content. If you ask about these images, such as whether there are any pictures of plants or to identify an animal picture, the person can quickly provide the answers. The key to quickly getting answers lies in how a person's memory encodes image information, essentially extracting features from those images. With this encoded foundation, we then extract key information from the question itself. This key information is then used to retrieve historical data containing relevant features, ultimately providing the answer. This can be compared to how a database functions: the computer's role is to clearly remember all data and quickly retrieve answers when queried.

To handle unstructured data, it must first be encoded, a process also known as **embedding**. This involves converting the data into a fixed-length numerical array, referred to as a vector, which contains the features of the unstructured data. However, these features are not human-readable. The encoding process typically requires specific models, many of which can be found on platforms such as Hugging Face or GitHub. If suitable models are not available, it may be necessary to train new ones based on existing data, a task that can be time-consuming and resource-intensive.

So what is the encoding process?

Exploring the encoding process

To understand the encoding process, we will focus on text encoding first. There are two methods for converting a segment of text into vectors: **one-hot encoding** and **TF-IDF encoding**.

Let's understand the fundamental principles behind these two methods.

One-hot encoding

In one-hot encoding, each word in the text is represented as a binary vector. The length of the vector is equal to the total number of unique words in the vocabulary. For each word, the vector contains a 1 in the position corresponding to that word and 0s in all other positions. This method is simple and intuitive, but does not capture any semantic relationships between the words.

The following is some sample code for one-hot encoding in Python:

```
import numpy as np
def one_hot_encode(words, vocab):
    vector = np.zeros(len(vocab))
    for word in words:
        index = vocab.index(word)
        vector[index] = 1
    return vector
vocab = ["apple", "banana", "cherry", "orange", "kiwi", "melon", "mango"]
words = ["apple", "cherry", "kiwi", "mango", "apple"]
encoded_vector = one_hot_encode(words, vocab)
print(encoded_vector)
```

The core method is one_hot_encode, which creates a one-dimensional array with the same length as vocab, then loops over the words, and if the word exists in vocab, sets the corresponding position to 1, and finally returns the array.

By running the preceding code in Google Colab, you will get the following results: *Figure 1.1* shows the final running result.

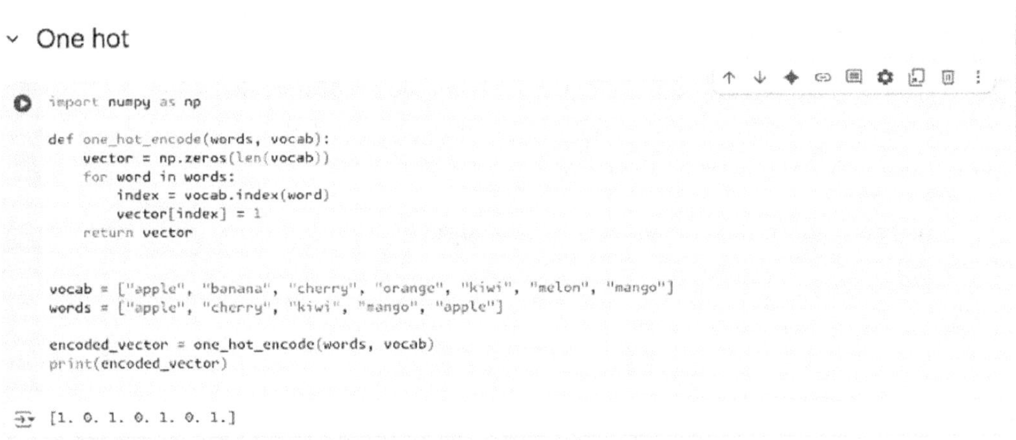

Figure 1.1: One-hot encoding results

As shown in the screenshot, the correct output is as follows:

```
[1. 0. 1. 0. 1. 0. 1.]
```

Another popular text encoding method is TF-IDF encoding.

TF-IDF encoding

TF-IDF assigns a weight to each word based on its frequency in a specific document relative to its frequency across all documents. The **term frequency** (**TF**) quantifies how frequently a word occurs in a specific document, while the **inverse document frequency** (**IDF**) evaluates how common or rare a word is across a broader collection of documents. For a deeper understanding, you can visit this resource, which explains these concepts in detail: `https://milvus.io/ai-quick-reference/what-is-tfidf-and-how-is-it-calculated`.

By combining these two metrics, TF-IDF highlights words that are important to the document while diminishing the weight of common words. These common words, often referred to as stop words, are typically articles, prepositions, and conjunctions such as *the*, *a*, *an*, *is*, *and*, *but*, and *or*. Because these words appear frequently across almost all documents in a collection, TF-IDF assigns them a very low weight, effectively making them less significant in determining a document's unique content or topic.

Now that we have a basic understanding of one-hot and TF-IDF encoding, let's proceed to convert a sample text into vectors using these two methods.

The following is sample code for TF-IDF encoding. These examples use the `gensim` Python third-party library, which is an easy-to-use Python library to create efficient semantic vectors of text documents. The following example is relatively simple and directly uses the example of `gensim`.

We'll run this demo to experience the principle of this process.

1. Perform the necessary imports for `corpora` and the `tfidf` model:

```
from gensim import corpora, models, similarities
```

2. Create a list of the text documents to be analyzed:

```
text_corpus = [
    "the cat in the hat",
    "the cat sat on the mat",
    "the dog sat on the log",
    "dogs and cats are great pets"
]
```

3. Preprocess the documents by converting them into lowercase and tokens:

```
texts = [doc.lower().split() for doc in text_corpus]
```

4. Map each unique word to an integer ID:

```
dictionary = corpora.Dictionary(texts)
corpus = [dictionary.doc2bow(text) for text in texts]
```

5. Convert each document into a **bag-of-words** format, which is a list of tuples (`word_id`, `word_frequency`) for each document:

```
tfidf = models.TfidfModel(corpus)
```

6. Compute the TF-IDF scores and construct a sparse matrix similarity index for efficient similarity calculations:

```
index = similarities.SparseMatrixSimilarity(
    tfidf[corpus], num_features=len(dictionary))
```

7. Define a query document as a list of words and transform the query into a bag-of-words format using the dictionary:

```
query_document = 'cat hat'.split()
query_bow = dictionary.doc2bow(query_document)
```

8. Calculate similarity scores between the query and all documents in the corpus:

```
sims = index[tfidf[query_bow]]
```

9. Sort and print the similarity scores in descending order for ranking:

```
for document_number, score in sorted(
    enumerate(sims), key=lambda x: x[1], reverse=True):
    print(document_number, score)
```

10. With our previous Python environment, it is very convenient to run. Remember to install the `gensim` third-party library before running. The following is the result of the run:

```
[1] from gensim import corpora, models, similarities

    text_corpus = [
        "the cat in the hat",
        "the cat sat on the mat",
        "the dog sat on the log",
        "dogs and cats are great pets"
    ]

    texts = [doc.lower().split() for doc in text_corpus]
    dictionary = corpora.Dictionary(texts)
    corpus = [dictionary.doc2bow(text) for text in texts]

    tfidf = models.TfidfModel(corpus)
    index = similarities.SparseMatrixSimilarity(tfidf[corpus], num_features=len(dictionary))

    query_document = 'cat hat'.split()
    query_bow = dictionary.doc2bow(query_document)
    sims = index[tfidf[query_bow]]
    for document_number, score in sorted(enumerate(sims), key=lambda x: x[1], reverse=True):
        print(document_number, score)

    0 0.71836466
    1 0.16127957
    2 0.0
    3 0.0
```

Figure 1.2: TF-IDF encoding results

As shown in the preceding screenshot, the correct output is as follows:

```
0 0.71836466
1 0.16127957
2 0.0
3 0.0
```

The next step is to utilize similarity search algorithms.

Similarity search algorithms

Once we have obtained the vectors, how do we use them for retrieval? This process is known as similarity search, which involves algorithms for **approximate nearest neighbor search** (**ANNS**). ANNS is a method used to quickly find data points in high-dimensional spaces that are like a given query point.

It's important to note that *approximate nearest* does not mean *exact nearest*. For example, in a two-dimensional coordinate system with many points, if we input a random coordinate to find the nearest point, the typical approach would be to traverse all existing points, calculate the distance from the input coordinate to each point, and select the one with the smallest distance. This is known as **exact nearest neighbor search**. However, if there are tens of thousands of points, finding this exact point can be very time-consuming.

In contrast, the ANN algorithm optimizes for speed and efficiency, often sacrificing some precision to achieve quicker responses, which is particularly crucial when dealing with large-scale data.

While there are many ANN algorithms, let us first talk about the **locally sensitive hashing** (**LSH**) algorithm.

LSH

LSH is principally similar to the **hash map**, which makes it easier for us to begin with ANN. A key characteristic of LSH is that it differs from conventional hash functions. While traditional hash functions aim to minimize hash collisions, LSH intentionally increases the probability of collisions to group similar items together. By mapping similar data points into the same *buckets*, LSH accelerates the search process.

LSH works by using hash functions to map high-dimensional data into a lower-dimensional space, ensuring that similar data points have a higher probability of colliding in the hash table. This allows us to search only within the same bucket rather than traversing the entire dataset.

The basic steps of the LSH algorithm are as follows:

1. **Choose a hash function**: Select a hash function suitable for the characteristics of the data. In our example, we will use coordinate points and calculate distances using *Euclidean distance*, employing **random projection** as the hash function. If you want to learn more about this, you can visit `https://en.wikipedia.org/wiki/Locality-sensitive_hashing#Random_projection`.
2. **Build a hash table**: Map the data points into different buckets using the hash function.
3. **Query**: Map the query point into the corresponding bucket using the same hash function and search for the nearest neighbors within that bucket, which may require distance calculations.
4. **Return results**: Return the found approximate nearest neighbors.

Note

Random projection hashing

Hashing is a process that maps data of arbitrary size to fixed-size values, facilitating fast data retrieval and comparison.

Random projection hashing is a technique that reduces the dimensionality of data by projecting it onto a lower-dimensional space using random matrices, preserving the distances between points with high probability.

Let's put this knowledge into practice:

1. **Initialization**: Takes `n_hashes` (number of hash functions) and `n_buckets` (number of buckets) as parameters, and initializes multiple empty hash tables and random vectors for subsequent hash calculations:

```
import numpy as np
class LSH:
    def __init__(self, n_hashes, n_buckets):
        self.n_hashes = n_hashes
        self.n_buckets = n_buckets
        self.hash_tables = [{} for _ in range(n_hashes)]
        np.random.seed(0)
        self.random_vectors = np.random.randn(n_hashes, 2)
```

2. **Hash function**: Computes a binary hash value for an input point by taking the dot product of random vectors. If the dot product is greater than zero, the corresponding bit is set to 1; otherwise, it is set to 0, returning a tuple as the hash value:

```
    def _pairwise_distances(self, X, Y=None):
        X = np.array(X)
        Y = np.array(Y)

        dist_matrix = np.zeros((X.shape[0], Y.shape[0]))
        for i in range(X.shape[0]):
            for j in range(Y.shape[0]):
                dist_matrix[i, j] = np.linalg.norm(X[i] - Y[j])
        return dist_matrix

    def _hash(self, point):
        bits = (
            np.dot(self.random_vectors, np.array(point)) > 0
        ).astype(int)
        return [
            int(''.join(map(str, bits[i:i+1])), 2) % self.n_buckets
            for i in range(self.n_hashes)
        ]
```

3. **Inserting data**: For each input point, calculate its hash value and store it in the corresponding hash table. If the hash value does not exist, it initializes a bucket and adds the point to that bucket:

```
def insert(self, point):
     bucket_ids = self._hash(point)
     for i in range(self.n_hashes):
         bucket_id = bucket_ids[i]
         if bucket_id not in self.hash_tables[i]:
             self.hash_tables[i][bucket_id] = []
         self.hash_tables[i][bucket_id].append(tuple(point))
```

4. **Querying and returning results**: Compute the hash value for the query point and retrieve candidate points from the hash table. If candidates exist, calculate their distances to the query point and return the nearest one; if no candidates are found, it returns `None`:

```
def query(self, query_point):
    candidates = set()
    bucket_ids = self._hash(query_point)
    for i in range(self.n_hashes):
        bucket_id = bucket_ids[i]
        if bucket_id in self.hash_tables[i]:
            candidates.update(self.hash_tables[i][bucket_id])

    candidates = np.array(
        [np.array(candidate) for candidate in candidates])
    if candidates.size == 0:
        return None
    distances = self._pairwise_distances(
        candidates, [query_point])
    nearest_index = np.argmin(distances)
    return candidates[nearest_index]
```

Finally, here's a simple code example that demonstrates how to use the LSH class to insert data and perform queries:

```
data = [[1, 2], [3, 4], [5, 6], [7, 8]]
query_point = [4, 5]
```

```
lsh = LSH(n_hashes=5, n_buckets=10)
for point in data:
    lsh.insert(point)

result = lsh.query(query_point)
print("lsh query result:", result)
```

Since we understand the steps of the algorithm, I believe the whole process of reading the code will be easier. The following is the running result of the code. Let's run it together.

Figure 1.3: LSH results

As shown in *Figure 1.3*, the correct output is as follows:

```
lsh query result: [3 4]
```

The LSH algorithm found `[3, 4]` as the nearest neighbor to the query point `[4, 5]`, which has a Euclidean distance of $\sqrt{2} \approx 1.41$. This demonstrates LSH's ability to quickly find approximate nearest neighbors by hashing similar points into the same buckets.

The advantages of LSH are as follows:

- **Efficiency in high dimensions**: LSH is particularly efficient when dealing with high-dimensional data, significantly reducing query times
- **Scalability**: It can handle large-scale datasets effectively

But, there are some disadvantages too:

- **Selection of hash functions**: The performance of LSH can be affected by the choice of hash functions and parameters, which requires careful tuning
- **Approximate results**: The results returned are approximate and may not always represent the most accurate nearest neighbors

In addition to LSH, other common ANNS algorithms include **inverted file** (**IVF**) and **hierarchical navigable small world** (**HNSW**). There are also various strategies to reduce computational load for high-dimensional vectors, such as **product quantization** (**PQ**). Many of these implementations are available in open source libraries, such as **FAISS**, a highly recommended option for efficient similarity search.

> Note
>
> If you are unfamiliar with ANNS-based algorithms, you can refer to *Chapter 18* of this book for a deeper dive.

In this section, you have gained a preliminary understanding of databases and vector databases. In the next section, let's explore our main focus: Milvus.

Introducing Milvus

You may have guessed by now that Milvus is undoubtedly a vector database, designed as an open source project specifically for handling and managing large-scale vector data.

As the most popular and powerful vector database in the world, Milvus has many advantages. Here is a brief overview of each advantage, which will help us to have a deeper understanding of Milvus later:

- **High speed**: Milvus achieves fast performance due to its distributed architecture, which separates read and write operations, a powerful indexing engine, and efficient data storage methods.

- **Scalability and high performance**: The system is designed with multiple node types, each serving a specific function. Various coordinator roles facilitate task and resource scheduling through service discovery.
- **Multiple deployment modes**, including Lite (a Python library), standalone (a single-machine server deployment), and Distributed (which is deployed on Kubernetes clusters).
- **Rich SDK support**: Milvus provides SDKs for popular programming languages, including Python, Go, Java, and Node.js, all maintained officially.
- **Support for various data types and indexing methods**: This versatility extends to handling diverse data types such as integers (int), floating-point numbers (float), booleans (bool), strings (str), and even specialized dense and sparse vectors crucial for machine learning. To efficiently manage and retrieve this data, it offers various indexing strategies, including `IVF_PQ`, `HNSW`, and `DISKANN`, each optimized for different performance needs and scales.
- **Flexible data consistency**: Milvus offers multiple consistency guarantees, allowing users to choose based on their specific business scenarios.
- **Development and operations tools**: Milvus includes various tools for management and monitoring:
    - `Attu` for GUI management: `https://github.com/zilliztech/attu`
    - `Birdwatcher` for metadata viewing: `https://github.com/milvus-io/birdwatcher`
    - Integration with Prometheus and Grafana for monitoring metrics and logs
    - Milvus `Backup` tool: `https://github.com/zilliztech/milvus-backup`
    - Milvus `CDC` for incremental data migration: `https://github.com/zilliztech/milvus-cdc`

For a deeper understanding of Milvus's features, you can refer to the Milvus overview: `https://milvus.io/docs/overview.md`

Milvus is utilized across various fields, including **retrieval-augmented generation** (**RAG**) in large models, text and multimodal search, image search, and recommendation systems. You can explore related demo cases at *Milvus Demos and Tutorials*: `https://github.com/milvus-io/milvus#demos-and-tutorials`.

While Milvus has many strengths, it also faces some challenges, including the following:

- Dependency on multiple services, which makes deployment complex

- Milvus consumes high computational resources
- Milvus has limited self-healing capabilities, and there is still room for improvement in error recovery

At present, to tackle these challenges, Milvus is continuously evolving by doing the following:

- Reducing dependencies by developing proprietary components
- Exploring efficient indexing methods such as DiskANN and optimizing task scheduling
- Enhancing system robustness through error prevention, recovery, and detection
- Implementing dynamic request throttling based on resource usage
- Improving upgrade processes to allow for rolling upgrades without service interruptions

This was a brief run-down of vector databases and features Milvus offers as a vector database, and how it is continually evolving to tackle challenges and improve its capabilities.

Throughout this book, we will focus on how you can configure and interact with Milvus, understand Milvus' architecture, perform writes and reads to Milvus, and explore its underlying mechanisms. We will also cover advanced concepts such as vector indexing and searching in Milvus, and gain a deeper understanding of evaluating performance and scaling operations in Milvus. Stay tuned!

Summary

In this chapter, we explored the concept of vector data, demonstrated how to obtain vectors through two Python examples, and explained how vector search—the core functionality of vector databases—works with another Python example. Building on this foundation, we introduced you to Milvus, the primary focus of this book, detailing what Milvus is, its various deployment modes, and highlighting its numerous advantages. I'm sure you're eager to dive deeper into Milvus.

In the next chapter, we will guide you through the process of various ways to deploy Milvus.

Get this book's PDF version and more

Scan the QR code (or go to `packtpub.com/unlock`). Search for this book by name, confirm the edition, and then follow the steps on the page.

UNLOCK NOW

Note: Keep your invoice handy. Purchases made directly from Packt don't require an invoice.

2

Deploying Milvus in Multiple Ways

In this chapter, we will focus on deploying Milvus, which means making the database available and ready to handle queries in a production or testing environment. First, we need to understand common deployment methods, which include open source tools such as Docker, Docker Compose, Kubernetes Operator, and Helm charts. Along with introducing these technologies, we will highlight the advantages of each of them and suitable application scenarios, providing a comparative analysis to aid in technology selection. After discussing the theoretical aspects, we will proceed with practical operations to deploy Milvus using each of these methods. This chapter covers the following:

- Understanding common service deployment methods
- Deploying Milvus through Docker Compose
- Deploying Milvus through Helm charts/operators

Technical requirements

This chapter focuses on learning how to deploy services using open source tools. You will need to install the following tools to learn how to deploy Milvus in this chapter:

- **Docker**: Install Docker Compose either as a standalone tool or as a plugin. For this guide, we'll be using Docker Compose v2, which is typically integrated directly into Docker Desktop and accessed via the `docker compose` command. If you're using an older Docker installation or have installed Docker Compose as a standalone tool, the command might be `docker-compose`.

For more detailed information, you can refer to the official Docker documentation:

- **Docker**: `https://docs.docker.com/get-started/docker-overview/`
- **Docker Compose**: `https://docs.docker.com/compose/`

Use the following commands to verify your installation:

- For standalone installation, use this command:

```
docker --version
docker-compose version
```

- For plugin installation, use this command:

```
docker --version
docker compose version
```

- **Minikube**
- **Kubectl**
- **Helm**

The code used in this chapter can be found on our GitHub repository: `https://github.com/PacktPublishing/The-Architecture-Handbook-for-Milvus-Vector-Database`.

Understanding common service deployment methods

In this section, we will not only introduce frequently used technologies for deploying Milvus but also highlight the advantages of each of them, providing a comparative analysis to help you select the appropriate tool.

Introducing Docker and Docker Compose

Docker is an open source platform designed for automating the deployment, scaling, and management of applications. It uses containerization to package applications and their dependencies, enabling them to run consistently across different computing environments. This allows applications to be delivered efficiently and reliably. Two core concepts in Docker are **containers** and **images**. Containers are lightweight, portable runtime environments that encompass an application and all its dependencies. Compared to traditional virtual machines, containers share the host operating system kernel, resulting in faster startup times. Images, on the other hand, are read-only templates used to create containers. They allow the packaging of applications and their environments, facilitating distribution and version control. This is similar to the concepts of classes and objects in programming, where a class serves as a template and an object is an instantiated class.

> **Note**
>
> To learn more about Docker containers, refer to this resource:
>
> `https://www.docker.com/blog/containers-are-not-vms/.`

Additionally, while using Docker, you will often encounter **Dockerfiles** and **Docker Hub**. A Dockerfile is a text file containing instructions for building images, enabling users to define the application's environment and dependencies. Docker Hub is a public container image repository where users can upload and download images, making sharing and management easier. Many companies also set up their own private Docker image repositories to provide faster upload and download speeds, as well as to conduct internal image testing.

Docker offers numerous advantages, including the following:

- **Consistency**: Since containers encapsulate all dependencies, applications behave consistently across development, testing, and production environments, reducing the "it works on my machine" problem
- **Lightweight**: Containers share the host's kernel, allowing startup times of just a few seconds and significantly lower resource usage compared to traditional virtual machines
- **Portability**: Containers can run in any environment that supports Docker, including local development setups, private data centers, and public clouds
- **Scalability**: Docker facilitates rapid scaling up or down of applications, making it easier to respond to traffic fluctuations and load demands
- **Microservices architecture**: Docker is well-suited for microservices architecture, enabling the breakdown of applications into multiple services that can be deployed independently

Docker has a variety of use cases, such as application development and testing, microservices deployment, **continuous integration and continuous delivery** (**CI/CD**), and unified management across multi-cloud environments. By simplifying the development, delivery, and deployment processes, Docker enhances development efficiency and system stability, making it an essential tool in modern software development.

Introducing Docker Compose

In complex application systems, there is often a dependency on various third-party services, such as messaging services, key-value stores, and caching services. This means that our application services can only start successfully if these third-party services are running properly. **Docker Compose** is a tool that allows users to define and run multi-container Docker applications. With

Compose, users can configure application services, networks, and volumes using a YAML file, simplifying the management and deployment of multi-container environments. A few simple commands can quickly start or stop all services in an application; for example, you can use `docker-compose up` to start services and `docker-compose down` to stop them.

Docker Compose has a number of benefits:

- **Rapid development**: Developers can quickly set up and test multiple components of an application without manually managing each container
- **Reproducibility**: By using configuration files, the deployment and runtime environments of an application can remain consistent across different machines, reducing environment-related issues
- **Ease of scaling**: Adding or removing services is straightforward, making it easy to scale applications
- **Integration testing**: It is well-suited for integration testing, allowing the testing of interactions between multiple services in the same environment

Currently, using Docker alone has become less common; it is often paired with Compose to define and run multiple Docker containers. You may notice two command formats: sometimes `docker-compose` and sometimes `docker compose`. This distinction arises from two installation methods:

- One method is a standalone installation, where the command is `docker-compose`, functioning independently from Docker. It is worth noting that this one has been deprecated; please use the other one.
- The other is as a plugin, where the command is `docker compose`, which operates as a subcommand of Docker.

We will now move on to understanding the Kubernetes operator.

Introducing the Kubernetes operator

Kubernetes (sometimes called **K8s**) is an open source container orchestration platform that automates the deployment, scaling, and management of containerized applications. It groups containers that make up an application into logical units for easy management and discovery.

In Kubernetes, an **Operator** is a controller that uses **Kubernetes Custom Resources** to install and manage applications. To better understand this definition, let's break down two key terms: **controller** and **custom resource**.

A controller in Kubernetes is a routine that monitors the desired state of Kubernetes configurations and the actual state of cluster resources. When it detects a discrepancy between the desired and actual states, whether due to administrative changes or internal failures, the controller attempts to reconcile them. For instance, if a configuration describing the desired state of an application is deployed, the controller will recognize this configuration and apply it, provided it aligns with the overall state of the Kubernetes cluster, which is a set of nodes (worker machines) that run containerized applications and workloads, managed by Kubernetes.

Custom resources in Kubernetes are extensions of the Kubernetes API that allow you to add functionalities that are not available by default. This has been achieved by creating a **custom resource definition** (**CRD**). If you want to use a Kubernetes Operator to install or manage an application, you can create a CRD that embodies the functionalities required by that application. When you combine the CRD with the Operator's controller, the Kubernetes controller routine will detect and deploy it accordingly.

Operators help automate complex application management tasks, making it easier to deploy and maintain applications in a Kubernetes environment.

Here are some key features of Kubernetes:

- **Container orchestration**: Kubernetes can automatically deploy and manage thousands of containers, ensuring they run seamlessly within a cluster
- **Load balancing**: It automatically distributes traffic to maintain application availability and performance
- **Self-healing**: If a container fails, Kubernetes automatically restarts or replaces it to ensure continuous application operation
- **Rolling updates**: This feature allows seamless application updates, ensuring users remain unaffected during the process

- **Service discovery and load balancing**: Kubernetes automatically assigns IP addresses to containers and provides DNS names for communication between them
- **Storage orchestration**: It can automatically mount various storage systems, including local and cloud storage

Introducing Helm charts

A **Helm chart** is a package format that contains the resources needed to deploy applications on Kubernetes, encapsulated in what is called a chart. Helm is the package manager and configuration management tool for Kubernetes, allowing users to install Helm charts easily.

Helm charts and the Helm package manager are analogous to **Debian packages** and `apt-get` on **Ubuntu** or **RPM packages** and **DNF** on **Red Hat**. However, there is a key difference: unlike operating system application packages, Helm charts typically do not include application binaries. Instead, they contain files that point to the container images or images needed to deploy the application.

Using Helm charts streamlines the process of deploying and managing applications in Kubernetes, making it easier to define, install, and upgrade complex applications with a single command.

Helm charts and operators are two deployment methods that rely on Kubernetes.

> **Tip**
>
> You can use `docker compose` when you want the local testing to be as simple as possible. For operation and maintenance, you might have to deal more with Helm as it provides more scalability, such as resource expansion and contraction, which is more critical for an online business.

Let's now see how the Helm charts and Kubernetes deployment methods differ.

Comparing Helm charts and Kubernetes operators

Docker Compose is the simplest deployment method. It is typically used for development and testing. It lacks resource control capabilities, meaning it can only install applications. In contrast, Helm charts and Kubernetes operators can both install and manage applications.

We will focus on comparing the latter two in the following table:

Features	Helm chart	Kubernetes operator
Scope and functionality	**Narrower scope**: Its primary purpose is to install standard applications that can run based on existing container images. **Limited configuration options**: You can pass parameters to customize the application during installation, but only if the chart is designed to support those parameters.	Provides much greater customization capabilities through written code, allowing virtually limitless custom logic in application deployment.
Complexity and flexibility	**Simpler to create**: You can build a Helm chart using relatively straightforward YAML code. Installation is also less complex, as you can install a chart with a single command.	While offering increased flexibility, Operators are inherently more complex. Creating an Operator requires writing CRDs, and the installation process usually involves longer `kubectl` commands.
Automation	Automate application installation and management tasks that would otherwise be manual. However, Helm's automation capabilities are limited to managing standard applications. While you can install or update applications based on container images automatically, you cannot automate custom configuration changes beyond Helm's built-in functionalities.	Automate application installation and management tasks and automate any operation supported by the Kubernetes API and controllers, making them more versatile for complex deployments.

Features	Helm chart	Kubernetes operator
Lifecycle management	Support application lifecycle management, including installation, updates, and deletions. You manage the application lifecycle using built-in commands such as `install`, `upgrade`, and `uninstall`. You can replace old versions with new ones or completely remove applications.	Like Helm charts, it supports lifecycle management well. In contrast, modifying an application's Operator allows finer adjustments, enabling more detailed control over the application lifecycle.

Table 2.1: Comparison of Helm chart and Kubernetes operator features

In summary, the choice between Helm charts and Kubernetes Operators depends on your specific flexibility, complexity, and automation needs in deploying and managing applications in Kubernetes environments.

You now have some understanding of the common deployment methods. Let's start trying it out.

Deploying Milvus

To deploy Milvus, we will first focus on Docker Compose deployment as it is relatively simple. You don't need to go through both Milvus deployment options right away; feel free to choose the method that you find easier to learn from. Later, if you need to use a specific approach, you can always return to this section as a refresher or reference point.

Deploying Milvus with Docker Compose

Using Docker Compose simplifies the deployment of services such as Milvus, making it easier to experiment and understand its functionality. Single Docker deployments can be cumbersome and impractical, so Docker Compose is a preferred method for testing and learning.

To deploy Milvus with Docker Compose, follow these steps:

1. Open your browser and go to the following link to download the Milvus Docker Compose file: `https://github.com/milvus-io/milvus/releases/download/v2.4.17/milvus-standalone-docker-compose.yml`.
2. Save this YAML file in an empty directory on your local machine and rename the `milvus-standalone-docker-compose.yaml` file to `docker-compose.yaml`.
3. Open your terminal and navigate to the directory where you saved the `docker-compose.yaml` file.
4. Depending on your installation method, use one of the following commands to start the service:
    - For standalone installation (This installation method has been deprecated. Please use another method.):

    ```
    # Start the Docker service
    docker-compose up -d
    ```

    - For plugin installation:

    ```
    # Start the Docker service
    docker compose up -d
    ```

5. Next, we need to verify whether the service is normal by sending a request to Milvus. Here, we use the `curl` command to send a post request to Milvus. Of course, you can also use other UI tools, such as Postman. It should be noted that the body of the post needs to be a JSON string:

```
# Get the collection list to see if the milvus service is normal

curl -X POST http://localhost:19530/v2/vectordb/collections/list -d '{}' -H
"Content-Type: application/json"
```

If the request result returns a normal JSON with no exceptions, it means that Milvus has been deployed.

```
{
    "code":0,"data":[]
}
```

6. To stop Milvus and its related services, use the following commands based on your installation method:

   ◦ For standalone installation (This has been deprecated. Please use another method.):

   ```
   # Stop the Docker service
   docker-compose down
   ```

   ◦ For plugin installation:

   ```
   # Stop the Docker service
   docker compose down
   ```

Now, let's move on to the Kubernetes deployment of Milvus.

Deploying Milvus through Kubernetes

There are many methods for local Kubernetes deployment. Common methods for local Kubernetes deployment are as follows:

- **Minikube**: A tool that quickly runs a single-node Kubernetes cluster on your local machine, supporting various virtualization drivers (e.g., VirtualBox, VMware)
- **kind**: **Kubernetes in Docker** (**kind**) allows you to run Kubernetes clusters in Docker containers, making it ideal for development and testing environments
- **K3s**: A lightweight Kubernetes distribution that is suitable for resource-constrained devices or local development environments
- **Docker Desktop**: For those using Docker Desktop, Kubernetes support can be enabled through the settings
- **Manual installation**: You can also manually install Kubernetes on physical or virtual machines using tools such as kubeadm

For our upcoming deployment, we will use Minikube to set up Kubernetes locally. First, you need to install Minikube. For detailed installation steps, please refer to the Minikube start page in the

Minikube documentation (`https://minikube.sigs.k8s.io/docs/start`). Once the installation is complete, you can verify it by running the following command:

```
minikube version
```

Using operators to deploy Milvus

Milvus Operator defines Milvus cluster custom resources on top of Kubernetes custom resources to ensure its scalability and high availability. So, let's start using it to deploy Milvus:

1. Before we begin, we'll need to start Minikube. We can do this using the following command:

   ```
   minikube start --driver=docker
   ```

2. We then need to install `cert-manager`, as the Milvus Operator uses it to provide a certificate for the webhook server. Run the following command:

   ```
   kubectl apply -f https://github.com/jetstack/cert-manager/releases/download/
   v1.5.3/cert-manager.yaml
   ```

3. Once this command has completed, verify the installation by checking the status of the pods:

   ```
   kubectl get pods -n cert-manager
   ```

   If all pods are in the `Running` state, the installation was successful.

4. Next, we will install the Milvus Operator:

   ```
   kubectl apply -f https://raw.githubusercontent.com/zilliztech/milvus-
   operator/main/deploy/manifests/deployment.yaml
   ```

5. After this command has executed, check the pod statuses again:

   ```
   kubectl get pods -n milvus-operator
   ```

   If all pods are in the `Running` state, the installation was successful.

6. Now, we can deploy Milvus using the Milvus Operator pod. Create a file named `demo_operator.yaml`.

You can find this file in the book's official repository at https://github.com/PacktPublishing/The-Architecture-Handbook-for-Milvus-Vector-Database/blob/main/ch2/demo_operator.yaml.

```
# This is a sample to deploy a milvus cluster in milvus-operator's default
configurations.
apiVersion: milvus.io/v1beta1
kind: Milvus
metadata:
  name: my-release
  labels:
    app: milvus
spec:
  config: {}
  components:
    image: milvusdb/milvus:v2.4.17
    standalone:
      replicas: 1
      serviceType: LoadBalancer
  dependencies:
    msgStreamType: "rocksmq" # or "pulsar"
    etcd:
      inCluster:
        values:
          replicaCount: 1
        deletionPolicy: Delete
        pvcDeletion: true
    storage:
      inCluster:
        values:
          resources:
            requests:
              memory: 100Mi
          persistence:
              size: 20Gi
        deletionPolicy: Delete
        pvcDeletion: true
```

7. Execute the following command:

```
kubectl apply -f demo_operator.yaml
```

8. After running this command, check the status of the Milvus cluster:

```
>>kubectl get milvus my-release -o yaml
{
  ...
  "updatedReplicas": 1
  },
  "conditions": [
    {
      "lastTransitionTime": "2024-12-18T03:33:17Z",
      "message": "All Milvus components are healthy",
      "reason": "ReasonMilvusHealthy",
      "status": "True",
      "type": "MilvusReady"
    },
    {
      "lastTransitionTime": "2024-12-18T03:33:17Z",
      "message": "Milvus components are all updated",
      "reason": "MilvusComponentsUpdated",
      "status": "True",
      "type": "MilvusUpdated"
    },
    {
      "lastTransitionTime": "2024-12-18T03:32:53Z",
      "message": "Etcd endpoints is healthy",
      "reason": "EtcdReady",
      "status": "True",
      "type": "EtcdReady"
    },
    {
      "lastTransitionTime": "2024-12-18T03:32:53Z",
      "reason": "StorageReady",
      "status": "True",
      "type": "StorageReady"
    },
    {
      "lastTransitionTime": "2024-12-18T03:32:53Z",
```

```
        "reason": "MsgStreamReady",
        "status": "True",
        "type": "MsgStreamReady"
      }
    ],
    "ingress": {
      "loadBalancer": {}
    },
    "observedGeneration": 3,
    "rollingModeVersion": 2,
    "status": "Healthy"
  }
```

9. Once your Milvus cluster is ready, the `status` field should be `Healthy`. If it remains `Unhealthy` or `Pending`, your Milvus cluster is still being created.
10. You can also check the status of all Milvus services and related services with the following command. Pods with names containing `"init"` should have a status of `Completed`, while all other pods should be in the `Running` state:

```
kubectl get pods

NAME                                            READY   STATUS    RESTARTS   AGE
my-release-etcd-0                               1/1     Running   0          8m39s
my-release-milvus-standalone-5b554989df-4rlb5 1/1 Running 0 8m28s
my-release-minio-697b74df-98lqj   1/1     Running   0        8m39s
```

11. To find the port at which your Milvus cluster serves, run the following command:

> **Note**
>
> You should replace the pod name with the one output from the previous step.

```
# Replace the pod name in this command with the actual name of your own pod
kubectl get pod my-release-milvus-standalone-5b554989df-4rlb5 --
template='{{(index (index .spec.containers 0).ports 0).containerPort}}
{{"\n"}}'
```

The output will indicate that the Milvus instance serves at the default port 19530.

12. Then, run the following command to forward a local port to the Milvus service:

```
# Replace the pod name in this command with the actual name of your own pod
kubectl port-forward my-release-milvus-standalone-5b554989df-4rlb5  :19530
```

13. Finally, we verify whether the service is normal by sending a request to Milvus. To do this, follow step 5 in the *Deploying Milvus with Docker Compose* section:

```
curl -X POST http://localhost:19530/v2/vectordb/collections/list -d '{}' -H
"Content-Type: application/json"
```

14. If the request result returns a normal JSON with no exceptions, it means that Milvus has been deployed:

```
{"code":0,"data":[]}
```

15. If you wish to uninstall Milvus, use the following command:

```
kubectl delete -f demo_operator.yaml
```

Let's see how to use Helm charts for deployment.

Using Helm charts to deploy Milvus

Before we begin, we need to prepare the runtime environment:

- **Installing the Helm CLI tool**: If you are using a Mac, you can install it using the following command:

  ```
  brew install helm
  ```

  If you are using a different operating system, installation is straightforward. Please refer to the official site for details: `https://helm.sh/docs/intro/install/`.

- **Creating a Kubernetes cluster**: You were introduced to this in the previous section. Once helm is installed, you can start the cluster with the following command:

  ```
  minikube start
  ```

- Also, install the kubectl command-line tool. If you are on a Mac, use the following:

  ```
  brew install kubectl
  ```

For other operating systems, installation is easy as well. More information can be found here: `https://kubernetes.io/docs/tasks/tools/`.

- After starting the cluster, verify its status with the following:

```
kubectl cluster-info
```

- Before installing Milvus Helm charts, you need to add the Milvus Helm repository:

```
helm repo add milvus https://zilliztech.github.io/milvus-helm/
```

- Then, fetch or update Milvus charts from the repository:

```
helm repo update
```

Next, let's begin deploying Milvus. The steps are as follows:

1. Use the following command to start the deployment, but do not execute it just yet:

```
helm install my-release milvus/milvus --set cluster.enabled=false --set
etcd.replicaCount=1  --version 4.2.25
```

   Let's first understand what these parameters mean. In this command, `my-release` is the release name, and you can replace `my-release` with a name of your choice. To avoid potential conflicts, especially if you're experimenting or running multiple deployments, it's recommended to customize this name to ensure its uniqueness (e.g., `my-release-yourname`).

   `milvus/milvus` refers to the chart repository. `cluster.enable` indicates that the deployed Milvus is in standalone mode, `etcd.replicaCount` indicates that `etcd` is also standalone, not multiple copies, and `version` indicates the Milvus Helm chart version used, where `4.2.25` refers to Milvus `2.4.17`.

2. To check the status of all the pods in your Milvus cluster, run this command:

```
kubectl get pods
```

If all pods are in the `Running` state (except for the `pulsar-zookeeper-metadata` pod), everything is functioning normally.

```
kubectl get pods -o wide

NAME                                               READY   STATUS
RESTARTS        AGE     IP            NODE         NOMINATED NODE   READINESS
GATES
my-release-etcd-0                                  1/1     Running
0               3m46s   172.17.0.8    minikube     <none>           <none>
my-release-milvus-standalone-59565d99d-jq4v8       1/1      Running    2 (3m22s
ago)  3m46s   172.17.0.4   minikube    <none>           <none>
my-release-minio-0                                 1/1     Running
0               3m46s   172.17.0.3    minikube     <none>           <none>
my-release-minio-1                                 1/1     Running
0               3m46s   172.17.0.5    minikube     <none>           <none>
my-release-minio-2                                 1/1     Running
0               3m46s   172.17.0.7    minikube     <none>           <none>
my-release-minio-3                                 1/1     Running
0               3m46s   172.17.0.6    minikube     <none>           <none>
```

This is how the output looks on screen:

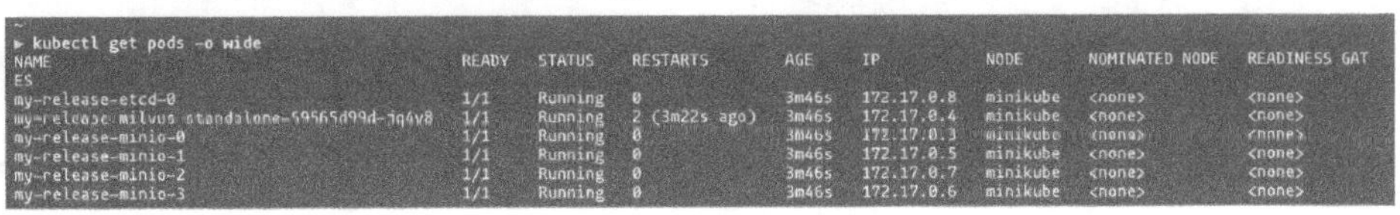

Figure 2.1: Milvus health pod state

3. To find the port at which your Milvus cluster is serving, use the following command. Note that you should replace the pod name in this command with the one you received in the previous step:

```
# Replace the pod name in this command with the actual name of your own pod
kubectl get pod my-release-milvus-proxy-6bd7f5587-
ds2xv --template='{{(index (index .spec.containers 0).ports
0).containerPort}}{{"\n"}}'
```

The output will indicate that the Milvus instance serves at the default port 19530. Then, run the following command to forward a local port to Milvus:

```
# Replace the pod name in this command with the actual name of your own pod
kubectl port-forward my-release-milvus-standalone-59565d99d-jq4v8 :19530
```

Note

You need to use your personal pod name.

4. In addition, when executing this command, it will keep the terminal occupied (it won't return to the command prompt). Therefore, we need to create a new terminal window to verify the status of Milvus:

```
# Replace the pod name in this command with the actual name of your own pod
>>kubectl port-forward my-release-milvus-standalone-59565d99d-jq4v8 :19530

Forwarding from 127.0.0.1:63897 -> 19530
Forwarding from [::1]:63897 -> 19530
```

5. Finally, we verify whether the service is normal by sending a request to Milvus. To do this, follow step 5 in the *Deploying Milvus with Docker Compose* section:

```
 curl -X POST http://localhost:19530/v2/vectordb/collections/list -d '{}' -H
"Content-Type: application/json"
```

If the request result returns a normal JSON with no exceptions, it means that Milvus has been deployed:

```
{"code":0,"data":[]}
```

6. If you wish to uninstall Milvus, use the following command:

```
helm uninstall my-release
kubectl delete milvus my-release
```

And that concludes our deployment.

Summary

In this chapter, we explored various common deployment methods for Milvus, including Docker Compose, Helm chart, and Kubernetes operators. We learned their basic functions and features, made a simple functional comparison, and then used them to deploy Milvus one by one. Now that you understand these approaches, you can choose the most suitable deployment method for different application scenarios. For instance, if you only need to test certain functionalities locally, Docker Compose is a good option. If customization of resources is not required, the Helm chart is a simple and quick choice. However, if more granular control over resources is needed, then the Kubernetes operator is your best option. Now that you have deployed Milvus, we will cover how to communicate with Milvus in the next chapter, specifically looking at how we can use the SDK to send various requests.

Subscribe for a free eBook

New frameworks, evolving architectures, research drops, production breakdowns – *AI_Distilled* filters the noise into a weekly briefing for engineers and researchers working hands-on with LLMs and generative AI systems. Subscribe now and receive a free eBook, along with weekly insights that help you stay focused and informed.

Subscribe at `https://packt.link/8Oz6Y` or scan the QR code below.

3

Interacting with Milvus

In the previous chapter, we covered several deployment methods for Milvus. Now we can move on to the practical part: how to effectively interact with Milvus.

This chapter will walk you through the fundamental concepts of Milvus, including collections, schemas, fields, and indexes. We will also explain the basic workflow of using Milvus, which you can implement via the Python SDK. In addition, we will introduce a more lightweight way of accessing Milvus: the built-in REST service.

So, this chapter mainly covers the following three topics:

- Introducing the core objects of Milvus
- Interacting with Milvus via the Python SDK
- Interacting with Milvus via REST APIs

Technical requirements

The code used in this chapter can be found in our GitHub repository: `https://github.com/PacktPublishing/The-Architecture-Handbook-for-Milvus-Vector-Database`.

Introducing the core objects of Milvus

In this section, we will introduce some fundamental concepts of Milvus. Understanding these concepts is essential for working with Milvus, and they play a critical role in real-world business scenarios. The core concepts we will cover include collections, schemas, fields, and indexes.

Here is a brief overview of each concept:

- A **collection** is equivalent to a **table** in a relational database. As the top-level data container in Milvus, it stores logically related data.

- A **schema** is the structural definition of a collection, which consists of detailed data descriptions of multiple fields.
- A **field** corresponds to an individual column in the data structure, defining column attributes such as the column name and data type.
- An **index** is an auxiliary data structure used to speed up data queries. It can be built on both scalar columns and vector columns.

To help your understanding, we will explain them in a bottom-up order. Let's start with fields.

Fields

A **field** is the foundational unit for defining data attributes in Milvus, corresponding to a single column in a relational database table. It describes the characteristics of a specific category of data within a collection, and the set of all fields in a collection forms the core metadata of that collection.

To define a valid field, you must specify at least two mandatory attributes:

- **Field name**: A unique identifier for the field within the collection (must be a string)
- **Field type**: The data type of the values stored in the field (e.g., `INT64`, `VARCHAR`, or `FLOAT_VECTOR`), which must be explicitly declared

Depending on the chosen field type, you may need to configure additional type-specific properties (e.g., `max_length` for `VARCHAR` fields or `dim` for `FLOAT_VECTOR` fields). Beyond these, you can also set optional attributes to enhance functionality, such as marking a field as a primary key, enabling auto-increment for a primary key field, or designating a field as a partition key to optimize query performance.

To help you understand the concept of a field more intuitively, let's use a real-world example. Suppose we create a collection (analogous to a *table* in a relational database) for storing movie information. We need to record core details for each movie, including a globally unique movie ID, the director's name, the film's duration, and a 128-dimensional floating-point feature vector extracted from the movie poster. For the sake of simplicity, this collection only includes the preceding information; we can define the following corresponding fields:

```
field0 = FieldSchema(name="movie_id", dtype=DataType.INT64,
    is_primary=True),
field1 = FieldSchema(name="movie_director", dtype=DataType.VARCHAR,
    max_length=64),
field2 = FieldSchema(name="movie_duration", dtype=DataType.DOUBLE),
field3 = FieldSchema(name="movie_picture", dtype=DataType.FLOAT_VECTOR,
    dim=128),
```

The following is a detailed explanation of the definition of each field:

- `field0`: The field name is `movie_id` with a data type of `INT64`. The `is_primary=True` property indicates that this field is the primary key of the entire collection, and its values are globally unique across the collection, which can be used to uniquely identify each movie.
- `field1`: The field name is `movie_director` with a data type of `VARCHAR` (variable-length string). `max_length=64` sets the maximum byte length of the director's name stored in this field to 64.
- `field2`: The field name is `movie_duration` with a data type of `DOUBLE`, which is used to store the numerical value of the movie's duration.
- `field3`: The field name is `movie_picture` with a data type of `FLOAT_VECTOR`. The `dim=128` property indicates that this field stores the 128-dimensional floating-point feature vector generated after embedding the movie poster.

The definitions of `field0`–`field3` that we've given are just basic examples. Field definitions in Milvus support a wider range of configurable attributes to finely constrain the behavior and characteristics of fields.

A detailed breakdown of the core attributes is provided in the following table:

Attribute	Description
Name	The unique name of the field in the collection (string; mandatory).
Data type (dtype)	The data type of the field (e.g., `INT64`, `VARCHAR`, `FLOAT_VECTOR`; mandatory).
Description	An optional string that explains the purpose of the field (improves readability).
is_primary	Boolean (default: `false`). Marks the field as the primary key for the collection; at least one primary key field must be defined to uniquely identify entities.
auto_id	Boolean (default: `false`). Only applicable to primary key fields. Enables auto-incrementing values for the field (eliminates the need to manually assign primary key values).

Attribute	Description
is_partition_key	Boolean (default: `false`). Designates the field as a partition key (similar to an enum). Partitions are physically isolated in storage, so querying by partition key is faster than conditional filtering.
max_length	The maximum byte length of string values for `VARCHAR` fields (mandatory for the `VARCHAR` type).
Dim	The dimension of vector values for vector-type fields (e.g., `FLOAT_VECTOR`; mandatory for all vector fields).

Table 3.1: Field attributes

The data type is a mandatory parameter when defining a field, so let's provide more details about it.

Milvus supports a diverse set of data types, with distinct valid data type ranges for different field categories (primary key, scalar, and vector fields). The following is a breakdown of the supported data types by field category:

- **Primary key fields**: A primary key field must satisfy two requirements:
    - Its values must be unique across the entire collection
    - It can be used to quickly locate and retrieve corresponding entities

  Not all data types are eligible to be used as a primary key. Currently, only fields of type `INT64` or `VARCHAR` can be defined as the primary key in Milvus:
    - **INT64**: Occupies 8 bytes of memory and represents 64-bit integers
    - **VARCHAR**: Stores character strings of a user-specified maximum length
- **Scalar fields**: Scalar fields are used to store non-vector structured data, typically single-valued data such as numbers, strings, and Booleans, rather than high-dimensional vectors. They represent the most basic form of structured data in Milvus.
  Scalar fields support the following data types:
    - `BOOL`: Boolean value (`true` or `false`)
    - `INT8`: 1-byte integer that represents 8-bit signed integers
    - `INT16`: 2-byte integer that represents 16-bit signed integers
    - `INT32`: 4-byte integer that represents 32-bit signed integers

  - `INT64`: 8-byte integer that represents 64-bit signed integers
  - `FLOAT`: 32-bit (4-byte) floating-point number with approximately 7 significant digits of precision
  - `DOUBLE`: 64-bit (8-byte) floating-point number with approximately 15–17 significant digits of precision, higher than `FLOAT`
  - `VARCHAR`: Variable-length string with a user-specified maximum length
  - `JSON`: Composite data type composed of key-value pairs, where keys are strings and values can be numbers, strings, Booleans, arrays, or nested structures
  - `Array`: Ordered collection of homogeneous values
- **Vector fields**: Vector fields are purpose-built for storing high-dimensional vector data, Milvus' core data type for AI/ML and similarity search use cases, and support the following vector types:
  - `BINARY_VECTOR`: Stores binary vectors represented as a sequence of 0s and 1s (ideal for binary similarity matching)
  - `FLOAT_VECTOR`: Stores 32-bit single-precision floating-point vectors (the most commonly used vector type for general-purpose similarity search)
  - `FLOAT16_VECTOR`: Stores 16-bit half-precision floating-point vectors (balances precision and memory efficiency)
  - `BFLOAT16_VECTOR`: Stores 16-bit floating-point vectors with reduced precision but the same exponent range as `FLOAT32` (optimized for AI/ML workloads such as neural network embeddings)
  - `SPARSE_FLOAT_VECTOR`: Stores sparse vectors as a list of non-zero elements and their corresponding indices (highly efficient for representing sparse data such as text embeddings)

Now that we have covered the definition of fields and their supported data types, we can turn to schemas, which are a critical component that organizes these fields into a unified structural definition for a collection.

Schemas

In most data systems, effective data management relies on clear rules for organizing data within a dataset. For example, Excel spreadsheets use the first row to define column headers (specifying the type of data each column holds), while traditional relational databases require explicit definition of columns and their attributes (e.g., data types or nullability constraints) when creating a table.

In Milvus, a collection **schema** serves as the formal structural blueprint for a collection. Put simply, a schema is a structured combination of all field definitions for a collection, plus a small set of collection-level configuration properties (e.g., description) that govern data organization. Building on our detailed discussion of fields in the previous section, let's examine how to define a schema for a Milvus collection. Note that the `fields` variable in the following code references the field definitions we covered earlier (not redefined here for brevity). The code also demonstrates that, beyond the list of fields, the schema supports configurable properties such as `description`:

```
fields = [field0, field1, field2, field3]
schema = CollectionSchema(
    fields,
    description="movie info",
)
```

Given Milvus' core positioning as a vector-native database (designed exclusively for managing high-dimensional vector data), a critical rule applies to collection schema definition: every Milvus collection schema must include at least one vector field (e.g., `FLOAT_VECTOR` or `BINARY_VECTOR`). This is a fundamental requirement that distinguishes Milvus schemas from those of traditional relational databases (which focus on scalar data alone).

With a solid understanding of fields (individual data columns) and schemas (the structural blueprints for data), we can now explore collections, which are the top-level containers for storing data in Milvus.

Collection

In Milvus, a **collection** is the fundamental unit for users to manage data. We can create multiple collections, insert data into them, and perform retrieval or other operations on them. Building on our understanding of fields (individual data columns) and schemas (the structural blueprints for data), the meaning of a collection becomes clear; it is Milvus' equivalent of a table in a traditional relational database, where each row in the table corresponds to an entity (a single data record) in Milvus.

Building on the movie example we've been using, where we defined the fields for movie data and then created a schema for it, we can now easily create a movie collection, as shown in the following code:

```
milvus_client = MilvusClient("http://localhost:19530")
milvus_client.create_collection(
    collection_name="movie", dimension=128, schema=schema)
```

The preceding code creates a `"movie"` collection with the predefined schema and a 128-dimensional vector field.

Index

An **index** is an optional, additional specialized data structure built on top of specific columns (fields) in a collection. While the original fields only store raw data, an index leverages dedicated algorithms and optimized data structures to drastically reduce the time required for data retrieval. This optimization can apply to either scalar fields or vector fields: scalar indexes speed up filtering on fields such as movie IDs or release years, while vector indexes (the hallmark of Milvus) enable fast similarity search on high-dimensional vector data (e.g., movie embeddings). While indexes are not mandatory for creating or using a collection, they are critical for achieving high-performance queries, especially with large datasets.

For more details regarding vector indexes, you can refer to *Chapter 10*.

With these fundamental concepts in place, we will now explore how to operate and interact with Milvus in practice.

Interacting with Milvus via the Python SDK

For any database, the most critical capability is data querying—and for Milvus (a vector-native database), its core strength lies in enabling efficient querying of vector data. In the following sections, we will walk through a complete end-to-end data operation workflow to demonstrate how to use the Python SDK to interact with Milvus and achieve high-performance vector data querying.

Before interacting with Milvus, we need to complete two preparatory steps:

1. Start a Milvus service locally. As discussed in *Chapter 2*, there are multiple ways to launch a Milvus service; for example, we can use Docker Compose to start a standalone Milvus service on our local machine.
2. Install the PyMilvus SDK (the official Python SDK for Milvus) locally. We can do this by running the `pip install pymilvus` command in the terminal. This command will automatically install the latest stable version of the PyMilvus SDK.

Then, we can run through the end-to-end data operation workflow, which includes the following steps:

1. Connecting to Milvus
2. Creating a collection
3. Viewing collections
4. Inserting data

5. Querying the data with an ID of 2
6. Upserting the data with an ID of 2
7. Running a query with filtering
8. Deleting an entity
9. Carrying out vector search
10. Deleting the collection

The complete code can be found in the GitHub repository: `https://github.com/PacktPublishing/The-Architecture-Handbook-for-Milvus-Vector-Database/blob/main/ch3/hello_milvus.py`.

Let's get started!

Step 1: Connecting to Milvus

These two lines of code are the core operations for connecting to the Milvus service using the Python SDK:

```
from pymilvus import MilvusClient
milvus_client = MilvusClient("http://localhost:19530")
```

`pymilvus` is the official Python SDK for Milvus. The first line imports the `MilvusClient` class from the library; it is the core client tool provided by `pymilvus`, and all interactions with Milvus (creating a collection, inserting data, querying data, creating an index, etc.) must be performed through an instance of this class.

The second line instantiates the `MilvusClient` class, where `"http://localhost:19530"` is the specified Milvus service connection address (endpoint). When connecting to a local Milvus instance on macOS or Linux (non-Docker environment), this is the correct address to use. `19530` is the default fixed HTTP port for Milvus.

Step 2: Creating a collection

This code is used to create a Milvus collection with straightforward and easy-to-understand logic:

```
collection_name = "hello_milvus"
schema = milvus_client.create_schema()
schema.add_field("id", DataType.INT64, is_primary=True)
schema.add_field("vector", DataType.FLOAT_VECTOR, dim=8)
schema.add_field("score", DataType.INT64)
```

```
index_params = milvus_client.prepare_index_params()
index_params.add_index(
    field_name = "vector",
    Index_type="HNSW",
    metric_type="L2"
)
milvus_client.create_collection(
    collection_name,
    schema=schema,
    index_params=index_params,
    consistency_level="Strong"
)
```

This collection consists of three fields: the `"id"` field is of the `INT64` data type and serves as the primary key of the collection, the `"vector"` field is a vector column with the `FLOAT_VECTOR` data type, and the `"score"` field is also of the `INT64` data type.

As mentioned in the previous section, a Milvus collection must contain one primary key field and at least one vector field, and the preceding field definitions fully comply with these requirements. It should be noted that the syntax for defining fields and schemas here is slightly different from that introduced earlier, which is perfectly normal, as the Milvus Python SDK supports multiple syntax forms. You can choose which to use according to your personal preferences.

In addition, while creating this collection, we also specify the creation of a vector index for the `"vector"` field: the index type is `HNSW`, and the distance calculation method is `L2` (Euclidean distance). For more details about vector indexes, you may refer to *Chapter 10*.

In the preceding sample code, a key parameter, `consistency_level="Strong"`, is specified when calling the `create_collection()` method. This parameter is used to set the default consistency level of the collection to *strong consistency*, which means all data written to the collection will be synchronized in real time, and any subsequent query operations will be able to read the latest written results. If you wish to learn more about consistency levels, please refer to the detailed explanations in the official documentation: `https://milvus.io/docs/consistency.md#Set-Consistency-Level-upon-Creating-Collection`.

Step 3: Viewing collections

After creating a collection, we can use the `list_collections()` method provided by the SDK to verify whether the collection has been created successfully, and we can also use the `describe_collection()` method to check whether the data structure (fields, indexes, data types, etc.) of the collection is consistent with the definition specified during creation.

```
print(fmt.format(" all collections "))
print(milvus_client.list_collections())
print(fmt.format(f"schema of collection {collection_name}"))
print(milvus_client.describe_collection(collection_name))
```

The following is the output:

```
===  all collections                ===
['hello_milvus']

=== schema of collection hello_milvus ===
{'collection_name': 'hello_milvus', 'auto_id': False, 'num_shards': 1,
'description': '', 'fields': [{'field_id': 100, 'name': 'id', 'description': '',
'type': <DataType.INT64: 5>, 'params': {}, 'is_primary': True}, {'field_id': 101,
'name': 'vector', 'description': '', 'type': <DataType.FLOAT_VECTOR: 101>,
'params': {'dim': 8}}, {'field_id': 102, 'name': 'score', 'description': '',
'type': <DataType.INT64: 5>, 'params': {}}], 'functions': [], 'aliases': [],
'collection_id': 464678310267870512, 'consistency_level': 0, 'properties':
{'timezone': 'UTC'}, 'num_partitions': 1, 'enable_dynamic_field': False,
'created_timestamp': 464792252544450578, 'update_timestamp': 464792252544450578}
```

From the output of `list_collections()`, we can see that the collection hello_milvus has been successfully created.

From the result of `describe_collection()`, we can verify that the field structure of the collection matches the field schema defined in `create_collection()`.

In addition to the field schema information, `describe_collection()` also returns extra configuration details, such as `consistency_level`, `num_partitions`, and `enable_dynamic_field`. These are configurable parameters that can be specified during collection creation. Since we did not set them explicitly in this example, the SDK applied the default values automatically.

We will not explain each of these parameters in detail here; readers interested in further information may refer to the official Milvus documentation.

Step 4: Inserting data

After successfully creating a collection, we can insert data into it. The following code inserts six pieces of entity data into the target collection, with the core requirement that the structure of each data record must be consistent with the schema definition of the collection:

```
rng = np.random.default_rng(seed=42)
rows = [
    {"id": 1, "vector": rng.random((1, dim))[0], "score": 100},
    {"id": 2, "vector": rng.random((1, dim))[0], "score": 200},
    {"id": 3, "vector": rng.random((1, dim))[0], "score": 300},
    {"id": 4, "vector": rng.random((1, dim))[0], "score": 400},
    {"id": 5, "vector": rng.random((1, dim))[0], "score": 500},
    {"id": 6, "vector": rng.random((1, dim))[0], "score": 600},
]
print(fmt.format("Start inserting entities"))
insert_result = milvus_client.insert(
    collection_name, rows, progress_bar=True)
print(fmt.format("Inserting entities done"))
print(insert_result)
```

The following is the output:

```
=== Start inserting entities        ===

=== Inserting entities done         ===
{'insert_count': 6, 'ids': [1, 2, 3, 4, 5, 6]}
```

Upon successful insertion, Milvus returns an insertion result object containing key information: the total number of successfully inserted entries and the list of primary key IDs corresponding to the inserted data. In the preceding example, we print this result object to demonstrate that the data has been inserted successfully.

Step 5: Querying the data with an ID of 2

query is one of the most commonly used interfaces in the Milvus Python SDK, used to retrieve raw data from a collection. In this example, we specify the primary key value (`ids=[2]`) to precisely query and obtain the entity data with the primary key value of 2.

```
print(fmt.format("Start query by specifying primary keys"))
query_results = milvus_client.query(collection_name, ids=[2])
print(query_results[0])
```

The following is the output:

```
=== Start query by specifying primary keys ===
{'vector': [0.12811362743377686, 0.4503859281539917, 0.3707980215549469,
0.926764965057373, 0.6438651084899902, 0.822761595249176, 0.44341421127319336,
0.2272387146949768], 'score': 200, 'id': 2}
```

From the output of the query command above, we can see that the command retrieves the complete information of an entity in full, including the contents of the id, score, and vector columns.

Step 6: Upserting the data with an ID of 2

`upsert` is a core interface in the Milvus Python SDK for data updates (or insertion). If an entity with the specified primary key already exists, the content of that entity will be updated; if it does not exist, a new entity will be inserted.

In this example, we call the `upsert` interface to update the entity data with the primary key of 2 (modifying its vector value and score value), and then invoke the query interface again to retrieve the entity corresponding to this primary key.

```
upsert_ret = milvus_client.upsert(
    collection_name,
    {"id": 2, "vector": rng.random((1, dim))[0], "score": 220}
)
print(upsert_ret)
print(fmt.format("Start query by specifying primary keys"))
query_results = milvus_client.query(collection_name, ids=[2])
print(query_results[0])
```

The following is the output:

```
{'upsert_count': 1, 'primary_keys': [2]}

=== Start query by specifying primary keys ===
{'score': 220, 'id': 2, 'vector': [0.6824954748153687, 0.13975247740745544,
0.19990819692611694, 0.007362269796431065, 0.7869243621826172, 0.6648508310317993,
0.7051653861999512, 0.7807290554046631]}
```

We can see that the data has been updated successfully.

Step 7: Running a query with filtering

In *Steps 5–6*, we demonstrated the query method based on primary keys, while this example showcases another commonly used query method in Milvus — a scalar filtering query.

```
print(fmt.format("Start query by specifying filtering expression"))
query_results = milvus_client.query(
    collection_name,
    filter="score ==600")
for ret in query_results:
    print(ret)
```

The following is the output:

```
=== Start query by specifying filtering expression ===
{'id': 6, 'vector': [0.4371519088745117, 0.8326781988143921, 0.700265109539032,
0.31236663460731506, 0.8322597742080688, 0.8047643303871155, 0.38747838139533997,
0.2883281111717224], 'score': 600}
```

In above code, we specify the `filter="score == 600"` filter condition to filter and retrieve all entities in the collection where the value of the `score` field equals `600`.

Step 8: Deleting an entity

The following code demonstrates the usage of the *delete* interface in the Milvus Python SDK, deleting a specified entity by its primary key:

```
print(f"start to delete by specifying filter in collection {collection_name}")
delete_result = milvus_client.delete(collection_name, ids=[6])
print(delete_result)
print(fmt.format("Start query by specifying filtering expression"))
query_results = milvus_client.query(
```

```
    collection_name, filter= "score == 600")
assert len(query_results) == 0
```

The following is the output:

```
start to delete by specifying filter in collection hello_milvus
{'delete_count': 1}

=== Start query by specifying filtering expression ===
```

In this example, we call the delete interface to remove the entity with the primary key of 6 (the value of the `score` field for this entity is `600`); after the deletion operation is completed, we query the collection again using the `filter="score == 600"` scalar filter condition and use an `assert` statement to verify that the query result is empty, thereby confirming that the entity has been deleted successfully.

Step 9: Carrying out vector search

The following code demonstrates the most basic vector similarity search operation in Milvus:

```
rng = np.random.default_rng(43)
vectors_to_search = rng.random((1, dim))
print(fmt.format(f"Start search with retrieve serveral fields."))
result = milvus_client.search(
    collection_name,
    vectors_to_search,
    limit=3,
    output_fields=["score"]
)
for hits in result:
    for hit in hits:
        print(f"hit: {hit}")
```

The following is the output:

```
Start search with retrieve several fields.
hit: {'id': 3, 'distance': 1.1954224109649658, 'entity': {'score': 300}}
hit: {'id': 2, 'distance': 1.2375965118408203, 'entity': {'score': 220}}
hit: {'id': 5, 'distance': 1.5500348806381226, 'entity': {'score': 500}}
```

First, we randomly generate a vector to be searched (`vectors_to_search`), then perform a vector similarity search on the specified collection. We set `limit=3` to request the return of the three entities most similar to the vector to be searched and specify `output_fields=["score"]` to require the return of the values of the `score` field in the search results.

Step 10: Deleting the collection

`drop_collection` is a core interface in the Milvus Python SDK for deleting an entire collection. After executing this operation, the target collection will be completely removed, including all raw entity data, vector index data within the collection, as well as the schema metadata of the collection.

```
milvus_client.drop_collection(collection_name)
```

Please pay attention; this operation is irreversible.

Through these steps, we hope you have gained a basic grasp of how to interact with Milvus using the Milvus Python SDK. The complete runnable code can be obtained by accessing the following link: `https://github.com/PacktPublishing/The-Architecture-Handbook-for-Milvus-Vector-Database/blob/main/ch3/hello_milvus.py`.

We have explained in detail how to complete various core interaction operations with Milvus by means of the Milvus Python SDK through a series of examples. With its advantages of ease of use and high performance, the Milvus Python SDK is the preferred solution for Python developers to connect to Milvus. However, in actual development scenarios, the demand for cross-language and cross-system integration with Milvus is very common. Therefore, in the following section, we will introduce another universal interaction method, that is, interacting with Milvus via REST APIs.

Interacting with Milvus via REST APIs

There are scenarios where we may not have access to a programming language environment (e.g., for product team members) or do not wish to open a code editor for just one or two simple operations. In such cases, a common option is the REST API (provided that the service exposes RESTful endpoints). In this section, we will introduce how to use the REST API. Similar to the Python SDK, we will not elaborate on every parameter in detail here; for details on the full usage of each API, please refer to the official Milvus documentation: `https://milvus.io/api-reference/restful/v2.6.x/About.md`.

Step 1: Creating a collection

If you check the documentation linked previously, you will find that the example request in the link has the authorization header, which is mainly used for user password verification. By default, Milvus turns off this verification, so we don't set this header here:

```
curl --request POST \
--url "http://localhost:19530/v2/vectordb/collections/create" \
--header "Content-Type: application/json" \
-d '{
    "collectionName": "hello_milvus_http",
    "dimension": 5
}'
```

The response should be as follows:

```
{"code":0,"data":{}}
```

Step 2: Describing the collection

We can display all of the detailed information of a collection via the `describe` interface of the REST API:

```
curl --request POST \
--url "http://localhost:19530/v2/vectordb/collections/describe" \
--header "Content-Type: application/json" \
-d '{
"collectionName": "hello_milvus_http" }'
```

The response should be as follows:

```
{"code":0,"data":{"aliases":[],"autoId":false,"collectionID":
454786685267084134,"collectionName":"hello_milvus_http","consistencyLevel":"Bounde
d","description":"","enableDynamicField":true,"fields":
[{"autoId":false,"clusteringKey":false,"description":"","id":
100,"name":"id","partitionKey":false,"primaryKey":true,"type":"Int64"},
{"autoId":false,"clusteringKey":false,"description":"","id":
101,"name":"vector","params":
[{"key":"dim","value":"5"}],"partitionKey":false,"primaryKey":false,"type":"FloatV
ector"}],"indexes":
```

```
[{"fieldName":"vector","indexName":"vector","metricType":"COSINE"}],"load":"LoadSt
ateLoaded","partitionsNum":1,"properties":[],"shardsNum":1},"message":""}
```


Step 3: Listing all collections

We can use the following command to list all created collections:

```
curl --request POST \
--url "http://localhost:19530/v2/vectordb/collections/list" \
--header "Content-Type: application/json" \
-d '{}'
```

The response should be as follows:


```
{"code":0,"data":["hello_milvus_http"]}
```


Step 4: Checking the index information and load status of the collection

The REST API in *Step 1* will create an index and load the collection by default:

```
curl --request POST \
--url "http://localhost:19530/v2/vectordb/indexes/describe" \
--header "Content-Type: application/json" \
-d '{
    "indexName": "vector",
    "collectionName": "hello_milvus_http"
}'
```

The response should be as follows:


```
{"code":0,"data":
[{"failReason":"","fieldName":"vector","indexName":"vector","indexState":"Finished
","indexType":"AUTOINDEX","indexedRows":0,"metricType":"COSINE","pendingRows":
0,"totalRows":0}]}
```


We can also check the load status:

```
curl --request POST \
--url "http://localhost:19530/v2/vectordb/collections/get_load_state" \
--header "Content-Type: application/json" \
-d '{
```

```
    "collectionName": "hello_milvus_http"
}'
```

The response should be as follows:

```
{"code":0,"data":{"loadProgress":100,"loadState":"LoadStateLoaded"},"message":""}
```

Step 5: Carrying out a data query or search

It is not recommended to use REST APIs to insert or delete data, since these operations involve large vector inputs that result in excessively large and unreadable REST requests. A similar issue also applies to quer, because query responses return the full vector column data, which can be extremely large.

For example, we can convert the following Python statement into a REST request:

```
milvus_client.query(collection_name, ids=[2])

curl --request POST \
--url "http://localhost:19530/v2/vectordb/entities/query" \
--header "Content-Type: application/json" \
-d '{
    "collectionName": "hello_milvus",
    "filter": "id in [2]",
    "outputFields": ["id"],
    "limit": 1
}'
```

The response should be as follows:

```
{"code":0,"cost":0,"data":[{"id":2}]}
```

The search request will not be demonstrated here, because it involves vectors and is not very meaningful.

Step 6: Dropping the collection

We can drop the collection using the drop REST API:

```
curl --request POST \
--url "http://localhost:19530/v2/vectordb/collections/drop" \
--header "Authorization: Bearer ${TOKEN}" \
--header "Content-Type: application/json" \
```

```
-d '{
"collectionName": "hello_milvus_http"
}'
```

The response should be as follows:

```
{"code":0,"data":{}}
```

Generally speaking, we use REST APIs to perform only simple operations, such as creating/dropping indexes, loading/releasing collections, or checking the status of a collection.

Operations related to **Data Manipulation Language** (**DML**), which primarily include inserting, deleting, and upserting data (a subset of SQL used to insert, update, and delete data in a database), are difficult to implement via HTTP requests as the request payloads are hard to construct, the readability of such requests is poor, and errors are difficult to troubleshoot. For this reason, we recommend using an SDK for these types of operations.

Summary

In this chapter, we have introduced the core entity concepts in Milvus, including collections, schemas, fields, and indexes, as well as their associated API operations.

To reinforce these concepts, we walked through a basic practical example using Milvus' Python SDK, with a detailed breakdown of each step. Furthermore, we explored Milvus' built-in REST APIs, which enable quick execution of collection-related query operations.

At this point, you should have a general understanding of Milvus and a preliminary grasp of its basic usage. In the next chapter, we will learn about the configuration of Milvus, focusing on how to optimize its settings to ensure it runs more efficiently and stably.

Get this book's PDF version and more

Scan the QR code (or go to `packtpub.com/unlock`). Search for this book by name, confirm the edition, and then follow the steps on the page.

UNLOCK NOW

Note: Keep your invoice handy. Purchases made directly from Packt don't require an invoice.

4

Configuring the Milvus System

Before we begin this chapter, let's briefly recap the content we've previously covered, including an overview of vector databases, how to deploy Milvus, and how to interact with it. By this point, you should have a clear understanding of vector databases and Milvus. In this chapter, we will dive deeper into practical aspects of using Milvus, including the following:

- Understanding dependency services and startup configurations for Milvus
- Managing core system and service configurations in Milvus
- Modifying configuration

Technical requirements

We will continue to use fundamental tools, all of which are open source, including the following:

- **VS Code**: For installation, please refer to the *Technical requirements* section in *Chapter 1*
- **Docker**: For installation, please refer to the *Technical requirements* section in *Chapter 1*

In addition to these basic tools, we will also utilize some open source services to monitor system logs and metrics, including the following:

- **Prometheus**
- **Grafana**
- **Promtail**
- **Loki**

We will also use a Milvus development tool, **Attu**. Its download address is `https://github.com/zilliztech/attu`. Its function is to easily communicate with Milvus.

The code used in this chapter can be found on our GitHub repository: `https://github.com/PacktPublishing/The-Architecture-Handbook-for-Milvus-Vector-Database`.

Understanding dependency services and startup configurations for Milvus

To better understand Milvus, it's important to recognize the services it relies on and their primary functions. This knowledge will help in selecting appropriate dependency services for production environments. Here are the main services that Milvus depends on and their roles:

- **etcd**: etcd is an open source distributed key-value store primarily used for storing and managing configuration data, service discovery, and coordinating the state of distributed systems. Its core features include the following:
    - **Consensus algorithm**: Uses the **Raft** consensus algorithm (`https://raft.github.io/Raft`) to ensure data consistency and reliability.
    - **Simple key-value storage**: Facilitates easy data storage and retrieval through key-value pairs.
    - **Event notification mechanism**: Implements an observer pattern for event notifications, commonly used for service discovery.

  In Milvus, etcd is utilized for metadata storage, recording essential system information and data management details during operation. It also aids in service discovery and node health checks. Notably, etcd is a critical dependency for Milvus; if etcd becomes unavailable, Milvus will not function properly, leading to request failures and abnormal internal metrics. If etcd experiences slow service (e.g., due to high disk latency), it can increase response times or cause request timeouts in Milvus. However, once etcd recovers, Milvus will automatically return to normal operation.

- **Pulsar/Kafka/RocksMQ**: These options are all **message queue** (**MQ**) services, and you can choose one based on your needs during Milvus operation. MQs serve as a communication mechanism for transmitting data in distributed systems, allowing asynchronous information exchange between different applications or services. This helps alleviate system load, enhance performance, and achieve decoupling.

  RocksMQ is a lightweight MQ based on **RocksDB**, designed for minimalism. It is the default option in Milvus's standalone mode, but it is not suitable for cluster mode since it currently only supports file storage. Pulsar and Kafka are better suited for large-scale applications. *Table 4.1* shows the similarities and differences between them.

Similarity/ Difference	Kafka	Pulsar
Model support	Both support publish/subscribe models, allowing producers to send messages to topics and consumers to subscribe to those topics.	
Message storage	Both provide persistent message storage to ensure no loss of messages after system crashes.	
Horizontal scaling	Both utilize distributed architectures that can scale horizontally to handle large volumes of messages.	
Message delivery	Both are capable of managing high-throughput message delivery.	
Architecture design	Kafka employs a single-broker architecture that combines data storage and message delivery, with each broker responsible for storing and processing messages. (`https://kafka.apache.org/`)	Pulsar uses a separated architecture consisting of brokers and BookKeeper, allowing independent scaling of storage and computation. (`https://pulsar.apache.org/`)
Message model	Kafka primarily uses a log-structured message storage system, where consumed messages are retained by default until they expire or are deleted.	Pulsar supports multiple consumption models (including shared, exclusive, and failover) and allows configuration of message retention policies.
Processing latency	Kafka typically has lower latency in high-throughput scenarios but can be affected under certain conditions.	Pulsar, due to its architecture, usually performs better in terms of processing latency, making it suitable for low-latency applications.

Table 4.1: Similarities and differences between Kafka and Pulsar

When choosing between Pulsar and Kafka, it's vital to consider your specific application scenarios, requirements, and the technical stack of your team. Pulsar is better for multi-tenant and low-latency scenarios, while Kafka excels in high throughput and maturity.

In Milvus, an MQ is primarily used for logging services. All data writes first go to the MQ, where messages are consumed by two services within Milvus: **DataNode** and **QueryNode**. DataNode is responsible for data persistence, while QueryNode ensures the timely visibility of incremental data to guarantee query correctness.

- **MinIO/S3**: These are object storage services designed for managing and storing large volumes of data, especially unstructured data such as images, videos, documents, and backups. Unlike traditional filesystems, object storage does not use hierarchical directory structures but stores all objects in a flat namespace. Object storage is capable of handling massive data amounts, making it suitable for cloud computing and big data applications, with support for horizontal scaling.
  S3 is an object storage service provided by **Amazon Web Services** (**AWS**), widely used for cloud storage, offering various security and compliance options such as data encryption and access control.

  MinIO is an open source high-performance object storage server that is compatible with the Amazon S3 API. It is simple to deploy and suitable for both cloud and on-premises environments.

  In Milvus, object storage is used for data persistence. DataNode periodically retrieves data from the MQ and writes it in bulk to the object storage.

> Note
>
> **DataNode**
>
> DataNode is a server type that makes up Milvus. Its core function is to store data on disk. Milvus contains many roles, which are divided by function, such as `Proxy/RootCoord/DataCoord/DataNode/QueryCoord/QueryNode/IndexNode`.
>
> This concept will further be discussed in *Chapter 5*.

We will now focus on how to manage the Milvus system and configurations.

Managing core system and service configurations in Milvus

Configuration is a fundamental aspect of any system, allowing it to provide appropriate service capabilities in various application scenarios. This enhances scalability and enables dynamic adjustments to control system behavior in case of errors, effectively minimizing business losses.

Moreover, configuration is not only a backup method for problem resolution but also a means to adjust task scheduling and concurrency capabilities based on system load, thereby improving resource utilization. It can also control how the system responds to user requests, such as setting valid parameter ranges and resource limitations.

In Milvus, **system configuration** is managed through a YAML file located in the `configs` directory of the Milvus binary files, specifically named `milvus.yaml`. In the previous section, we discussed that Milvus supports three types of MQ: RocksMQ, Pulsar, and Kafka. When starting Milvus, you can select one of these options through the configuration. Additionally, a series of configurations is required to interact with dependency services, which are also specified in the `milvus.yaml` file.

The configuration organization in `milvus.yaml` groups similar-purpose configurations under specific nodes. For example, configurations for the `etcd` connection method and storage root path are all found under the `etcd` node.

The configuration file is structured as follows:

```
etcd:
  endpoints: localhost:2379
  rootPath: by-dev
  metaSubPath: meta
  kvSubPath: kv
  log:
    level: info # Only supports debug, info, warn, error, panic, or
fatal. Default 'info'.
    path: stdout
```

Of course, the preceding examples are not complete etcd-related configurations. Milvus also supports secure links by configuring etcd's auth and its SSL. Of course, if it is not needed, just delete it or leave it blank. Similarly, for other application services, it is similar. For example, to choose a service, the type configuration under the MQ node is used. The default value is default, which means that it is in standalone mode. You could also select RocksMQ or Pulsar based on the services you want to configure. If you want to customize it, select one of Pulsar, Kafka, or RocksMQ. For the specific service configuration of MQ, it depends on the selected MQ type. If you choose RocksMQ, configure the parameters for linking it under the `'rocksmq'` node; if you choose Pulsar or Kafka, set the link parameters under the `'pulsar'` and `'kafka'` nodes.

In addition to some class service configurations, Milvus' internal services also include some class configurations. We do not need to know the meaning and function of these services for the time being. We only need to understand that Milvus is composed of these services: `proxy`, `rootcoord`, `datacoord`, `querycoord`, `datanode`, `querynode`, and `indexnode`. Sometimes we also refer to these services as nodes.

Of course, these nodes are not static. As the architecture of Milvus evolves, new nodes may appear, or existing nodes may be deleted. For example, `indexcoord` still exists in the early version of Milvus.

> Note
>
> The version referenced in this book is Milvus 2.4.17. Careful readers will have also noticed that when introducing the deployment of Milvus in *Chapter 2*, we all use Milvus 2.4.17.
>
> The configuration of the service also follows the preceding configuration rules. The composition of Milvus services, such as `proxy`, `rootcoord`, and so on, is collectively referred to as a **node**.

For example, the configuration related to the `proxy` service is all in the proxy node in the `milvus.yaml` file. This would include configurations such as the proxy port, task queue length, task-specified scheduling concurrency, and basic verification of some fields in user requests, such as name length, restrictions on some attributes of collection, and so on. The following are common configurations in `proxy`:

```
proxy:
  maxNameLength: 255
# The maximum length of the name or alias that can be created in Milvus, including
the collection name, collection alias, partition name, and field name.
  maxFieldNum: 64 # The maximum number of field can be created when creating in a
collection. It is strongly DISCOURAGED to set maxFieldNum>= 64.
  maxVectorFieldNum: 4
# The maximum number of vector fields that can be specified in a
collection. Value range: [1, 10].
  maxShardNum: 16
# The maximum number of shards can be created when creating in a collection.
```

```
  maxDimension: 32768
# The maximum number of dimensions of a vector can have when creating in a
collection.
  maxTaskNum: 1024 # The maximum number of tasks in the task queue of the proxy.
  ddlConcurrency: 16 # The concurrent execution number of DDL at proxy.
  dclConcurrency: 16 # The concurrent execution number of DCL at proxy.
  port: 19530 # TCP port of proxy
```

The aforementioned configurations are not exhaustive for the proxy; their meanings will become clearer as you deepen your understanding of Milvus. For the complete system configurations, you can refer to `https://milvus.io/docs/system_configuration.md#Milvus-System-Configurations-Checklist`.

Additionally, common configurations that may be utilized by multiple nodes are placed under the `common` section in the configuration file.

Adjusting configurations before starting Milvus

Before starting Milvus, we need to adjust some configurations. We will use Docker Compose to redeploy Milvus, modify the configurations, and verify whether the changes take effect:

1. Before deployment, the `docker-compose.yml` file needs to be adjusted. Since we need to modify the `milvus.yaml` file before starting, we must map the `milvus.yaml` file to a local directory. This requires adjusting the volumes configuration in `standalone`. You can refer to the files in the `004-docker-compose` directory of the book's GitHub repository (*Chapter 4*) for the completed configuration file:

```
standalone:
    ...
    volumes:
      - ${DOCKER_VOLUME_DIRECTORY:-.}/volumes/milvus:/var/lib/milvus
      - ${DOCKER_VOLUME_DIRECTORY:-.}/configs/milvus.yaml:/milvus/configs/
milvus.yaml
    ...
```

2. Adjust the configuration in `milvus.yaml`. We will modify the `maxNameLength` setting under `proxy`. The default value is 255, and we will change it to 10, meaning that the name length for creating a collection cannot exceed 10. Please remember to save the file.

3. Start Milvus by navigating to the directory where the `docker-compose.yml` file is located and then executing the following command:

```
docker compose up -d
```

4. Use Attu to connect to Milvus.
5. The next step is to create a collection. When creating a collection, you need to specify collection-related attributes, one of which is the collection name. You can create collection names of different lengths.

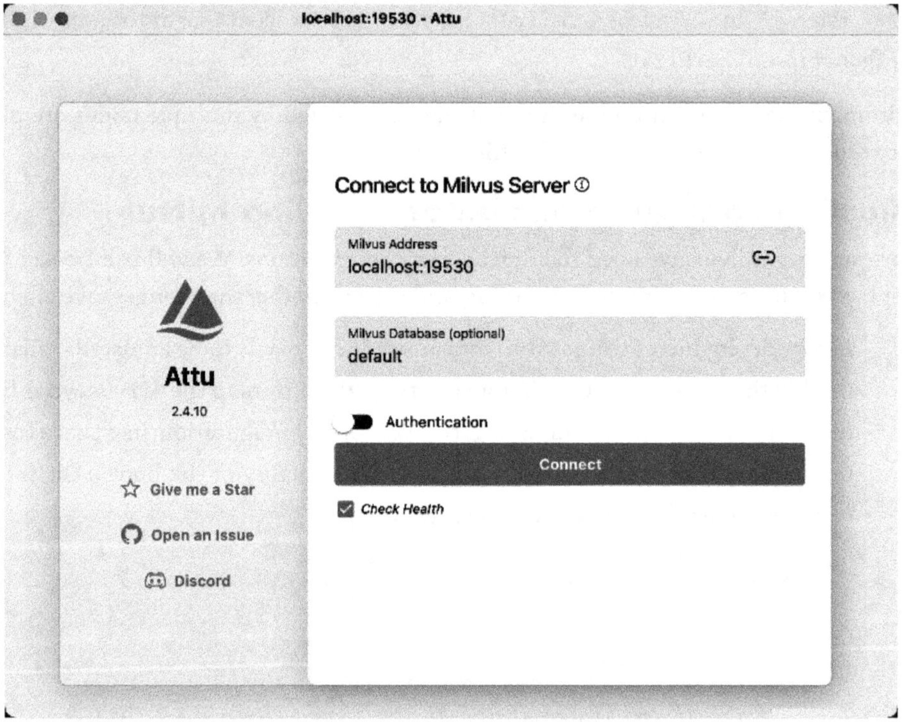

Figure 4.1: Getting started with Attu

6. Once you've connected, you'll see the home page. Click **default** under **Databases**.
7. When Attu is running inside a container, do not use `localhost:19530` to connect to Milvus, as it will cause a connection failure. Instead, specify the actual address of Milvus, such as `milvus-container-name:19530` or `host-IP:19530`.

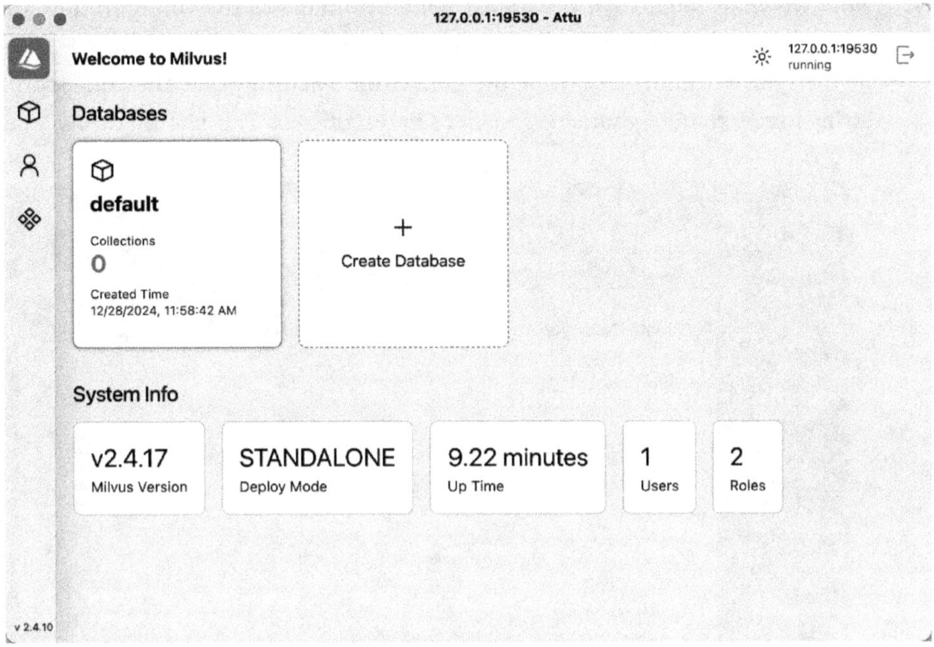

Figure 4.2: Attu home page after login

8. Next, click **Collection** to create a collection.

Figure 4.3: Attu Create Collection

9. Now we want to check if the adjustments we made to the configuration are in effect. Remember that we updated the filename maximum length to 10 in *step 2*. To test this, fill in the relevant information for the collection, ensuring that the collection name is a string longer than 10 characters, such as **hello_milvus**. This should throw an error.

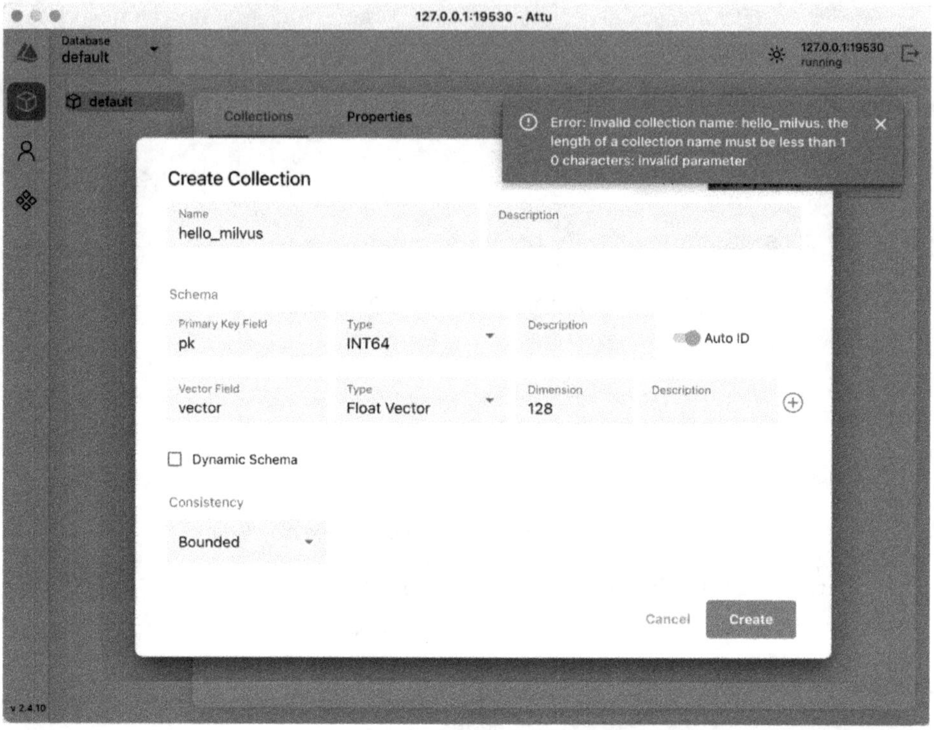

Figure 4.4: Attu Create Collection error

10. This error shows that the adjustments to the configuration are in effect.

Through this example, we have learned how to configure Milvus before startup. The method of setting other configurations is similar. This allows us to adjust Milvus settings based on specific production needs. Of course, we don't need to understand all of Milvus's configurations at once; we can refer to the Milvus configuration documentation and make adjustments as needed for specific requirements.

Let's now see how to modify a configuration during runtime.

Modifying configuration

In the previous section, we discussed how to adjust configurations before starting Milvus. Milvus also supports modifying configurations at runtime.

Parameters that can be dynamically adjusted usually require checking the configuration each time they are used, such as when validating the length of a collection name. Generally, parameters related to validation and thresholds (such as the maximum collection size) in Milvus can be dynamically adjusted.

Here's a brief overview of how Milvus implements dynamic configuration: at startup, Milvus reads the configuration file, formats the data, and stores it in variables. It periodically refreshes the file and compares its contents with the in-memory configurations. If changes are detected, the in-memory configuration values are updated, and events are triggered. Thus, Milvus allows for the registration of configuration change listeners, which will receive signals and execute corresponding logic when configurations change.

Remember that during the previous environment setup, we updated `maxNameLength` to 10. We will now directly adjust the `maxNameLength` configuration in `proxy` to 15 from 10:

```
maxNameLength: 15
```

After making this change, we can attempt to create a collection again. If the collection creation is successful, everything will work as expected. However, if you encounter a connection error when trying to create the collection, you should check whether the Milvus pods are running correctly. If they are not, simply restart the pods.

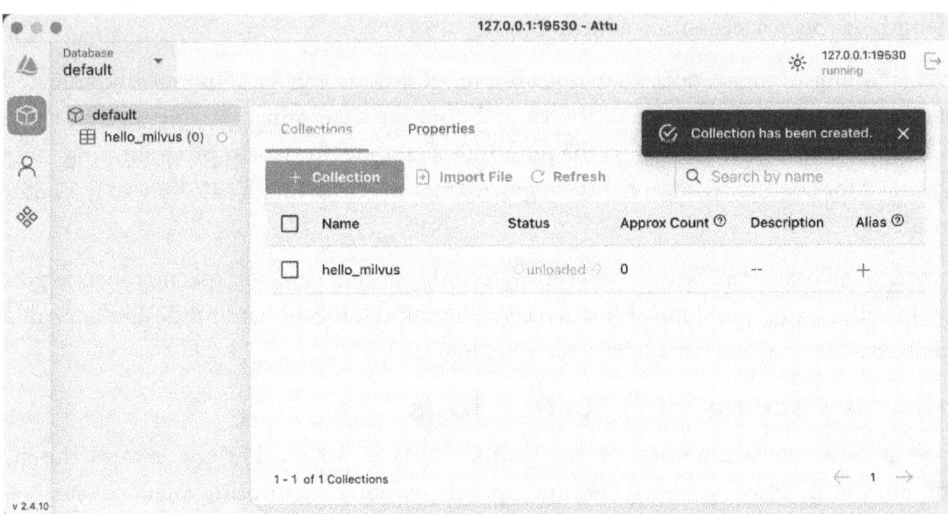

Figure 4.5: Attu Create Collection success

Next, if we try to create a collection with a name longer than 15 characters, such as **hello_milvus_backup**, it will result in an error, but **hello_milvus** will not. The error message will confirm that the maximum name length has been successfully adjusted to 15:

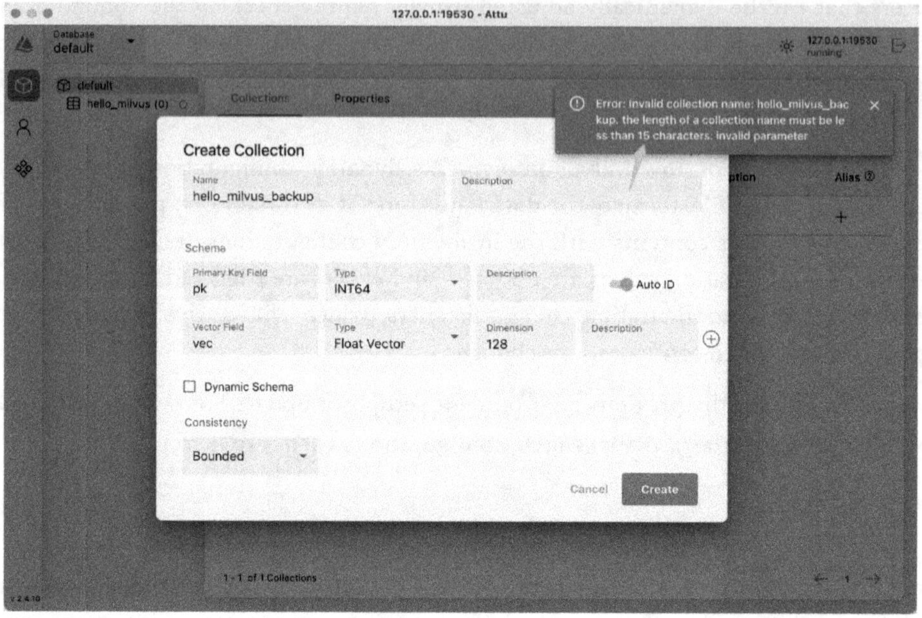

Figure 4.6: Attu Create Collection error

From the error message shown in the preceding figure, we can see that the current maximum name length has been successfully adjusted to 15.

However, it's important to note that not all configurations can be dynamically adjusted. For example, settings such as the size of the thread pool are determined at startup and cannot be changed afterward. This is similar to the length of a channel in the **Go** programming language, which is used for communication between **goroutines** and provides a safe way to pass data and synchronize.

Moreover, not all issues can be resolved through configuration changes; it is merely one potential method for addressing problems. Effective error handling requires careful design consideration for exceptional cases, along with robust recovery logic.

Monitoring access and system logs

Logs are an essential component of any mature system. To quickly understand the current operational status, most systems also incorporate various monitoring metrics, such as the number of collections in Milvus at any given moment and request latencies. A popular open source solution for logging and monitoring is the combination of Prometheus, Grafana, Loki, and Promtail.

Let's look at these services in more detail:

- **Prometheus**: Prometheus is an open source monitoring and alerting system designed for recording time series data. It pulls metric data via HTTP and supports various data storage and querying functionalities.
  Prometheus is well known for its **powerful query language** (**PromQL**) and flexible data model, making it suitable for monitoring microservices and containerized environments.
- **Grafana**: Grafana is an open source data visualization and monitoring platform. It supports multiple data sources (such as Prometheus, InfluxDB, and Elasticsearch), allowing users to monitor and analyze data through charts, dashboards, and alerting systems.
- **Loki**: Loki is an open source log aggregation system, designed similarly to Prometheus but focused on log data. It integrates seamlessly with Grafana, enabling users to query and visualize logs directly within Grafana, allowing for a consolidated view of metrics and logs.
- **Promtail**: Promtail is the log collection tool for Loki, responsible for gathering logs from various sources (such as files and system logs) and sending them to Loki.

By using this combination of tools, you can effectively monitor and log the performance and behavior of your Milvus system, gaining insights into its operational health and troubleshooting potential issues.

Deploying Prometheus and Grafana

Here, we will deploy Prometheus and Grafana to monitor Milvus metrics. We will use Docker Compose for this setup. Before we begin the deployment, we need to prepare the following:

1. Create an empty folder and name it `004-docker-compose-monitor`.
2. Enter the newly created folder and create a new `prometheus.yaml` file with the following content:

```
global:
  scrape_interval: 10s
scrape_configs:
  - job_name: 'prometheus'
    static_configs:
      - targets: ['standalone:9091']
```

Here, we use a very simple configuration, where `scrape_interval` represents the interval for collecting indicators. It is worth noting that the address in targets needs to be filled in as `standalone:9091`, because we need to interact with another Docker instance and use the network built in Docker Compose.

3. Modify `docker-compose.yml`, add Prometheus and Grafana services, and let Prometheus apply the configuration file. The completed configuration file can be found in the `004-docker-compose-monitor` directory in `ch4` of the GitHub repository of the book:

```
prometheus:
    container_name: milvus-prometheus
    image: prom/prometheus
    volumes:
      - ${DOCKER_VOLUME_DIRECTORY:-.}/prometheus.yml:/etc/prometheus/
prometheus.yml

    ports:
      - "9090:9090"
    command:
      - '--config.file=/etc/prometheus/prometheus.yml'
    depends_on:
      - "standalone"

  grafana:

    container_name: milvus-grafana
    image: grafana/grafana
    ports:
      - "3002:3000"
    environment:
      - GF_SECURITY_ADMIN_PASSWORD=admin
    depends_on:
      - "standalone"
 - "prometheus"
```

Note that the port mapped by Grafana is adjusted here to map port `3000` in Docker to local port `3002`, because local port `3000` may be occupied. For example, the Attu tool uses port `3000` internally. In other words, if Attu is opened, if port mapping also uses port `3000`, this will make Grafana inaccessible.

4. Access `http://localhost:3002/` locally through the browser. You will see a login page, and you can then log in. The username and password are both `admin`, which is the `GF_SECURITY_ADMIN_PASSWORD` setting in `docker-compose.yml`.
5. Add a data source to the Grafana service (that is, our Prometheus instance), and then you can operate according to the page.

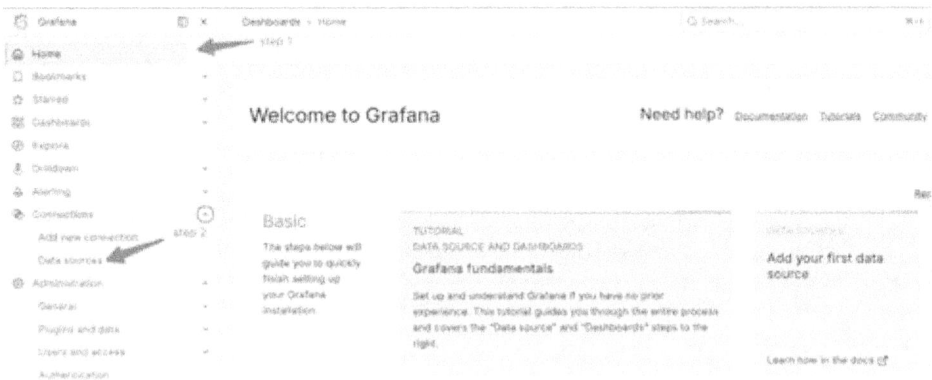

Figure 4.7: Grafana data source

6. When adding the address of Prometheus, fill in `http://prometheus:9090`. After filling this in, scroll down to the bottom of the page and click the **Save** button.

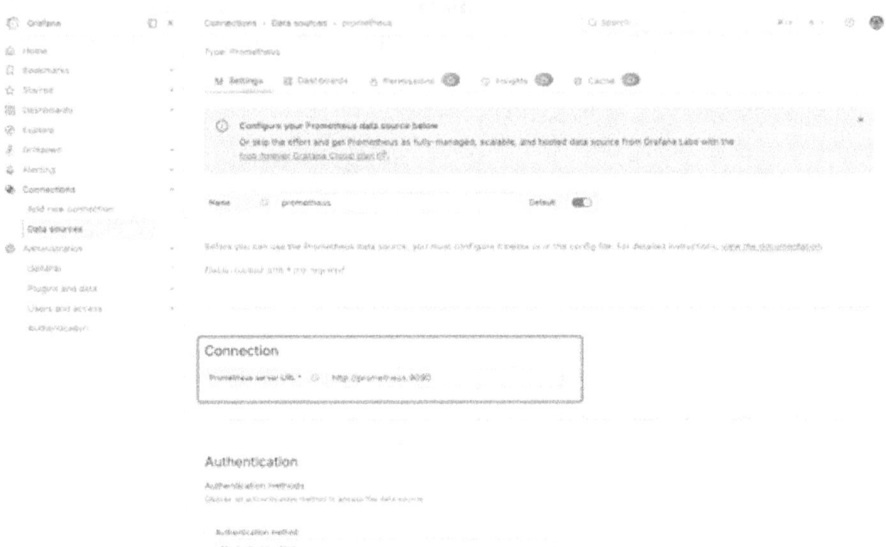

Figure 4.8: Adding Prometheus data source

7. Import the JSON of the Milvus dashboard; the file is `milvus-dashboard.json` in the `004-docker-compose-monitor` directory in *Section 4* of the book's GitHub repository. It is worth noting that the dashboard configuration file here is for a k8s deployment, but it doesn't matter. Let's import the dashboard first. Here, we mainly want to understand which panels there are and how to view them.

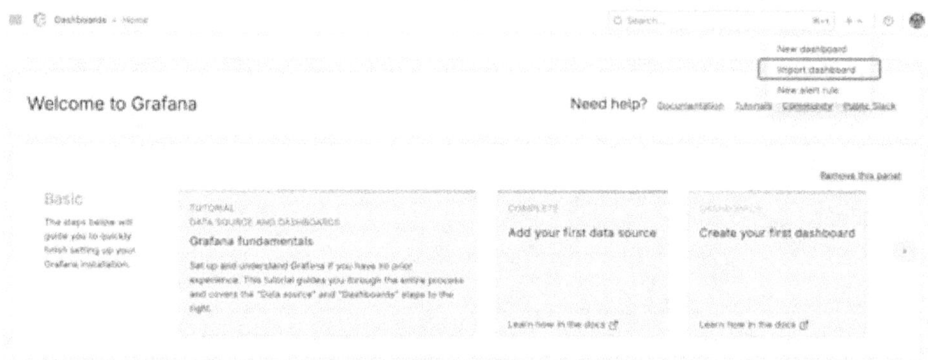

Figure 4.9: Grafana import dashboard

8. After the panel is imported, if there is no error message, it means it is successful. It is expected that there will be no data displayed. We find the **Root Coordinator** panel row and then find a **Collection Num** panel. After finding this panel, click it according to the following figure to enter the **Explore** page. Because we have successfully created a collection in the previous chapter, use this monitor to check whether this information can be seen.

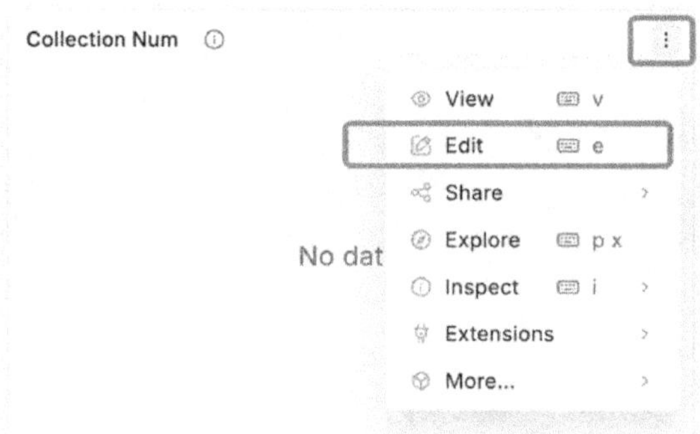

Figure 4.10: Grafana Explore page

9. Then, modify the statement to `milvus_rootcoord_collection_num{}`, and then click the **Run Query** button in the upper-right corner. If successful, you should see a page similar to the following figure:

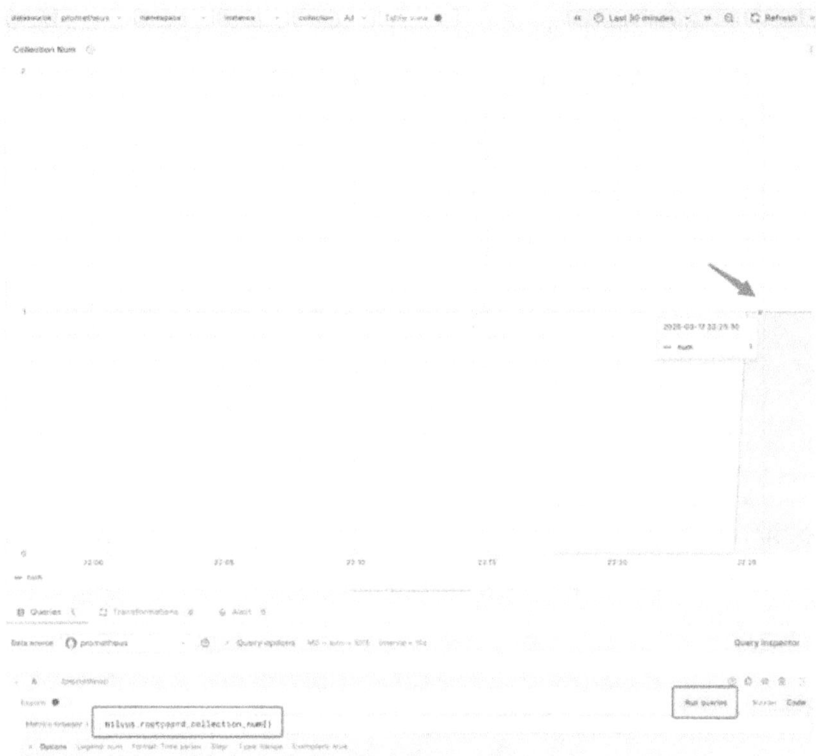

Figure 4.11: Grafana collection number metric

Through the steps outlined, we have successfully connected to the Milvus metrics. It's important to emphasize that since our dashboard is based on Kubernetes, it may not be compatible if deployed with Docker Compose. However, this is not an issue; we simply need to remove Kubernetes-related filtering conditions, such as `app_kubernetes_io_instance`, `app_kubernetes_io_name`, and `namespace`.

At first, it may not be clear which conditions are Kubernetes-related, but that's okay. Our main focus is on how to set up the entire metrics system.

If you want to learn more about metrics, such as how to write monitoring queries, it's advisable to read related books or visit the Grafana official website: `https://grafana.com/docs/grafana/latest/`.

Deploying Loki and Promtail

After successfully deploying Prometheus and Grafana, we can now focus on deploying Loki and Promtail. These services will allow us to query logs effectively. Using Loki, we can leverage LogQL to filter logs based on various conditions, which is extremely helpful for troubleshooting:

1. Adjust the configuration of Milvus and modify the log root node in `milvus.yaml`. Mainly, set `rootPath` to `/tmp` and `stdout` to `false`:

```
log:
  level: info
  file:
    rootPath: /tmp
    maxSize: 300
    maxAge: 10
    maxBackups: 20
  format: text
  stdout: false
```

2. Modify the file mapping of the Milvus standalone Docker instance in `docker-compose.yml` and map the log file to the current directory to facilitate the collection of the Promtail service:

```
  standalone:
    container_name: milvus-standalone
    ...
    volumes:
      - ${DOCKER_VOLUME_DIRECTORY:-.}/volumes/milvus:/var/lib/milvus
      - ${DOCKER_VOLUME_DIRECTORY:-.}/configs/milvus.yaml:/milvus/configs/
milvus.yaml
      - ${DOCKER_VOLUME_DIRECTORY:-.}/tmp:/tmp
    ....
```

3. Create two new files, `loki-config.yaml` and `promtail-config.yaml`, in the current directory. Loki uses the official default configuration, which can be found in the `004-docker-compose-monitor` directory in the fourth chapter of the GitHub repo corresponding to this book. Here, we emphasize the `promtail-config.yaml` file. When

configuring the client address, its domain name should use `loki`, and finally, set the log file for monitoring Milvus:

```
server:
  http_listen_port: 9080
positions:
  filename: /tmp/positions.yaml
clients:
  - url: http://loki:3100/loki/api/v1/push
scrape_configs:
  - job_name: milvuslog
    static_configs:
      - targets:
          - localhost
        labels:
          job: milvuslog
          __path__: /tmp/milvus/*.log
```

4. Add two services, Prometheus and Grafana, in `docker-compose.yaml`, which involves the mapping of configuration files:

```
  loki:
    container_name: milvus-loki
    image: grafana/loki
    ports:
      - "3100:3100"
    volumes:
      - ${DOCKER_VOLUME_DIRECTORY:-.}/loki-config.yaml:/etc/loki/loki-
config.yaml
    command: -config.file=/etc/loki/loki-config.yaml
  promtail:
    container_name: milvus-promtail
    image: grafana/promtail
    ports:
      - "9080:9080"
    volumes:
      - ${DOCKER_VOLUME_DIRECTORY:-.}/promtail-config.yaml:/etc/promtail/
config.yaml
      - ${DOCKER_VOLUME_DIRECTORY:-.}/tmp:/tmp/milvus
    command: -config.file=/etc/promtail/config.yaml
```

5. Start all services through the command, then access Grafana. As in the previous section, add a data source. This time, we select **Loki**. Fill in the address of the Loki service as `http://loki:3100`, and then click **Save**:

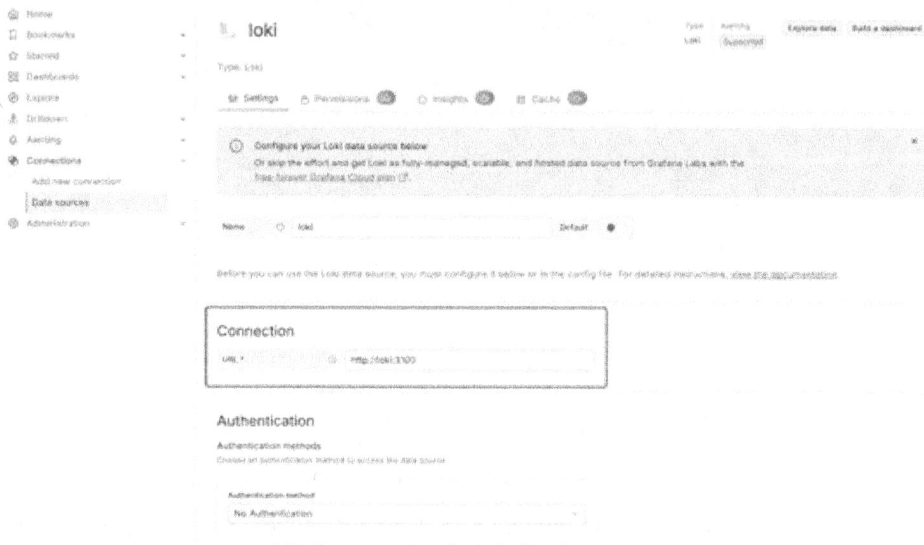

Figure 4.12: Adding a Loki data source

6. Go to the **Explore** page:

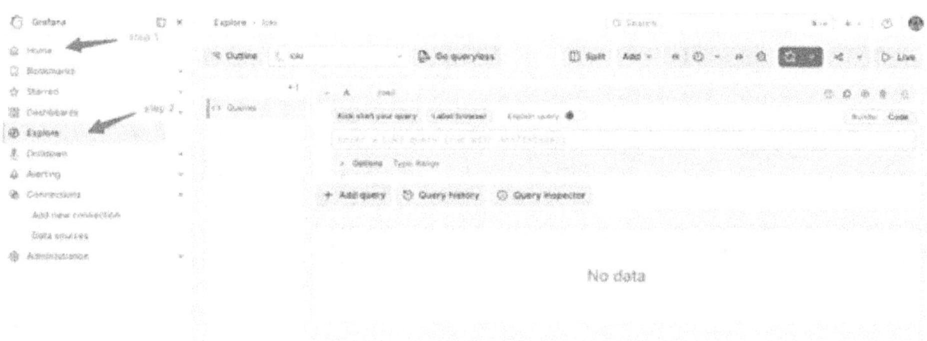

Figure 4.13: Grafana Explore page

7. Enter a query page, enter `{service_name="milvuslog"}` in the query box, and click **Run Query** to see the Milvus log:

Figure 4.14: Grafana-Loki Milvus log

Congratulations – you have now successfully completed the setup of the logging and monitoring services for Milvus!

Summary

In this chapter, we provided an overview of Milvus, focusing on its dependency services, configuration setup, and the deployment of related monitoring and logging services. These services are widely utilized in open source projects and can be applied across various cloud service scenarios.

With this knowledge, when encountering related issues while using Milvus, you will be able to address them more swiftly, whether by configuring different validation rules or leveraging the extensive monitoring metrics and powerful logging query system to pinpoint problems.

This concludes the first part of our discussion centered on the use of Milvus. In the next chapter, we will go deeper into the various internal process designs of Milvus, which will further enhance your understanding. I believe this will be an exciting journey!

Subscribe for a free eBook

Part 2

System Architecture and Data Lifecycle Management

Part 2 delves into Milvus' underlying architecture and core operating mechanisms, unpacking its data model, distributed, layered design, and end-to-end read-write data workflows. It elaborates on critical background maintenance processes, including data compaction and garbage collection, while clarifying the full lifecycle of data within the system. By studying this part, readers will gain a thorough understanding of how Milvus organizes, stores, and manages data stably at the architectural level, moving beyond surface-level usage to comprehend the system's internal operating logic.

This part contains the following chapters:

- *Chapter 5, Understanding the Milvus Data Model and Architecture*
- *Chapter 6, Data Modification and Maintenance in Milvus*
- *Chapter 7, Reading Data in Milvus*
- *Chapter 8, Compaction and Garbage Collection*

5

Understanding the Milvus Data Model and Architecture

In previous chapters, we covered how to get started with Milvus and use it to build applications. From this chapter through *Chapter 7*, we'll deepen our understanding of Milvus by exploring both its external interactions and internal workings.

In modern AI and data-driven applications, the ability to store, index, and query massive amounts of vector data efficiently is paramount. **Milvus' architecture** is designed from the ground up to grow with your needs, whether you're handling a few million embeddings for a recommendation engine or trillions of vectors for large-scale image search. In this chapter, we will dive deep into Milvus' scalable design, from the data model that defines how your data is organized to the multilayered architecture and the **message queue** (**MQ**).

We will cover the following topics in this chapter:

- Milvus data model
- Milvus' layered architecture
- MQ – the lifeline of streaming data

Technical requirements

The code used in this chapter can be found on our GitHub repository: `https://github.com/PacktPublishing/The-Architecture-Handbook-for-Milvus-Vector-Database`. To run these code examples, you'll need a Python >= 3.8 environment, which you can download from `https://www.python.org/downloads/`, and you should install all dependencies from the `ch5` directory using the `requirements.txt` file in *Chapter 5*:

```
pip install -r requirements.txt
```

In addition to Python dependencies, you'll need a running Milvus instance to execute the code in this chapter. For instructions on starting Milvus, refer to *Chapters 2* and *3*. Some examples can run directly on Milvus Lite without requiring a running Milvus instance; check Milvus' official documentation for more information on Milvus Standalone: `https://milvus.io/docs`. These examples will be specifically noted in the text.

Milvus data model

At the heart of any database lies its **data model**, which defines how data is structured, stored, and accessed. **Milvus' data model** is a **vector model**, specially designed for managing vector data, that enforces structure while allowing for dynamic fields. It's structured into **collections**, **entities**, and **fields**.

In this section, we will introduce the concepts of collection, entity, field, and schema with examples. Then, we're going to introduce how partitions and shards subdivide the collection for parallelism and efficient retrieval. Let's first talk about the key concepts of collection, entity, and schema.

Collection, entity, and schema

Collection, **entity**, and **schema** are equivalent to table, row, and column in relational databases. For example, a collection named `movies` may store one entity for each movie, with fields such as ID, title, genre, release year, and embedding, just as a `movies` table in a relational database stores one row per movie with corresponding columns. The schema defines these fields and their data types, much like a table definition in a relational database.

A **collection** in Milvus is the logical container of data; it's where entities are actually stored, indexed, and queried. All read and write operations in Milvus are performed on a specific collection. Each collection contains vector embeddings, metadata fields, and index information. A collection stores entities (records) that follow a defined schema.

An **entity** is a single row of data in a collection. A field defines the attributes of an entity. Each collection has a name: a schema that defines its structure, shards, partitions, and segments. It's the actual data itself, plus metadata and the schema definition. Here's a code example:

```
{
    "id": 101,
```

```
    "title": "Milvus Tutorial",
    "embedding": [0.12, 0.55, 0.91, ...]
}
```

This entity contains a **primary key** (**PK**) ID, a metadata title, and a vector embedding – a total of three fields.

A **schema** of a collection describes the structure and constraints of the entity inside a collection. It describes what fields exist, their types, and roles. When you create a collection, you must provide a schema that specifies field definitions that define the name, data types, and other properties of the field.

For example, consider a collection named `articles`. Its schema contains three fields: `id`, `title`, and `embedding`. The `id` field uses the `INT64` data type and serves as the PK. The `title` field uses the `VARCHAR` data type with a maximum length of 128 bytes. The `embedding` field uses the `FLOAT_VECTOR` data type with a dimension of 768. Here's an example:

```
Collection: articles
Fields:
id(INT64, primary key)
title(VARCHAR, max_length=128)
embedding(FLOAT_VECTOR, dim=768)
```

Milvus enforces a strict **schema model** for collections while allowing for one special dynamic field to allow flexibility, which is represented with a JSON data type. A strict schema model means every field must be declared up front in the collection schema. Each field has a fixed name, type, and role (e.g., PK, partition key). When you insert data, entities must conform to the schema.

In Milvus, a collection schema must have at least two fields: a **PK** field and a **vector** field.

Next, let us use the real open source dataset *Cohere wikipedia-2023-11-embed-multilinguul-v3* (`https://huggingface.co/datasets/Cohere/wikipedia-2023-11-embed-multilingual-v3`) as an example to create a Wikipedia collection in Milvus. The dataset uses Cohere's multilingual embedding model (`embed-multilingual-v3`), supports multiple languages, and each document contains a title, body text, and a pre-computed 1024-dimensional vector embedding.

To simplify the demonstration, let's focus on the English (`"en"`) subset and get familiar with the dataset:

```
# Import the load_dataset function from the HuggingFace datasets library
# This function allows us to download and load datasets directly from HuggingFace
```

```
Hub
from datasets import load_dataset

# Import Polars library
# Polars is a fast DataFrame library (similar to pandas but faster for large data)
# It is often used for high-performance data processing
import polars as pl

# Name of the dataset hosted on HuggingFace Hub
# This dataset contains Wikipedia text embeddings generated using Cohere's
multilingual embedding model
DS = " Cohere/wikipedia-2023-11-embed-multilingual-v3"

# Load the dataset
wiki_ds = load_dataset(
    DS, # Dataset name on HuggingFace Hub
    "en", # Configuration / subset of dataset of dataset (English Wikipedia)
    split="train", # Which split of the dataset to load(train/test/validation)
    streaming=True # Enables streaming mode so the dataset is not fully downloaded
                   # instead, it is read lazily row-by-row which saves memory.
)

# Print the schema / structure of the dataset
# This shows the dataset fields such as text, title, embeddings, etc.
print(wiki_ds.features)
```

After executing the preceding code, you'll see an output similar to the following. This dataset contains five attributes – `_id`, `url`, `title`, `text`, and `emb`:

```
{'_id': Value('string'), 'url': Value('string'), 'title': Value('string'), 'text':
Value('string'), 'emb': List(Value('float32'))}
```

Next, we use the Wikipedia dataset as an example to create a collection named `coll_wiki` with only the `id` and `emb` fields in Milvus. This example uses Milvus Lite for demonstration. As long as you have PyMilvus with Milvus Lite installed (see the `requirements.txt` file in the `ch5` directory), you don't need to run a Milvus instance:

```
# Import MilvusClient to interact with the Milvus vector database
# Import DataType to define types in the schema
from pymilvus import MilvusClient, DataType
```

```
# Create a schema object that will define the structure of the collection
# A schema describes what fields exist in the collection and their data types.
schema = MilvusClient.create_schema()

# Add a field name "id" to the schema
# datatyp=INT64 means the field stores 64-bit integers
# is_primary=True means this field is the primary key (unique identifier for each
record)
schema.add_field(field_name="id", datatype=DataType.INT64, is_primary=True)

# Add a vector field named "emb"
# datatype=FLOAT_VECTOR means this field will store vector embeddings
# dim = 1024 means each vector contains 1024 floating point values
# This dimension must match the embedding model output size.
schema.add_field(field_name="emb", datatype=DataType.FLOAT_VECTOR, dim=1024)

# Initialize a Milvus client connection
# uri="./milvus.db" creates or connects to a local Milvus Lite database file
# This is useful for local development and testing without running a full Milvus
server
client = MilvusClient(uri="./milvus.db")

# Create a new collection named "coll_wiki"
# The collection will follow the schema defined above
# If the collection already exists, Milvus may throw an error depending on
configuration.
client.create_collection(collection_name="coll_wiki", schema=schema)
```

In the preceding code, we have the following:

- The `id` field is declared as the PK field with `is_primary=True`, corresponding to the `_id` attribute in the dataset.
- The `embed` field is set to the vector field, whose data type is set to `FLOAT_VECTOR` with a dimension of 1024. The `FLOAT_VECTOR` data type is one of the vector data types supported by Milvus, which internally uses `float32` to store each floating-point value.

Now that we know about the basic concepts of collection and schema, let's talk about what an entity may consist of.

Entity composition

An entity is a single data point in a collection. Each entity contains the following four types of fields:

1. **Required fields**: Required fields are fields that must be present in every entity inserted into a collection. These fields are defined in the collection schema and cannot be omitted during insertion. Milvus entities require one PK field, and as a vector database, at least one vector field. Milvus doesn't guarantee the uniqueness of the PK value if you provide your own PKs.
2. **Predefined fields**: Predefined fields are fields that are explicitly defined in the schema before the collection is created. These fields store structured metadata along with vectors. Defined by the schema, Milvus entities may contain optional fields of scalar data types, such as `INT64`, `VARCHAR`, `JSON`, `ARRAY`, `AND`, and so on.
3. **Dynamic fields**: Dynamic fields allow the storage of additional fields that are not predefined in the schema. Defined by the schema, Milvus entities may contain one optional schema-less field for flexibility, which is stored as a `JSON` data type. It is useful when some entities need to store additional data.
4. **System-reserved fields**: System-reserved fields are fields that are automatically managed by Milvus and cannot be used as user-defined field names. Reserved by the system, Milvus adds these two fields to all collections: `RowID` and `Timestamp`. The `RowID` field ensures uniqueness, while `Timestamp` enables **multi-version concurrency control** (**MVCC**) and query consistency. Unlike the PK field, the `RowID` field is guaranteed to be unique.

> Note
>
> **MVCC** is a technique that allows concurrent data access without locking. In Milvus, the Timestamp field serves as the version. When a query runs, it sees only data committed before that timestamp, ensuring consistent reads even during ongoing writes.

Figure 5.1 illustrates what an entity contains:

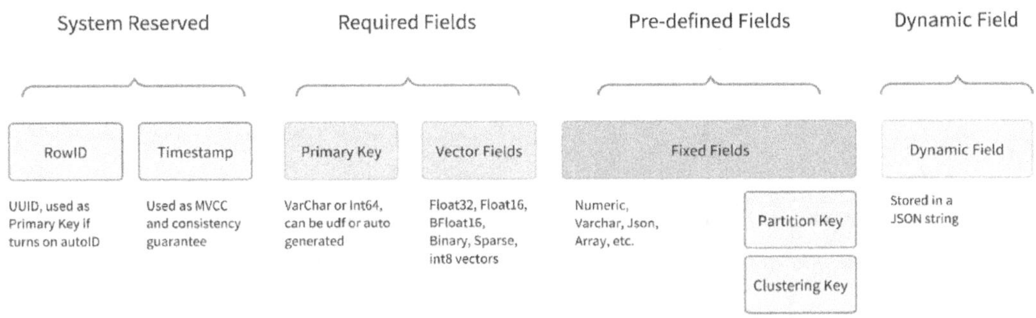

Figure 5.1: What an entity contains

Let's take an example to create a `coll_wiki_2` collection with all four types of fields and insert one entity into the collection using the Wikipedia dataset.

Following the previous code, let us get the first row from the dataset and insert it into the collection. We won't download the full dataset, so don't worry if it's too big to download:

```
# Import the Milvus client and DataType definitions
# MilvusClient is used to connect and interact with the Milvus database
# DataType helps define the type of each field in the schema
from pymilvus import MilvusClient, DataType

# Create a connection to a local Milvus Lite database
# "./coll_wiki.db" is the local database file where Milvus will store the
collection
client = MilvusClient(uri="./coll_wiki.db")

# Create a schema for the collection
# enable_dynamic_field=True allows inserting fields that are not predefined in the
schema
# These additional fields will automatically be stored in Milvus' internal $meta
field
schema = MilvusClient.create_schema(enable_dynamic_field=True)

# Add a primary key field called "id"
# datatype=VARCHAR means the id will be stored as a string
# is_primary=True indicates this is the unique identifier for each entity
# max_length=128 defines the maximum allowed string
```

```
lengthschema.add_field(field_name="id", datatype=DataType.VARCHAR,
is_primary=True, max_length=128)

# Add a vector field called "emb"
# datatype=FLOAT_VECTOR indicates that this field stores vector embeddings
# dim=1024 means each vector contains 1024 float values
# The dimension must match the embedding model output
schema.add_field(
    field_name="emb", datatype=DataType.FLOAT_VECTOR, dim=1024)

# Add a "title" field to store the title of the document/article
# VARCHAR allows storing string text
# max_length=256 defines the maximum character limit
schema.add_field(
    field_name="title", datatype=DataType.VARCHAR, max_length=256)

# Add a "url" field to store the source URL of the article
# A very large max_length is used since URLs can be long
schema.add_field(
    field_name="url", datatype=DataType.VARCHAR, max_length=65535)

# Add a "text" field to store the full content of the article
# Again using VARCHAR with a large max_length to support long documents
schema.add_field(
    field_name="text", datatype=DataType.VARCHAR, max_length=65535)

# Create the collection in Milvus using the defined schema
# "coll_wiki_2" will store Wikipedia embeddings along with metadata
client.create_collection(collection_name="coll_wiki_2", schema=schema)

# Extract the primary key value from the dataframe
# df['_id'][0] gets the first record's id
pk = df['_id'][0]
entity = {
    "id": pk,                  # Primary key
    "emb": df['emb'][0],       # 1024-dimension embedding vector
    "title": df['title'][0],   # Article title
    "text": df['text'][0],     # Article content
    "url": df['url'][0],       # Source URL
    # This field is NOT defined in the schema
    # Because dynamic fields are enabled, Milvus will store this inside the
```

```
internal $meta field
    "extra": "This will go into dynamic field".
}

# Insert the entity into the collection
# data must be a list of entities even if inserting a single record
client.insert(collection_name="coll_wiki_2", data=[entity])
```

Milvus will create a field named `$meta` with a `JSON` data type when you set `enable_dynamic_schema = True`, as the example shows. The extra information in the example entity will be inserted into this dynamic field.

The `title` field is set to the `VARCHAR` data type with `max_length = 256` properties to constrain the max size of variable character fields.

Then, let's get the inserted row from the `coll_wiki_2` collection and output the entity, except for the `emb` field because it's too large to display:

```
# Retrieve an entity (record) from the collection using the primary key
# "coll_wiki_2" is the collection name from which the record will be fetched
# pk is the primary key value of the entity we want to retrieve
# output_fields specifies which fields we want
res = client.get(
    "coll_wiki_2", pk,
    output_fields=["id", "title", "text", "url", "extra"])

# Print the retrieved entity
# The result will usually be a list of dictionaries
print(res)
```

Here's the output:

```
data: ["{'id': '20231101.en_13194570_0', 'text': 'The British Arab Commercial Bank
PLC (BACB) is an international wholesale bank incorporated in the United Kingdom
that is authorised by the Prudential Regulation Authority (PRA) and regulated by
the PRA and the Financial Conduct Authority (FCA). It was founded in 1972 as UBAF
Limited, adopted its current name in 1996, and registered as a public limited
company in 2009. The bank has clients trading in and out of developing markets in
the Middle East and Africa.', 'title': 'British Arab Commercial Bank', 'url':
'https://en.wikipedia.org/wiki/British%20Arab%20Commercial%20Bank', 'extra': 'This
will go into dynamic field'}"], extra_info: {}
```

Now that we know about what an entity may consist of in Milvus, let's talk about two ways to physically divide a collection for parallelism and scalability: partitions and shards.

Partitions and **shards** are two types of physical subdivisions of a collection. They are used in conjunction with each other, meaning if a collection has two partitions and two shards, the data will be physically divided into four parts. In *Figure 5.2*, *Collection A* contains two shards (*Shard 1* and *Shard 2*) and two partitions (*Partition A* and *Partition B*). Each shard holds four segments. Each partition also holds four segments. Inside each shard and partition combination, there are two segments.

From the perspective of shards, the collection's data consists of *Shard 1* and *Shard 2*. From the perspective of partitions, it consists of *Partition A* and *Partition B*:

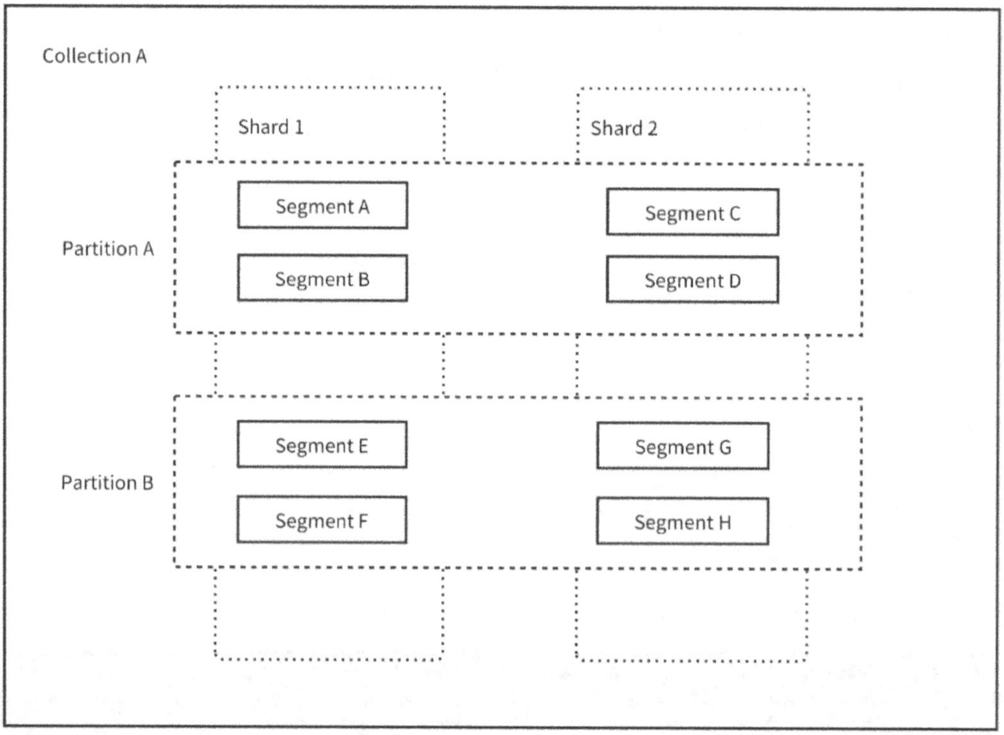

Figure 5.2: Collection layout

Let's first dive into partitions.

Partition

Partitions are used to logically divide a collection into smaller segments of data. This helps organize data and improve search efficiency by restricting queries to specific subsets. Partitions allow you to group data based on some criteria relevant to your application (e.g., by date, category, or user group). There are two ways to manage partitions in a collection.

However, partitions should not be overused; creating too many partitions can increase management overhead and negatively impact performance. Instead, design partitions around meaningful data segmentation and keep the number of partitions relatively small while ensuring balanced data distribution across them.

Partition APIs

The first way to divide your collection into partitions is by **user-defined partitions** that are fully controlled and managed via **partition-related APIs**. Partitions in a collection are small collections sharing the same schema. You can manage partitions to, for example, create, drop, load, search, insert, and so on, just like managing a collection.

The following example creates two partitions named `"p1"` and `"p2"` and inserts an entity into each partition using the Wikipedia dataset. Note that partition-related APIs are not supported in Milvus Lite; you need to deploy a Milvus Standalone or cluster instance first before running this code:

```
# Create two partitions named "p1" and "p2"
client.create_partition(
    collection_name="coll_wiki_2", partition_name="p1")
client.create_partition(
    collection_name="coll_wiki_2", partition_name="p2")

# Get two rows from Wikipedia dataset
rows = list(dataset.take(2))

# Insert first entity into partition "p1"
entity1 = {
    "id": rows[0]['id'],
    "emb": rows[0]['emb'],
    "title": rows[0]['title'],
    "text": rows[0]['text'],
    "url": df['url'][1],
    "extra": "This entity is in partition p1"}
res1 = client.insert(
```

```
    collection_name="coll_wiki_2", data=entity1, partition_name="p1")
print(f"Inserted into p1: {res1}")

# Insert second entity into partition "p2"
entity2 = {
    "id": rows[1]['id'],
    "emb": rows[1]['emb'],
    "title": rows[1]['title'],
    "text": rows[1]['text'],
    "url": df['url'][2],
    "extra": "This entity is in partition p2"}
res2 = client.insert(
    collection_name="coll_wiki_2", data=entity2, partition_name="p2")
print(f"Inserted into p2: {res2}")
```

The entities in different partitions are separated physically. To insert data into a certain partition, you need to provide a partition name in the insert API. Milvus would write entities to the collection's default partition if you left the partition name empty. To get data from certain partitions, you also need to provide the partition names when querying, or Milvus will go through the entire collection.

By providing partition names in these APIs, you can narrow down the API scope to the partition level, saving lots of resources while increasing performance.

However, due to the physical subdivision, Milvus can only maintain up to 4096 (configurable) partitions per collection. To address these issues, Milvus introduces a second way to divide the collection into partitions, which requires no maintenance for the user while supporting millions of partition keys.

Partition key field

The second way to partition a collection is to use a **partition key field**. When creating a collection with a schema, you designate one field as the partition key field, and Milvus uses it to automatically distribute data across internal partitions.

Because the partition key field manages partition placement internally, you can no longer manually create or drop individual partitions, nor can you target a specific partition directly in a search. The full lifecycle of those partitions (that is, their creation, data routing, and deletion) is delegated entirely to Milvus.

When you insert entities, Milvus computes a hash of each entity's partition key field value and routes the entity to the appropriate partition automatically. The partition key is a lightweight logical concept: multiple distinct key values may map to the same underlying physical partition.

To make this concrete, imagine building a semantic movie search engine over the MongoDB `embedded_movies` dataset, available via the Hugging Face `datasets` library. The dataset includes a `plot` field, a pre-computed `plot_embedding` vector (generated with OpenAI's `text-embedding-ada-002` model at 1536 dimensions), and a `genre` field. By designating genre as the partition key, Milvus automatically groups movies by genre at insert time; so, a search for films similar to a given action movie plot never needs to scan the `Drama` or `Comedy` partitions at all:

```
# create collection with partition-key enabled
schema = client.create_schema(auto_id=True, enable_dynamic_field=False)
schema.add_field("id", DataType.INT64, is_primary=True)
schema.add_field("title", DataType.VARCHAR, max_length=512)
schema.add_field("plot", DataType.VARCHAR, max_length=4096)
schema.add_field(
    "genre", DataType.VARCHAR, max_length=64, is_partition_key=True)
schema.add_field("embedding", DataType.FLOAT_VECTOR, dim=1536)

client.create_collection(
    collection_name="coll_enables_partitionkey", schema=schema)
```

Next, let's dive into shards, which are another method to physically divide a collection.

Shards

A shard is also a physical subdivision of a collection, designed to process streaming data efficiently. In conjunction with partitions, the underlying resources of a shard are **virtual channels (VChannels)** in the MQ (see the *MQ – the lifeline of streaming data* section later in this chapter). Shards are defined once at collection creation time and are immutable; you cannot change the number of shards after a collection has been created.

Milvus creates one VChannel for each shard when creating a collection, and every new collection starts with one shard by default. You can override this when creating the collection. The following example code creates a collection with four shards:

```
client.create_collection(
    "coll_enables_four_shards", schema=schema, num_shards=4)
```

When you insert an entity, Milvus hashes the PK value to determine which shard receives it. For a collection with four shards, the routing rule is `Hash(PK) % 4`. Entities whose PK is 0, 4, or 8 all hash to shard 0.

We'll talk about MQs and VChannels in detail in the last section of this chapter.

Let us walk through a concrete example of how shard and partition key routing work together when inserting four entities into a collection.

First, let's define a schema and create a collection with a partition key field with two shards and two partitions:

```
client = MilvusClient(uri="http://localhost:19530")
schema = MilvusClient.create_schema()
schema.add_field(
    field_name="id", datatype=DataType.INT64, is_primary=True)
schema.add_field(
    field_name="title", datatype=DataType.VARCHAR, max_length=512)
schema.add_field(
    field_name="plot", datatype=DataType.VARCHAR, max_length=4096)
schema.add_field(
    field_name="genre", datatype=DataType.VARCHAR,
    max_length=64, is_partition_key=True)
schema.add_field(
    field_name="embedding", datatype=DataType.FLOAT_VECTOR, dim=1536)
client.create_collection(
    collection_name="coll_2_shards_2_partitions",
    schema=schema,
    num_shards=2, # 2 shards
    num_partitions=2  # 2 partitions for partition key
)
```

In this collection, genre is the partition key field that Milvus uses to route each row into a partition automatically, and two shards means Milvus uses two VChannels for this collection. Next, stream the first four drama movies from the MongoDB embedded_movies dataset:

```
import itertools
from datasets import load_dataset

dataset = load_dataset(
    "MongoDB/embedded_movies", streaming=True, split="train")

drama_rows = (
    row for row in dataset
    if row.get("plot_embedding") and row.get("genres") and "Drama" in
row["genres"]
)
```

```
rows = list(itertools.islice(drama_rows, 4))
# Now preview the 4 rows with polars
import polars as pl

preview = pl.DataFrame([
    {"id": i, "title": row["title"], "genre": row["genres"][0]}
    for i, row in enumerate(rows)
])
print(preview)
```

You are going to get an output like the following:

```
id[AC1.1]   title                   genre
i64         str                     list[str]
-------------------------------------------------------------------------
0           "Beau Geste"            ["Action", "Adventure", "Drama"]
1           "Men Without Women"     ["Action", "Drama"]
2           "The Crowd Roars"       ["Drama", "Action"]
3           "Scarface"              ["Action", "Crime", "Drama"]
```

Now, insert all four rows into the `coll_movies` collection:

```
drama_entities = [
    {
        "id":        i,
        "title":     row["title"],
        "plot":      row.get("plot", ""),
        "genre":     "Drama", # just use Drama because the original dataset has a 
list of genres
        "embedding": row["plot_embedding"],
    }
    for i, row in enumerate(rows)
]

for entity in drama_entities:
    print(f"Entity {entity['id']}: genre={entity['genre']} (partition key)")

res = client.insert(collection_name="movies", data=drama_entities)
print(f"Insert result: {res}")
```

All four rows are routed into the same partition because they all share the same genre value `"Drama"`, producing the same hash value for the partition key. The shard assignment, however, is determined by the PK. With two shards, the rule is `Hash(id) % 2`: entities with IDs 0 and 2 land on Shard 0, while entities with IDs 1 and 3 land on Shard 1.

Understanding the Milvus data model is fundamental to building high-performance vector databases. You've learned how collections, fields, and schemas provide structural integrity and type safety, while partitions and shards enable massive scalability by distributing data across nodes.

Typical number of shards

In most deployments, the number of shards is typically **between 1 and 16**, depending on the scale of the system and the number of available Query or Data nodes. Smaller systems may use **1-4 shards**, while larger distributed systems may use **8-16 shards** to support higher ingestion and query parallelism.

> **Note**
>
> The shard number is usually fixed when a collection is created and cannot be changed later, so it should be chosen carefully based on expected data volume and cluster capacity. Setting too many shards may introduce unnecessary overhead, while too few shards can limit parallel processing and reduce performance.

This knowledge empowers you to design collections that are not only semantically rich but also optimized for efficient storage, indexing, and querying.

Now that you have a solid grasp of how Milvus organizes data, we will explore the underlying architecture that brings it all to life.

Milvus' layered architecture

Milvus is an open source, cloud-native, distributed vector database. The core design philosophy of its architecture is to achieve a high degree of flexibility and scalability. To accomplish this, Milvus strictly adheres to several key principles: **separation of data and control**, **separation of storage and computation**, and **separation of read and write operations**. This design allows different parts of the system to be scaled independently according to the actual workload, thereby ensuring high throughput and low latency while also significantly improving resource utilization and overall system resilience.

To put these design principles into practice, Milvus is built on a four-layer architecture with a clear division of labor, as shown in *Figure 5.3*. These four layers are the **access layer**, responsible for handling client interactions; the **coordination layer**, which acts as the system's brain; the **worker layer**, which executes specific computational tasks; and the **storage layer**, which ensures data persistence. Each layer encapsulates specific functionalities and collaborates with the others through clearly defined interfaces, collectively forming a complete and powerful vector database:

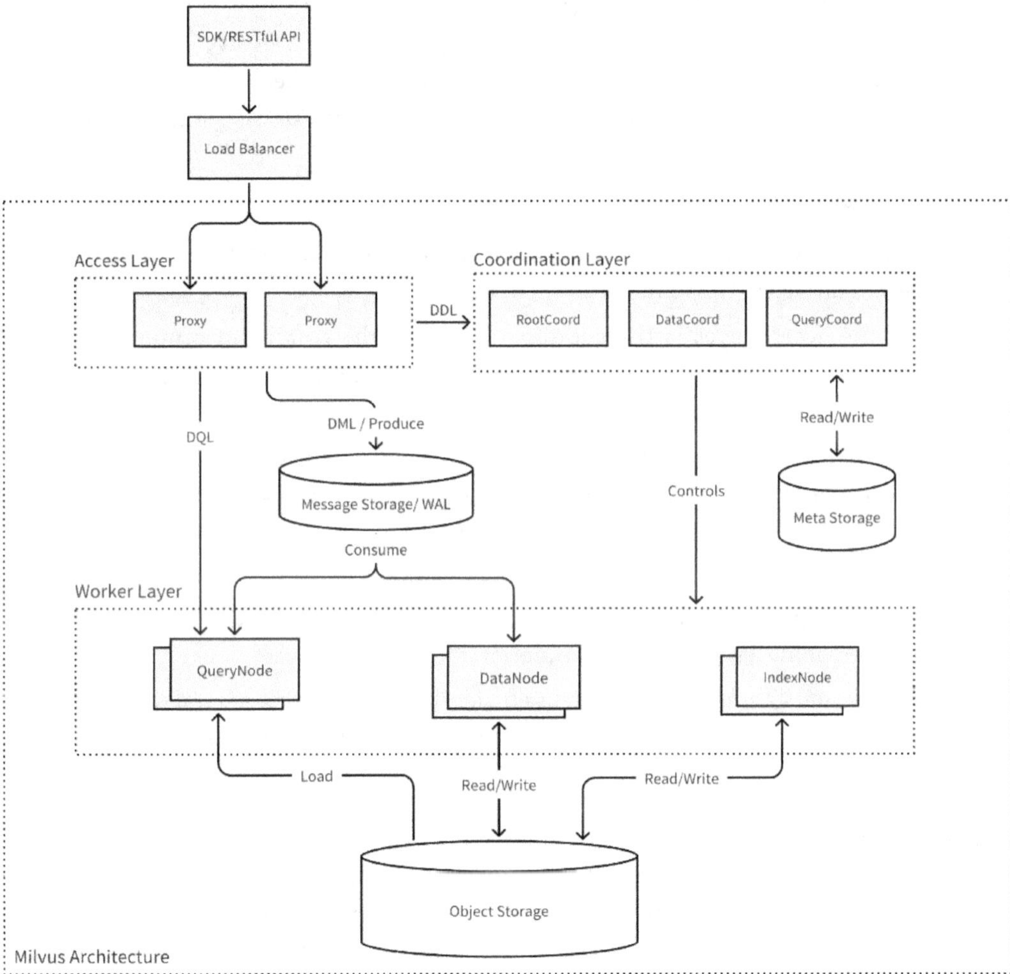

Figure 5.3: Milvus' layered architecture

This layered design brings significant engineering advantages:

- First, it endows the system with exceptional elastic scalability. When faced with high-concurrency connection requests, nodes of the access layer can be scaled out independently. When compute-intensive query or indexing tasks increase, nodes of the worker layer can be added. This **on-demand scaling model** avoids the resource waste of *all-or-nothing* scaling seen in traditional monolithic architectures.

- Second, the clear layer boundaries naturally form **fault isolation**. The failure of any single layer or component is confined locally and will not easily trigger a chain reaction across the entire system, making it more robust and easier to maintain.
- Finally, this modular structure makes the system easy to evolve. Each layer can be technologically upgraded or have its components replaced independently without affecting the others, ensuring that Milvus can continuously integrate the latest technological advancements.

Now, let's take a closer look at the role each layer plays:

1. The access layer is the system's gateway, composed of a set of stateless proxy nodes that serve as a unified entry point for all client requests.
2. Below the access layer is the coordination layer, the command center of the entire cluster, responsible for managing metadata, assigning tasks, and coordinating the activities of all distributed components.
3. Next is the worker layer, the system's powerhouse, consisting of various types of compute nodes that execute all core data processing tasks such as data insertion, compaction, index building, and vector retrieval.
4. Finally, all data and system states rely on the storage layer for persistence. This layer is typically composed of infrastructure such as object storage, metadata storage, and a log broker, providing a reliable data foundation for the upper layers.

To gain a deeper understanding of how Milvus efficiently processes vector data, we will start with the access layer and dissect the functions, design points, and key roles of each layer one by one.

Access layer

The **access layer** is the gateway to the Milvus architecture and the first point of interaction with the user. It is essentially a stateless proxy gateway whose core responsibility is to receive all requests from various language SDK clients and act as a central hub for request dispatching. It accurately forwards them to the appropriate internal services within Milvus for processing and then aggregates and returns results to the user. Because the access layer is composed of a group of **stateless proxy nodes**, it possesses excellent horizontal scalability and can gracefully handle high volumes of concurrent requests by simply adding or removing nodes.

Proxy nodes in the access layer classify requests into three main categories based on their nature: **Data Definition Language** (**DDL**) requests, **Data Modification Language** (**DML**) requests, and **Data Query Language** (**DQL**) requests.

DDL requests, also known as **Data Control Language** (**DCL**) requests, are primarily used to define and manage the logical structure of data, such as creating or deleting a collection. These operations directly affect the metadata of data organization and, therefore, have extremely high requirements for consistency and order. To ensure the determinism of operations and the consistency of results, the access layer serializes received DDL requests, queues them in chronological order, and then dispatches them sequentially to the coordination layer for execution. This strict sequential execution mechanism prevents potential metadata state conflicts that could arise from concurrent operations.

DML requests, on the other hand, are focused on modifying data within a collection and cover common operations such as insert, upsert, and delete. Unlike DDL requests that require strict ordering, DML operations can often be processed concurrently to maximize write throughput. When the access layer receives a DML request, it immediately writes the incoming data change to the **write-ahead log** (**WAL**) in the storage layer to ensure data durability and recoverability. Once the data is safely recorded in the log, the access layer can return a confirmation to the client, while the worker nodes in the background process these logs asynchronously to apply the data to the final storage files.

DQL requests are used to retrieve data from Milvus and primarily include operations such as vector search, scalar query, get by PK, and hybrid search. When handling these requests, the access layer showcases its intelligent routing capabilities. It analyzes the current load of the backend query nodes in real-time and selects the most appropriate node to handle the current query request to achieve load balancing. In a distributed execution environment, a complex query may be distributed to multiple worker nodes for parallel processing. After all nodes return their partial results, the access layer is also responsible for aggregating and merging these fragmented results into a final, unified response to be sent back to the client.

Using Python in the access layer of Milvus allows applications to interact with Milvus easily through client libraries such as **PyMilvus**. The Python SDK acts as a bridge between the application and the Milvus server, enabling developers to perform operations such as creating collections, inserting vector data, building indexes, and executing similarity searches. Through simple Python APIs, requests are sent to the Milvus service via gRPC, where they are processed by internal coordinators and worker nodes. Using Python in the access layer simplifies integration with **machine learning** (**ML**) pipelines, data processing frameworks, and **Retrieval-Augmented Generation** (**RAG**) systems, making it a common choice for applications that require vector storage and retrieval.

Next, we will introduce the coordination layer.

Coordination layer

If the access layer is the gateway of Milvus, then the **coordination layer** is the brain and command center of the entire Milvus cluster. This is a stateful layer with broad and critical responsibilities. Being **stateful** means that the coordination layer must maintain and persist all critical information about the cluster itself. This information, such as collection schemas, the distribution of data segments, and the progress of background tasks, collectively forms the *memory* of the cluster. Unlike stateless worker nodes that can be replaced at will, the state of the coordination layer must be fully recovered after a node restart or a failover; otherwise, the entire cluster cannot function properly. It is this maintenance of state that gives the coordination layer the ability to make global decisions and perform precise scheduling. It not only handles DDL operations passed from the access layer but also centrally manages all metadata in the system. At the same time, the coordination layer acts as a supervisor, continuously monitoring the topology and status of all worker nodes and intelligently generating and assigning background tasks such as index building and data compaction based on system load and data conditions. Furthermore, features such as resource quota management, user credentials, and **role-based access control** (**RBAC**) also fall under the jurisdiction of the coordination layer.

The core of the coordination layer consists of three functionally distinct components known as **coordinators**. When deployed, these three coordinators can either run as separate services or be merged into a single hybrid coordinator service called the **Mix Coordinator** (**MixCoord**). Regardless of the deployment model, to ensure the consistency of metadata and system state, there can only be one active instance of each coordinator type running at any given time. To achieve **high availability** (**HA**), the system allows for standby instances to be launched. When a primary coordinator goes offline due to a failure or a rolling upgrade, a standby instance can immediately take over its duties, ensuring service continuity.

When deployed as separate services, the three coordinators are the **Root Coordinator** (**RootCoord**), the **Data Coordinator** (**DataCoord**), and the **Query Coordinator** (**QueryCoord**):

- **RootCoord** is responsible for managing core functions and global state necessary for Milvus to operate as a distributed database. One of its key tasks is to execute global DDL requests, such as the creation of databases or collections and the management of security credentials, in a strictly sequential order, while also maintaining associated metadata. More importantly, the RootCoord acts as the central **Time Stamp Oracle** (**TSO**) for the entire cluster. By issuing globally unique and monotonically increasing timestamps, it provides a fundamental guarantee for data visibility and transactional consistency in a distributed environment.
- **DataCoord** focuses on managing the system's data modification path. All tasks and metadata related to data ingestion, storage, persistence, and modification are under its

control. It tracks the entire lifecycle of a data segment from its creation, growth, and flushing to its eventual compaction or indexing. When a segment meets certain criteria, the DataCoord triggers and dispatches corresponding compaction or index-building tasks to worker nodes in the background. It is worth noting that in earlier architectural versions, the management of indexing tasks was handled by a separate **Index Coordinator** (**IndexCoord**). To simplify the architecture, the functionality of this component was subsequently merged into the DataCoord, making it responsible for the entire process from data writing to index construction. Additionally, it is responsible for maintaining the topology of all worker nodes on the write path and performing load balancing to ensure that data can be written into the system efficiently and evenly.

- **QueryCoord** is responsible for managing the read path of the system, with all its work revolving around optimizing query performance and availability. It supervises the loading and unloading of data segments on query nodes, ensuring that the data required for user queries is pre-loaded into memory. At the same time, it is responsible for balancing the query load among multiple query nodes, managing replicas to improve query concurrency and **fault tolerance** (**FT**), and isolating query workloads from different tenants or applications by managing resource groups, thereby ensuring that the entire system's query service is efficient, stable, and fair.

These three coordinators do not operate in isolation; instead, they are closely linked through a coordination mechanism that jointly ensures cluster data consistency and a smooth flow of state. An informational dependency exists among them: the RootCoord acts as the authoritative source for global metadata, managing top-level information such as collections. When the DataCoord or QueryCoord requires this information, they request it from the RootCoord. Similarly, the DataCoord is the authority on data distribution, managing the detailed state of all data segments. The QueryCoord, in turn, periodically fetches the latest segment information from the DataCoord and uses it to guide query nodes in loading new segments or releasing old ones, ensuring that queries always operate on the latest data view.

Next, let's look at the worker layer that the coordination layer manages.

Worker layer

The **worker layer** is the core component in the Milvus architecture, where the heavy lifting of data manipulation and queries is performed. This layer is primarily composed of three different types of stateless nodes: the query node, the data node, and the index node, which are uniformly managed and scheduled by the QueryCoord and DataCoord, respectively.

Stateless is a core design feature of the worker layer. This means the compute nodes themselves do not store persistent data or metadata; they act more like pure execution units. This design brings tremendous flexibility: when the system's workload increases, the number of nodes can be dynamically increased on demand to share the pressure; when the load decreases, nodes can be scaled down accordingly to save resources. These worker nodes, following instructions assigned by the coordination layer, interact directly with the underlying storage layer to read and write data. They can handle both real-time (streaming) data and historical (batch) data, making them key to Milvus' ability to achieve rapid scalability and high elasticity. Let's explore the functions of all the key worker nodes:

- The **query node** is the executor on the read path, responsible for handling all search and query requests. In practice, the QueryCoord assigns roles to different query nodes based on task requirements. Some nodes act as standard query nodes, focusing on querying historical data. Others are designated as a more specialized **shard delegator** role, with each data shard having its own dedicated delegator. The shard delegator extends the functionality of a standard query node in several key ways, enabling it to efficiently handle complex query scenarios involving a mix of real-time and historical data. It not only processes real-time data streams, builds temporary intermediate indexes for this new data, and manages real-time deletions, but it is also responsible for enforcing the user-specified consistency level for queries. Lastly, it maintains and provides a list of all historical segments belonging to its shard, offering precise guidance for query routing to ensure that queries efficiently reach the correct data scope.
- The **data node** plays a dual role on the write path. Its primary responsibility is to act as an executor for streaming data, handling real-time data modification. It subscribes to the **log broker**, consumes persisted DML logs, and then transforms this incremental data into Milvus' proprietary columnar file format, forming new segments, which are finally written to object storage. In addition to processing real-time data streams, the data node also undertakes important background maintenance tasks, the most critical of which is compaction. As data is continuously written, the system generates a large number of small segment files. To prevent performance degradation and increased metadata management overhead caused by excessive file fragmentation, the DataCoord periodically triggers compaction tasks. A data node receiving the task reads multiple small segments from object storage, merges them into one or a few larger segments, and, in the process, physically removes data that has been marked for deletion. This process not only optimizes the data layout and improves subsequent query efficiency but also effectively reclaims storage space.
- The **index node** is a compute node specifically responsible for building indexes. When a data segment is written to object storage and meets the conditions for index building, the DataCoord dispatches an index-building task to an index node. Upon receiving the task, the index node fetches the corresponding data segment from object storage and then executes a user-specified vector index algorithm on it, such as `HNSW` or `IVF_FLAT`.

This process is typically compute-intensive. After the index is built, the index node writes generated index files back to object storage for subsequent loading and use by query nodes, thereby greatly accelerating the speed of vector retrieval.

> Note
>
> It is worth mentioning that to further simplify the architecture and optimize resource scheduling, the upcoming Milvus `2.6` release has merged the functionalities of the data node and index node. This evolutionary step aims to unify the closely related tasks of data writing and index building into a single type of node, thereby reducing the number of node types and improving resource utilization and operational efficiency.

Having understood the worker layer responsible for various computations, we now turn our attention to the storage layer, which provides the data persistence foundation for the entire system.

Storage layer

The **storage layer** is the persistence cornerstone of the Milvus architecture, providing a safe and reliable home for all data and metadata in the system. A core design philosophy of this layer is **pluggability**, which means Milvus does not bundle a specific storage implementation. Instead, it allows users to freely choose from a variety of mature third-party external services based on their own business needs, technology stack preferences, or cost considerations to build the most suitable storage solution.

Data assets handled by the storage layer can be clearly divided into three different categories, each supported by a dedicated component:

- The first category is the *streaming messages* (**transaction log**) of system operations, which includes recent DML and DDL operations, stored as a log message in a highly available *log broker*.
- The second category is the system's *household register* (**master record**), which comprises all critical system-level metadata, stored in a dedicated **metastore**.
- The third and by far the largest category in terms of data volume is all processed and solidified **data archives**, including immutable vector and scalar data files, index files built for accelerated retrieval, and related statistical information. All these large files are ultimately archived in an infinitely scalable object storage.

The Meta Store, with `etcd` as its default implementation, acts as the *registration center* and *configuration center* of the Milvus cluster. The `etcd` store is a highly consistent key-value store widely used in distributed systems. It is not only responsible for persisting all Milvus' core metadata, such as collection schema definitions, partition statuses, and segment information, but also provides crucial service registration and discovery functions for all components in the system. Each node in the cluster registers its information with `etcd` upon startup and relies on `etcd` to discover the presence and address of other nodes, thereby forming a cohesive, collaborative whole.

The **log broker** is the lifeblood of Milvus' real-time data processing capabilities. It's one of the third-party servers on which Milvus depends. In Milvus, it first serves as a WAL to ensure data reliability. Any insert, upsert, or delete requests from the SDK client must have their corresponding log message successfully written to the log broker before the proxy returns the requests. This ensures that a successful DML request is persisted in the log broker and will never be lost. Furthermore, the log broker is also the underlying pillar that supports Milvus' sophisticated distributed timestamp model and its read-write separation architecture.

Milvus adopts a different server as the default log broker for different deployment methods:

- For standalone mode, the built-in log broker is **RocksMQ**, a lightweight, embedded MQ based on **RocksDB**, which relieves users from the burden of deploying and maintaining complex message middleware.
- For cluster mode, the default deployment uses **Apache Pulsar** as the log broker. Pulsar is a cloud-native distributed messaging and streaming platform known for its powerful enterprise-grade features such as multi-tenancy, tiered storage, and a flexible messaging model.

Additionally, for teams that already have a mature Kafka technology stack, Milvus also supports using **Apache Kafka** as its log broker, offering a richer ecosystem of integration choices.

Object storage is the cornerstone of Milvus' cloud-native design. Its default implementation is MinIO, and it also seamlessly supports major public cloud object storage services such as Amazon S3 and Google Cloud Storage. All large-volume batch data in the system, such as columnar data files generated by data nodes after consuming logs and index files generated by index nodes after computation, are ultimately stored here. This design pattern of completely separating computation from storage is the key to Milvus' ability to achieve extreme elasticity. Since the **source of truth** (**SoT**) for the data resides in object storage, stateless worker nodes in the upper layers can be freely created and destroyed based on load demands without fear of data loss. For example, when a query node needs to process a query, it can load the required data and indexes from object storage into its own memory on demand and can even release these resources after the task is completed, making the entire process highly efficient and flexible.

At this point, we have completely dissected the four-layer architecture of Milvus. Next, we will focus on the data flow process and delve into how Milvus cleverly uses its MQ to drive its complex internal data processing and distribution workflows.

MQ – the lifeline of streaming data

In Milvus, not all data is static. The continuous stream of recent, real-time data operations (that is, all DML requests and parts of DDL requests) collectively constitute what is known as streaming data. To handle this constant influx, Milvus has designed a specialized infrastructure with the MQ at its core. The MQ is not only key to achieving high-throughput, distributed writes but is also the cornerstone for ensuring data durability, scalability, and supporting various levels of query consistency. Common MQ systems used by Milvus include Apache Pulsar, Kafka, or RocksDB (for standalone deployments). This design enables Milvus to handle large-scale data ingestion and distributed query processing efficiently.

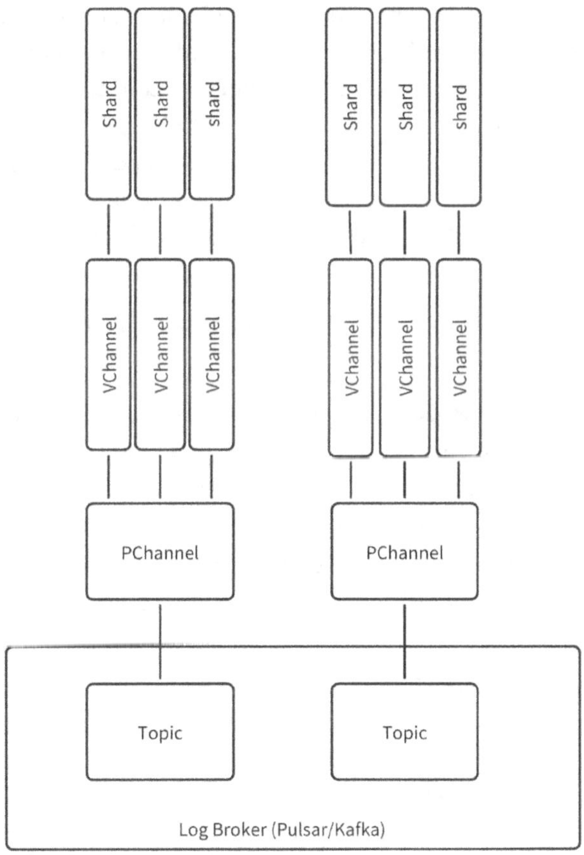

Figure 5.4: MQ architecture

The **MQ architecture** in Milvus also adopts a sophisticated layered design (as shown in *Figure 5.4*), built upon a foundational **log broker**. On top of the native **topic** resources provided by the log broker, Milvus constructs its layer of **physical channels** or **PChannels**. In messaging systems such as Kafka or Pulsar, a topic is a named channel or category used to organize messages. Producers write messages to specific topics, and consumers subscribe to those topics to read the messages. In Milvus, each PChannel corresponds one-to-one with an underlying topic, thereby ensuring complete physical data isolation between them. However, since topics in systems such as Pulsar or Kafka are relatively resource-intensive, the number of PChannels that can be created in a cluster is objectively limited.

To overcome this limitation while providing isolated channels for a massive number of collections, Milvus introduces a more lightweight abstraction layer: the VChannel. Multiple VChannels can share a single PChannel. As lightweight logical resources, an almost infinite number of VChannels can theoretically be created. Milvus cleverly binds this VChannel mechanism to its sharding mechanism: each shard of every collection is assigned to a dedicated VChannel. This means that all streaming data destined for a specific shard is guaranteed to be written to the same VChannel. Since downstream data nodes and query nodes can independently subscribe to and process data from specific VChannels, this design of binding shards to VChannels forms the basis of Milvus' ability to achieve shard-level load balancing and elastic scalability.

Having understood its layered structure, let's delve deeper into the two core roles MQ plays in the Milvus ecosystem:

- **Persistence of streaming data**: The MQ serves as the guarantee for the persistence of streaming data. In Milvus, the success of a writer operation is marked by its corresponding log message being successfully produced to the MQ. In this capacity, the MQ functions as a WAL, a concept we will explore in detail in a later chapter. It ensures that any data change is durably recorded, allowing for rapid data recovery by replaying these logs even in the event of a system failure, thus guaranteeing data correctness and preventing data loss.
- **Support for multiple consistency levels**: The MQ is fundamental to implementing multiple data consistency levels. It underpins Milvus' ability to support various isolation levels, ranging from eventual consistency to strong consistency. For the strictest level, strong consistency, the MQ ensures that once data is confirmed as written, it is immediately visible to all subsequent queries, regardless of which SDK clients or proxy nodes are being used.

The foundation supporting this powerful multiple consistency levels feature is the global event ordering capability, which is jointly realized by MQ and Milvus' own time synchronization mechanism. We'll explore this in the next section.

Global event ordering

Every record that flows through MQ, whether we call it a *log* or a *message*, represents an event that has occurred in the system. To achieve strong consistency and guarantee the global ordering of events, Milvus must solve two fundamental problems:

- First, mark the precise time at which each event occurred.
- Second, ensure that any service can read these messages in the same, consistent order. Although the underlying log broker can, to some extent, guarantee message order from a single producer, this guarantee does not hold in a distributed scenario with multiple proxy nodes writing concurrently.

In Milvus' architecture, the design of using multiple stateless proxy nodes in the access layer, while providing HA and load distribution, introduces a fundamental challenge: how to establish a global, consistent temporal order for all requests coming from different proxies. This challenge manifests in two main ways:

- First is the problem of physical clock inconsistency. In a distributed system, physical clocks on different machines can never be perfectly synchronized; there is always a slight difference between them, known as **clock skew**. If Milvus were to rely on the local server clocks of individual proxy nodes to determine the order of events, this skew would become a root cause of data inconsistency, ultimately leading to serious data integrity issues.
- Second is the out-of-order problem caused by network and processing latency. Even if events have a clear logical sequence, their physical arrival order at the MQ can be completely different from their logical order of occurrence due to variations in proxy processing speeds and network uncertainties. This misalignment of time and order makes time-based consistency control extremely difficult.

Let's use a concrete scenario to understand the severity of these problems. Suppose *Client A* sends an insert request via *Proxy A* at time `t1`, and subsequently, *Client B* sends a delete request via *Proxy B* at time `t2` (where `t2 > t1`), targeting the very data inserted by *Client A*. Logically, the delete operation should be executed after the insert operation. However, due to differences in network latency, proxy processing time, or internal scheduling, the delete operation from *Proxy B* could very well be processed before the insert operation from *Proxy A*, leading to an attempt to delete a record that does not yet exist, which clearly violates the logical intent.

Similarly, when *Client C* successfully inserts data via *Proxy A* and then immediately executes a query via *Proxy B* to retrieve that data, the query might hit a query node that has not yet been updated with the new insertion due to data propagation delays within the cluster, resulting in an incomplete result set.

To completely solve these timing and consistency problems in a distributed environment, Milvus has introduced two key technologies: the **timestamp** and the **Timetick**.

Let's first explore how Milvus uses the timestamp mechanism to solve the problem of physical clock inconsistency.

Timestamp in Milvus

To fundamentally solve the problem of clock inconsistency in a distributed environment, Milvus employs a centralized, hybrid timestamp scheme that combines physical and logical time. The elegance of this solution is that it no longer requires the physical clocks of different machines in the cluster to be perfectly synchronized. Instead, by cleverly combining physical time with a logical counter, it provides a continuous, monotonically increasing, and reliable source of event timing for the entire distributed system.

As shown in *Figure 5.5*, a timestamp is a 64-bit unsigned integer. These 64 bits are divided into two parts: the high 46 bits store the physical time in milliseconds, derived from the system time of the timestamp-generating node, while the low 18 bits serve as a logical counter.

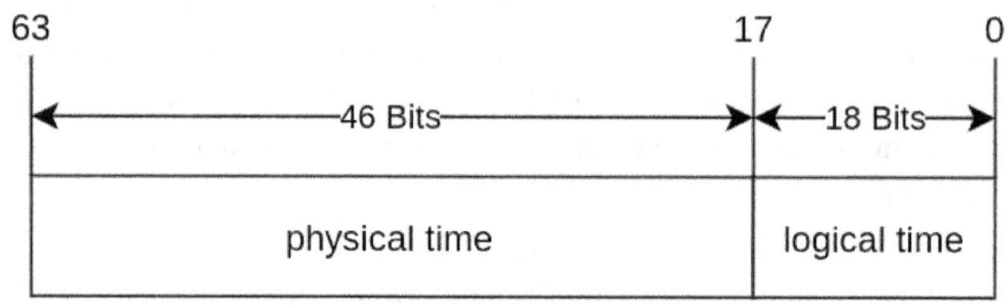

Figure 5.5: Timestamp

The generation of all timestamps for the entire Milvus cluster is centrally managed by the RootCoord, which in this capacity acts as the global TSO. When a component needs a timestamp, it sends a request to the TSO. The TSO then gets its current physical time and combines it with an internal logical counter to generate a unique timestamp. If multiple requests arrive within the same millisecond, the TSO increments the logical counter to ensure the uniqueness of each timestamp.

Through this centralized design, Milvus decouples the event time of the entire cluster from the physical clock of any single compute node, thereby mitigating risks associated with physical clock skew and providing a stable, reliable, and globally ordered time base for all events.

Having solved the problem of *when* an event occurs, we will now explore how Milvus uses the Timetick mechanism to solve the problem of "ordered reading" of events.

Timetick mechanism

To support high-throughput DML requests, proxy nodes in the access layer process them concurrently and write resulting log messages to the MQ. However, as previously described, the time of an event's occurrence, its execution, and its final physical write to the MQ can all differ due to network latency and processing speed variations. This can lead to a disordered sequence of messages in the queue, as *Figure 5.6* shows:

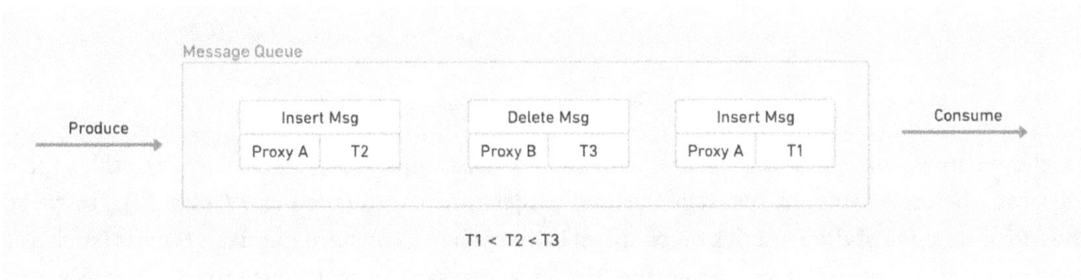

Figure 5.6: Messages inside the MQ

In the preceding diagram, the delete message from *Proxy B* has a later timestamp, *T3*, but its physical position in the queue appears before the insert message with an earlier timestamp, *T2*. If a downstream consumer (such as a data node) were to simply process messages in their physical order, logical errors would occur. To address this potential disorder and establish a global, consistent event consumption sequence, Milvus employs the Timetick mechanism. This can be understood as a mechanism for setting global checkpoints or watermarks within the stream. Specifically, the RootCoord periodically generates a special type of message, a Timetick message, and broadcasts it to all physical channels of MQ.

Each Timetick message carries a single timestamp, *T*, and the meaning of this timestamp is crucial: it represents a global consensus that all requests with timestamps less than or equal to this Timetick's timestamp have been completely processed by all proxy nodes and sent to the MQ.

So, how is this globally consensus-based Timetick timestamp generated? It comes from an elegant synchronization process. Each proxy node in the cluster periodically reports its most recently processed request timestamp to the RootCoord. After collecting reports from all proxy nodes, the RootCoord selects the minimum timestamp among all the reported ones. This global minimum represents the *bottleneck* of the entire system's current processing progress, which is a safe point in time that all proxy nodes have collectively reached. The RootCoord then uses this minimum value as the timestamp for the next Timetick message. In this way, the Timetick mechanism ensures that the timestamp it publishes is an absolutely reliable global watermark.

Therefore, the conceptual view of a data stream containing Timetick messages might look like *Figure 5.7*:

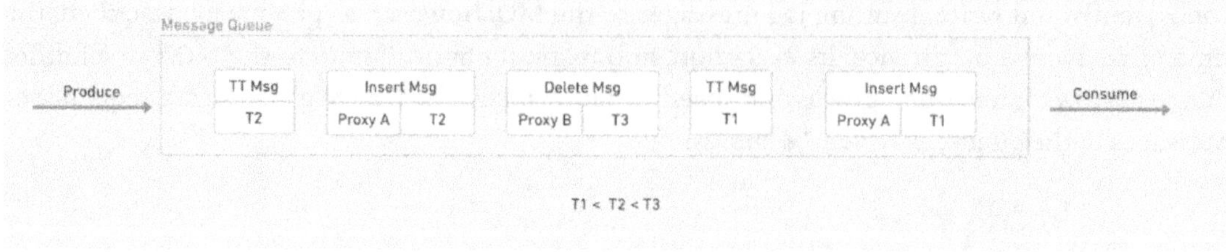

Figure 5.7: Messages inside MQ with Timeticks

As shown in *Figure 5.7*, some events with later timestamps (such as *T3*) might still appear physically before a Timetick message with an earlier timestamp (such as *TT Msg T2*). However, the core guarantee of the Timetick mechanism is this: when a consumer node in Milvus (such as a data node or query node) processes the Timetick message with timestamp *T2*, it receives a deterministic signal that all event messages with timestamps less than or equal to *T2* are guaranteed to have arrived in the queue. At this point, the consumer can safely perform a global sort on all the messages in its internal buffer with timestamps no later than *T2* and then process them in the correct logical order.

By leveraging this consensus mechanism, downstream services in Milvus are able to process data in discrete **beats** defined by Timeticks. Within each beat (the time window between two consecutive Timetick messages), a service node consumes and buffers all arriving messages. When the signal for the next Timetick beat arrives, the node performs a complete, ordered processing of all messages buffered from the previous time window. In this way, the Timetick mechanism cleverly transforms a physically disordered data stream into a logically ordered, batch-processed data stream, thereby achieving strong data processing consistency while maintaining high throughput. In simple terms, the Timetick mechanism acts as a synchronization signal that keeps all Milvus components aligned on the same timeline, ensuring correct query results and consistent data visibility in distributed vector search operations.

Summary

Milvus' power comes from how its core architectural components work together. This chapter explored how the power and resilience of Milvus stem directly from its disaggregated, four-tier layered design. We saw how the stateless access layer serves as the unified gateway, the coordination layer acts as the central brain, worker nodes perform the heavy computational lifting, and the pluggable storage layer provides a persistent foundation. Tying this entire architecture together is the MQ, the system's central nervous system. Functioning as a durable log stream, the MQ enables the asynchronous communication that fully decouples these layers for immense resilience and scalability. Most importantly, through its sophisticated timestamp and Timetick mechanisms, the MQ guarantees data reliability and establishes a consistent, global order for all events, making Milvus a powerful, scalable, and cloud-native vector database.

In the next chapter, we will focus on one of the most fundamental operations: writing data. We will trace the journey of an insert request, following it from the client, through the layers and channels we've discussed in this chapter, to see exactly how Milvus prepares data for future queries.

Get this book's PDF version and more

Scan the QR code (or go to `packtpub.com/unlock`). Search for this book by name, confirm the edition, and then follow the steps on the page.

UNLOCK NOW

Note: Keep your invoice handy. Purchases made directly from Packt don't require an invoice.

6

Data Modification and Maintenance in Milvus

In *Chapter 5*, we explored the layered architecture that Milvus designed for high scalability. Starting with this chapter, we will shift our focus from static components to dynamic data flow, exploring the complete lifecycle of data within Milvus from both the write and read perspectives. This chapter will focus on the data writing process. We will first unveil the core data organization unit within Milvus, which is the **segment**, and clarify the key distinctions between streaming and historical data. Next, we will detail the complete lifecycle management of a segment, from its birth, growth, and consolidation to its eventual demise. Finally, from a developer's point of view, we will follow **insert**, **delete**, and **upsert data manipulation language** (**DML**) requests through their entire journey inside Milvus, helping you gain a deep understanding of how the Milvus write path works. In this chapter, we will cover the following main topics:

- The core of data organization – the segment
- The lifecycle of a segment
- The journey behind DML requests
- Channel checkpoints

Let's begin with the most fundamental form of data organization within Milvus.

Technical requirements

The code used in this chapter can be found on our GitHub repository:`https://github.com/PacktPublishing/The-Architecture-Handbook-for-Milvus-Vector-Database`. To run these code examples, you'll need a Python >= 3.8 environment, which you can download here: `https://www.python.org/downloads/`. You should install all dependencies from the ch5 directory using the `requirements.txt` file in ch5.

The core of data organization – the segment

In Milvus, all data within a collection is ultimately organized into numerous segments. A **segment** is the smallest unit of data organization and management within Milvus. The vast majority of services in the cluster, such as data nodes and query nodes, process data at the segment level. Segments play a key role in Milvus performance because they enable parallel processing, scalable storage, and efficient indexing, making them the core structure that organizes vector data internally. Therefore, to deeply understand Milvus' data management mechanism, we must first understand this core concept.

To understand a segment, we can examine it from three interconnected dimensions: its data state, its internal structure, and the role it plays within the system.

Data states – streaming vs historical

First, based on the stage of data in its lifecycle, Milvus logically divides the data within a collection into two states: **streaming data** and **historical data**.

Streaming data typically refers to real-time, recently inserted data in Milvus. It mainly consists of growing segments and anonymous deletes. It is worth noticing that the physical storage location of the data is not the definitive boundary between streaming and historical data.

A growing segment might still have some data in the message queue's vChannel, while the other part may have already been persisted to object storage. The same applies to delete records.

In contrast, historical data represents the part of the system that has been consolidated. In the context of the write path, any segment that is no longer in a growing state can be considered historical data. The entities in these segments are immutable, and they are the primary objects for building indexes, performing queries, and undergoing data compaction. One of the core goals of the entire Milvus write path is to efficiently transform streaming data into structured historical data. In simple terms, streaming data represents real-time incoming data, while historical data represents stable, stored, and indexed data. This separation allows Milvus to support both high-speed data ingestion and efficient large-scale vector search at the same time.

Let's now take a look at the segment structure in Milvus.

Internal structure – the file composition of a segment

Internally, a segment is not a single file but a logical collection of various types of files that work together to fully describe the state of a portion of data (see *Figure 6.1*):

```
+----------------------------------------------------------------+
|                   SEGMENT FILE STRUCTURE                       |
+----------------------------------------------------------------+
|                                                                |
|  +------------------+          +------------------+            |
|  |    BINLOGS       |          |   STATS LOGS     |            |
|  | (Core Data)      |          | (Optimization)   |            |
|  |                  |          |                  |            |
|  | - chunk_0/       |          | - Bloom Filters  |            |
|  |   * field_1      |          | - Min/Max PK     |            |
|  |   * field_2      |          |                  |            |
|  |   * field_N      |          |                  |            |
|  | - chunk_1/       |          |                  |            |
|  |   * ...          |          |                  |            |
|  +------------------+          +------------------+            |
|                                                                |
|  +------------------+          +------------------+            |
|  |  INDEX FILES     |          |   DELTA LOGS     |            |
|  | (Fast Search)    |          |  (Deletions)     |            |
|  |                  |          |                  |            |
|  | - Vector Index   |          | - Delete PKs     |            |
|  | - Scalar Index   |          | - Timestamps     |            |
|  |                  |          |                  |            |
|  +------------------+          +------------------+            |
|                                                                |
+----------------------------------------------------------------+
```

Figure 6.1: Segment file structure

A segment file structure can be broadly categorized into four parts:

1. **Binlogs**: They form the core of the segment, storing all the entities it contains in a *columnar* storage format. For efficient reading and writing, the data within a segment is split into multiple data chunks. Each chunk contains multiple rows organized by columns, and each column is a separate binlog file.

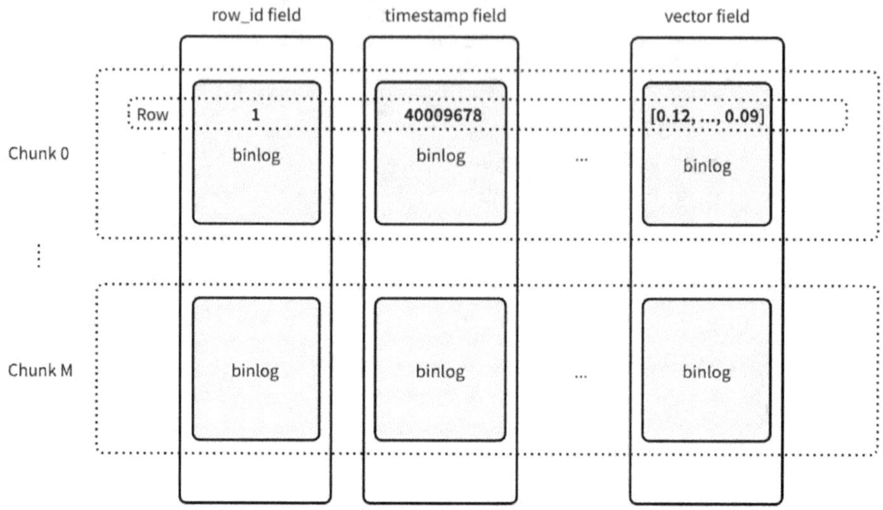

Figure 6.2: A segment with M number of chunks

Each binlog file follows a standardized event format:

- **4-byte magic number**: This is a fixed identifier (`0xfffabc`) that marks the beginning of every binlog file, allowing Milvus to quickly validate that a file is indeed a valid binlog.
- **A descriptor event that contains segment metadata**: This event stores essential information about the data, including `collectionID`, partition ID, segment ID, field ID, data type, and timestamp range. It acts as the file's header, providing context about what data the binlog contains and how it should be interpreted when reading the file.
- **An insert Event that contains an actual data payload in Parquet format**: This event stores the actual data rows in Apache Parquet format, which is a columnar storage format that provides efficient compression and encoding. The insert event includes timestamp information and wraps the Parquet-encoded data, allowing Milvus to efficiently store and retrieve large volumes of vector and scalar data.

2. **Statistics logs (stats logs)**: These are used for query optimization and data filtering. They enable Milvus to quickly determine whether a segment might contain relevant data without scanning the entire segment. This mainly includes bloom filters calculated based on the primary key. A **bloom filter** is a space-efficient probabilistic data structure that tests whether an element is a member of a set. It can produce false positives (saying

an element is present when it's not) but never false negatives (if it says an element is absent, it's definitely absent). In Milvus segments, bloom filters are calculated based on the primary key field, which contains the bloom filter and minimum and maximum primary key values. Purpose: It improves query efficiency by enabling Milvus to quickly filter out irrelevant segments during search operations.

Stats logs are widely used to locate which segment contains the primary keys to be deleted. This lookup capability is essential for both standard delete operations on read path and background data compaction in write path; see *Chapter 8* for details.

3. **Index files:** These store index data generated for fields that can be indexed (such as vector fields). Query nodes load these files to greatly accelerate ANN search speed. Purpose: It enables fast vector similarity search and significantly reduces search latency. It shares the same binlog format as binlogs, except that the event data stores data payload in insert binlog stores indexed data. There are many index types, including vector indexes and scalar indexes, which we'll discuss in *Chapter 9* in detail.
4. **Delta logs**: Also known as delete logs, these are specifically used to store delete records. A delete record is a JSON string that contains a primary key and a timestamp, indicating an entity of the same primary key that was inserted before the timestamp is deleted. Purpose: It supports logical deletion of records while maintaining data consistency using timestamps. The use of delta logs will be detailed in the delete process in chapters *6* and *7*.
5. **Segment levels:** Finally, to achieve more refined data management, especially to optimize the efficiency of compaction and delete operations, Milvus introduces the concept of segment levels, dividing segments into three different levels:
    - **Level zero (L0) segment**: This is a special level used exclusively for storing anonymous delete records. L0 Segment is a channel level segment, which stores delta logs only. When a `delete` request comes in, Milvus cannot immediately know which segments the deleted primary keys are distributed in. These deleted records are grouped into delta logs that belong to an L0 segment.
    - **Level one (L1) Segment**: This is the most standard segment level. The growing segments we discussed earlier are L1 segments. An L1 segment can store entity data and also record delete entries for itself. The data distribution among L1 segments is usually random.
    - **Level two (L2) segment**: This is an optimized L1 segment. An L2 segment is generated when multiple L1 segments are merged through an operation called **clustering compaction**. The data inside an L2 Segment is no longer randomly distributed but is reorganized according to a specific rule (e.g., based on vector

similarity). This ordered organization can significantly improve retrieval efficiency in specific query scenarios.

Through this analysis, we have understood how a segment undergoes a dynamic evolution from streaming to historical, has an internal structure composed of various files, and plays different roles within the system. With this holistic image of a segment, we can better understand its complete lifecycle in the next section.

The lifecycle of a segment

In this section, we will follow the complete life journey of a segment, observing from a dynamic perspective how it is created, managed, and ultimately recycled by Milvus.

The journey can be summarized as a clear state transition path:

Growing -> Sealed -> Flushed -> Dropped

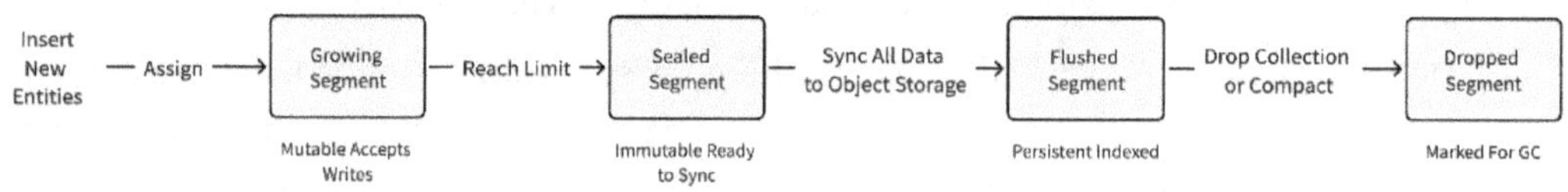

Figure 6.3: Segment lifecycle management

Let's explore the phases of a segment lifecycle in detail.

Phase one – the growing state

When you insert some new entities into a collection, Milvus will assign these entities to growing segments. Since shards and partitions represent physical divisions of data, a collection with *m* shards and *n* partitions can contain up to *m*n* growing segments at any given time, one growing segment per shard-partition combination.

A new growing segment is created under two conditions: when all existing growing segments have reached their maximum capacity, or when no growing segments exist yet for a particular shard-partition pair in such a collection. The DataCoord monitors segment states and makes the decision to allocate a new segment when needed. This newly created segment enters the growing state immediately upon creation. Segments in the growing state are mutable, meaning they can continuously receive incoming entity data. Growing segments are part of the streaming data pipeline, meaning they handle real-time data ingestion before the data is finalized. Although the data in this state is not yet sealed or indexed, it is still searchable. Milvus ensures that queries consider both growing segments and sealed segments so that newly inserted data can be retrieved immediately.

This phase continues until the segment reaches a predefined size threshold, or a flush operation occurs. Once that happens, the segment transitions to the next stage in its life cycle, where it is sealed and prepared for persistent storage and indexing.

Phase two – the sealed state

A growing segment does not grow indefinitely. When certain conditions are met, the DataCoord will automatically seal a growing segment, changing its state from growing to sealed. This transition means that the data writing gate for this segment is officially closed, and it will no longer accept new entities.

The conditions that trigger sealing are varied, aiming to balance the real-time nature of data writing, memory usage efficiency, and file management overhead:

- **Size threshold**: When the size of a growing segment exceeds a predefined capacity limit (calculated by two configs: `dataCoord.segment.maxSize*` `dataCoord.segment.sealProportion`).
- **Time threshold**: When a growing segment has remained in the growing state for too long, even if its size has not reached the threshold.
- **System pressure**: When a large amount of streaming data has accumulated in its shard, Milvus may seal the segment prematurely. This is mainly to alleviate the memory pressure on related components in the query path (Delegator), the detailed mechanism of which will be discussed in *Chapter 7*.

The sealed state is a brief intermediate state. At this point, some of the segment's data may still be in the message queue and not fully processed. Therefore, it cannot yet be considered a complete, independently recoverable historical data segment from object storage. It is like a package awaiting final processing, waiting for the DataNode to complete all its related sync work. A sealed segment is immutable, and no new data can be written into it.

Phase three – the flushed state

The transition from sealed to flushed is a crucial step in the segment's lifecycle. It marks the official transformation of a segment from dynamic streaming data to static, content-consolidated historical data. The core of this process is flush.

A flush operation essentially ensures that all related data of a sealed segment in the message queue has been consumed by the DataNode and successfully persisted to object storage. Only when the DataCoord confirms that this process is thoroughly complete will it officially update the segment's state to *flushed*.

Once it becomes a flushed segment, it enters the longest and most stable mature phase of its lifecycle. All its entity data is completely saved on object storage, and its content is immutable. As an effective unit of historical data, it can participate in various background tasks, such as:

- Being loaded by a QueryNode to provide query services
- Having persistent indexes built for it
- Participating in compaction tasks, being merged with other segments to optimize storage and performance (this will be detailed in *Chapter 8*).

Phase four – the dropped state

A segment's journey ends when it is dropped. There are two main ways a segment can enter this state:

- **Active deletion**: When a user executes a drop collection or drop partition operation, all contained segments, regardless of their current state, are marked as Dropped by the DataCoord.
- **Passive merging**: When one or more Flushed Segments participate in a Compaction task, the old segments are marked as Dropped because the Compaction generates a brand-new segment to contain their merged data.

Segments in the dropped state are immutable. They cannot be selected for indexing or compaction in the write path. However, the data from the dropped segments is still available. They can still be loaded, balancing in the read path, and still serve queries. The dropped state is merely a logical marker; the physical files of the segment have not yet been deleted. It is like *logical garbage* waiting to be cleaned up, and in some cases, the data may even still be queryable. The lifecycle of this segment is not truly complete until the background **garbage collection (GC)** process, guided by this marker, thoroughly removes all its related physical files, indexes, and metadata from the system.

Although the lifecycle of a segment is managed automatically by Milvus in most cases, Milvus also provides an important API, `flush()`, that allows users to actively intervene in this process:

```
c.flush(collection_name = "test_collection")
```

Calling the `flush()` method triggers a synchronous operation that forces all currently growing segments in a collection to complete the ***Growing*** → ***Sealed*** → ***Flushed*** process. The significance of this operation is that it provides a deterministic guarantee to the user. After the `flush()` call successfully returns, all data written before this call has been safely and completely persisted to object storage, forming an immutable snapshot of historical data. This is crucial for application scenarios that require a clear point-in-time between data writes and subsequent operations (such as queries or backups).

Having understood the lifecycle of a segment, it is now time to look at how the DML requests are executed.

The journey behind DML requests

After understanding the static structure and dynamic lifecycle of segments, this section starts from the three DML requests, which are insert, delete, and upsert, and follows the Milvus write path to trace the full journey of data from the SDK to segment binlogs persisted in object storage (such as S3). We begin with the most basic insert operation.

Insert request

Using the following simple insert as an example, we will focus on three questions:

1. How is an insert routed to the correct shard and vChannel?
2. When does the data become queryable?
3. When is it turned into a segment binlog and persisted to object storage?

Using the same dataset from *Chapter 5*, let's load the dataset to create a collection and insert four entities into it:

```
# Create a schema object for the Milvus collection
# A schema defines the structure of the data that will be stored
# including fields names, data types, vector dimensions, and primary keys
schema = MilvusClient.create_schema()

# Add a primary key field named "id"
# datatype=VARCHAR means the ID will be stored as a string
# max_length=64 limits the maximum allowed characters for the ID
# is_primary=True indicates this field uniquely identifies each entity in the
collection
schema.add_field(
    field_name="id", datatype=DataType.VARCHAR,
    max_length=64, is_primary=True)

# Add a field to store the movie title
# VARCHAR is used because titles are text values
# max_length=512 allows relatively long movie titles
schema.add_field(
    field_name="title", datatype=DataType.VARCHAR, max_length=512)

# Add a field to store the movie plot/description
# max_length=65536 allows storing very long text descriptions
```

```
# This is useful for storing full movie summaries
schema.add_field(
    field_name="plot", datatype=DataType.VARCHAR, max_length=65535)

# Add a field to store the movie genre
# Only one genre is stored here (first genre from dataset)
# VARCHAR with max_length=64 is sufficient for genre names
schema.add_field(
    field_name="genre", datatype=DataType.VARCHAR, max_length=64)

# Add a vector field named "embedding"
# datatype=FLOAT_VECTOR means this field stores vector embeddings
# dim=1536 indicates each vector contains 1536 floating point values
# This dimension matches the embedding model used for the dataset
schema.add_field(
    field_name="embedding", datatype=DataType.FLOAT_VECTOR, dim=1536)

# Create a new collection in Milvus named "ch6_movies"
# The collection will store movie information along with vector embeddings
# Milvus will internally create partitions, segments, and storage structures
client.create_collection(collection_name="ch6_movies", schema=schema)

# --------------------------------
# Load Dataset
# --------------------------------

# Load the dataset from HuggingFace
# "MongoDB/embedded_movies" contains movie metadata and embeddings
# split ="train" loads the training portion of the dataset
# streaming=True enables streaming mode meaning the dataset is read row-by-row
# instead of downloading the entire dataset into memory
dataset = load_dataset(
    "MongoDB/embedded_movies", split="train", streaming=True)

# --------------------------------
# Prepare Entities for Insertion
# --------------------------------

# Initialize an empty list to store processed rows
# These rows will later be inserted into Milvus
rows = []
```

```
# Iterate over the dataset using itertools.islice
# This allows use to read only a limited number of records from the streaming
dataset
for row in itertools.islice(dataset, 10):

    # Stop once we collect 4 valid rows
    # This avoids inserting too many records during testing
    if len(rows) >= 4:
        break

    # Check if the current row contains both embedding and genre information
    # Some dataset entries might have missing values
    # We skip those entries to prevent insertion errors
    if row.get("plot_embedding") and row.get("genres"):

        # Append a properly structured entity dictionary
        # Each key must match the field names defined in the schema
        rows.append({

            # Use dataset _id as the primary key
            "id": row["_id"],

            # Movie title
            "title": row["title"],

            # Movie plot/description
            # row.get("plot", "") ensures an empty string if plot is missing
            "plot": row.get("plot", ""),

            # Select the first genre from the genres list
            "genre": row["genres"][0],

            # Vector embedding representing the movie plot
            # This vector will be used for similarity search
            "embedding": row["plot_embedding"],
        })

# ------------------------------
# Insert Data into Milvus
# ------------------------------
```

```
# Insert the prepared rows into the Milvus collection
# data must be prepared as a list of entity dictionaries
insert_res = client.insert(collection_name="ch6_movies", data=rows)

# Print the insertion result
# This usually includes information such as number of rows inserted
print(f"Insert result: {insert_res}")
```

Inside Milvus, this piece of data goes through three main stages:

1. **Synchronous phase (Proxy)**: The Proxy receives the request, parses it, and routes it to the corresponding vChannel, requests a timestamp from RootCoord, requests or extends a growing segment from DataCoord and allocates a `SegmentID` for this write, and finally writes the data annotated with the timestamp and `SegmentID` into the message queue. This stage ensures the request is valid and structured correctly before it enters the internal pipeline. Once the validation is complete, the proxy forwards the request to the next stage.
2. **WAL phase (message queue)**: In the **write-ahead log** (**WAL**) phase, the data is written into a **message queue system** such as Kafka, Pulsar, or RocksMQ. This acts as a persistent log that records all operations before they are processed. The WAL ensures durability and fault tolerance—if any component fails, the system can recover the operations from the log without losing data. Once the insert message has been successfully appended to the underlying log service, the Proxy returns success to the client. At the same time, QueryNodes subscribe to the same vChannel and can start querying this data as soon as they consume the message.
3. **Asynchronous phase (DataNode)**: In the asynchronous phase, DataNodes consume insert messages per vChannel, aggregate them by `SegmentID` into in-memory writer buffers, and, once certain conditions are met, turn the buffered data into binlog files and write them to object storage, thus completing the transformation from *streaming data* into *historical data*. This asynchronous processing allows Milvus to handle high ingestion throughput while maintaining system scalability.

Now let's examine the first of these stages in detail to understand exactly what happens from the moment the client initiates a request until it is safely enqueued.

Synchronous processing (during the API call)

This part of the process occurs in the brief time between the `insert()` method call and its successful return. Its core goal is to determine the target segment for the data and reliably write it into the message queue (see *Figure 6.4*):

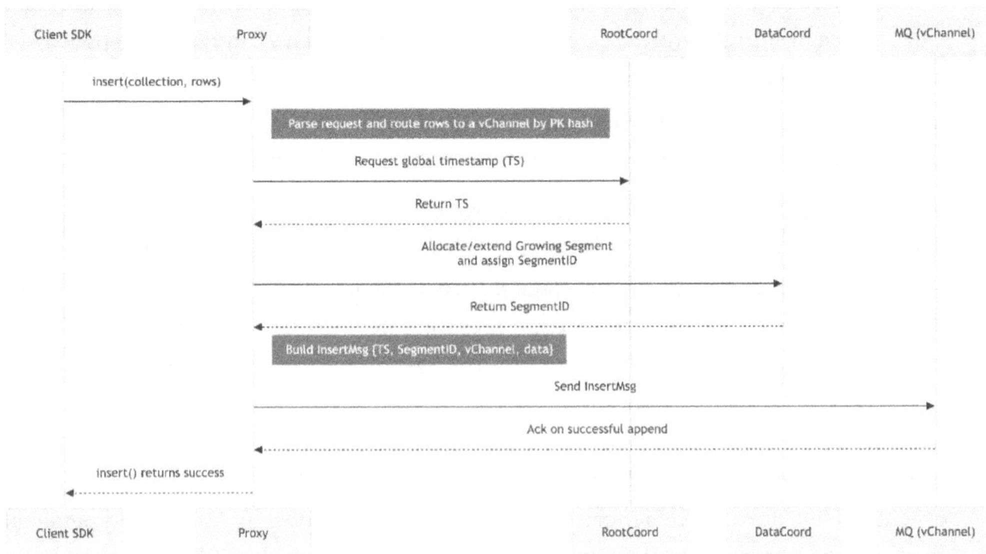

Figure 6.4: An overview of the synchronous processing of insert

The synchronous processing phase consists of four key steps:

1. **Proxy reception and pre-processing**: The Proxy parses the incoming request and, based on the collection metadata (for example, the number of shards) and the primary key of each row, computes a hash over the **primary key** (**PK**). It uses this hash value to decide which shard the row belongs to. Each shard corresponds to one vChannel, and the Proxy groups the rows into their respective vChannels accordingly. Downstream DataNodes and QueryNodes subscribe to and consume data per vChannel. At this point, the data has been batched and grouped according to their target vChannels.
2. **Timestamp acquisition**: To guarantee global ordering and consistency, Milvus relies on a global timestamp service provided by RootCoord (see *Chapter 5*). The Proxy requests a monotonically increasing, globally unique timestamp from RootCoord. This timestamp marks the logical time of this write. The Proxy attaches this timestamp to the batch of rows being inserted, turning them into timestamped insert records.
3. **Segment space allocation**: Next, the system needs to decide which segment these rows will ultimately belong to. The Proxy sends a request to DataCoord, specifying the target

collection, partition, shard/vChannel, and the number of rows in this insert. DataCoord then makes a decision based on the current segment state of that shard:

- If there is an existing writable growing segment with enough remaining space, it reserves a contiguous range in that segment for this insert;
- If there is no suitable growing segment, or the existing one does not have enough space, it immediately creates a new growing segment and reserves space in it for this write.

DataCoord then returns the SegmentIDs allocated for this batch of rows to the Proxy. At this point, every row that is about to be written has been bound to a concrete SegmentID.

4. **Writing to the message queue and returning the response:** With the timestamp and SegmentID in hand, the Proxy constructs insert messages and produces them to the appropriate vChannels in the message queue. Once the underlying log service (such as Pulsar or Kafka) confirms that the messages have been successfully appended, the Proxy considers the write durably accepted by the system, returns a success response to the client, and the `insert()` call completes.

   At this moment, the data has been persisted in the message queue and will not be lost, even if the Proxy or a DataNode fails. At this point, the `insert()` method has finished executing. For the user, this means the data has been received by Milvus and persisted in the message queue. Since the QueryNode also subscribes to the vChannel, this data will become visible and queryable very quickly (the exact visibility depends on the consistency level settings). However, ensuring data durability and long-term storage involves further steps that happen in the background.

Asynchronous processing (after the API returns)

After the API returns, the write path moves from foreground synchronous processing to background asynchronous processing (see *Figure 6.5*):

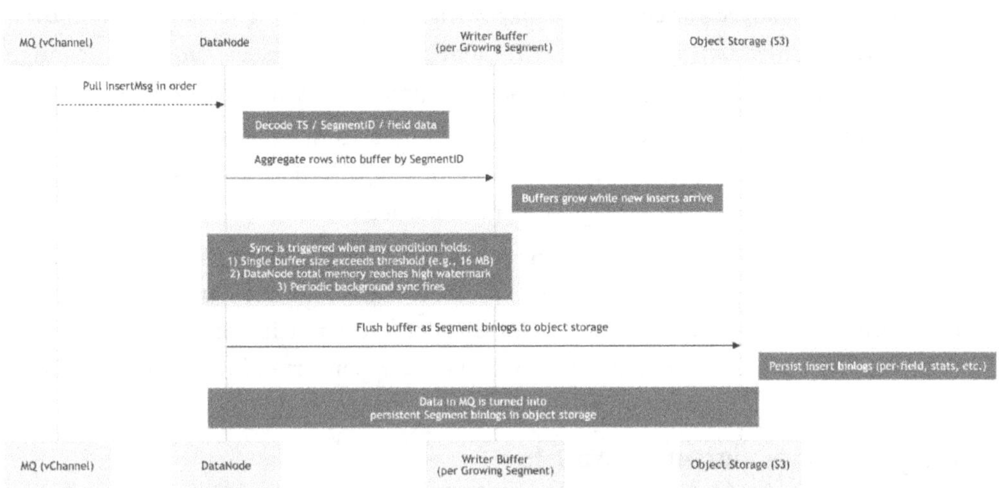

Figure 6.5: An overview of the asynchronous processing of insert

At this point, DataNodes take over and turn the streaming data in the message queue into segment binlogs, which are then persisted to object storage. Let's explore the steps involved in this process:

1. **DataNode vChannel consumption and buffering**: DataNode consumes the vChannel and aggregates into writer buffers. Each vChannel has exactly one DataNode instance responsible for consuming it. The DataNode subscribes to the corresponding vChannel and consumes InsertMsgs in timestamp order. For each message, it parses the `SegmentID` and caches rows belonging to the same growing segment in an in-memory writer buffer. At this point, the data exists in two places: in the message queue log and in the DataNode's in-memory buffers.
2. **Triggering sync**: turning buffered data into binlogs: A writer buffer will trigger a sync operation once certain conditions are met, flushing the in-memory insert data to object storage. Typical trigger conditions include:
    - Single-buffer size exceeds a threshold. For example, when the writer buffer for a given segment grows beyond 16 MB, the DataNode proactively triggers a sync to prevent unbounded growth and flushes the current buffer to disk as binlog files.

  - Total DataNode memory reaches a high watermark. The system monitors the overall memory usage of each DataNode. When usage crosses a configured threshold, the DataNode selects some segments to sync to free memory.
  - **Periodic background sync**: To prevent data from lingering in memory for too long under low write load, a background task periodically forces syncs so that data is persisted to object storage within a bounded time.

Once a sync is triggered, the DataNode drains the writer buffer for that segment, builds binlog and statistics files per field, writes these files to object storage, and finally notifies DataCoord to update the corresponding segment metadata. At this point, the portion of streaming insert data that originally only existed in the message queue has been converted into binlog files in object storage.

Visibility and persistence points

Putting the synchronous and asynchronous phases together, we can summarize the key moments in the lifetime of an insert request:

- **API return time**: The condition for this is that the insert messages have been successfully written to the message queue. At this moment, the data is reliably stored in MQ. QueryNodes subscribed to the same vChannel can, in principle, consume these messages shortly afterwards and serve queries over them (the exact visibility depends on the chosen consistency level and the progress of each QueryNode).
- **Sync completion time**: The condition for this is that the DataNode has turned the buffered data into binlogs and successfully written them to object storage. At this moment, the data has become part of a segment and is persisted as binlog files. QueryNodes can then use these on-disk binlogs to build indexes or load historical data, further improving query performance and stability.

Through this combination of synchronous and asynchronous processing, Milvus splits a single insert request into two stages: a fast "ingest into the message queue" stage and a "batch flush to object storage" stage in the background. This design keeps frontend write latency low while still completing the full evolution from streaming data to historical data.

Next, let's look at the delete request.

Delete request

Compared with insert, the delete operation in Milvus takes a different path. Milvus uses a soft delete mechanism: a delete request does not immediately remove data physically. Instead, it first records a "delete record" request, and only later, during compaction, are these delete records merged with the actual data segments to complete physical cleanup.

The following example shows two common delete styles in the Milvus Python SDK: deleting by primary keys and deleting by a filter expression. While the `delete()` method returns as the request is persisted in the WAL (synchronous phase), the actual data persistence happens in the background (asynchronous phase)

```
ids_to_delete = rows[0]['id']
client.delete(collection_name="ch6_movies", ids=[ids_to_delete])
client.delete(
    collection_name="ch6_movies", filter=f"id < {ids_to_delete}")
```

As with insert, the processing of a delete is also divided into synchronous and asynchronous phases.

Synchronous processing (during the API call)

The synchronous phase happens between the start and successful return of the `delete()` call. Its main goal is to determine the set of primary keys to be deleted and reliably write the corresponding delete records into the message queue. Most of the infrastructure is shared with insert (see *Figure 6.6*):

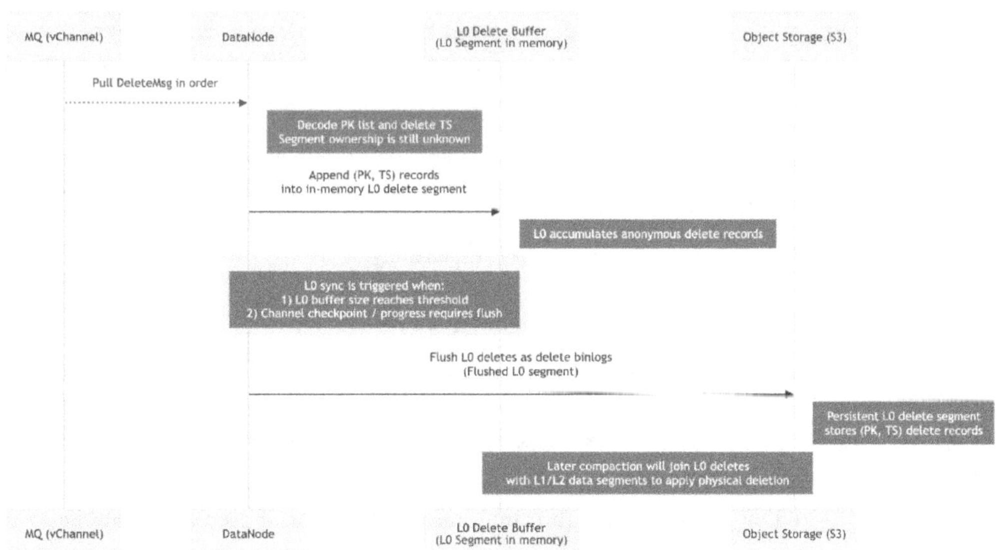

Figure 6.6: An overview of the synchronous delete process

Let's look at the steps involved in the process:

1. **Proxy receives and parses the request**: After receiving a delete request from the client, the Proxy first parses its content. There are two cases:
   - Delete by PK list (e.g., `ids=[1]`), The request explicitly specifies the set of primary keys to delete, so the Proxy can directly use this PK list in subsequent steps.
   - Delete by filter expression (e.g., `filter="year > 1999"`). The request contains a Boolean filter expression. The Proxy must issue an internal query, parse and execute this filter, and obtain the set of PKs that satisfy it. The subsequent delete is still just a delete of this PK set.
2. **Obtaining a timestamp and writing delete messages**: Once the Proxy has determined the PK set to delete, it requests a timestamp for these PKs and constructs delete messages (`DeleteMsg`). As with insert, it hashes the PKs to route the delete messages to the corresponding vChannels and produces them to MQ. When the message queue confirms that the delete messages have been durably appended to the log, the Proxy returns success to the client, and the `delete()` call completes. At this point, there is a crucial detail: delete messages are "anonymous". Unlike insert, a `DeleteMsg` only contains PKs and a timestamp; it does not yet know which concrete segments these PKs belong to. Which segments actually contain these PKs will only be determined later in the asynchronous phase, using segment metadata and segment-level bloom filters.

> Note
>
> **Expression-based delete is not atomic**
>
> For a delete like filter="year > 1999", the flow is essentially:
>
> 1. The Proxy runs an internal query and obtains a PK list.
> 2. It then sends a delete message based on that list.
>
> Between these two steps, there is a time window. If new rows that also satisfy year > 1999 are inserted during this window, their PKs are not in the original list and therefore will not be affected by this delete request. In other words, a filter-based delete applies once to "the set of entities that existed at query time"; it does not guarantee deletion of entities inserted later that also match the filter.

Asynchronous processing (after the API returns)

After the API returns, the delete processing enters the asynchronous phase and is taken over by DataNodes. The core goal of this phase is to accept these *anonymous* delete records and persist them as a special L0 segment, see *Figure 6.7*:

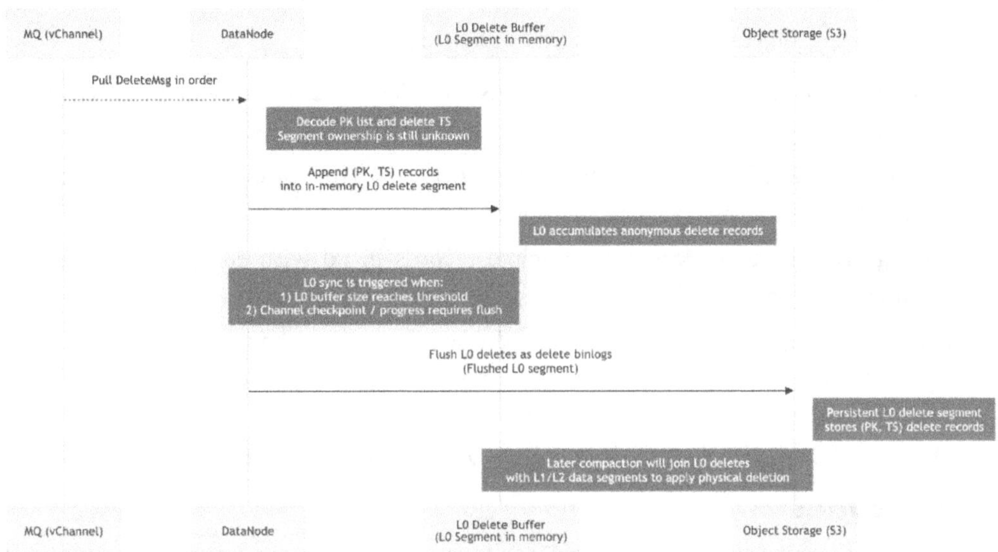

Figure 6.7: An overview of the asynchronous delete process

Let's look at the steps involved in detail:

1. **Consume and buffer to L0 segment**: The DataNode consumes these anonymous delete messages from the vChannel. Since it cannot immediately determine which segment of these delete records belongs to, the DataNode uniformly caches them in a special memory buffer, which corresponds to an L0 segment.
2. **Syncing the L0 segment**: When the L0 segment's buffer accumulates to a certain size, or is triggered by a channel checkpoint, the DataNode will sync this anonymous delete information to object storage, forming a persistent flushed L0 segment.

So, when does delete take effect, and how is physical cleanup completed?

From the user's perspective, the semantics of delete have two layers:

1. **Logical deletion (visibility)**: Once a `DeleteMsg` has been written to the message queue and has been consumed and applied by a QueryNode, subsequent queries will use the PK and delete timestamp information to filter out deleted entities. After the QueryNode

has processed the relevant delete records, those entities disappear from query results and are logically deleted.

2. **Physical deletion (via compaction)**: The L0 segment is only a persistent carrier for delete records; it does not itself remove any data. Later, background compaction tasks will take care of this part as described in detail in the compaction chapter.

Putting this together, delete in Milvus is a multi-stage process:

- **Synchronous phase**: Determine the PKs to delete and write delete records into the vChannel
- **Asynchronous phase (DataNode)**: Aggregate anonymous delete records into an L0 segment and sync them to object storage
- **Background compaction**: Merge delete records in L0 with concrete data segments, ultimately completing physical cleanup

Along this entire path, delete and insert share the same message channel (vChannel), but they follow different data paths on the DataNode and beyond. Insert data goes directly into the writer buffers of growing segments, whereas delete records are first collected into the writer buffer of an L0 segment and only affect data segments indirectly through later compaction

Upsert request

In Milvus, upsert is not a separate internal DML type; it is a composite operation built on top of existing delete and insert. Conceptually, an upsert is broken down into two steps: delete first, then insert, and these two steps together provide a convenient way to realize an eventual replacement semantics. The target semantics are straightforward: if a row with the given PK already exists, its fields should be replaced by the new values. If it does not exist, a new row should be inserted.

The following code demonstrates how to upsert entities into the same collection "`ch6_movies`" created in the insert section:

```
upsert_entities = []

# Update existing entity (row 2)
if len(rows) > 2:
    upsert_entities.append({
        "id": rows[2]['id'],
        "title": "Updated Title",
        "plot": "Updated plot content",
        "genre": rows[2]['genre'],
        "embedding": rows[2]['embedding']
```

```
    })

# Insert new entities (rows 4-5)
for i in range(4, min(6, len(rows))):
    upsert_entities.append({
        "id": rows[i]['id'],
        "title": rows[i]['title'],
        "plot": rows[i]['plot'],
        "genre": rows[i]['genre'],
        "embedding": rows[i]['embedding']
    })
upsert_res = client.upsert(
    collection_name="ch6_movies", data=upsert_entities)
print(f"Upsert result: {upsert_res}")
```

When an upsert request reaches the Proxy, the Proxy first extracts all PKs from the request payload and builds an internal delete request for this PK set; it then builds an insert request based on the original upsert data. To preserve the ordering between the old and new versions for the same PK, the Proxy asks RootCoord for a globally unique timestamp and assigns this timestamp to both the internal delete and the internal insert.

These two messages are then written to the corresponding vChannel in order: delete first, insert second. Downstream DataNodes and QueryNodes do not need any special handling for upserts; they simply process a normal delete message and a normal insert message as described in the previous sections. For a given PK, with the same timestamp and a defined message order, Milvus ensures that the final view retains only the new version introduced by the insert.

In summary, upsert fully reuses the write and recovery paths of delete and insert: on the write path, both operations share the same vChannel and the same timestamp; at the DataNode, the delete half still goes into an L0 segment and affects data segments later through compaction, while the insert half is written as binlogs into the corresponding growing segments. With the behaviors of insert, delete, and upsert in place, we can now trace a row throughout its entire lifecycle on the write path, from being accepted, to being marked, to being persisted. The next question is, in the face of failures, restarts, and load migration, how does Milvus recover the processing position on a given channel precisely and keep read and write segment views consistent? To answer this, we introduce the core concept for the rest of this chapter: the channel checkpoint.

Channel checkpoints

As a distributed architecture with read-write separation, Milvus must, by design, solve two inherent core challenges.

The first challenge is **component fault recovery**. Both DataNodes, which handle writes, and shard delegators, which serve real-time queries, continuously consume data from the message queue. Whenever one of these nodes crashes and restarts, or takes over a new vChannel due to load balancing, it must know exactly from where to resume processing. That starting point cannot be too early, or the system will waste resources reprocessing large amounts of already-persisted data; nor can it be too late, or it will miss data that has not yet been synced to object storage. If every recovery had to start replaying from a very old point in the log, recovery times would become unacceptable, and the resulting load on the system would be prohibitive.

The second challenge, an essential requirement of a read-write separation architecture, is **read-write path synchronization**. If the read path relied solely on consuming streaming data to provide query services, all data would remain in memory as a growing segment for a long time. While this form is ideal for fast ingestion, it is unsatisfactory for production workload in terms of query performance, memory footprint, and cold-start costs. The whole point of the write path is to continuously flush these growing segments, build indexes, and run compaction, gradually evolving them into a set of flushed segments or larger, merged segments with much better layout and query efficiency. For the read path to actually benefit from this work, it must be able to reliably observe the write path's progress and, at the right time, replace its segments with the higher-quality segments, so that its own view of the data converges toward the write path's latest and best state. To uniformly address these two core challenges, Milvus introduces one of the most critical reliability mechanisms on the write path: the **channel checkpoint**.

The core idea of a channel checkpoint is to establish a constantly advancing **safe watermark** in the data stream of each vChannel. This watermark is, in essence, a timestamp that is durably recorded. It provides a clear guarantee to the entire system: all streaming data with timestamps less than or equal to the checkpoint's timestamp has already been fully and reliably persisted to object storage. As long as this condition holds, any component in the system, when facing recovery, replay, or ownership transfer, can treat the checkpoint as a trustworthy reference point.

For fault recovery and load balancing, the effect of the checkpoint is immediate. When a new subscriber needs to start consuming a vChannel, whether due to a node restart or because it has taken over a new task due to the cluster's load balancing strategy, it no longer has to start from the head of the message queue and chase the log all the way forward. Instead, it can simply obtain the latest checkpoint for that channel from the DataCoord. The checkpoint timestamp then defines the precise point at which it must begin active processing: all historical data up to and including this timestamp can be safely reconstructed directly from object storage. *Figure 6.8* shows that messages from `T_1` to `T_k` are all persisted in the object storage, and only data after that point needs to be replayed from the message queue. This greatly improves the system's availability and elasticity.

At the same time, the checkpoint is also the foundation for synchronizing the read and write states. By periodically observing how the checkpoint advances and comparing it with the segments it has already loaded, the read path can infer exactly what the write path has completed. For example, when the checkpoint moves beyond the time range of a given growing segment, the read path knows that this segment has been flushed and is now available as a safely loadable flushed segment. When the checkpoint confirms that a set of old segments has been compacted into a new one, the read path unloads the old segments and switches to the new one. By repeatedly applying this kind of comparison and replacement, the read path can continuously evolve its in-memory view toward a more optimal data layout, achieving high query performance. The detailed mechanisms behind this process will be discussed in depth in *Chapter 7*.

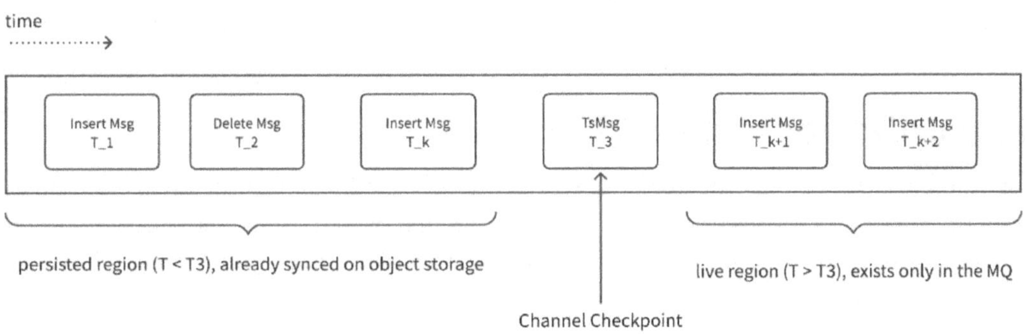

Figure 6.8: An overview of the vChannel timeline (ordered by timestamp)

Therefore, the channel checkpoint mechanism is not just a technical detail; it is the cornerstone designed by Milvus to solve the two core challenges of fault tolerance and read-write synchronization in its distributed, read-write separated architecture. By establishing a continuously advancing and absolutely reliable ***safe watermark***, it endows the components within the system with the ability to recover quickly and allows the read path to stay synchronized with the continuous optimizations of the write path. It is this mechanism that ensures the entire write path is not only efficient but also robust and resilient, fully capable of operating reliably in a production environment.

Summary

In this chapter, we explored the complex and intricate inner world of the Milvus write path, completely mapping the journey of data from an API call to a persistent record. Our exploration began with the cornerstone of its data organization, the segment, for which we built a three-dimensional cognitive model based on its state, structure, and role. We then followed a segment through its entire lifecycle from birth (growing) to demise (dropped), understanding the automated management mechanisms by which Milvus transforms streaming data into historical data. With this foundation, we analyzed the behind-the-scenes flow of DML requests like insert, delete, and upsert from a developer's perspective, witnessing the close collaboration of components like the proxy, coordinators, and data nodes. Finally, we unveiled the core mechanism that ensures the reliability of the entire write path, which is the Channel Checkpoint, and understood its critical role in fault recovery, resource management, and read-write state synchronization. Through this chapter, we have not only learned how to write data to Milvus but, more importantly, have gained an insight into how data is organized and managed internally, laying a solid foundation for exploring Milvus' high-performance reading capabilities in the next chapter.

7

Reading Data in Milvus

In *Chapter 6*, we detailed the process of writing data into Milvus. This chapter shifts our focus to the other side of the equation: how to efficiently retrieve that data.

To understand the read path, we must revisit the core design principle from *Chapter 5*: read-write separation. This separation is crucial because it endows the read path with a powerful dual capability. On one hand, it has the ability to provide stable, high-performance queries on optimized, persistent historical data, completely unaffected by complex tasks on the write path, such as segment state transitions, compaction, or index building.

On the other hand, it also possesses the flexibility to provide near-real-time visibility for the new data. This is achieved because QueryNodes subscribe to the same vChannels and apply insert/delete messages in memory immediately after consumption, allowing data to be queried right after it is written, long before it is flushed or indexed.

The components responsible for orchestrating and executing this entire complex read path, enabling it to masterfully handle both historical and streaming data, are two core components we have met before: **QueryCoord**, which acts as the cluster manager, and **QueryNode**, which serves as the frontline worker.

This chapter will walk you through the process of querying the data and the role Query Coord and QueryNode play in this workflow. You will also learn about how the query mechanism works in Milvus. We will then move our focus to handling deletes and how to ensure consistency across reads and writes.

In this chapter, we will cover the following main topics:

- The query scatter-gather pattern
- Loading and balancing
- Handling deletes
- Ensuring multi-level consistency

The query scatter-gather pattern

Assuming a collection's data has been successfully loaded into memory (we will discuss this loading process in detail in the next section), how does Milvus leverage its distributed architecture to efficiently process a query request when it arrives? The answer is a classic computing pattern: **scatter-gather**. This section will first give you a bird's-eye view of the complete end-to-end journey of a query.

> Note
>
> **Meaning of "read" and "query"**
>
> In this chapter, unless otherwise specified, we refer to read or query as the general procedure for accessing data in Milvus, encompassing **approximate nearest-neighbor (ANN)** search, scalar retrieval, and multi-vector hybrid search.

The core of this process is to take a single, high-level query request and break it down layer by layer; that is, scattering it into micro-search tasks that can be executed in parallel across a large number of data shards. Then, the results of these parallel tasks are gathered layer by layer, ultimately forming a meaningful global result for the user.

Figure 7.1 shows a visual representation of the **query scatter-gather pattern**:

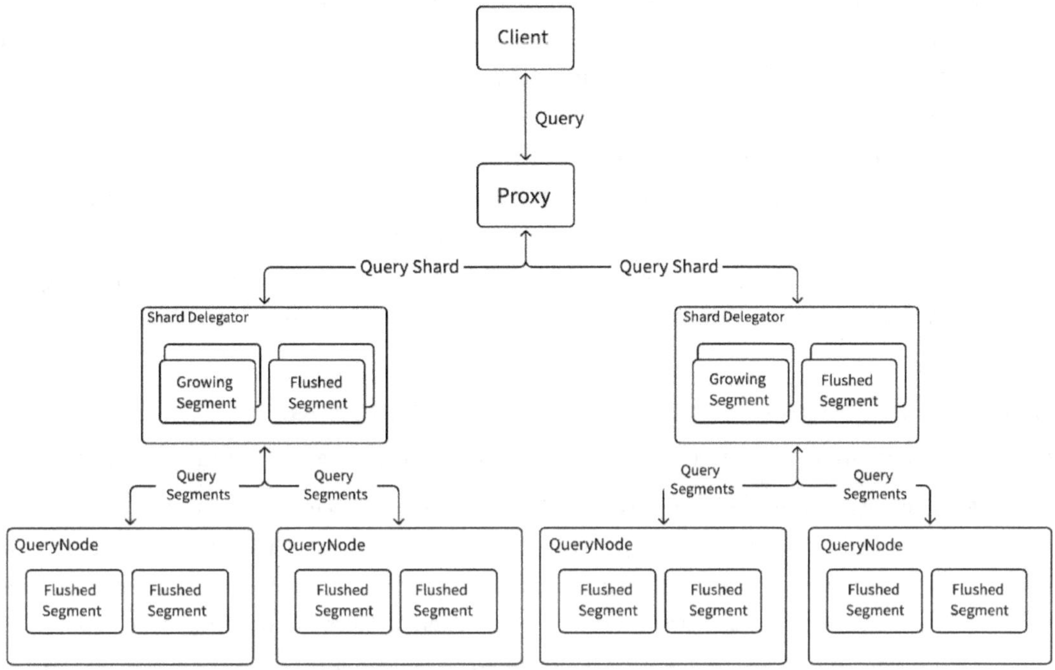

Figure 7.1: The query scatter-gather pattern

First, let's get to know the key participants in a query.

Query participants

The primary actors involved in processing a query are Proxy node, QueryCoord, Shard Delegator, and QueryNode:

- **Proxy node**: As the entry point for user requests, it is responsible for receiving queries, performing validation, parsing expressions, selecting an available collection replica to query, and finally aggregating the sub-results from all parallel compute nodes to form the final response to be returned to the client.
- **QueryCoord**: As the central coordinator of the query cluster, it maintains the cluster's topology and the metadata of the data distribution. It does not participate in the actual computation but provides the Proxy node with the routing information needed to execute the query, such as which node is responsible for which data shard.
- **Shard Delegator**: This is essentially a QueryNode that has taken on additional coordination responsibilities. In addition to loading and querying historical data segments (flushed segments), such as other QueryNodes, it is also assigned by the QueryCoord to subscribe to a specific shard's vChannel. This enables it to process real-

time streaming data and organize this data into in-memory growing segments. During a query, it is responsible for both querying the data it holds (both streaming and historical) and for further distributing the query request to other QueryNodes that hold data for that shard.

- **QueryNode**: As the *worker node* for executing queries, it loads specific historical data segments (flushed segments) into memory or onto disk and is responsible for performing underlying search and computation operations on this local data.

With these key participants in place, the query process kicks off by systematically distributing the workload. This is the scatter part of the pattern, where a single request is fanned out for parallel execution.

The scatter phase – distributing the workload

In Milvus, a query undergoes a two-tiered **scatter process** to achieve maximum parallelism:

- **First-level scatter is from Proxy to Delegators**: When the Proxy receives a query, it first asks the QueryCoord for the target collection's routing table. This table identifies which QueryNode is acting as the Shard Delegator for each shard in the selected replica. The Proxy then scatters the entire query request to each of these Shard Delegators in parallel.
- **Second-level scatter is from Delegators to QueryNodes**: Upon receiving the query, each Delegator breaks it down further. It initiates three parallel sub-searches simultaneously:
    - A search on its own in-memory **growing segments**
    - A search on any **flushed segments** it happens to be holding locally
    - A scatter of the request to all other QueryNodes that hold the remaining flushed segments for that specific shard

After this **two-level scatter**, a single query has been decomposed into parallel search tasks running on individual segments across the entire cluster.

The gather phase

The **gather phase** mirrors the **scatter phase**, consolidating results from the bottom up to produce the final answer:

1. **First-level gather (at the Shard Delegator level)**: Each Shard Delegator waits for the results from all the QueryNodes to which it dispatched tasks. It then performs a reduction, merging these results with the results from its own local search (on its

growing and flushed segments). This produces a single, consolidated top-K result for its entire shard.

2. **Second-level gather (at the Proxy level)**: The Proxy, in turn, waits to receive the consolidated top-K result from each Shard Delegator. It then performs the final reduce, merging the results from all shards to produce the global top-K result, which is then returned to the client.

For example, a query with a limit of 100 will cause each QueryNode to return its local top 100 results. The Shard Delegator merges these results to find the shard's top 100. Finally, the Proxy merges the top 100 results from each shard to find the global top 100.

This scatter-gather pattern gives Milvus immense horizontal scalability. As data volume or query traffic grows, you can simply add more QueryNodes or load more replicas to scale out the query processing power. However, at extreme scales, the gathering step at the Proxy and Delegator can become a bottleneck, which can be mitigated by increasing CPU and memory (RAM) resources for the Proxy or QueryNodes.

Now that we have a bird's-eye view of the entire query journey, let's delve into the starting point of this journey and see how the system prepares for a query through **loading** and **balancing**.

Loading and balancing

To understand the necessity of a **load operation**, we must first revisit a core design philosophy of Milvus: in-memory computation built for speed. In the realm of vector retrieval, even a millisecond of latency difference can have a huge impact on user experience. Therefore, to achieve ultimate query performance, Milvus prioritizes utilizing memory for its core computations.

However, considering the conflict between massive datasets and limited memory in a production environment, Milvus also provides advanced solutions such as disk-based indexes (e.g., DiskANN) and **memory-mapping (mmap)**. These allow users to make a trade-off between memory and high-speed SSDs to support high-performance queries on datasets that far exceed memory capacity.

However, whether it's a pure in-memory or a memory-plus-disk solution, they all follow a common prerequisite: data must first be pulled from remote, low-cost object storage to the local QueryNode to become *computable*. This process involves downloading index and data files from remote storage to the QueryNode's local disk or cache.

The `load_collection` API is the API that formally executes this process. It acts like a switch, telling Milvus, *I am about to query this collection. Please prepare the data on the QueryNodes.*

This design gives users active control over their resources. You can choose to load only hot collections that need to be queried frequently, while letting less-used cold data rest quietly in object storage. This allows for the most cost-effective use of valuable memory or local disk resources across the entire cluster. Loading is the first step to unlocking high-performance queries and a direct reflection of Milvus' resource management philosophy.

Before you can query a collection, Milvus requires you to first load at least one **replica** of it into the memory or disk of the QueryNodes.

So, what exactly are we loading when we execute a load operation? The answer is replicas. Let's understand the anatomy of a replica.

Replicas

A replica in Milvus is a complete, queryable copy of a collection's data, encompassing both immutable historical data stored in object storage and the continuous stream of real-time data flowing in from the **message queue** (**MQ**).

It's not a simple static snapshot but is composed of two parts: all the **historical segments** stored in object storage, and **streaming data** continuously flowing in from the MQ.

Furthermore, a complete replica of a collection is composed of a replica for each of its shards. The data for a single shard's replica, in turn, also comes from its historical segments and its real-time stream. It is the design of the MQ that ensures when multiple subscribers (i.e., QueryNodes) consume the same channel, they receive the exact same data in the exact same order, thus guaranteeing that each replica maintains a precise copy of the streaming data.

As demonstrated in *Figure 7.2*, a complete replica of a collection is composed of a replica for each of its shards.

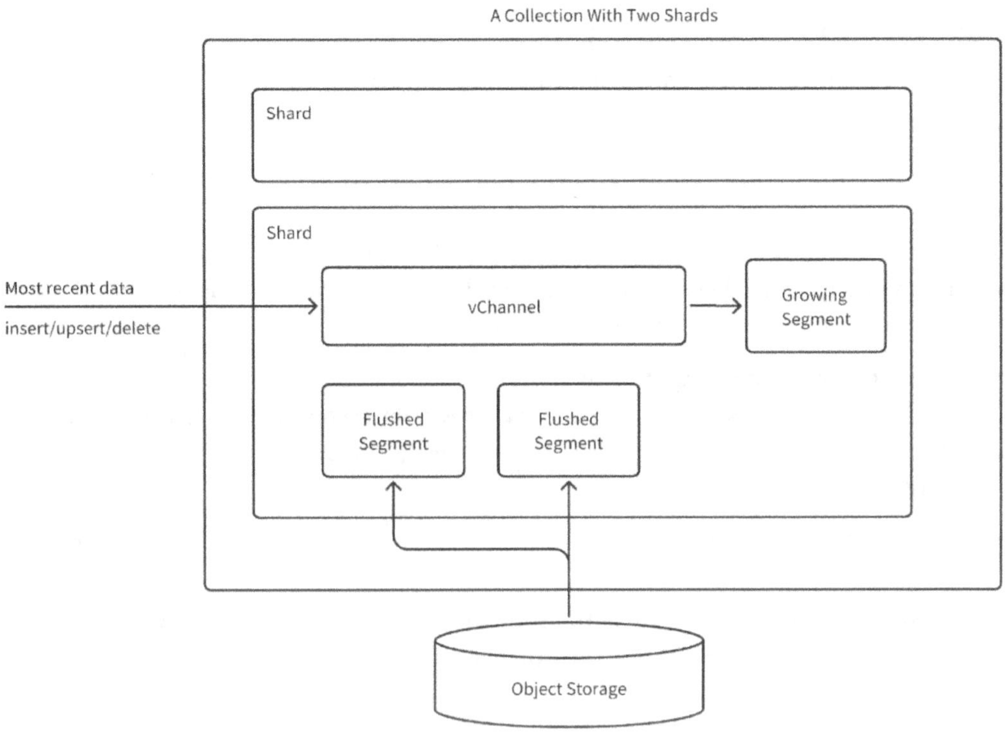

Figure 7.2: A visual representation of a replica of a collection with two shards

The complete dataset for a single shard is sourced from two locations:

- **The Shard's vChannel**: This MQ topic holds the most recent, real-time data that has not yet been synced to object storage
- **The Shard's segments**: These immutable files in object storage hold historical data

The design of the MQ (covered in *Chapter 5*) is what allows a channel to serve as a source for a replica. When multiple subscribers of the same channel consume data at the same timestamp, they are guaranteed to receive the exact same data in the exact same order. This ensures that every QueryNode subscribing to a channel maintains an identical copy of the streaming data.

For example, if two replicas (Replica A and Replica B) subscribe to the same vChannel, and two users (User A and User B) insert or query data on that collection at the same time, both replicas will process the incoming messages in the same order and produce the same state. This guarantees that User A and User B will see consistent results regardless of which replica serves their query.

Now, we will take a look at how to load and release replicas in Milvus.

Loading and releasing replicas

The PyMilvus client provides a simple API to manage the loading process:

```
client.load_collection("test_collection")
client.load_collection("test_collection", replica_number=3)
```

To load a collection, you can specify the number of replicas you wish to create. Choosing the right number of replicas for a collection is a crucial trade-off between performance, availability, and cost. You should typically consider the following points:

- **Target query throughput**: This is the most common reason to scale replicas. Each replica can handle a certain number of **queries per second** (**QPS**). If a single replica can handle 1,000 QPS but your application needs 3,000 QPS, you will need at least three replicas.
- **High availability (HA)**: If your application cannot tolerate downtime, you need at least two replicas.
- **Resource constraints**: This is the most important limiting factor. Replicas consume memory and disk. Three replicas means three times more resources.

> Note
>
> Milvus enforces that the number of QueryNodes must be greater than the number of replicas you intend to load. Attempting to load more replicas than available QueryNodes (or running in standalone mode) will result in an error.
>
> Ensure you have created an index for your vector field(s) on the collection before loading it; otherwise, the load will fail.

The process of loading a collection is a coordinated effort between the Proxy, QueryCoord, and QueryNodes. When a user's load request is forwarded from the Proxy to the QueryCoord, the entire loading process is immediately organized and dispatched by the QueryCoord.

Here is how this process works:

1. First, the QueryCoord retrieves the collection's metadata, especially how many shards it contains.
2. Then, for each replica requested by the user, it will select a QueryNode from the available pool to act as the Shard Delegator for each shard.

3. Simultaneously, based on its load-balancing strategy, it will evenly distribute the loading tasks for all flushed segments of that shard among all available QueryNodes, including the Delegator itself.
4. The QueryCoord then issues specific tasks to all relevant QueryNodes. At this point, the loading work begins in parallel across the entire query cluster.
5. The node assigned as a Shard Delegator will immediately subscribe to its shard's vChannel starting from the latest checkpoint, consume the real-time data, build and maintain growing segments in memory, and automatically create temporary in-memory indexes for them to accelerate queries.
6. At the same time, all QueryNodes (including the Delegator) will begin pulling their assigned flushed segment data and indexes from object storage. After these files are downloaded, they are handed over to Milvus' core execution engine, **Knowhere** (see *Chapter 9*).

Only when every shard of a replica has a corresponding Delegator handling its real-time stream, and all of its flushed segments have been successfully loaded on the various QueryNodes, will the QueryCoord mark the replica as available, and the load operation is considered complete.

When you no longer need to query a collection, use the `release_collection` API to free up its occupied memory and disk resources:

```
client.release_collection("test_collection")
```

This action unloads all data associated with the collection from all QueryNodes. The collection becomes unqueryable until it is loaded again.

Loading a collection is the crucial first step to enabling queries. However, in a dynamic environment where data is continuously written, and nodes may change, Milvus must continuously optimize the data distribution to maintain high performance and resilience. This automatic process, managed by the QueryCoord, is known as dynamic load balancing.

Let's talk about it in detail.

Dynamic load balancing

In a multi-node cluster, Milvus automatically balances the data distribution across QueryNodes to maximize resource utilization and maintain query performance. This balancing act occurs continuously and is managed by the QueryCoord. It balances streaming data at the channel level and historical data at the segment level. First, let's look at **channel balancing**.

Channel balancing

As the consumer of streaming data, the Shard Delegator's CPU and memory resources are particularly valuable. Therefore, ensuring an even distribution of subscribing to vChannels' responsibilities across QueryNodes is critical to prevent bottlenecks.

When the cluster topology changes (e.g., node scaling, failures, or upgrades), the QueryCoord automatically triggers a rebalancing of vChannels. This process strictly adheres to the **load-before-release** principle, ensuring that a subscription task is successfully started on a new node before it is released from the old one, guaranteeing service continuity and preventing query interruptions.

Next up is **segment balancing**.

Segment balancing

The goal of segment balancing is more granular: it aims to ensure each QueryNode handles a roughly equal number of entity rows, not just the number of segments, as this more accurately reflects the true query workload. Balancing is triggered in several key scenarios:

- **Growing to flushed transition (handoff)**: When the write path transforms a growing segment into a flushed segment, the read path needs to replace the in-memory growing segment on the Shard Delegator with this new, immutable flushed one. This process, known as a **handoff**, also follows the load-before-release principle. It ensures that the new flushed segment is fully loaded and ready on a QueryNode before the old growing segment stops serving queries, guaranteeing a seamless transition.
  This process is demonstrated in *Figure 7.3*:

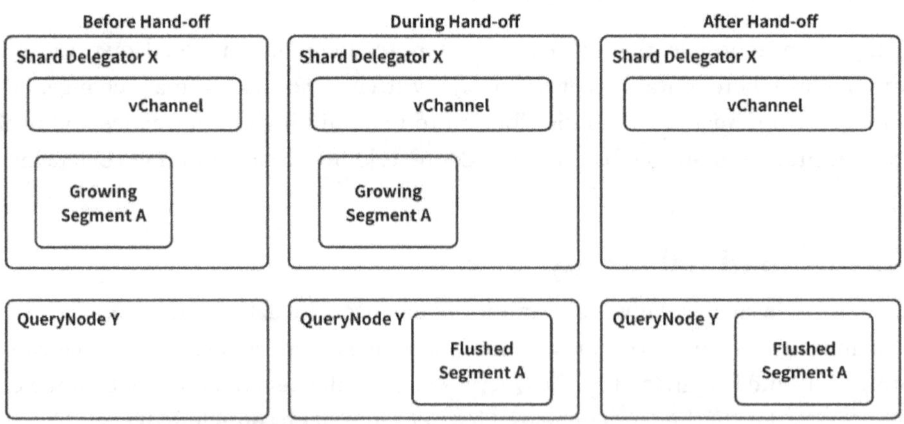

Figure 7.3: The handoff process from growing to flushed transition

Here is how the handoff process works:

1. **Before handoff**: Shard *Delegator X* has one in-memory growing *Segment A*. *QueryNode Y* does not yet host the flushed copy of *A*.
2. **Flush**: *Segment A* transfers from growing to flushed states, and is written to object storage by DataNode.
3. **Rebalance (handoff)**: The new flushed *Segment A* is loaded into *QueryNode Y* *before* the growing segment is released. Initially, all queries for this collection are routed to the growing *Segment A*. While these queries are being served, Milvus loads the new flushed *Segment A* onto a QueryNode. Once this flushed segment is fully loaded and ready, the QueryCoord and Delegator update the current target segments, directing all new queries to it. The original growing *Segment A* is safely released only after all in-flight queries that were targeting it have completed, guaranteeing a seamless transition without interrupting any ongoing queries.

- **Flushed segment replacement (compaction)**: When the write path merges several small segments into a more optimal large one (compaction), the read path also needs to perform a synchronous replacement. Adhering to the load-before-release principle, QueryNodes will load the new segment first before releasing old ones, ensuring queries are not disrupted.
  Figure 7.4 depicts the flushed segment replacement process:

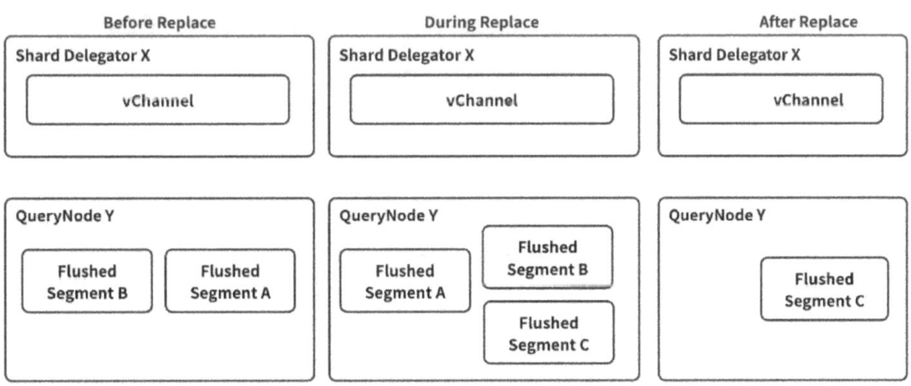

Figure 7.4: Segment replacement process

Here's how it works:

1. **Before**: *QueryNode Y* serves flushed *Segments A* and *B*. All queries for this collection are routed to *Segments A* and *B*.

2. **During**: *Segment C* is not in the *Before Replace* image. It means that the flushed *Segment C* is created by merging flushed *Segments A* and *B*, and loaded into *QueryNode Y*.
3. Before *Segment C* is fully loaded, the queries are still routed to *Segments A* and *B*.
4. **After**: Once *C* is fully loaded, and all queries on *A* and *B* are done, *A* and *B* are ready to be safely released, and all queries go to *C*.

- **Balancing on node topology changes**: When a QueryNode is added, removed, or fails, the QueryCoord redistributes its segments among the remaining active nodes. If there's only one replica loaded, a node failure will cause a temporary service interruption for the data it held until that data is reloaded on other nodes. With multiple replicas, or during planned scaling and upgrades, the load-before-release approach ensures continuous query availability.

  Figure 7.5 depicts the process of load balancing:

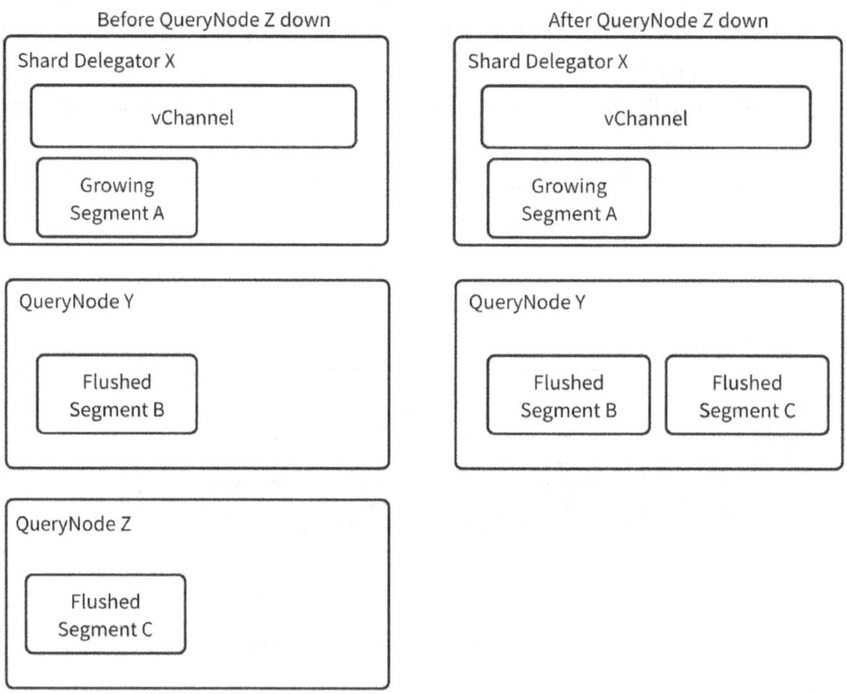

Figure 7.5: Load balancing of QueryNodes

Here's how it works:

1. **Before failure**: Initially, *QueryNode Z* hosts flushed *Segment C*, and Shard *Delegator X* routes all relevant queries to it.
2. **During failure**: Refers to if *QueryNode Z* unexpectedly goes down.
3. **Rebalance**: QueryCoord detects the failure and initiates a rebalance process to reload flushed *Segment C* onto *QueryNode Y*. Once loaded, the delegator updates its routing table, allowing queries to continue seamlessly against the newly loaded segment.

Now, we have a clear understanding of how queryable data is prepared and organized in Milvus. However, this blueprint only describes the *addition of data*; that is, how entities are loaded and distributed. A complete system must also efficiently handle the *subtraction of data*. So, what happens when a `delete` command is issued to ensure that this data is not seen during a query? This is the core mechanism we will explore in the next section – the handling of delete operations in Milvus.

Handling deletes

From the previous section, we have a clear understanding of how queryable data is prepared and organized in Milvus. Now, we face a deeper question: What happens when a `delete` command is issued?

To answer this, we must return to two of Milvus' core architectural principles. First, its historical data is persisted on immutable object storage such as S3, which means that once a data file is generated, it cannot be modified in place. Second, its read-write separation architecture dictates that the components responsible for querying (the read path) do not *own* the data themselves and have no authority to alter original files generated by the write path.

These two principles collectively determine one thing: when processing a delete, the responsibility of the read path is not to physically erase the data, but to efficiently *mask* it during a query. This section will delve into how Milvus achieves this goal through an elegant soft-delete mechanism. This presents a new challenge for the read path: during query execution, the system must be able to identify and hide data that has been marked as deleted in real time.

When you issue a `delete` command, targeted entities are not immediately purged from storage. Instead, Milvus records their **primary keys** (**PKs**) in a deltalog associated with the relevant segments.

There are many possible sources of deletion. When a user issues a delete command, the information does not immediately affect the data files. Instead, it is recorded as a **delete marker**.

On the read path, to construct a complete view of what data has been deleted, the QueryNodes need to collect these delete markers from three different sources:

- **From the vChannel**: These are the latest, real-time, anonymous delete records. Like insert records, they are first written into the vChannel.
- **From L0 segment**: These are recently flushed deletions. As we learned in *Chapter 6*, anonymous delete operations are centrally written into special L0 segments.
- **From deltalogs**: For older, flushed segments, delete records pertaining to their internal data are stored in a set of deltalog files associated with each segment.

The key challenge here lies in handling the anonymous deletes from the first two

sources. These records only contain the PK of the deleted entity and the timestamp, but they don't know which data segment the PK actually belongs to.

So, how do anonymous deletions happen? Let's find out.

The delegator's role and Bloom filters

The Shard Delegator is central to processing these anonymous deletions. It consumes real-time delete messages from its assigned vChannel, loads relevant L0 segment data from object storage, and then caches all this anonymous deletion information in an in-memory structure called the delete buffer.

Now, the question is: For each PK to be deleted in the buffer, how can the delegator quickly locate which segment it might belong to without scanning all data segments (which would be a computationally astronomical task)? The answer is the **Bloom filter**.

A Bloom filter is a space-efficient, probabilistic data structure used to test whether an element is a member of a set. Instead of storing elements directly, a Bloom filter maintains a bit array and uses multiple hash functions to map each element to several bit positions.

When inserting an element, the element is hashed by *k hash* functions, and the corresponding bits in the array are set to 1. To test membership, the same hashes are computed, and the corresponding bits are checked.

A Bloom filter has the following characteristics:

- **Definitive negative**: If any of the corresponding bits is 0, the element is definitively not in the set.
- **Probabilistic positive**: If all corresponding bits are 1, the element might be in the set. In this case, there is a very small chance of a false positive, where the filter reports that the element exists even though it was never inserted.

The false positive probability depends on the size of the bit array (m), the number of inserted elements (n), and the number of hash functions (k). It can be approximated as follows:

$$p = \left(1 - e^{-\frac{kn}{m}}\right)^k$$

For example, with a Bloom filter of 10,000 bits and 7 hash functions storing about 1,000 elements, the false positive rate is typically below 1%.

Milvus pre-generates a Bloom filter based on all PKs for every flushed segment at the time of flushing. For growing segments in memory, the Shard Delegator also dynamically generates one for them. During query processing, the Shard Delegator's workflow is as follows:

For each PK in its delete buffer, the delegator checks the Bloom filters of all relevant segments. While a Bloom filter may produce a low false positive rate, it is extremely fast and guarantees no false negatives. When a Bloom filter indicates a potential match, the delegator forwards the delete operation (the PK and timestamp) to the QueryNode responsible for that segment.

These forwarded deletions are applied during query by the Knowhere execution engine (discussed in *Chapter 9*). Milvus converts delete records into bitmaps that mark the corresponding entities as deleted. During the final stage of query execution, the results are filtered using these bitmaps so that entities marked as deleted are excluded from the result set. This allows deletes to affect ongoing queries without physically modifying the underlying segment data.

Through this mechanism, Milvus implements soft deletion: deleted entities remain in storage but are masked at query time according to their delete timestamps. Bloom filters make this process efficient by quickly narrowing down segments that may contain deleted entities.

This design raises an important question: When a query is executed, which writes and deletes are visible to it? In other words, to what point in time does the query's data view correspond? Milvus answers this through its multi-level consistency model, which we introduce in the next section.

Ensuring multi-level consistency

In any distributed system, there is an inherent delay between when data is written and when it becomes available for reading on all nodes. Does the system choose to wait for the data to be fully synchronized to guarantee the latest results, or does it choose not to wait and immediately execute the query on the currently visible data to get the fastest response? This is the classic trade-off between data freshness and query latency.

Milvus does not adopt a one-size-fits-all approach. Instead, it empowers the user to choose the consistency level, allowing an optimal balance between performance and freshness for different application needs. Queries carry a guarantee timestamp, and the system ensures that only data with <= *this value* timestamps is visible. The Shard Delegator maintains a *tSafe* timestamp representing the progress of the read path. A query is executed once *tSafe >= Guarantee Ts*.

The four consistency levels are summarized in the following table:

Consistency level	Guarantees	Execution logic	tSafe versus Guarantee Ts
Strong	Query sees all writes up to the latest global timestamp	Waits until the read path has processed all relevant data	tSafe >= latest global timestamp
Session	Query sees all writes from the same client session	Waits only for the client's own writes	tSafe >= timestamp of last write in session
Bounded Staleness (default)	Query sees data that may be slightly outdated (e.g., 5 seconds)	Executes once tSafe is within the staleness window	tSafe >= current_time - staleness_period
Eventual	Query sees whatever data is currently visible; all writes will eventually appear	Executes immediately	tSafe >= 0 (always true)

Table 7.1: Consistency levels and execution timing

Here's a discussion on the consistency levels in some detail:

- **Strong consistency**: The highest level of consistency. It guarantees that queries will see all data written before the query begins. This provides the freshest possible view but may incur the highest latency due to waiting for background data synchronization.
- **Session consistency**: A very practical level. It guarantees that a client will see their own writes within the same session. It provides an intuitive read-your-writes experience without waiting for other clients' data to sync.
- **Bounded staleness consistency**: This is the default consistency level in Milvus. It guarantees that the data seen by a query is outdated by at most a configured time

window (e.g., 5 seconds). This is a practical option that offers a great balance between performance and freshness.

- **Eventual consistency**: The lowest consistency level, offering the highest performance. It provides no guarantees about data freshness, and queries execute immediately on data currently visible to the node. It only guarantees that all written data will eventually become visible.

Next, we will introduce how Milvus achieves these consistency levels.

How Milvus ensures consistency

Milvus manages consistency using a timestamp-based mechanism. The principle can be summarized as follows: have every query carry a timestamp requirement and then wait for the system's data progress to catch up to that requirement.

This mechanism revolves around two key timestamps:

- **Serviceable timestamp (tSafe)**: This is a timestamp maintained and continuously advanced by the Shard Delegator. It represents the data progress that the read path has currently processed and is ready to serve. All data with timestamps less than or equal to `tSafe` is visible to queries.
- **Guarantee timestamp (Guarantee Ts)**: This is a timestamp attached to each query request, representing how new the data for this query needs to be. In other words, the query result must reflect all write and delete operations with timestamps less than or equal to this guarantee timestamp.

Here is what the mechanism entails.

When a query arrives, the Delegator compares these two timestamps. The query is only executed when `tsafe >= Guarantee Ts`. If the system's progress has not yet caught up to the query's requirement, the query needs to wait. The essential difference between the four consistency levels lies in how the Guarantee Ts for each query are calculated:

1. For **strong consistency**, the Proxy will use the latest global timestamp issued by the system's TSO RootCoord (covered in *Chapter 5*). The query must therefore wait until the read path has processed all data before this point and `tSafe` advances past it, ensuring absolute freshness.
2. For **session consistency**, the Proxy will use the timestamp of the last write from that specific client's session as the guarantee timestamp.

3. For **bounded stateless consistency**, the Guarantee Ts is calculated as `current_time - staleness_period`. Since `tSafe` is usually ahead of this slightly delayed time, queries can often execute with little to no waiting.
4. For **eventual consistency**, the Guarantee Ts is set to a very small value (e.g., 0). Since `tSafe` is always greater, the query never needs to wait and executes immediately.

Here's how to specify the desired consistency level in your query calls:

```
# Query with Strong Consistency: See all the latest data
results = client.query(collection_name, consistency_level="Strong")
# Query with Session Consistency: See your own recent writes
results = client.query(collection_name, consistency_level="Session")
# Query with Bounded Staleness Consistency (default): Allow minor data lag for
speed
results = client.query(collection_name)
# Query with Eventual Consistency: Prioritize speed above all.
results = client.query(collection_name, consistency_level="Eventually")
```

Choosing the right level is a critical design decision. Use *Strong* when data freshness is non-negotiable, *Session* for interactive applications, and *Bounded Staleness* or *Eventual* when performance is the primary concern.

The following table captures the mechanics behind each consistency level: *Strong* ensures queries see all recent updates, *Session* focuses on a client's session, *Bounded Staleness* tolerates minor delays, and *Eventual* prioritizes speed over freshness.

Consistency level	Example applications	Trade-offs
Strong	Access control (face recognition), development/ testing	Highest freshness, but highest latency and lowest throughput
Session	Interactive personalization (saved articles, user content)	Guarantees "read-your-writes" for individual users, moderate latency
Bounded Staleness	Recommendation engines, near-real-time news feeds	Balances performance with slightly stale data (e.g., 5 seconds)

Consistency level	Example applications	Trade-offs
Eventual	Batch analytics, **machine learning (ML)** training, reporting	Maximum throughput and lowest latency, but may see stale data

Table 7.2: Typical use cases for each consistency level

Here are some guidelines you can follow:

- **Strong consistency** guarantees every client sees the absolute latest data that has been successfully written to Milvus across the entire system. Suitable for use cases such as critical access control using face recognition, if an administrator revokes a user's access, that change must be reflected immediately. The next time the user tries to authenticate, the system must read from the updated state to deny access.
  It provides the highest data accuracy and integrity, and is also simple to reason about from a developer's perspective, so it's commonly used in development or tests. However, it also has the highest query latency and lowest throughput.
- **Session consistency** guarantees that a single client session sees all previous writes from that same session. It provides an intuitive "read-your-writes" experience for an individual user, but makes no guarantees about seeing writes from other users immediately. Suitable for use cases such as interactive content personalization when a user likes or saves an article, generating a vector. If they immediately go to their *saved articles* page, this consistency level ensures the article they just saved appears instantly for them.
  It's crucial for creating a good, logical user experience in interactive applications, as it provides better performance than *Strong* consistency.
- **Bounded staleness consistency** is the default consistency level; it guarantees to see data that's outdated by at most 5 seconds. It avoids waiting for the absolute latest data, trading a small amount of freshness for much better performance. Suitable for recommendation engines and near-real-time news feeds or social media. It's the best balance of performance and data freshness for most applications.
- **Eventual consistency** provides no guarantee of data visibility other than that the data will eventually become visible. Queries execute immediately on the data currently available to the QueryNode, offering the best possible performance. Suitable for use cases such as batch data analytics, reporting, ML model training, and offline system audits. It can provide the lowest possible query latency and the highest throughput.

To conclude, Milvus doesn't force a single consistency choice on you. By using its smart timestamp system, it turns the difficult problem of data consistency into a simple option. This gives the developer the power to decide what's more important for the application: getting the absolute latest data or getting the fastest possible query speed. Making the right choice is a key part of building a great application with Milvus.

Summary

In this chapter, we journeyed through the complete read path of Milvus. Our journey began with a bird's-eye view of the query process through the scatter-gather pattern, then delved into the preparation phase, understanding the necessity of loading collection replicas and the automated mechanism of dynamic load balancing. Next, we revealed how the system cleverly handles soft deletes using designs such as the Bloom filter. Finally, we explored how multi-level consistency empowers users to trade off between data freshness and query performance. In the next chapter, we will talk about compaction and garbage collection in Milvus for efficient memory management.

Get this book's PDF version and more

Scan the QR code (or go to `packtpub.com/unlock`). Search for this book by name, confirm the edition, and then follow the steps on the page.

UNLOCK NOW

Note: Keep your invoice handy. Purchases made directly from Packt don't require an invoice.

8

Compaction and Garbage Collection

In previous chapters, we explored how to write and read data in Milvus. While these processes are highly efficient for real-time operations, they introduce underlying challenges like segment fragmentation and obsolete files.

In this chapter, we will explore two critical, automated background processes that ensure the long-term health and efficiency of Milvus: compaction and **garbage collection** (**GC**). Without these mechanisms to continuously clean and organize data, Milvus would suffer a gradual decay in performance, with queries slowing down and storage costs spiraling upwards due to unpruned data. We will explore strategies such as mix compaction, L0 compaction, and clustering compaction that work under the hood to merge segments and permanently remove deleted data to ensure data consistency, reduce system overhead, and enhance query performance. Meanwhile, GC plays a vital role in cleaning up obsolete data, freeing up storage, and maintaining resource efficiency. This chapter is designed for Milvus administrators, developers, and system architects who want to deepen their understanding of Milvus' internal data management strategies and optimize their clusters for real-world workloads.

In this chapter, we will cover the following topics:

- Why compaction matters in Milvus
- Compaction in detail
- Managing obsolete data with GC

Technical requirements

Before diving into this chapter, readers should have a foundational understanding of:

- Collections, partitions, and clustering keys (covered in *Chapter 5*)
- Basic concepts of flushed segments and L0 segments (covered in *Chapter 6*)

Let's first start by understanding the importance of compaction in Milvus and the challenges it addresses.

Why compaction matters in Milvus?

Compaction is integral to Milvus' read-write disaggregation architecture (covered in *Chapter 5*), and is specifically designed to address several critical challenges in data management: segment fragmentation, inefficient queries, and the buildup of obsolete or soft-deleted data. By continuously optimizing data organization, compaction enhances query performance, reduces resource overhead, and ensures the system scales effectively with growing workloads. Compaction helps solve this by merging smaller segments into larger ones and permanently removing logically deleted records. By doing this, Milvus reduces the number of segments that QueryNodes need to scan during searches, which improves query efficiency and lowers latency. It also optimizes storage usage by eliminating redundant or obsolete data. In essence, compaction keeps the system clean, efficient, and performant, ensuring that vector searches remain fast even as the dataset grows and evolves.

In the following sections, we will explore how compaction addresses these challenges.

Segment fragmentation

As described in *Chapter 6*, Milvus seals and flushes a growing segment when it reaches 15% of its target size (`dataCoord.segment.maxSize`). This early sealing strategy provides clear operational advantages:

- **Controlling memory pressure**: By limiting the size of growing segments, it reduces the memory burden on the Shard Delegator that handles growing segments. Fragmentation increases memory overhead and can lead to inefficient resource usage. Compaction helps reduce memory pressure by merging smaller segments into larger ones, minimizing the number of active segments that need to be loaded into memory.
- **Accelerating index building**: Fragmented segments can slow down index construction because indexes may need to be built separately for many small segments. By merging segments through compaction, Milvus can build indexes on larger, consolidated datasets. Data is persisted faster, enabling index construction to improve query performance. However, this strategy introduces a significant trade-off: frequent sealing

at the 15% threshold produces many small segments, leading to severe segment fragmentation.

How fragmentation impacts query performance

Segment fragmentation affects query performance in multiple ways. Let's understand this from the query path perspective. Recall the scatter-gather query pattern from *Chapter 7* – queries must be distributed to all segments, and then results are merged and returned. The number of segments directly determines the overhead of this process. Consider a shard with 100 small segments versus 10 large segments. In this case, the query engine must perform significantly more scatter-gather operations. The former requires:

- 10x the number of per-segment query invocations
- 10x more intermediate result sets to merge
- 10x more metadata overhead to process

Second, from an index efficiency perspective, indexes on small segments perform worse than those on large segments. Take **hierarchical navigable small world** (**HNSW**) indexes as an example; they accelerate nearest neighbor search by building multi-layer graph structures. On large segments, HNSW can construct deeper, more optimized graph hierarchies with shorter search paths and higher query efficiency. In this case, the query engine must perform significantly more scatter-gather operations.

Finally, each segment in a QueryNode must contain independent metadata and memory state, including bloom filters, statistical information, etc. When there are too many segments, the memory footprint and management overhead of this metadata increase, further squeezing the memory available for query caching.

Mix compaction's performance optimization

Mix compaction merges multiple small segments into larger ones, fundamentally reducing segment count. Specifically, when mix compaction merges 10 small segments into 1 large segment, the following takes place:

- **Simplified query path**: Query and merge operations drop from 10 to 1, dramatically reducing latency and overhead.
- **Improve index quality**: Indexes built on larger datasets are more optimized. For HNSW, graph structures on large segments have deeper hierarchies and denser connections, yielding shorter search paths and higher query efficiency. Similarly, IVF indexes built on larger datasets can generate more representative clusters, improving both recall and query efficiency.

Without changing the underlying data content, mix compaction significantly improves query performance and system resource utilization by optimizing data organization.

The next challenge that compaction addresses is inefficient intra-partition queries. When you apply filters like `partition_key == '2025-02-11'`, Milvus can efficiently perform partition pruning at the collection level, reducing the scan range by excluding entire partitions. This collection-wise pruning is a powerful optimization that reduces unnecessary data scanning, but Milvus' partition key mapping mechanism introduces a challenge.

Partition key mapping logic

In Milvus, partition keys are not directly mapped to physical partitions. Instead, they are hashed and distributed across a limited number of partitions (typically 32). This means that multiple logical partition key values may map to the same physical partition. See *Figure 8.1*:

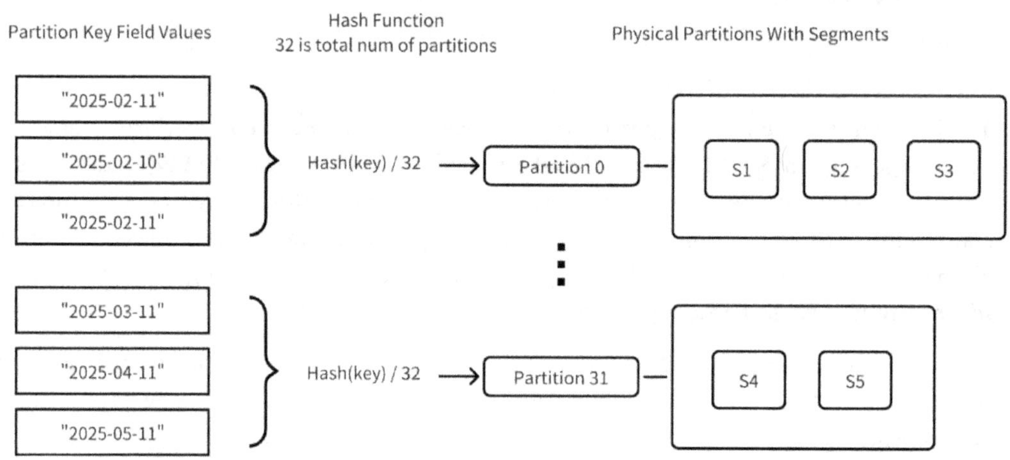

Figure 8.1: How partition keys map to partitions

While this enables efficient partition-level pruning, it creates a challenge. Even when a query targets only a specific partition key value, all segments within the selected partition must be scanned. Because the partition may contain data for other partition key values that also map to the same partition, queries must still scan segments containing data unrelated to the target key value. If a partition contains a significant amount of data, random entity distribution across segments leads to excessive read amplification and unnecessary computations.

For example, when querying `partition_key == "2025-02-11"`, the system locates partition 0, but that partition may store data for multiple dates (see *Figure 8.2*):

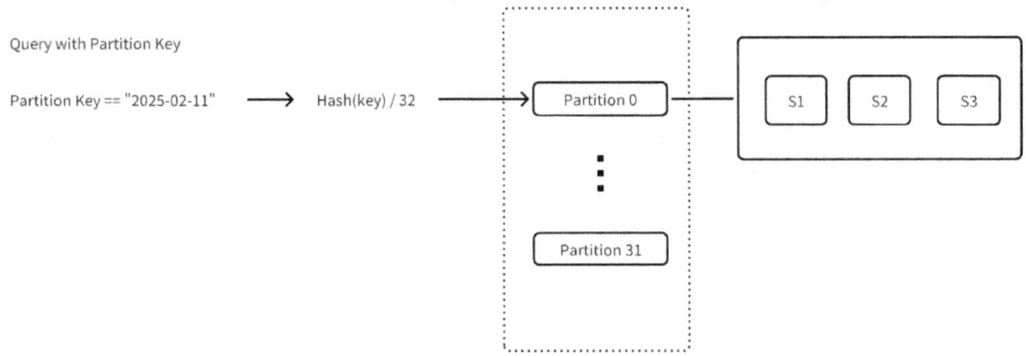

Figure 8.2: Query with partition key == "2025-02-11" scans all segments in partition 0

Therefore, the actual data accessed is much larger than needed, and every segment in the partition must be accessed and searched.

Clustering compaction enables intra-partition segment pruning

Clustering compaction is designed to solve this problem. Its core idea is to reorganize data within physical partitions around a clustering key. This clustering key is typically the most frequently used filter field in queries, ensuring data is ordered and clustered according to that field's value.

Specifically, clustering compaction reorganizes entities with identical or similar clustering key values into the same segments. After reorganization, data for the same date that was previously scattered across multiple segments is now tightly clustered in just a few segments. Meanwhile, the system maintains clustering key value range metadata for each segment, recording the minimum and maximum clustering key values that the segment contains.

This reorganization's greatest benefit is enabling segment-level data pruning. When a query specifies `partition_key == "2025-02-11"`, the system first locates the physical partition via hashing. Then, instead of blindly scanning all segments in that partition, it checks each segment's clustering key value range metadata. Only segments whose value range includes `"2025-02-11"` are actually accessed and searched, while other segments are safely skipped. This segment-level pruning dramatically reduces the amount of data accessed, significantly lowering query latency and computational overhead, especially for scenarios with many segments and high-cardinality partition keys, where performance improvements are particularly pronounced.

Now, let's examine the third challenge compaction faces: the storage and performance overhead of soft deletes.

Storage and performance overhead of soft deletions

Milvus uses soft deletion to handle delete operations. However, as deletions accumulate, soft deletes gradually become a performance burden, manifesting in two main ways.

The first issue is the continued resource occupation by deleted entities. Although these entities are logically deleted, their data physically remains in segments, continuing to occupy storage and potentially QueryNode memory when segments are loaded. In applications with frequent deletions, this accumulation of *zombie data* causes memory utilization to continuously decline while storage costs keep rising.

More serious is the impact on query performance. When executing search operations, queries carrying deletions always need to generate bitmaps, perform additional checks, and traverse more data compared to queries without deletions when searching for the same top-k results. This filtering process adds extra computational overhead, and as the proportion of soft-deleted data increases, this overhead becomes increasingly significant. In extreme cases, if most data in a segment has been deleted, the query engine may need to scan large amounts of invalid data to find sufficient valid results, severely slowing query speed.

The second issue comes from the handling mechanism for orphan deletes (introduced in *Chapters 6* and *7*). When delete requests arrive, the system writes delete messages to the vChannel and subsequently to L0 segments. These delete messages are called **orphan deletes** because they only contain the primary keys of deleted entities, not which specific segment contains the entity.

This uncertainty places a heavy routing burden on the shard delegator. For each orphan delete message, the delegator must execute a lookup process: it needs to traverse bloom filters for all segments in the shard, checking one by one which segment might contain the entity corresponding to that primary key. Once the target segment is located, the delegator forwards the delete information to the corresponding segment in the appropriate QueryNode.

This lookup process has computational complexity that grows linearly with the number of segments in the shard. In high-deletion-rate scenarios, large volumes of orphan delete messages continuously trigger global bloom filter queries, generating significant CPU overhead and network communication costs. As the collection scale expands and the segment count increases, this routing work becomes a serious performance bottleneck, especially in applications requiring large-scale dynamic dataset processing.

L0 and mix compaction address soft delete overhead

Milvus compaction alleviates the burden of soft deletes in multiple ways. First, L0 compaction converts orphan deletes into definite in-segment delete markers. Second, during the segment merging process of mix compaction, compaction physically deletes all entities marked as deleted, completely removing them from segments. This not only immediately frees memory and storage space but also eliminates the overhead of filtering this invalid data during queries.

Next, we'll dive into the specific compaction types in Milvus, and understand how these optimizations are implemented in the actual system.

Compaction in detail

Compaction in Milvus is a collection of processes tailored to address specific challenges within the system. This section explores the fundamental aspects of compaction, breaking down its common procedures and introducing the three primary types: mix compaction, L0 compaction, and clustering compaction.

Let's begin with an overview of the common procedures that underpin all compaction types.

The common process

Even though Milvus has three different types of compactions for different situations, they all follow the same execution framework. This framework is jointly handled by DataCoord and DataNodes, encompassing three core phases: triggering, scheduling, and execution. This works as follows:

- **Triggering (in DataCoord)**: DataCoord regularly checks the metadata of all flushed segments. Based on a set of predefined rules specific to each compaction type, it identifies eligible segments and groups them into a compaction task. This task is then submitted to a compaction task queue, awaiting scheduling. We'll cover the specific rules for each compaction type in the next section.
- **Scheduling (in DataCoord)**: After the tasks enter the queue, the compaction scheduler determines when and where to run the task. It makes this decision based on the task's priority and the resource availability (slots) of the DataNodes. The scheduler then assigns the chosen compaction task to a specific DataNode.
- **Execution (in DataNode)**: The assigned DataNode carries out the compaction task received from the DataCoord. While the exact logic differs between compaction types, the fundamental principle is the same: compaction is an immutable operation. It always writes data to new segments and never modifies or deletes existing files.

We will explore the execution details for each type in the upcoming sections.

Taking a closer look at the scheduling process

Since all compaction types share the scheduling algorithm, we will cover it in detail here to avoid repetition. The scheduler in DataCoord relies on a robust system of priorities and resource allocation via slots:

1. **Priority-based scheduling**: The DataCoord's scheduler always dispatches the highest-priority task in the queue first. By default, the priority policy is **first-in-first-out** (**FIFO**), meaning tasks generated earlier have higher priority than those generated later, and the scheduler schedules them based on their creation time. The priority policy is configured via `dataCoord.compaction.taskPrioritizer`, which offers three options: level, mix, and default. The default option represents the standard FIFO strategy, which prioritizes L0 compaction tasks, while the mix option sets mix compaction tasks to the highest priority.

   For workloads with frequent deletions or L0 compaction backlogs, setting the configuration to level prioritizes L0 compaction task scheduling to alleviate backlogs and prevent deletion accumulation. For high-write scenarios with severe fragmentation, using mix prioritizes `MixCompaction` task scheduling to accelerate small segment merging.

2. **Slot-based resource management**: After selecting the highest-priority task, the scheduler must choose a DataNode to execute it. The slot mechanism is the core of the scheduler's resource management. Slots are units that measure a DataNode's available resources for concurrent task execution. Each DataNode's slot capacity determines how many tasks it can handle simultaneously, controlled by the configuration parameter `dataNode.slot.slotCap` with a default value of 16.

   Different compaction task types consume different slot counts, which are also configurable. When selecting a node to execute a compaction task, the scheduler assigns tasks to the DataNode with the most available slots, thereby achieving load balancing.

By adjusting related configuration parameters, you can precisely control compaction resource usage.

The following table lists the key configuration parameters for managing compaction resource allocation:

Configuration parameter	Default value	Description
`dataNode.slot.slotCap`	16	Total slots per DataNode
`dataCoord.slot.clusteringCompactionUsage`	16	Slot usage for each clustering compaction task
`dataCoord.slot.mixCompactionUsage`	8	Slot usage for each mix compaction task
`dataCoord.slot.l0DeleteCompactionUsage`	8	Slot usage for L0 compaction task

Table 8.1: Compaction resource configuration parameters

If you have sufficient memory and CPU resources, you can increase `slotCap` to raise the number of concurrent compaction tasks a DataNode can execute. For resource-intensive operations, increasing per-task slot consumption can prevent DataNode overload. Conversely, on resource-constrained nodes, reducing per-task slot consumption allows more concurrent tasks. For example, if you configure mix compaction to consume 4 slots on a DataNode with 16 total slots, four mix compaction tasks can execute in parallel. By properly tuning these parameters, you can optimize resource utilization, effectively scale the DataNode cluster, and ensure compaction tasks run efficiently and stably under various system loads. We will discuss mix compaction, L0 compaction, and clustering compaction in the upcoming sections in greater detail. Please note that the scheduling phase is common to all three types of compactions.

Mix compaction

Mix compaction merges multiple flushed L1 segments into fewer, larger segments while purging expired and marked-for-deletion data. This merging not only addresses segment fragmentation but also frees storage space and improves query performance by physically removing invalid data.

Expired data refers to entities that have surpassed their defined **time-to-live** (**TTL**). You can set a TTL for your collection by configuring the property `collection.ttl.seconds` when creating the collection. Once TTL is set for a collection, any entity within that collection that exceeds its specified duration will be marked as expired and will be permanently removed during the compaction process.

Mix compaction takes multiple flushed segments as inputs and merges their valid data into one or more output segments that are close to a predefined target size to avoid creating segments that are too small or too large. For example, if three segments are input with sizes of 200MB, 300MB, and 500MB, respectively, each with 10% deleted data, mix compaction will ultimately produce a new 900MB segment. It's worth noting that a single compaction task can merge multiple L1 segments. However, for L2 segments produced by clustering compaction, since their data distribution is specific and relatively stable, compaction tasks are only triggered when there's excessive deleted or expired data, and each task processes only one L2 segment to avoid frequently disrupting the data distribution among L2 segments.

Mix compaction can triggered automatically or be manually executed on demand. Automatic triggering takes place based on several conditions:

- **Deletion ratio:** When the proportion of soft-deleted data in a segment exceeds a configured threshold(default 20%), compaction is triggered. This threshold can be set based on the ratio of delete entries (`dataCoord.compaction.single.ratio`, default 20%), the total size of deleted data (`dataCoord.compaction.single.deltalog.maxsize`, default 16MB), or the number of delta log files (`dataCoord.compaction.single.deltalog.maxnum`, default 200 files). Similarly, if the size of expired data in a segment exceeds a configurable threshold (`dataCoord.compaction.single.expirelog.maxsize`, default 10MB), compaction is triggered.
- **Fragmentation**: When the total size of a group of small segments falls between 85% (`maxSize * dataCoord.segment.compactableProportion`) and 115% (`maxSize * dataCoord.segment.expansionRate`) of the target maximum segment size, the system triggers a compaction task, where `maxSize` is the configured target segment size. This range design avoids creating overly small segments and prevents generating oversized segments that put pressure on memory.

> **Note**
>
> In scenarios requiring higher performance, you can reduce fragmentation at the source by increasing `dataCoord.segment.maxSize` (e.g., to 2GB), allowing compaction to merge into larger, fewer segments. However, note that increasing `maxSize` correspondingly increases the size of segments when sealed, requiring more memory for growing segments and shard delegators. Alternatively, you can synchronously lower `dataCoord.segment.sealProportion` to a smaller ratio (e.g., 8%) to reduce the overall size of growing data in the system. It's important to note that Milvus provides an additional, larger size configuration specifically for segments with DiskANN indexes for compaction selection: `dataCoord.segment.diskSegmentMaxSize`. If you're using DiskANN indexes, adjust this parameter to generate larger segments. DiskANN indexes leverage disk storage for data and index creation, allowing them to support larger segment sizes compared to pure in-memory indexes under the same machine conditions.
>
> For scenarios with frequent deletions, the default configuration retains up to 20% obsolete data. In such cases, you should lower the delete ratio threshold (e.g., to 10-15%) to make the system more aggressive in cleaning deleted data, preventing invalid data from occupying resources long-term.

Next, let's move our focus to L0 compaction.

L0 compaction

L0 compaction is a specialized process designed to handle anonymous deletions in L0 segments. Its primary function is to apply these deletions to their corresponding L1 and L2 segments. This ensures that higher-level segments accurately reflect deletion through their own delta logs while reducing the computational and routing burden on the shard delegator.

The following figure shows how L0 segments are merged with flushed segments during this process:

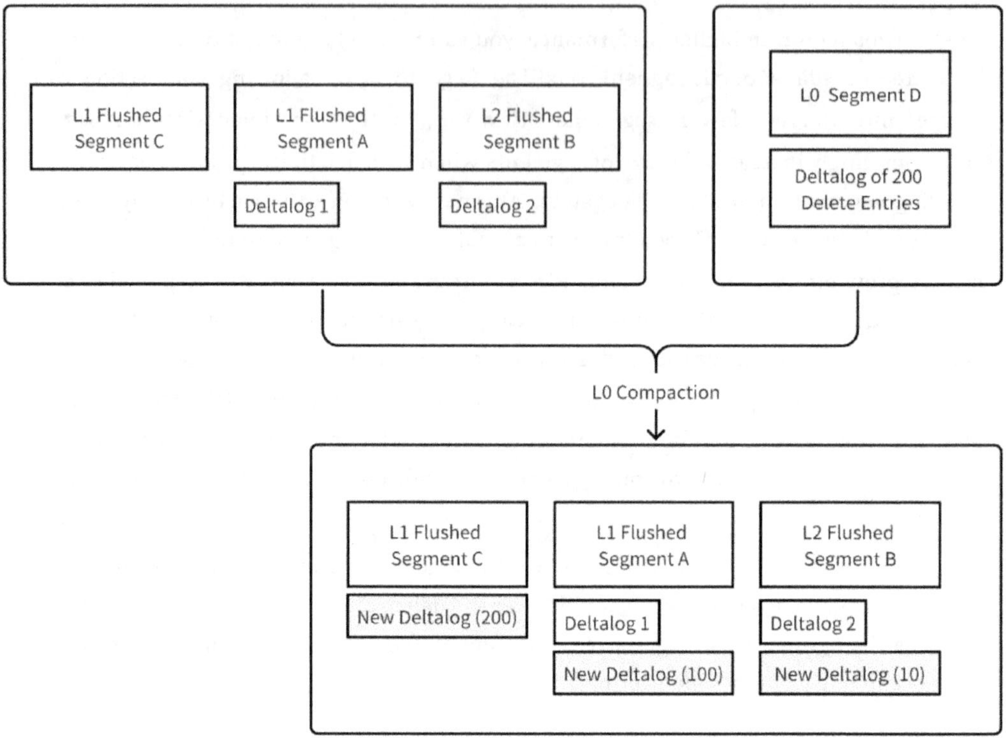

Figure 8.3: L0 compaction process – merging delete records with data segments

The inputs to L0 compaction include multiple L0 segments containing anonymous delta logs and the bloom filters of related L1 and L2 segments. The output consists of updated delta logs for the affected L1 and L2 segments, reflecting the deletion records propagated from the L0 segments.

L0 compaction uses L1 and L2 segment bloom filters to screen orphan deletes. If the bloom filter identifies that the primary keys of some orphan-deleted entities exist in **Segment A**, this indicates that these orphan deletes may have deleted data from **Segment A**. At this point, L0 compaction writes a new delta log for this segment, recording these deleted entities. L0 compaction is triggered under carefully defined conditions to balance data accuracy and resource efficiency:

- **Older timestamps**: Eligible L0 segments are those with timestamps older than the earliest data in the channel's growing segments.

- **Activity-based triggers**: During periods of heavy deletion, L0 compaction is triggered as soon as the total size or row count of eligible L0 segments exceeds a configured threshold. This proactively manages a high volume of deletes.
- **Inactivity-based triggers**: During periods of low or no deletion activity, a time-based trigger acts as a housekeeping mechanism. It ensures that even small batches of stale delete records are periodically cleaned up and don't linger in the system indefinitely.
- **Safety limits**: The total size and count of L0 segments in a single L0 compaction task are capped by maximum thresholds, ensuring the operation remains efficient and resource-friendly.

Generally speaking, L0 compaction triggering already covers all scenarios and is sufficiently optimized, requiring no additional configuration adjustments.

Now, let's turn our attention to clustering compaction.

Clustering compaction

Clustering compaction is a process designed to reorganize data based on clustering keys. This process enhances query performance by enabling efficient segment pruning, where irrelevant segments are skipped during queries.

The clustering key in Milvus is not automatically determined by the system. Instead, it must be explicitly specified by the user during collection creation. This is a deliberate design choice that puts the responsibility of optimizing query patterns in the hands of the developer who best understands their data access patterns.

When creating a collection, users must declare which field will serve as the clustering key through the collection schema configuration. This field becomes a permanent part of the collection's metadata and cannot be changed after creation. The clustering key selection is a one-time decision that has long-lasting implications for query performance.

The ideal clustering key should meet several criteria. First, it should be a field that appears frequently in query filters, as this maximizes the benefit of segment pruning. Second, it should have appropriate cardinality - not so high that each segment contains only a few records, but not so low that clustering provides no meaningful separation. Third, the field should have natural ordering or grouping patterns that align with how data is typically accessed.

Common choices for clustering keys include timestamp fields for time-series data, category or type fields for applications that frequently filter by classification, geographic fields for spatial queries, and user or tenant IDs for multi-tenant systems. Each of these choices reflects a different access pattern and optimization strategy.

For scalar-type clustering keys, Milvus adopts a range-based partitioning strategy. The system analyzes the value distribution of the clustering key field, then creates segments covering specific non-overlapping ranges. For example, if using timestamps as the clustering key, the system might organize all records from January 1-15 into one segment and January 16-31 records into another segment. This way, when queries specify a particular date range, the system can quickly identify relevant segments.

For vector-type clustering keys, Milvus adopts a different approach. The system uses the *k-mean* clustering algorithm to compute centroids representing different regions in vector space. During clustering compaction, each vector is assigned to its nearest centroid, and vectors assigned to the same centroid are organized into the same segment. This method is particularly suitable for vector similarity search scenarios because it ensures physical clustering of similar vectors, significantly improving approximate nearest neighbor search efficiency.

Triggers

Unlike the automatic triggering of mix and L0 compaction, clustering compaction requires manual triggering because it can be computationally expensive and depends heavily on workload patterns. You can explicitly invoke it through the SDK:

```
c = MilvusClient()
c.compact("test", is_clustering=True)
```

Clustering compaction is particularly valuable in multi-tenant SaaS applications. In such scenarios, you should set the tenant ID field as the clustering key when creating the collection. When combined with partition keys, optimal query performance can be achieved as partition keys enable partition-level pruning through hashing, while clustering keys enable segment-level pruning within each partition. After clustering compaction completes, queries like `tenant_id = 'tenant_123'` can precisely locate the few segments containing that tenant's data, dramatically reducing the scan range. For time-series data scenarios, using timestamp fields as the clustering key enables efficient time-range queries. Regardless of the scenario, administrators need to manually trigger clustering compaction periodically based on data growth and query performance needs to maintain optimization benefits.

With compaction setting the stage for efficient data organization, we now turn to the critical role of managing obsolete data through GC in the next section.

Managing obsolete data with garbage collection

Compaction improves Milvus performance by organizing and optimizing data layout, but it inevitably leaves behind a side effect, namely large amounts of obsolete data residue. However, compaction is not the only source of digital garbage in a Milvus system. In a long-running Milvus deployment, multiple operations leave traces that require cleanup.

To address this problem, Milvus introduces the final and crucial link in its data lifecycle management, known as **garbage collection** (**GC**). GC is a core functionality within the DataCoord component, responsible for identifying and safely deleting all files no longer used by the system, thereby freeing up storage space in object storage and the meta store. It is triggered periodically at a configurable fixed interval. Specifically, the targets of GC primarily include the following categories of data:

- **Dropped segments**: This is the primary category. Whether due to compaction tasks replacing old segments with new ones, or users actively deleting data through drop collection or drop partition APIs, these operations do not immediately physically delete the related segments and their files. They are only marked as *dropped* in the metadata. GC's primary task is to clean up these marked segments, including all their files: entity data (`binlogs`), statistics, index files, and delta logs.
- **Abandoned index files**: User operations can be more granular. For example, when a user uses the `drop_index` API to delete an index on a specific field while retaining the data itself, the old index files being replaced become garbage to be reclaimed. GC's other important responsibility is to periodically scan and clean up these orphaned garbage files, preventing storage space from being silently consumed by invalid data.
- **Orphaned garbage files**: Some background tasks in Milvus (such as data import and index building) may fail or be retried for various reasons. These abnormal processes sometimes leave temporary, invalid, or incomplete *orphaned files* in object storage.

Therefore, GC is a systematic and comprehensive cleanup process that ensures the long-term health and efficiency of the Milvus storage environment. Next, we will discuss its working principles.

GC working principles

A seemingly simple question arises: how does the system know when an old file can be safely deleted? For instance, when a segment is soft deleted by a compaction task, when can it be physically deleted without affecting ongoing queries? In a distributed system like Milvus, the answer is far more complex than "delete immediately." The GC mechanism must ensure data safety while efficiently reclaiming storage space and maintaining query performance. To achieve this, Milvus implements a multi-check delayed deletion mechanism that strictly follows the principle of *safety first and performance priority*.

Safety first – multi-layer protection ensuring data integrity

The Milvus GC mechanism prioritizes data safety above all else. The system employs multiple time windows and checking mechanisms to ensure that any data deletion operation does not jeopardize normal system operation.

The first line of defense is the orphaned file protection period. When data is written to object storage, a subtle time gap emerges where the file physically exists, but the metadata system has not yet completed its update. During this brief window, these files appear *orphaned*. The `dataCoord.gc.missingTolerance` config (default 86400 seconds, or 24 hours) provides an umbrella of protection for the temporarily orphaned files. The system must wait long enough to confirm that a file is genuinely orphaned, not merely experiencing metadata update delays, before marking it for deletion. This mechanism effectively prevents newly written data from being mistakenly deleted before metadata synchronization is complete.

The second line of defense is the dropped segment buffer period. Even when a segment is explicitly marked as *dropped*, the `dataCoord.gc.dropTolerance` parameter (default 10800 seconds, or 3 hours) still requires the system to retain these files for a period of time. This *grace period* design is filled with practical wisdom; it provides a buffer for the system to handle exceptional situations and reserves an operation window for administrators to intervene or recover data when issues are discovered. In production environments, this buffer period has repeatedly proven its value, preventing permanent data loss due to operational errors or system anomalies.

Performance priority – intelligent scheduling and query protection

Building on the foundation of safety, the Milvus GC mechanism also carefully considers performance impact through intelligent scheduling strategies that minimize disruption to the read path.

The most typical example is the delayed replacement strategy in compaction scenarios. When small segments A and B are merged into a large segment C, intuition suggests immediately deleting A and B to free up space. However, Milvus opts for a more cautious approach. The system first checks whether the new segment C has already established its indexes. Only when C's indexes are fully ready and can provide query performance comparable to or better than A and B does the system delete the old segments. This mechanism prevents a serious performance pitfall: if indexed old segments are deleted and replaced with an unindexed new segment, query latency would skyrocket.

Going further, even if new segment C's indexes are ready, if old segments A and B are still serving queries on QueryNodes, GC still delays the deletion operation. The system waits for QueryNodes to complete the segment switchover, ensuring that no queries depend on these old segments before physically deleting them. This meticulous checking mechanism ensures query service continuity and stability.

At the execution level, GC employs a hierarchical scheduling strategy to optimize resource usage. Scanning for orphaned files requires traversing the entire storage system and comparing it with metadata, which is a relatively time-consuming operation. Therefore, the system uses the `dataCoord.gc.scanInterval` parameter (default 168 hours, or 7 days) to separately control the frequency of orphaned file checks. For already-marked-for-deletion segments and their associated files, the `dataCoord.gc.interval` parameter (default 3600 seconds, or 1 hour) controls the check frequency. This separation design enables the system to perform targeted optimization based on different types of garbage.

Fine-tuning GC behavior

After understanding GC's operating principles, DevOps teams using Milvus can adjust configuration parameters based on specific business characteristics and resource conditions to find the optimal balance between storage efficiency and system stability.

For adjusting check frequency, consider the system's data change patterns. In **online transaction processing** (**OLTP**) systems with high-frequency writes and deletes, the garbage collection interval (`dataCoord.gc.interval`) can be shortened to 15-30 minutes. This accelerates GC and prevents rapid storage space growth. Conversely, in **online analytical processing** (**OLAP**) systems that are primarily query-focused with relatively stable data, intervals can be lengthened to 2-4 hours. This strategy reduces GC overhead, allowing more system resources to be allocated to query services.

For retention period configuration, balance safety and cost considerations. The `dataCoord.gc.dropTolerance` parameter directly affects data recovery capability. If your business has extremely high data safety requirements or has established comprehensive disaster recovery procedures, extend this retention period to 48-72 hours to provide sufficient time for problem diagnosis and data recovery. Conversely, if storage costs are a significant concern and the system experiences frequent compaction operations that produce many pending-deletion segments, you can appropriately shorten the retention period to 1 hour to accelerate space reclamation.

Through this carefully designed GC mechanism, Milvus achieves automated and intelligent storage management. It not only efficiently reclaims unused storage space, but more importantly, the entire process is completely transparent to users and does not affect normal system operations.

Summary

In this chapter, we covered how compaction and garbage collection work together to manage data in Milvus. We looked at how compaction reduces segment fragmentation, improves query performance, and handles deletions, while garbage collection cleans up unused data to free storage and maintain efficiency.

These processes form the backbone of Milvus' data management, ensuring a well-organized and resource-efficient system. This knowledge prepares us to explore more advanced Milvus features in the next chapter.

Subscribe for a free eBook

New frameworks, evolving architectures, research drops, production breakdowns – *AI_Distilled* filters the noise into a weekly briefing for engineers and researchers working hands-on with LLMs and generative AI systems. Subscribe now and receive a free eBook, along with weekly insights that help you stay focused and informed.

Subscribe at `https://packt.link/8Oz6Y` or scan the QR code below.

Part 3

Vector Computing Engine, Indexing, and Advanced Query Mechanisms

Focused on the core kernel of vector retrieval, *Part 3* explores Milvus' vector computing engine, the principles and selection strategies of vector indexing, and optimization methods for high-dimensional data retrieval. It also breaks down advanced search processing logic, such as conditional filtering and performance acceleration, to resolve complex query demands. This part equips readers with the expertise to optimize retrieval efficiency and accuracy while tackling the core technical challenges of high-dimensional vector data processing.

This part contains the following chapter:

- *Chapter 9, Exploring Milvus' Vector Engine*
- *Chapter 10, How to Select a Vector Index*
- *Chapter 11, Handling Complicated Search Requests*

9

Exploring Milvus' Vector Engine

In this chapter, we will delve into one of the core components of Milvus, which is the vector engine, Knowhere. Knowhere is a high-performance vector search engine specifically designed for vector databases, responsible for handling critical tasks such as index construction and searching of vector data. Through this chapter, you will gain an understanding of Knowhere's architectural design, core functionalities, and its unique advantages in high-dimensional vector search. Whether you are a beginner or an experienced practitioner, this chapter will provide you with a comprehensive perspective on Knowhere, helping you to deeply master the core engine of Milvus' vector search system.

In this chapter, we will cover the following topics:

- Introducing Milvus' core engine: Knowhere
- Working with Knowhere's main APIs
- Understanding Knowhere's functionality

Technical requirements

Before starting this chapter, we believe that you should have a general understanding of what a vector is, what a vector index is, and what a vector index algorithm library is. You should also be clear about the difference between vector similarity search and traditional exact search. This chapter will not spend space introducing these basic concepts. If you are not familiar with these concepts, you can start by learning from Wikipedia:

`https://en.wikipedia.org/wiki/Vector_database`.

Let's start with the definition of the vector operation engine.

Introducing Milvus' core engine: Knowhere

The relationship between Milvus and Knowhere can be summarized in one sentence. If Milvus is likened to a sports car, then Knowhere is the engine of this sports car. The speed at which a sports car can run largely depends on the power and efficiency of its engine; similarly, the performance of Milvus as a vector database, such as its **queries per second** (**QPS**) or latency, largely depends on the performance of Knowhere.

> Note
>
> **QPS and latency**
>
> QPS refers to the number of queries or requests a system can handle per second. It is a metric used to measure the throughput of a system. A higher QPS rate indicates stronger processing capability.
>
> Latency refers to the time taken from sending a request to receiving a response. It is typically measured in milliseconds and indicates the responsiveness of a system. Lower latency means faster response times and better user experience. High latency can lead to long waiting times, negatively impacting system performance.

Understanding the functional scope of Knowhere

There are two types of functional scopes of Knowhere: narrow and broad. When Milvus was initiated, it was designed to conveniently integrate with all popular vector index algorithm libraries on the market. Therefore, in the system architecture design of Milvus, a layer of encapsulation was designed between the lower-level vector index algorithm libraries (such as Faiss, HNSWlib, DiskANN, etc.) and the upper-level service, such as scheduling. It provides a unified interface for all index-related operations to the upper layer.

In this way, the upper-layer module can select different indexes and perform different index operations through the unified interfaces, thereby achieving decoupling between the upper-layer scheduling and the specific lower-level index algorithms. This layer of interface encapsulation is the early narrow sense of Knowhere.

Heterogeneous computing is also controlled by the interface encapsulation layer of Knowhere, which is used to manage where the construction and query of vector indexes are executed, on a CPU, GPU, or perhaps on a **data processing unit** (**DPU**)/**tensor processing unit** (**TPU**) in the future. This is also the origin of the name Knowhere: *know where*.

We will touch upon more details about the Knowhere layer in the upcoming section, *Knowhere architecture*.

In its earliest form, Knowhere only provided a layer of interface encapsulation above all third-party index libraries without making any changes to the code of the third-party libraries. However, as the project evolved, we, the core development and maintenance team at Milvus, made more and more functional improvements within the third-party index libraries. For example, we made the **Inverted File Index** (**IVF**) series of indexes in Faiss to be thread-safe; we enhanced HNSWlib to support the new metric type, `COSINE`; we implemented Range Search in DiskANN, and so on. In addition, more functions such as version control and thread management have also been added to the Knowhere layer. If you are interested in these topics, you can find more detailed introductions in the following section, *Understanding Knowhere's functionality*. Therefore, we have expanded the meaning and scope of Knowhere. Now, in the broad sense, Knowhere is not just a simple wrapper for third-party index libraries, but a general term for all modules related to vector operations, including third-party index libraries.

From the preceding definition of the broad sense of Knowhere, we can understand the functional scope of Knowhere. Knowhere only deals with tasks related to vector operations. Other tasks, such as data sharding, load balancing, data storage, disaster recovery, query optimization, and so on, are handled by other modules in Milvus and are unrelated to Knowhere.

Milvus, as an AI-specific database, has data storage and data computation as one of its most basic functions. Data computation can be further divided into **scalar computation** and **vector computation**.

Milvus, as a dedicated vector database, focuses primarily on vector computations with scalar computations as a secondary function. Scalar computations are mainly used for attribute filtering. If your data table contains only scalar data and no vector data, Milvus may not be suitable for you; you can opt for other traditional relational databases such as Oracle or MySQL.

The scalar computations in Milvus deal with one-dimensional data and support the following types of operations:

- **Logical operations**:
  - **AND**: Combines multiple conditions that must all be true
  - **OR**: Combines conditions where at least one must be true
  - **NOT**: Negates a condition

  Example: To find all products where `price` is greater than `100` and `stock` is greater than `50`, use this:

  ```
  filter = 'price > 100 AND stock > 50'
  ```

- **Arithmetic operations**:
  - + (addition)
  - - (subtraction)
  - * (multiplication)
  - / (division)
  - % (modulus)
  - ** (exponentiation)

  Example: To find entities where the `total` price is the sum of `base_price` and `tax`, use this:

```
filter = 'total == base_price + tax'
```

- **Comparison operations**:
  - == (equal to)
  - != (not equal to)
  - > (greater than)
  - < (less than)
  - >= (greater than or equal to)
  - <= (less than or equal to)

  Example: To find all entities with `rating` greater than or equal to 4, use this:

```
filter = 'rating >= 4'
```

- **Others**:
  - IN (contain in)
  - LIKE (match to pattern)

  Example: To find all entities with specified colors, use this:

```
filter = 'color in ["white", "red", "yellow"]'
```

The vector computations in Milvus handle high-dimensional data, with dimensions ranging from dozens to tens of thousands. Vector data does not have a well-defined mathematical order, so we cannot accelerate vector queries through sorting as with traditional numerical or string data. We need special index structures and storage methods. Moreover, vector computations are approximate queries rather than exact queries, typically using vector L2 distance, inner product distance, and so on, to determine whether the query conditions are met.

All vector computations in Milvus are managed in Knowhere, while scalar computations are executed in other modules.

Milvus data model

Let's understand the scope of Knowhere's functions from the perspective of the Milvus **data model**.

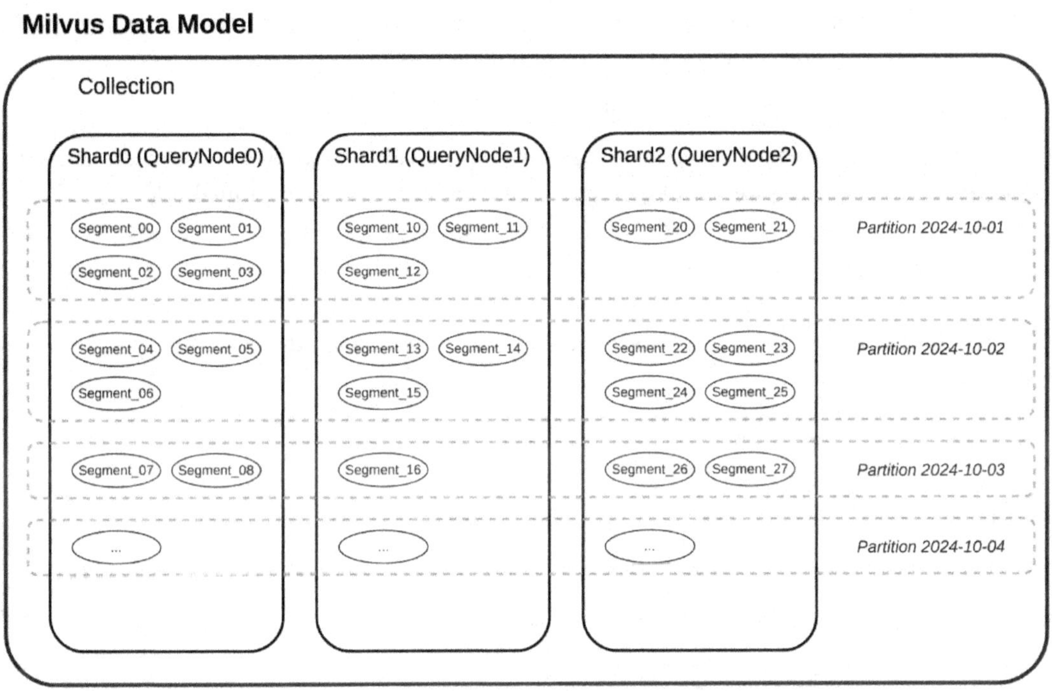

Figure 9.1: Milvus data model

Figure 9.1 shows the data model of Milvus. Remember that we discussed the following concepts in *Chapter 5*. Here is a brief overview of the concepts in the context of the Milvus data model:

- **Collection**: In Milvus, a collection can be likened to a table in a relational database. The collection is the largest data unit in Milvus.
- **Shard**: To fully utilize the distributed characteristics of the cluster during data writing, Milvus can distribute data writing across multiple nodes simultaneously. Each shard is a physical data partition of the collection. As shown in *Figure 9.2*, the collection is

distributed across three data nodes (`QueryNode0` to `QueryNode2`), corresponding to the physical data partitions: `Shard0`, `Shard1`, and `Shard2`.

- **Partition:** The data within each collection can also be logically divided into multiple partitions. Common methods for partitioning include dividing by date, gender, or user age, and so on. In *Figure 9.2*, the partition is created based on the data generation date. Data within a partition can span multiple shards.
- **Segment:** Each shard or partition is composed of multiple segments. The segment is the smallest unit for querying in Milvus. A query operation on a collection will ultimately be broken down into query operations on several segments, and then the query results from all segments are merged to obtain the final result.

Let's discuss more about why segments are important to Knowhere.

To support streaming data insertion, segments are divided into two categories: **growing segments** and **sealed segments**. Growing segments allow for the continued addition of data. Once the size or time reaches a certain threshold, a growing segment becomes a sealed segment. Each segment is composed of multiple fields. Here, `id` and `timestamp` are system-default fields that come with the segment. The remaining fields are specified by the user when creating a collection in the schema. The fields specified by the user must include one primary key column and one vector column.

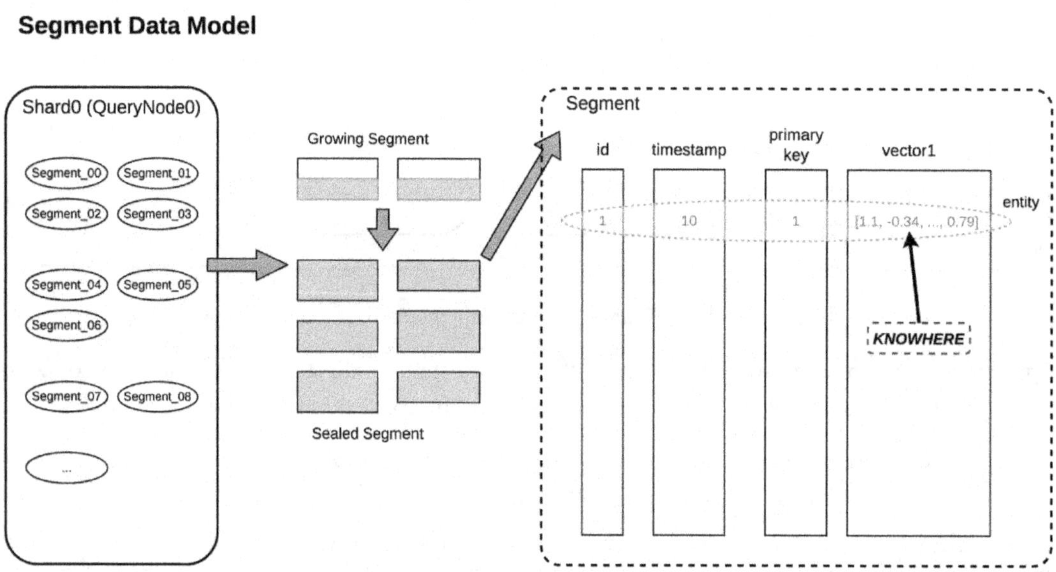

Figure 9.2: Segment data model

As shown in *Figure 9.2*, the fundamental unit of data that Knowhere can process is just the single vector column within a segment.

We will now take a look at the internal architecture of Knowhere.

Knowhere architecture

As the core vector search engine of Milvus, Knowhere interacts with `QueryNode`, which is responsible for query execution, and `IndexNode`, which handles index construction in the Milvus architecture. These two components are the sole callers of the API interfaces provided by Knowhere. *Figure 9.3* specifically illustrates the meaning and scope of Knowhere:

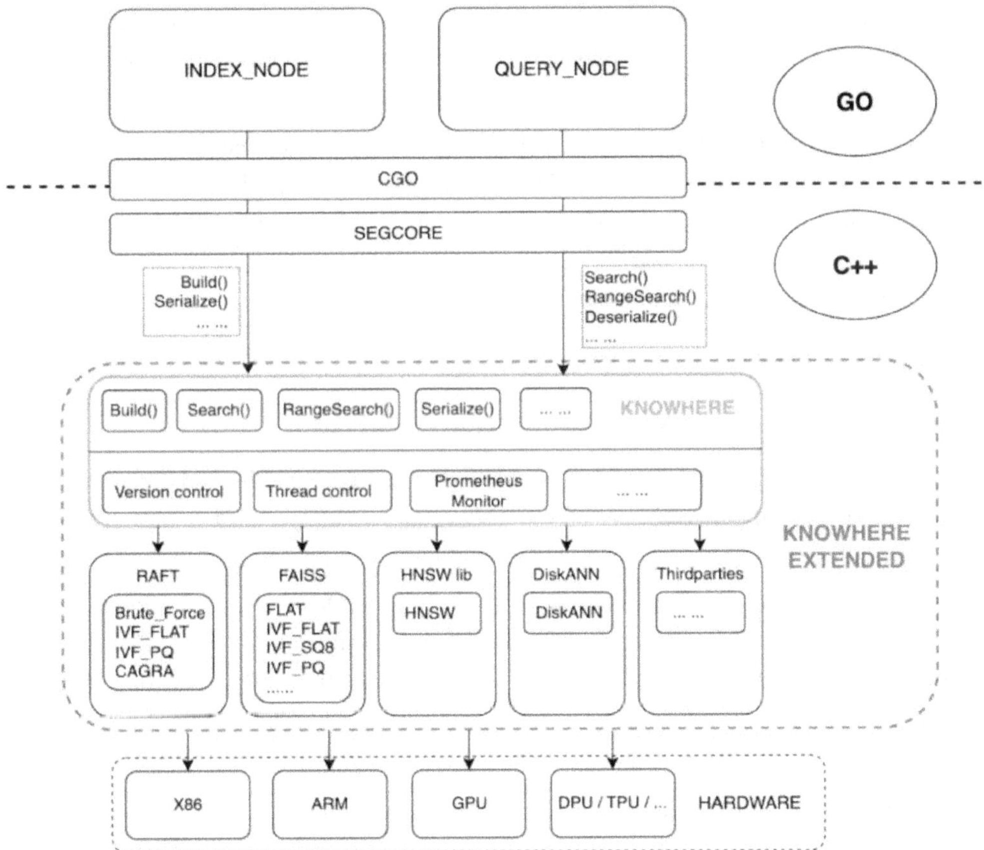

Figure 9.3: Internal architecture of Knowhere

The early narrow sense of Knowhere, as shown in the solid line box **KNOWHERE** in *Figure 9.3*, was only to provide a layer of interface encapsulation for the upper layer. The current broad sense of Knowhere, as shown in the dashed line box **KNOWHERE EXTENDED** in *Figure 9.3*, includes the narrow sense of Knowhere as well as all third-party index libraries.

Since the vector computations handled by Knowhere are computationally intensive tasks with strict requirements for program execution efficiency, the entire Knowhere module is written in C++. Knowhere is compiled into the Milvus binary in the form of a dynamic link library, `libknowhere.so`. All components of Milvus (including `IndexNode` and `QueryNode`) are implemented in Go. `IndexNode` and `QueryNode` call the interfaces provided by Knowhere through a layer of CGO.

Note that CGO serves as a critical interoperability layer in Go-based systems like Milvus: it allows Go components (IndexNode and QueryNode) to invoke native C/C++ interfaces from the Knowhere library, bridging the gap between Go's runtime environment and low-level C/C++ implementations.

Starting with Milvus 2.0, we have separated Knowhere and all third-party index libraries from the Milvus project and established an independent open-source project, Knowhere (`http://www.github.com/zilliztech/knowhere`). Knowhere has its own Python interface, `pyknowhere`, its own unit tests, and its own performance testing framework. Since then, the vector engine Knowhere and Milvus can be developed independently without affecting each other.

We will now move our focus to Knowhere's APIs.

Working with Knowhere's main APIs

You should already be familiar with what a **vector index** is. A vector index is a data structure that is independent of the original vector data.

As mentioned in the overview of this chapter, the initial introduction of Knowhere was to provide a layer of interface encapsulation above all third-party index libraries. This allows the upper-layer modules to select different indexes and perform various index operations through a unified interface. The interface names provided by different indexes may vary, but they all offer the following categories of interfaces:

- Interfaces related to index construction
- Interfaces related to index serialization and deserialization
- Interfaces related to querying
- Other interfaces

We will discuss these indexes in detail in *Chapter 10*.

Coming up is a general introduction and explanation of the interface parameters and these categories of interfaces.

Knowhere parameters

Since Knowhere's function interfaces need to be compatible with the function interfaces of all third-party index libraries, a semi-open design was adopted in the design of function parameters. The three most important interface parameters are as follows:

- **DataSet**: Essentially, `DataSet` is a **map** that stores key-value pairs. We use `DataSet` to store all vector-related information. `DataSet` can serve as an input parameter, containing the row number, dimension, and original data tensor of the vectors; or as an output parameter, holding query results such as IDs and distances.
- **JSON**: `JSON` can only be used as an input parameter, storing configuration parameters related to the index. The configuration parameters for different indexes vary greatly. Using `JSON`, a lightweight data interchange format, is undoubtedly the most suitable choice. This is because `JSON` is easy to read and write, and it also has excellent cross-language and cross-platform characteristics.
- **BitsetView**: `BitsetView` is a binary bitstream, with the number of bits corresponding one-to-one with the number of rows of the input vectors. For example, if the *n*th bit is `1`, it indicates that the *n*th row of the vector is invalid (it may have been deleted, or it does not meet the scalar filtering conditions) and will not participate in the query computation; and this row of the vector will not appear in the query results. `BitsetView` can only be used as an input parameter. When `BitsetView` is `null`, it has the same effect as when all bits in `BitsetView` are `0`, indicating that all input vectors are valid and will participate in the query.

If you are only a user of Milvus, you will not directly encounter these three parameter types, as they are not exposed in Milvus' SDK. However, if you delve into the code of Knowhere, you will find that these three parameter types are present in almost all of Knowhere's interface functions.

You can get all index-related interface definitions here: `https://github.com/zilliztech/knowhere/blob/main/include/knowhere/index/index.h`.

The following snippet is the interface code, which clearly shows how these three data types are used in the interface functions:

```
Status Build(const DataSetPtr dataset, const Json&json);
Status Train(const DataSetPtr dataset, const Json&json);
Status Add(const DataSetPtr dataset, const Json&json);
expected<DataSetPtr> Search(const DataSetPtr dataset, const Json& json, const
BitsetView& bitset) const;
expected<DataSetPtr> RangeSearch(const DataSetPtr dataset, const Json& json,
```

```
const BitsetView& bitset) const;
expected<DataSetPtr> GetVectorByIds(const DataSetPtr dataset) const;
bool HasRawData(const std::string& metric_type) const;
Status Serialize(BinarySet& binset) const;
Status Deserialize(const BinarySet& binset, const Json& json = {});
```

Let's take the most important interface function in Knowhere, `Search()`, as an example.

The input parameters of `Search()` include `dataset`, which holds all information about the input vector, such as rows, dimension, and the vector's raw data; `json`, which holds all information about the index specified search parameters, such as `nprobe` for IVF index; and `bitset`, which stands for each vector row's validation.

The output parameter of `Search()` is also of the `DataSet` type, which holds all information about the search result, such as result IDs and distances.

As mentioned earlier in this chapter, all indexes provide external interfaces for index creation, serialization and deserialization, querying, and more. Here is a brief explanation of these interfaces.

Train(), Add(), and Build()

Generally speaking, a vector index goes through four steps from creation to application, as shown in *Figure 9.4*: creating the index, training, adding data, and searching. The `Create()`, `Train()`, `Add()`, and `Search()` functions in the following figure correspond to four interface functions in Knowhere, respectively:

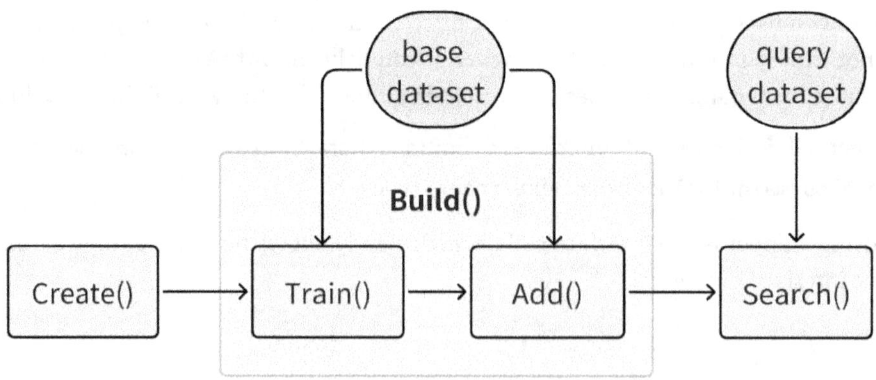

Figure 9.4: Index flow in Knowhere

The `Create()` function creates an empty index of a certain type, which does not contain any data at this point. The `Train()` and `Add()` functions are the ones that actually add real data to the index. After `Train()` and `Add()`, we can use this index to perform `Search()`.

In some AI applications, the datasets used for training and adding are separate. For example, in the public dataset `sift-128-euclidean` (`http://ann-benchmarks.com/sift-128-euclidean.hdf5`), there are separate training and testing datasets labeled as `train` and `test`, respectively. The training dataset is used first for training, and then, based on the training results, the testing data is inserted into the index.

However, Knowhere does not distinguish between training and testing data. The **base dataset** in *Figure 9.4* is the vector column data from a certain segment passed from the Milvus `IndexNode`. Knowhere first uses this data for training and then, based on the training results, inserts the same data into the index.

Since Knowhere performs training (`train`) first and then adds the same data (`add`) for all indexes, it also provides a new interface called `Build()`, which just combines the `Train()` and `Add()` interfaces. When building an index in Knowhere, you can directly call the `Build()` interface, which has the same effect as calling the `Train()` and `Add()` interfaces separately. The `Train()` and `Add()` interfaces are retained to maintain the semantic habits of AI applications and for extensibility considerations. This is also to support the possibility of future new indexes that may require special handling for `Train()` and `Add()` separately.

Since these interfaces, `Build()`, `Train()`, and `Add()`, are provided by Knowhere and Milvus, users will not directly interact with them; hence, code snippets demonstrating the usage of these interfaces are not provided here.

Next, we will learn about index serialization and deserialization.

Serialize() and Deserialize()

Index **serialization** and **deserialization** are essential for supporting the storage and transmission of indexes. Building an index is a computationally intensive and time-consuming task. Therefore, for a column of vector data in a segment, we typically build the index only once and serialize it to persist as a file in object storage, such as S3 or MinIO. When the index is needed, we read it from the object storage and then deserialize and load it into memory for query operations.

Specifically, in Milvus, `IndexNode` is responsible for index building and storage. `IndexNode` calls the `Create()` and `Build()` interfaces of Knowhere to create the index and uses the `Serialize()` interface of Knowhere to serialize the index into an index file, then persists it into the object storage. `QueryNode` is responsible for index loading and querying. `QueryNode` first loads the index file from the object storage and then calls the `Deserialize()` interface of Knowhere to deserialize it.

Finally, we call the search interface to perform queries, which is discussed next.

Since these interfaces, `Serialize()` and `Deserialize()`, are provided by Knowhere and Milvus, users will not directly interact with them; code snippets demonstrating the usage of these interfaces are not provided here.

Search() and RangeSearch()

The `Search()` interface is one of the most fundamental and earliest implemented interfaces in Knowhere. The input to `Search()` is the `nq` parameter names, which denote query vectors, and it performs **approximate nearest neighbor search** (**ANNS**) to find the `topk` most similar results for each input vector. Finally, it returns the IDs and corresponding distances of the total of *nq * topk* results.

The `Search` operation has certain limitations. Firstly, `Search` always returns the most similar results, but sometimes users may not always want the most similar results. Secondly, although Knowhere does not impose any restrictions on `topk`, Milvus, considering system overhead, limits the number of results returned per vector in a single search to a maximum of 16,384.

Due to these limitations of the `Search` operation, a user working on a recommendation system proposed the `RangeSearch` requirement in the community. They hope that Milvus can provide a range-based query function that returns results within a certain distance range. This is because a good recommendation system should provide results that are somewhat relevant but not too similar. Having some similarity means that the vector distance should not be too far. However, it should not be too similar either, as results that are too similar are likely to be identical news articles or products. Therefore, the vector distance should be within a range scope. Let's take a look at *Figure 9.5* that illustrates the concepts of `Search` and `RangeSearch`:

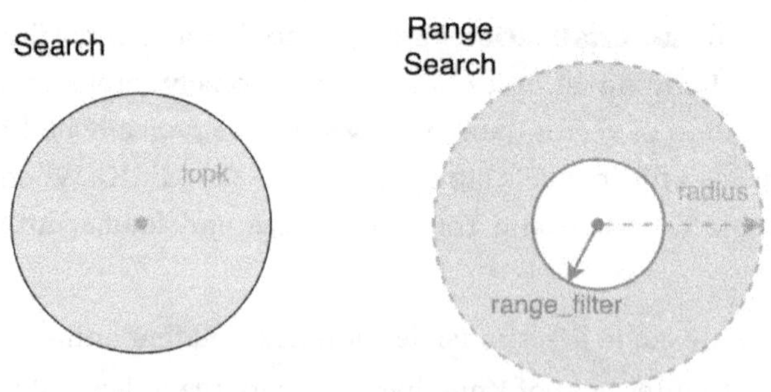

Figure 9.5: Search and RangeSearch

Search is akin to drawing the smallest circle in the vector space such that only the topk results fall within the circle. In contrast, RangeSearch is like marking an annular region in the vector space, where the similarity should lie between the inner and outer boundaries.

Since these interfaces, Search() and RangeSearch(), are provided by Knowhere and Milvus, users will not directly interact with them; hence, code snippets demonstrating the usage of these interfaces are not provided here.

Knowhere's query interfaces, Search and RangeSearch, return the IDs and corresponding distance values of the result vectors. However, some users would like Milvus to return the original vector data along with the query results, for verifying the accuracy of the query results or for other machine learning tasks. Let's see how we can do that.

HasRawData() and GetVectorByIds()

HasRawData() and GetVectorByIds() are the two interfaces that support Milvus in returning the original vector data along with the query results to users.

Milvus's query tasks are executed by QueryNode, which only loads the index files and does not load the original vector data. One solution is for DataNode to load the original vector data from the object storage and return it together with the query results from QueryNode. Although this solution meets the user's needs, it performs poorly.

Considering that some index data structures, such as FLAT, IVF_FLAT, and HNSW index type, actually store the original vector data, it is possible to directly read the original vectors from the index. Therefore, the HasRawData() interface is used to determine whether the index stores the original vector data. These indexes, such as FLAT, IVF_FLAT, and HNSW, return True for the HasRawData() interface. The GetVectorByIds() interface, as the name suggests, returns the original vector values for the specified IDs.

Since these interfaces, HasRawData() and GetVectorByIds(), are only provided by Knowhere and Milvus, users will not directly interact with them, so, code snippets demonstrating the usage of these interfaces are not provided here.

Moving on, we will discuss some important features that have been implemented at the Knowhere layer.

Understanding Knowhere's functionality

In the previous chapters, we mentioned that as the project evolved, we not only made more functional extensions and improvements in the third-party index libraries, but also added more features at the Knowhere layer.

In this section, we will introduce three features implemented at the Knowhere layer: **thread management**, **version management**, and **Prometheus monitor**.

Thread management

To understand why Knowhere needs to implement thread management, we should consider it from the Milvus system level.

Knowhere integrates multiple third-party index libraries, and these libraries often use multi-threading to maximize CPU utilization during ANNS. For example, the IVF series of indexes in Faiss creates a separate thread for each query vector during search operations. This approach is fine when Faiss is used as a standalone index algorithm library. However, when Faiss is integrated into Knowhere and becomes part of the entire Milvus system, this behavior can significantly impact query performance.

In the *Milvus data model* section, it was introduced that a segment is the smallest query unit in Milvus. A query operation on a collection is ultimately broken down into query operations on several segments.

Now, assume there is a `QueryNode` with *n* segments, and each segment has created an `IVF_FLAT` index. When a query request arrives, the `QueryNode` generates a thread for each segment to execute the query operation, resulting in a total of *n* query threads. These *n* query threads call the `Search` interface of Knowhere, which, in turn, calls the `Search` interface of the Faiss `IVF_FLAT` index. Consequently, each query thread internally generates *nq* sub-threads for the queries. Thus, a total of *(n * nq)* threads are created.

Each `QueryNode` has limited physical resources. For example, a node with 16 cores and 64 GB of memory can run a maximum of 16 threads simultaneously. With *(n * nq)* threads being created, this leads to frequent thread switching, which dramatically reduces computational efficiency.

Milvus, as a vector database, is capable of receiving and processing multiple user query requests simultaneously. Consequently, the number of threads generated on each `QueryNode` becomes *N1 * N2 * N3*, where *N1* is the number of query requests within a certain period, *N2* is the number of segments on the `QueryNode`, and *N3* is the average number of query vectors per request. This many threads further exacerbates the situation. This phenomenon has a specific term called **thread explosion,** as depicted in *Figure 9.6*:

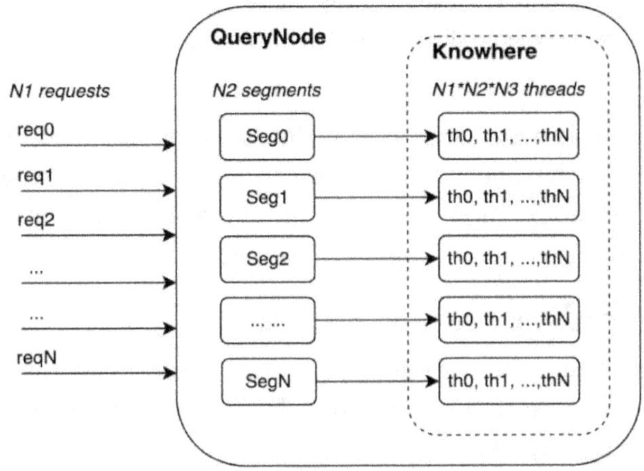

Figure 9.6: Thread explosion in Knowhere

To address the issue of thread explosion, Knowhere creates two thread pools during initialization: one for building indexes and one for querying.

The number of threads in each pool can be specified by the user based on the node resources through configuration parameters (`querynode.segcore.knowhereThreadPoolNumRatio` and `common.buildIndexThreadPoolRatio`) in the `milvus.yaml` configuration file.

Take, for example, the following code snippet, which updates `knowhereThreadPoolNumRatio`:

```
queryNode:
  segcore:
    knowhereThreadPoolNumRatio: 4
```

All third-party index libraries run in a single-threaded manner. This way, the multi-threaded concurrency on each physical node is uniformly managed by Knowhere, which can prevent the occurrence of thread explosion.

Version management

Version management is a challenge faced by any software that needs to persist data to object storage and also load data from storage into memory. As Milvus and Knowhere continuously introduce new features, the data structures of the indexes are bound to evolve. The version compatibility issues that Milvus and Knowhere currently face are primarily backward compatibility issues (i.e., how to open index files saved by older versions of Milvus using newer versions), such as how to open index files saved by *Milvus v2.3.x* using *Milvus v2.4.x*.

Knowhere has added a `version` field to the index data structure. With the information from this `version` field, Knowhere can deserialize the index files without relying on any additional external information.

The version control of index files is implemented internally within the code and is transparent to users. Therefore, this section will not delve into the technical details of version control. Interested readers can directly refer to the source code for more information: `https://github.com/zilliztech/knowhere/blob/main/include/knowhere/version.h`.

Prometheus monitor

Typically, we can determine whether Knowhere is running normally through logs. However, to achieve real-time monitoring and visualization for cloud services, we have introduced the **Prometheus monitoring system** in Knowhere.

Prometheus is an open source monitoring system and time-series database. It collects metric data from target systems through an *HTTP pull model* and stores this data in a local time-series database. This monitoring approach not only reflects the system's operational status in real time but also helps us quickly identify and resolve potential issues.

In Knowhere, we use the Prometheus C++ client to sample performance data. This data includes, but is not limited to, key metrics such as query latency, index build time, `topk` statistics, cache hit rates, and so on. Through the CGO layer, we send this performance data to the Milvus side and integrate it with the Prometheus data on the Milvus side. Ultimately, the integrated data is visualized through Grafana, allowing users to intuitively view the operational status of Knowhere and Milvus on a unified interface.

Summary

In this chapter, we introduced Milvus' core vector engine, Knowhere. We discussed the definition and scope of Knowhere, the main interfaces it provides externally, and the functionalities implemented at the Knowhere layer, specifically, thread management, version management, and the Prometheus monitor.

Understanding these concepts will lead you to fully grasp how Knowhere works internally, allowing you to use Milvus more effectively, troubleshoot underlying issues, and even extend or customize the vector engine to meet practical requirements.

In the next chapter, we will delve into vector indexing and the enhancements we have made to these indexes in Knowhere.

Get this book's PDF version and more

Scan the QR code (or go to `packtpub.com/unlock`). Search for this book by name, confirm the edition, and then follow the steps on the page.

UNLOCK NOW

Note: Keep your invoice handy. Purchases made directly from Packt don't require an invoice.

Get this book's PDF version and more

Scan the QR code (or go to packtpub.com/unlock). Search for this book by name, confirm the edition, and then follow the steps on the page.

10

How to Select a Vector Index

In modern data processing, whether it is a vector database or a traditional relational database, indexing is a key means of improving query efficiency. The core purpose of both is to quickly locate target information in a vast amount of data, thereby enhancing the overall data processing performance. Although there are differences in the implementation details of indexing between the two databases, the basic concept is the same; it is to reduce the amount of computation that must be processed to speed up the query process.

For a vector database, the necessity of building indexes is particularly prominent. Vector data usually has a high dimensionality, which means that the computational workload during queries is much greater than that of traditional scalar data. This difference in computational workload is especially evident when dealing with large datasets. Therefore, reducing the necessary computational space and load through indexing is crucial for improving the performance of vector databases.

Compared with a **scalar index** in a relational database, a **vector index** has a significant difference: a scalar index can guarantee the integrity and accuracy of query results, while a vector index cannot. Vector data is an approximate representation of unstructured data, which inherently allows a certain degree of *fuzziness*. Usually, queries performed on vector data are similarity queries. We do not pursue a 100% exact match but rather seek approximate results that meet specific recall and precision rates. This characteristic of **fuzzy query** provides greater flexibility and room for innovation in the design of vector indexes.

In this chapter, we will not delve into the implementation of specific indexing algorithms but instead aim to reveal the general principles behind various indexes. Our goal is to help you understand how to choose the appropriate index type and parameter configuration when facing specific business requirements and data characteristics, in order to achieve the best query efficiency and performance.

We will discuss the following topics:

- Introducing performance metrics
- Understanding vector types and metric types
- Measuring the performance of indexes

Introducing performance metrics

For vector indexes, performance metrics are used to evaluate how well the index can handle tasks such as data insertion, query execution, and resource management.

Here, we will introduce two performance metrics related to query execution.

Recall and accuracy

In the field of vector retrieval, we commonly use **recall** and **accuracy** to evaluate the quality of index retrieval.

Recall measures the proportion of relevant vectors that an indexing algorithm can find among the true result vectors. In other words, it focuses on whether the indexing algorithm can retrieve all relevant vectors, that is, the completeness of the retrieval. A high recall rate means that the indexing algorithm can find most or all relevant vectors, but it may also retrieve some irrelevant vectors, which means the accuracy may be relatively low.

Accuracy measures the proportion of actually relevant vectors among the vectors retrieved by an indexing algorithm. It focuses on the correctness (that is, the quality) of the retrieval results. A high accuracy means that most of the vectors retrieved by the system are relevant, but it may miss some relevant vectors, which means the recall rate may be relatively low.

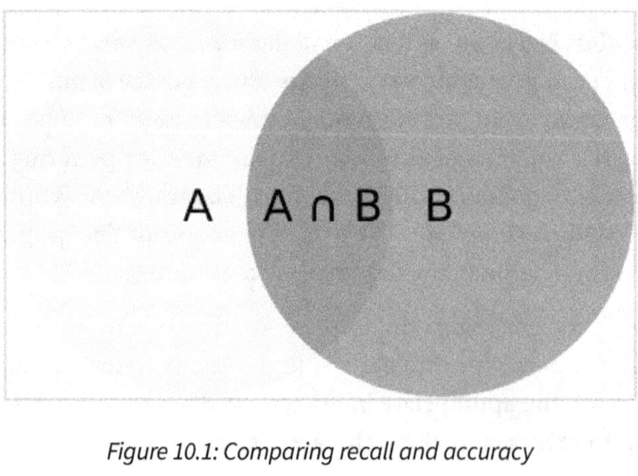

Figure 10.1: Comparing recall and accuracy

Taking *Figure 10.1* as an example, if *A* represents the set of true correct results, and *B* represents the set of retrieval results, then we have the following:

$$Recall = \frac{A \cap B}{A}$$

$$Accuracy = \frac{A \cap B}{B}$$

To illustrate with a specific example, suppose the benchmark result set contains 100 relevant vectors, and the query result set contains 200 vectors, of which 80 are correct. Then, we have the following:

$$Recall = \frac{80}{100} = 0.8$$

$$Accuracy = \frac{80}{200} = 0.4$$

However, in actual index queries, we usually expect the number of query results to match the number of true results. In this case, recall and accuracy are numerically equal, so we are more inclined to use recall to evaluate the query performance of the index.

Vector per second and latency

In the field of vector query, we commonly use **vectors per second** (**VPS**) and **latency** to evaluate the performance of index retrieval.

VPS measures the number of query vectors that a vector database can handle within a unit of time. This indicator reflects the throughput capacity of the index, that is, its ability to process a large number of query requests under high load. A high VPS value means that the index can quickly respond to multiple concurrent queries, which is particularly important for applications that need to handle large-scale data and high-concurrency requests.

In traditional relational databases, we often use **queries per second** (**QPS**) to measure the system's query performance, that is, the number of query requests that can be processed per second. However, when performing similarity queries on vectors, it is allowed to input *N* query vectors at once in a single query, and the returned results are *TOPK* query results for each of the *N* query vectors, totaling *N*TOPK* query results. Therefore, in vector databases, VPS has become a more appropriate performance evaluation indicator.

Latency refers to the time it takes from issuing a query request to receiving the query results. Low latency is key to enhancing user experience, especially in real-time search and recommendation systems where users expect to get query results swiftly.

VPS and latency jointly assess the performance of an index. VPS focuses on the index's ability to handle a large volume of queries, while latency is concerned with the response speed of individual queries. In practical applications, these two indicators often need to be balanced.

Assume there is an e-commerce website that uses a vector index to implement a product similarity search feature, allowing users to search for similar products by uploading an image.

A user uploads an image, and among all the products on the e-commerce website, 100 products are truly similar to the uploaded image (i.e., relevant products).

The system searches the database for similar products using the vector index and returns 120 products as search results. Upon manual verification, 90 of these 120 products are truly similar to the uploaded image, while 30 are not similar.

Here is how the performance metrics calculation looks for this system:

- **Recall**: *Recall = (90 / 100) × 100% = 90%.*
  This means that the system successfully retrieved 90% of all relevant products.
- **Accuracy**: *Accuracy = (90 / 120) × 100% = 75%.*
  This indicates that 75% of the returned search results are truly relevant.
- **VPS**: Assuming that the system can handle 100 such similarity search queries within 1 second, the QPS is 100. Since a single query only contains one vector, VPS is numerically equal to QPS, which is also 100. This reflects the number of queries the system can process in a unit of time, demonstrating the system's throughput.
- **Latency**: Assuming it takes an average of 0.5 seconds from the user uploading the image to the system returning the search results, the latency is 0.5 seconds. Lower latency means better user experience and faster system response.

In the field of vector retrieval, there is an inherent trade-off among performance indicators, particularly between recall and VPS. An increase in recall typically comes with a higher computational load, as the system needs to conduct a broader search to capture more relevant vectors, which, in turn, may reduce the VPS. Therefore, when designing and optimizing indexes, we must find a balance among these performance indicators.

Now, we will learn more about different types of vectors and metrics.

Understanding vector types and metric types

In AI domains, the elements in **embeddings** mostly exist in the form of floating-point numbers. However, with the rapid development of AI technology and the explosive growth of data volume, the issue of tight memory resources has become increasingly prominent. To accommodate more data within limited memory, embeddings are gradually introducing low-precision data types.

This transformation not only enhances memory utilization efficiency but also optimizes computational performance, effectively addressing the challenges of large-scale data processing.

Knowhere with version `2.5.0` supports a total of five vector types, each corresponding to a set of different vector distance calculation methods. The vector data types mentioned here refer to the data types of the original vector data input, which are different from the data types used for storing data in vector indexes.

These five vector data types are `FloatVector`, `Float16Vector`, `BFloat16Vector`, `BinaryVector`, and `SparseFloatVector`.

Let's look at each of them.

FloatVector series

For the `FloatVector` type, the data type of each individual element is a single-precision floating-point number. `FloatVector` is the most commonly used vector data type. The reason for using single-precision floating-point numbers is that the precision of such data is already sufficient. As mentioned at the beginning of this chapter, vectors are inherently a *fuzzy* representation of unstructured data, and vector index queries are also a **fuzzy similarity search**. If higher-precision data types such as `Double` were used, the benefits to the business would be limited, while the computation time and runtime memory usage would be doubled compared to single-precision data types.

In the early days of Milvus, the community received requests from users to support double-precision data types. However, as artificial intelligence has gradually matured, there are now very few users asking for increased data precision anymore.

For the `Float16Vector` or `BFloat16Vector` type, the data type of each individual element is `Float16` or `BFloat16`. The precision of these two data types is much lower than that of `Float`, but the computation volume and runtime memory are significantly reduced.

In the field of machine learning, it is common to use arithmetic with smaller bit widths (such as `float16`, `bfloat16`, `int8`, etc.) during the inference process to replace `float32` used in training in order to achieve better computational performance. The main reason is that for computations of the same complexity, the smaller the bit width, the less memory bandwidth is required, and the computational overhead of the operators is smaller. At the same time, **single instruction multiple data** (**SIMD**) registers, a type of parallel computing technology in computer architecture, can hold more arithmetic operations, thereby achieving higher parallelism. The downside is the precision loss due to insufficient precision during the computation process. Compared to the significant improvement in performance, the range of precision loss is acceptable.

For `FloatVector`, `Float16Vector`, and `BFloat16Vector`, Knowhere employs three vector distance calculation methods to measure vector similarity. We also use a specialized term to refer to these vector distance calculation methods, known as **metric type**.

These three vector distance calculation methods are also the most common, and almost all vector databases on the market can support them:

- **Euclidean distance (L2)**: Essentially, the Euclidean distance is the distance between two points in a high-dimensional space, and its calculation formula is as follows:

  $$d(A, B) = \sqrt{\sum_{i=0}^{n-1} (a_i - b_i)^2}$$

  Here, $A = (a_0, a_1, \ldots, a_{n-1})$ and $B = (b_0, b_1, \ldots, b_{n-1})$ are two points in an n-dimensional Euclidean space.

  In Knowhere, the returned L2 distance is actually not the true L2 distance, but the value before taking the square root. This is because taking the square root is a time-consuming computational operation, and directly returning the value before taking the square root does not affect the final result's ranking.

- **Inner product (IP) distance**: The calculation formula for the IP distance between two vectors is as follows:

  $$d(A, B) = A \cdot B = \sum_{i=0}^{n-1} a_i \cdot b_i$$

  Before using the IP metric type to calculate the similarity between embeddings, it is usually necessary to normalize the embeddings. The **normalization** of a vector is the process of scaling the length (or norm) of the vector to *1* while keeping the direction of the vector unchanged. The vector after normalization is called a **unit vector**. After normalization, the IP similarity distance is equal to the COSINE similarity distance.

- **COSINE distance (COSINE)**: *COSINE similarity* measures the similarity between two vectors by the COSINE of the angle between them. You can think of these two vectors as line segments starting from the same point, but pointing in different directions. To calculate the COSINE similarity between two vectors, *A* and *B*, use the following formula:

  $$d(A, B) = \frac{\sum_{i=0}^{n-1}(a_i \cdot b_i)}{\sqrt{\sum_{i=0}^{n-1} a_i^2} \cdot \sqrt{\sum_{i=0}^{n-1} b_i^2}}$$

COSINE similarity always lies within the interval *[-1, 1]*. For example, the COSINE similarity of two directly proportional vectors is *1*, that of two orthogonal vectors is *0*, and that of two opposite vectors is *-1*. The larger the COSINE value, the smaller the angle between the two vectors, indicating a higher degree of similarity between them.

L2 distance, IP distance, and COSINE distance are the most commonly used and fundamental distance metrics in vector calculations, and they are suitable for vectors whose elements are of numerical types.

The distance metric is not a parameter that users can choose arbitrarily. It is determined by the inherent properties of the vectors. Vectors are usually extracted from unstructured data by neural networks, and the metric used during extraction becomes an intrinsic attribute of the vectors. After vectors are inserted into Milvus, the same metric type must be used for both index building and querying; otherwise, the search results will be completely invalid.

There is another type of vector whose elements are not numerical values but individual bits. This type of vector is called `BinaryVector`.

BinaryVector

For `BinaryVector`, each element is just a single bit. The earliest demand for support of `BinaryVector` came from users in the pharmaceutical industry. They represent the molecular structure characteristics of drugs in binary form as chemical molecular fingerprints, where each bit indicates the presence or absence of a specific chemical bond or property. Therefore, by comparing the distance between two binary vectors, one can assess the chemical similarity between two molecular formulas.

Not all vector databases support `BinaryVector`. Milvus is one of the earliest vector databases to support `BinaryVector`.

For `BinaryVector`, Knowhere provides two methods for calculating vector distances to evaluate the vector similarity:

- **Hamming distance**: The Hamming distance is the number of differing bits between two binary strings of equal length. For example, consider two binary vectors, 1101 1001 and 1001 1101. The XOR operation between them is as follows:

  $$11011001 \bigoplus 10011101 = 01000100$$

  Since there are two positions where the bits differ, the Hamming distance is as follows:

  $$d(11011001,\ 10011101) = 2$$

- **Jaccard distance**: Let's first talk about the **Jaccard similarity coefficient**, which measures the similarity between two sample datasets. It is defined as the ratio of the number of elements in the intersection to the number of elements in the union of the two datasets:

$$J(A, B) = \frac{|A \cap B|}{|A| + |B| - |A \cap B|}$$

The Jaccard distance, on the other hand, is used to measure the dissimilarity between datasets. It is obtained by subtracting the Jaccard similarity coefficient from 1:

$$d_j(A,B) = 1 - J(A, B) = \frac{|A \cup B| - |A \cap B|}{|A \cup B|}$$

We'll use the same binaries as an example, A = 1101 1001 and B = 1001 1101.

The set represented by *A* contains five elements, and the set represented by *B* also contains five elements. Four elements are common to both sets.

Thus, the union of *A* and *B* has six elements, and the intersection has four elements. So, the equation is as follows:

$$d_j(A, B) = 1 - J(A, B) = \frac{|A \cup B| - |A \cap B|}{|A \cup B|} = \frac{6-4}{6} = 0.333333$$

In addition to Hamming distance and Jaccard distance for general binary vectors, **superstructure** and **substructure** metrics are specially designed for molecular structure matching in domains such as chemoinformatics.

When a chemical structure is embedded within a larger chemical framework, the smaller structure is referred to as a substructure, while the encompassing structure is termed a superstructure. To illustrate, ethanol serves as a substructure within the context of acetic acid, and conversely, acetic acid is recognized as the superstructure relative to ethanol.

Structural similarity is widely used to determine whether two chemical formulae are similar to each other in that one is the superstructure or substructure of the other.

To determine whether *A* is a superstructure of *B*, use the following formula (the symbol $\equiv$ means identically equal):

$$D = (A \,\&\, B \equiv B)\ ?\ 0 : \infty$$

Let's understand this formula:

- *A* is the binary representation of a chemical formula to be retrieved
- *B* is the binary representation of a chemical formula in the database

If it returns *0*, *A* is a superstructure of *B*.

To determine whether *A* is a substructure of *B*, use the following formula:

$$D = (A \,\&\, B \;\equiv\; A)\;?\;0 : \infty$$

If it returns *0*, *A* is a substructure of *B*.

Although the `FloatVector` series, introduced earlier, and `BinaryVector` have different element value types, they share a common characteristic. Almost all elements in their dimensions are non-zero values. Therefore, they are also referred to as **dense vectors**.

In contrast to dense vectors, there exists another type of vector. This vector has a single-element data type of `float`, and the majority of its elements across dimensions are zero. We call this type of vector `SparseFloatVector`.

SparseFloatVector

`SparseFloatVector` is a new vector type introduced to support direct text search. For dense vectors (the `FloatVector` series and `BinaryVector`), since every dimension has a valid value, it is necessary to record the data for each dimension completely. However, in sparse vectors, most dimensions have a value of *0*. Recording every dimension's data completely would waste a lot of storage space. Therefore, for `SparseFloatVector`, we store only the non-zero elements and their corresponding indices. This can significantly reduce storage space and computational costs.

For `SparseFloatVector`, Knowhere provides two vector distance calculation methods to evaluate vector similarity: **inner product distance** and **BM25 distance**. We discussed the inner product distance in the *FloatVector series* section of this chapter.

BM25 distance is a prevalent approach for measuring text relevance, originally developed for full-text search applications. It integrates the three key factors described here:

- **Term frequency** (**TF**): This measures how frequently a term appears in a document. While higher frequencies often indicate greater importance, BM25 uses the `k1` saturation parameter to prevent overly frequent terms from dominating the relevance score.
- **Inverse document frequency** (**IDF**): This reflects the importance of a term across the entire corpus. Terms appearing in fewer documents receive a higher IDF value, indicating greater contribution to relevance.
- **Document length normalization**: Longer documents tend to score higher due to containing more terms. BM25 mitigates this bias by normalizing document lengths, with the `b` parameter controlling the strength of this normalization.

  The BM25 scoring is calculated as follows:

$$score(D, Q) = \sum_{i=1}^{n} IDF(q_i) \cdot \frac{TF(q_i, D) \cdot (k_1 + 1)}{TF(q_i, D) + k_1 \cdot \left(1 - b + b \cdot \frac{|D|}{avgdl}\right)}$$

The parameter descriptions are as follows:

- Q: The query text provided by the user.
- D: The document being evaluated.
- $TF(q_i, D)$: Term frequency, representing how often the term q_i appears in document D.
- $IDF(q_i)$: Inverse document frequency, calculated as follows:

$$IDF(q_i) = \log\left(\frac{N - n(q_i) + 0.5}{n(q_i) + 0.5} + 1\right)$$

Here, N is the total number of documents in the corpus, and $n(q_i)$ is the number of documents containing the term *qi*.

- $|D|$: Length of document D (total number of terms).
- $avgdl$: Average length of all documents in the corpus.
- k_1: Controls the influence of term frequency on the score. Higher values increase the importance of term frequency. The typical range is *[1.2, 2.0]*, while Milvus allows a range of *[0, 3]*.
- b: Controls the degree of length normalization, ranging from *0* to *1*. When the value is *0*, no normalization is applied; when the value is *1*, full normalization is applied.

The following table lists all the combinations of vector data types and metric types supported by Knowhere, which you can use as a reference:

	BinaryVector	**FloatVector**	**Float16Vector**	**BFloat16Vector**	**SparseFloatVector**
L2		✔	✔	✔	
IP		✔	✔	✔	✔
COSINE		✔	✔	✔	
HAMMING	✔				
JACCARD	✔				

	BinaryVector	FloatVector	Float16Vector	BFloat16Vector	SparseFloatVector
SUBSTRUCTURE	✔				
SUPERSTRUCTURE	✔				
BM25					✔

Table 10.1: Vector and metrics supported by Knowhere

The vector data types and metric types are not set in stone, especially the metric types. Users can design and add new metric types according to their own needs.

The reason for first introducing the vector types and their corresponding metric types is that these form the foundation of vector retrieval. All vector query requests ultimately boil down to the calculation and comparison of vector distances. Through the preceding introduction, you will also gain an intuitive understanding that vector distance calculation is a computationally intensive task, with computational complexity proportional to the dimensionality of the vectors, far exceeding that of one-dimensional scalar calculations.

So, is there a way to efficiently store and retrieve this vector data? The answer is yes, and this is precisely the core value of vector indexing. The design of vector indexing aims to address the efficiency challenges in high-dimensional data retrieval by leveraging specific data structures and algorithms to quickly find the most similar results to the target vector. Next, we will delve into the fundamental principles behind vector indexing, revealing how it enables efficient similarity search in high-dimensional spaces.

Theory behind indexes

Let's start with a simple example. Suppose we have a dataset containing 1 million vectors, each with a dimension of 128. Now, we have a query vector, q, and the goal is to find the 100 vectors in the dataset with the closest IP distance to q.

Without an index, we can only use a brute-force search method, which means calculating the IP distance between q and each vector in the dataset. This entails performing 1 million IP distance calculations, each requiring 128 floating-point multiplications and 128 floating-point additions, totaling *1.28×10^9* floating-point multiplications and additions. Even with modern CPUs operating at GHz frequencies, such a computational load would still take several minutes.

Therefore, to improve the efficiency of vector queries, we can adopt the following two methods:

- **Reduce the number of times IP distance is calculated**: By optimizing algorithms and data structures, we can divide the vector space into multiple subspaces and perform calculations only within some of these subspaces. This method can significantly reduce the number of distances that need to be calculated, thereby improving query efficiency. Typical indexing algorithms include **hierarchical navigable small world** (**HNSW**), **inverted file** (**IVF**), and **DiskANN**. If you are unfamiliar with the HNSW or IVF algorithms, refer to the *HNSW Algorithm* and *IVF Algorithms* sections in the *Appendix*.
- **Simplify the computational load of each IP distance calculation**: Another approach is to use quantization techniques to reduce the precision and storage size of high-dimensional vectors, thereby lowering computational and memory overhead during distance calculation. Common quantization methods include **scalar quantization** (**SQ**) and **product quantization** (**PQ**).

Here, I do not wish to delve into the specific implementation details of quantization techniques such as SQ and PQ. If you are interested in the topic of quantization, you can refer to this technical document: `https://zilliz.com/learn/unlock-power-of-vector-quantization-techniques-for-efficient-data-compression-and-retrieval`.

In addition to the two methods just mentioned, there is another technique called **refinement**. It does not directly improve query efficiency, but it can mitigate the decline in recall rate caused by quantization. Quantization may lead to data distortion, thereby reducing the recall rate. The strategy of refine is to first query out `TOPK*ratio` results (for example, 1.5 or 2 times *TOPK*) using quantization methods, and then recalculate the vector distances of these candidate results using higher-precision data (such as the original data), and select the *TOPK* most similar results as the final answer.

In practical applications, indexes often combine some or all of the preceding three methods to balance recall rate and VPS. For example, the IVF algorithm can be used without quantization to form an `IVF_Flat` index; or the HNSW algorithm, SQ8 quantization, and refine can be combined to form an `HNSW_SQ8_Refine` index.

Next, we will briefly introduce the various indexes supported by Knowhere.

Measuring the performance of indexes

In this section, we will present the performance test results of these indexes. All test data was obtained on the same desktop computer, with the following configuration:

- **CPU**: Intel Core i7-8700 CPU @ 3.20GHz x 12
- **Memory**: 64 GB

- **Disk**: Samsung SSD 990 PRO 1TB
- **GPU**: GeForce GTX 1660

The absolute values of the test data are not important because they are influenced by factors such as CPU model, clock speed, memory, and storage media. What is truly valuable is the order of magnitude of the performance data and the relative comparison between different indexes. This information will provide a more practical reference for choosing the appropriate index type.

The test dataset used is the publicly available `sift-128-euclidean` dataset, which contains 1,000,000 training data points and 10,000 test data points, with each data point being 128-dimensional. This public dataset can be downloaded from the following URL: `http://ann-benchmarks.com/sift-128-euclidean.hdf5`.

It should be particularly noted that the performance test data presented in this section is based on the results of creating indexes and performing queries on a single segment using Knowhere. This differs from the query performance data obtained in the Milvus system. In a Milvus system, there can be multiple QueryNodes, and each QueryNode may load multiple segments. During a search query, each QueryNode first performs a local `reduce` operation to merge results from all its segments. After that, a global reduce operation is applied to aggregate results from all QueryNodes. Only then is the final merged result returned to the client. Additionally, the Milvus system must also consider the time consumed by the transmission of query requests between different components. Therefore, the performance test data in this section is only applicable for comparing the performance of different indexes and does not directly reflect the recall rate and latency during actual queries in the Milvus system.

The test code can be found here: `https://github.com/zilliztech/knowhere/blob/main/benchmark/hdf5/benchmark_float.cpp`.

If you want to verify this test data, you can refer to the following steps to run it on your own computer:

```
# clone knowhere repo
git clone https://github.com/zilliztech/knowhere/blob/main

# switch to knowhere v2.5.2
cd knowhere
git checkout v2.5.2

# build knowhere with benchmark test enabled
mkdir build
conan install .. --build=missing -o with_ut=True -o with_diskann=True -o
with_benchmark=True -s compiler.libcxx=libstdc++11 -s build_type=Release
```

```
conan build ..

# switch to benchmark directory, download sift dataset
cd Release/benchmark
wget "http://ann-benchmarks.com/sift-128-euclidean.hdf5"

# run benchmark tests
rm Makefile -f
ln -s ../../../benchmark/hdf5/ref_logs/Makefile .
make test_float
```

Now, let's look at how various indexing techniques impact the query performance.

FLAT index and BruteForce series

As mentioned earlier, all indexes are combinations of an indexing algorithm, a quantization strategy, and a refine technique. However, there is one index that does not use any algorithm, nor does it use any quantization or refine technique. This index is called the **FLAT index**. The FLAT index uses a brute-force search method, sequentially calculating the distance between the query vector and each vector in the index, then sorting and selecting the *TOPK* results (but it does use parallel computing and SIMD).

FLAT is the simplest index and has a low runtime efficiency. However, it has an advantage that no other index possesses: it is the only index that can guarantee a recall of 100%. This is very useful when building a baseline for results.

The query performance of the FLAT index on the public `sift-128-euclidean` dataset is shown in *Figure 10.2*:

```
Build index FLAT time: 0.227s

[0.919 s] sift-128-euclidean | FLAT(FP32)
================================================================================
  nq = 10000, k =  100, elapse = 52.313s, R@ = 0.9999
================================================================================
```

Figure 10.2: FLAT search performance

This is the first figure that demonstrates the index performance. Let me explain some of the information displayed in this figure:

- `Build index FLAT time` shows the time spent on building the index.
- `sift-128-euclidean` indicates that this performance data was obtained using the `sift-128-euclidean` dataset.

- `FLAT(FP32)` means that the index type is `FLAT` and the data type is `FP32` (`float`). The data type can also be `FP16` (`float16`) or `BF16` (`bfloat16`).
- `nq=10000` means that the query operation is a batch query with `nq=10000`.
- `k=100` means that for each query vector, 100 nearest neighbors are returned as the query results.
- `elapse=52.313s` indicates that the total query time is 52.313 seconds.
- `R@=0.9999` means that the recall rate of this query is 0.9999.

Since the FLAT index does not require any processing of vector data, the index-building time is almost negligible (0.227 seconds). For the 128-dimensional `sift` dataset with 1,000,000 base vectors and 10,000 query vectors, searching for the nearest 100 results requires *10^10* L2 distance calculations, which takes about 52 seconds (*Figure 10.2*).

The FLAT index does not process the original vector data, but as an index, it must hold the original vector data. Therefore, when building a FLAT index, the original vector data is copied into the FLAT index, doubling the runtime memory consumption. To reduce memory consumption, Knowhere has replaced the FLAT index with the `BruteForce` series of functions. The `BruteForce` series of functions does not hold the original vector data and does not consume additional memory. They use a brute-force search algorithm to directly query the input vector data.

The query performance of `BruteForce` on the `sift-128-euclidean` dataset is shown in *Figure 10.3*:

```
[0.348 s] sift-128-euclidean | BruteForce(FP32)
================================================================================
  nq = 10000, k =  100, elapse = 52.258s, R@ = 0.9999
================================================================================
```

Figure 10.3: BruteForce(FP32) search performance

The `BruteForce` algorithm is exactly the same as the algorithm used by the FLAT index, so the query performance is also the same:

```
[53.046 s] sift-128-euclidean | BruteForce(FP16)
================================================================================
  nq = 10000, k =  100, elapse = 29.636s, R@ = 0.9999
================================================================================
```

Figure 10.4: BruteForce(FP16, BF16) search performance

The two sets of tests (*Figure 10.4*) involved converting the data from the `sift-128-euclidean` dataset from `float` to `Float16` and `BFloat16`, respectively, and then testing the performance using the `BruteForce` function. The results show that the computational efficiency of half-precision floating-point numbers is about 40% higher than that of single-precision floating-point numbers.

Let's turn our focus to the IVF series indexes.

IVF series indexes

The IVF series indexes are the most commonly used indexes in **Facebook AI Similarity Search (FAISS)** and were among the first supported by Knowhere. Knowhere supports three IVF series indexes: `IVF_FLAT`, `IVF_SQ8`, and `IVF_PQ`. These three indexes all use the IVF algorithm but differ in their quantization methods.

IVF is a clustering-based index algorithm. Its basic principle is to divide the vector dataset into multiple smaller subspaces through clustering and then perform local searches in several subspaces to improve retrieval efficiency.

In `IVF_SQ8`, SQ is applied to individual vectors, mapping vector elements represented by floating-point numbers to a finite set of integer levels to reduce storage requirements and accelerate computation. For example, SQ8 quantization represents 32-bit floats using 8-bit `uint8_t`.

PQ is applied to multiple vectors in `IVF_PQ`, decomposing high-dimensional vectors into multiple low-dimensional sub-vectors and quantizing them separately for compression.

In addition to thread management, SIMD support, and BITSET support for deletions and scalar filtering, Knowhere has made a significant change by making the IVF series indexes thread-safe. In the native FAISS IVF index, query parameters such as `nprobe` are stored directly in the index data structure, leading to thread safety issues when multiple query requests are executed concurrently. Knowhere addresses this by passing query parameters as input arguments.

Another important optimization in Knowhere is the addition of support for **cosine similarity (COSINE)**. Native Faiss only supports L2 and IP. Although users can manually normalize vectors and use IP to achieve COSINE, this increases the complexity of use.

Integrating COSINE in Knowhere presented a new challenge. To support COSINE, Knowhere needs to normalize the raw vectors being inserted, which will alter the numerical values of the original vectors. Before supporting COSINE, the `IVF_FLAT` index, which did not quantize the vectors, supported the `GetVectorByIds()` interface (refer to *Chapter 9*, the *Working with Knowhere's main APIs* section). To maintain the `IVF_FLAT` index's support for the `GetVectorByIds()` interface, it is necessary to ensure that the inserted raw vector data remains unmodified. This creates a conflict between the two requirements.

To resolve this conflict, Knowhere adopted a compromise solution, storing both the original vector data and their norms in the IVF index. When calculating COSINE similarity, the IP distance is first calculated, and then the IP distance is divided by the vector norm to obtain the COSINE distance. This approach allows Knowhere to support both COSINE and the `GetVectorByIds` functionality simultaneously.

Knowhere has also developed `IVF_FLAT_CC` and `IVF_SQ8_CC` indexes based on `IVF_FLAT` and `IVF_SQ8`. These indexes allow concurrent data insertion, accelerating the index-building process while maintaining the same query performance as the original indexes. They are often used for temporary indexes built for growing segments.

An example of creating an `IVF_FLAT` index with a metric type of `L2` using Python SDK is shown in the following code snippets:

```
index_param = {
    "index_type": "IVF_FLAT",
    "metric_type": "L2",
    "params": {"nlist": 1024}
}

collection.create_index("vector_field", index_param)
```

And here's the output:

```
Build index IVF_FLAT time: 11.031s

[12.079 s] sift-128-euclidean | IVF_FLAT(FP32) | nlist=1024
================================================================================
  nprobe =    1, nq = 10000, k =  100, elapse =  0.207s, R@ = 0.2914
  nprobe =    2, nq = 10000, k =  100, elapse =  0.376s, R@ = 0.4403
  nprobe =    4, nq = 10000, k =  100, elapse =  0.728s, R@ = 0.6042
  nprobe =    8, nq = 10000, k =  100, elapse =  1.422s, R@ = 0.7587
  nprobe =   16, nq = 10000, k =  100, elapse =  2.784s, R@ = 0.8809
  nprobe =   32, nq = 10000, k =  100, elapse =  5.481s, R@ = 0.9564
  nprobe =   64, nq = 10000, k =  100, elapse = 10.729s, R@ = 0.9898
  nprobe =  128, nq = 10000, k =  100, elapse = 21.138s, R@ = 0.9988
  nprobe =  256, nq = 10000, k =  100, elapse = 41.261s, R@ = 0.9999
  nprobe =  512, nq = 10000, k =  100, elapse = 81.043s, R@ = 0.9999
================================================================================
```

Figure 10.5: IVF_FLAT(FP32) search performance

Figure 10.5 shows the build and query time for the `IVF_FLAT` index. Building the `IVF_FLAT` index took 11.031 seconds, which is a relatively short training time. The query time is linearly related to the `nprobe` query parameter. This is understandable because the training vectors are essentially uniformly distributed across each bucket. When `nprobe` is doubled, the number of buckets to be queried is doubled, and the number of vectors to be calculated is also doubled, resulting in a doubling of the query time. The recall rate increases significantly with the increase of `nprobe`.

When nprobe=32, which is equivalent to calculating only 1/32 of all vectors, the recall rate has already reached 0.9564, while the query time is only 1/10 of the full search of the FLAT index (IVF_FLAT 5.481s vs. FLAT 52.313s).

Take a look at *Figure 10.6*, which shows the build and query performance of the IVF_SQ8 index:

```
Build index IVF_SQ8 time: 11.308s

[11.698 s] sift-128-euclidean | IVF_SQ8(FP32) | nlist=1024
==================================================================================
  nprobe =    1, nq = 10000, k =  100, elapse =  0.118s, R@ = 0.2914
  nprobe =    2, nq = 10000, k =  100, elapse =  0.161s, R@ = 0.4401
  nprobe =    4, nq = 10000, k =  100, elapse =  0.249s, R@ = 0.6037
  nprobe =    8, nq = 10000, k =  100, elapse =  0.439s, R@ = 0.7577
  nprobe =   16, nq = 10000, k =  100, elapse =  0.792s, R@ = 0.8787
  nprobe =   32, nq = 10000, k =  100, elapse =  1.496s, R@ = 0.9519
  nprobe =   64, nq = 10000, k =  100, elapse =  2.893s, R@ = 0.9822
  nprobe =  128, nq = 10000, k =  100, elapse =  5.588s, R@ = 0.9892
  nprobe =  256, nq = 10000, k =  100, elapse = 10.946s, R@ = 0.9899
  nprobe =  512, nq = 10000, k =  100, elapse = 21.928s, R@ = 0.9899
==================================================================================
```

Figure 10.6: IVF_SQ8(FP32) search performance

Building the IVF_SQ8 index took 11.698 seconds, which is comparable to the building time of the IVF_FLAT index. The query time also increases linearly with the increase of nprobe. However, due to the increased computational efficiency brought by SQ8 quantization, when nprobe=32, the query time is only 1/3 of the IVF_FLAT query time (IVF_SQ8 1.496s vs. IVF_FLAT 5.481s), while the recall rate only decreases slightly (IVF_SQ8 0.9519 vs. IVF_FLAT 0.9564).

Figure 10.7 shows the build and query performance of the IVF_PQ index:

```
Build index IVF_PQ time: 16.806s

[17.009 s] sift-128-euclidean | IVF_PQ(FP32) | nlist=1024, nbits=8, m=8
==================================================================================
  nprobe =    1, nq = 10000, k =  100, elapse =  0.108s, R@ = 0.2476
  nprobe =    2, nq = 10000, k =  100, elapse =  0.120s, R@ = 0.3342
  nprobe =    4, nq = 10000, k =  100, elapse =  0.140s, R@ = 0.4019
  nprobe =    8, nq = 10000, k =  100, elapse =  0.187s, R@ = 0.4444
  nprobe =   16, nq = 10000, k =  100, elapse =  0.244s, R@ = 0.4655
  nprobe =   32, nq = 10000, k =  100, elapse =  0.418s, R@ = 0.4735
  nprobe =   64, nq = 10000, k =  100, elapse =  0.719s, R@ = 0.4753
  nprobe =  128, nq = 10000, k =  100, elapse =  1.280s, R@ = 0.4756
  nprobe =  256, nq = 10000, k =  100, elapse =  2.397s, R@ = 0.4757
  nprobe =  512, nq = 10000, k =  100, elapse =  4.586s, R@ = 0.4757
==================================================================================
```

Figure 10.7: IVF_PQ(FP32, m=8) search performance

The query performance of `IVF_PQ` is better than that of `IVF_SQ8`, but the recall rate drops significantly. Moreover, after `nprobe=32`, the recall rate hardly changes with the variation of `nprobe`. This is because when `nbits=8` and `m=8`, it corresponds to a data compression ratio of 1/64. The high data compression ratio leads to a significant loss of quantization precision.

By adjusting the `m` parameter, the recall rate can be improved to some extent. *Figure 10.8* adjusts the value of `m` to 16:

```
Build index IVF_PQ time: 19.744s

[105.074 s] sift-128-euclidean | IVF_PQ(FP32) | nlist=1024, nbits=8, m=16
================================================================================
  nprobe =    1, nq = 10000, k =  100, elapse =  0.103s, R@ = 0.2751
  nprobe =    2, nq = 10000, k =  100, elapse =  0.119s, R@ = 0.3946
  nprobe =    4, nq = 10000, k =  100, elapse =  0.150s, R@ = 0.5022
  nprobe =    8, nq = 10000, k =  100, elapse =  0.219s, R@ = 0.5776
  nprobe =   16, nq = 10000, k =  100, elapse =  0.338s, R@ = 0.6201
  nprobe =   32, nq = 10000, k =  100, elapse =  0.576s, R@ = 0.6389
  nprobe =   64, nq = 10000, k =  100, elapse =  1.034s, R@ = 0.6446
  nprobe =  128, nq = 10000, k =  100, elapse =  1.929s, R@ = 0.6457
  nprobe =  256, nq = 10000, k =  100, elapse =  3.638s, R@ = 0.6457
  nprobe =  512, nq = 10000, k =  100, elapse =  7.082s, R@ = 0.6457
================================================================================
```

Figure 10.8: IVF_PQ(FP32, m=16) search performance

In *Figure 10.9*, `m` has been adjusted to 32:

```
Build index IVF_PQ time: 26.316s

[222.182 s] sift-128-euclidean | IVF_PQ(FP32) | nlist=1024, nbits=8, m=32
================================================================================
  nprobe =    1, nq = 10000, k =  100, elapse =  0.116s, R@ = 0.2863
  nprobe =    2, nq = 10000, k =  100, elapse =  0.151s, R@ = 0.4245
  nprobe =    4, nq = 10000, k =  100, elapse =  0.217s, R@ = 0.5632
  nprobe =    8, nq = 10000, k =  100, elapse =  0.372s, R@ = 0.6723
  nprobe =   16, nq = 10000, k =  100, elapse =  0.574s, R@ = 0.7396
  nprobe =   32, nq = 10000, k =  100, elapse =  1.019s, R@ = 0.7710
  nprobe =   64, nq = 10000, k =  100, elapse =  1.890s, R@ = 0.7817
  nprobe =  128, nq = 10000, k =  100, elapse =  3.595s, R@ = 0.7840
  nprobe =  256, nq = 10000, k =  100, elapse =  6.946s, R@ = 0.7842
  nprobe =  512, nq = 10000, k =  100, elapse = 13.726s, R@ = 0.7842
================================================================================
```

Figure 10.9: IVF_PQ(FP32, m=32) search performance

As shown in *Figures 10.8* and *10.9*, adjusting `m` to 16 and 32 results in data compression ratios of 1/32 and 1/16, respectively. The upper limit of the recall rate is somewhat increased, but it is still far from reaching the recall rate level of `IVF_SQ8` (the data compression ratio for SQ8 is 1/4). Moreover, increasing the `m` parameter also leads to an increase in the index building time.

Due to the high data compression ratio of the `IVF_PQ` index, which leads to insufficient recall rates, it is typically not used as a standalone retrieval solution. However, considering the high efficiency of PQ quantization during the query process, it can be used for initial coarse ranking, followed by refinement to improve recall rates. This approach has been applied in indexes such as SCANN and DiskANN.

We will discuss SCANN next.

SCANN

Scalable nearest neighbors (**SCANN**) was introduced by Google in 2020, and Milvus has supported the **SCANN index** since version 2.3.0. The SCANN index is algorithmically similar to `IVF_PQ`, starting with clustering and bucketing, followed by quantization of vectors within the buckets using PQ. The difference is that SCANN is more aggressive in quantization, using a higher compression ratio to obtain smaller quantization codes that can fit into CPU registers, which, when combined with SIMD, results in higher computational efficiency, unlike the traditional `IVF_PQ`, which requires inefficient memory table lookups. However, the loss of precision is greater, and generally, the original vectors are needed for refinement to improve recall.

The parameters used for building the SCANN index are consistent with those of the `IVF_PQ` index. The parameters such as `m` and `nbits` are not exposed because SCANN has default requirements for these parameters; otherwise, there would be no performance advantage.

During query time, SCANN requires not only the specification of `nprobe` but also a new parameter, `reorder_k`. The algorithm first uses PQ distance to obtain `reorder_k` results, and then refines these results using the original vectors to get the final *TOPK* vectors.

An example of creating an SCANN index with the `L2` metric type using the Python SDK is shown in the following code snippets:

```
 index_param = {
     "index_type": "SCANN",
     "metric_type": "L2",
     "params": {"nlist": 1024, "reorder_k": 256}
 }
collection.create_index("vector_field", index_param)
```

And here's the output:

```
Build index SCANN time: 11.419s

[12.493 s] sift-128-euclidean | SCANN(FP32) | nlist=1024, reorder_k=256
================================================================================
  nprobe =    1, nq = 10000, k =  100, elapse =  0.135s, R@ = 0.2904
  nprobe =    2, nq = 10000, k =  100, elapse =  0.152s, R@ = 0.4371
  nprobe =    4, nq = 10000, k =  100, elapse =  0.177s, R@ = 0.5953
  nprobe =    8, nq = 10000, k =  100, elapse =  0.223s, R@ = 0.7376
  nprobe =   16, nq = 10000, k =  100, elapse =  0.300s, R@ = 0.8413
  nprobe =   32, nq = 10000, k =  100, elapse =  0.436s, R@ = 0.8984
  nprobe =   64, nq = 10000, k =  100, elapse =  0.685s, R@ = 0.9203
  nprobe =  128, nq = 10000, k =  100, elapse =  1.150s, R@ = 0.9252
  nprobe =  256, nq = 10000, k =  100, elapse =  1.965s, R@ = 0.9256
  nprobe =  512, nq = 10000, k =  100, elapse =  3.257s, R@ = 0.9256
================================================================================
```

Figure 10.10: SCANN(FP32, reorder_k=256) search performance

As can be seen from *Figure 10.10*, the SCANN index, due to its more aggressive quantization, has better query performance than `IVF_PQ`. Moreover, thanks to the `reorder_k` parameter for refinement, its recall rate is much higher than that of `IVF_PQ`.

```
Build index SCANN time: 12.559s

[80.145 s] sift-128-euclidean | SCANN(FP32) | nlist=1024, reorder_k=512
================================================================================
  nprobe =    1, nq = 10000, k =  100, elapse =  0.212s, R@ = 0.2914
  nprobe =    2, nq = 10000, k =  100, elapse =  0.221s, R@ = 0.4400
  nprobe =    4, nq = 10000, k =  100, elapse =  0.261s, R@ = 0.6034
  nprobe =    8, nq = 10000, k =  100, elapse =  0.324s, R@ = 0.7565
  nprobe =   16, nq = 10000, k =  100, elapse =  0.397s, R@ = 0.8757
  nprobe =   32, nq = 10000, k =  100, elapse =  0.551s, R@ = 0.9472
  nprobe =   64, nq = 10000, k =  100, elapse =  0.817s, R@ = 0.9772
  nprobe =  128, nq = 10000, k =  100, elapse =  1.326s, R@ = 0.9848
  nprobe =  256, nq = 10000, k =  100, elapse =  2.220s, R@ = 0.9856
  nprobe =  512, nq = 10000, k =  100, elapse =  3.675s, R@ = 0.9856
================================================================================
```

Figure 10.11: SCANN(FP32, reorder_k=512) search performance

As shown in *Figure 10.11*, by adjusting the `reorder_k` parameter, the recall rate can be further improved. When `reorder_k` is set to `512`, the recall rate approaches the level of `IVF_SQ`.

The next index we will talk about is the HNSW series index.

HNSW series indexes

HNSW is a graph-based approximate nearest neighbor search algorithm. It is renowned for its ultra-fast search speed and excellent recall rate. If a vector database supports only one vector index, it is likely to be `HNSW`.

Knowhere initially chose the HNSW implementation from this repository: `https://github.com/nmslib/hnswlib`. However, in the latest version of Faiss 1.9.0, the HNSW algorithm has seen significant improvements in both functionality and performance. Considering stability and maintainability, as well as the close collaboration between Knowhere and the Faiss community, Milvus 2.5 has officially migrated its support for `HNSW` from `hnswlib` to Faiss.

Milvus 2.5, based on Faiss, supports multiple quantization methods on `HNSW`, including SQ, PQ, and **product residual quantization** (**PRQ**). It also supports refine for various data types, including `SQ8`, `FP16`, `BF16`, and `FLAT`.

SQ and PQ are common quantization methods; SQ offers good query performance and build speed, while PQ provides better query performance at the same compression rate.

PRQ is a fusion of PQ and **additive quantization** (**AQ**). AQ is a further optimized quantization method that represents each vector as the sum of codewords from multiple codebooks. Unlike PQ, AQ does not assume the independence of subspaces and thus can represent vectors more accurately. While maintaining relatively high computational efficiency, AQ provides higher accuracy and is suitable for scenarios with high precision requirements. Compared to PQ, AQ requires a longer build time to offer better recall rates, especially at high compression rates.

`HNSW` is a graph-based index. During the graph construction process, the algorithm tries to ensure that all nodes are connected. However, as the amount of filtering increases, due to vector deletions or scalar filtering, the connectivity of the graph changes. When the filtering reaches a certain threshold, islands inevitably form in the graph, leading to a decrease in recall rate and a reduction in query performance. Therefore, Knowhere has made improvements to the `HNSW` algorithm. When the filtering reaches a certain threshold, it directly traverses all valid nodes in the `HNSW`, calculates the distances, and returns the results.

An example of creating a simplest HNSW index with a metric type of L2 using the Python SDK is shown in the following code snippets:

```
 index_param = {
     "index_type": "HNSW",
     "metric_type": "L2",
     "params": {"efConstruction": 200, "M": 16}
 }
collection.create_index("vector_field", index_param)
```

Figure 10.12 shows the build and query performance of the native `HNSW` index, without using any quantization or refine:

```
Build index HNSW time: 107.928s

[108.805 s] sift-128-euclidean | HNSW(FP32) | hnsw_M=16, efc=200
================================================================================
  ef =  128, nq = 10000, k =  100, elapse =  0.639s, R@ = 0.9562
  ef =  256, nq = 10000, k =  100, elapse =  1.120s, R@ = 0.9891
  ef =  512, nq = 10000, k =  100, elapse =  1.989s, R@ = 0.9980
================================================================================
```

Figure 10.12: HNSW(FP32) search performance

The HNSW index achieves a recall rate of 0.9562 at `ef=128`, with a query time of only 0.639 seconds, which is an order of magnitude faster than the query time of IVF indexes at the same recall rate. This demonstrates the ultra-fast query speed and excellent recall rate of the HNSW index. The only drawback of the `HNSW` index is its longer building time, which is an order of magnitude greater than that of IVF indexes. However, in most applications, index building time is not a primary performance metric compared to recall rate and VPS.

Now in Knowhere, the `HNSW` index can be freely combined with various quantization methods and refine methods. *Figure 10.13* shows the performance data of `HNSW` with `SQ8` quantization and `FLAT` refine:

```
HNSW SQ_TYPE: SQ8
HNSW Refine: FLAT
Build index HNSW_SQ time: 90.586s

[91.682 s] sift-128-euclidean | HNSW_SQ(FP32) | hnsw_M=16, efc=200, ef=128
================================================================================
  refine_k =  1, nq = 10000, k =  100, elapse =  0.559s, R@ = 0.9532
  refine_k =  2, nq = 10000, k =  100, elapse =  0.816s, R@ = 0.9814
  refine_k =  4, nq = 10000, k =  100, elapse =  1.473s, R@ = 0.9962
  refine_k =  8, nq = 10000, k =  100, elapse =  2.653s, R@ = 0.9993
  refine_k = 16, nq = 10000, k =  100, elapse =  4.819s, R@ = 0.9998
================================================================================
```

Figure 10.13: HNSW_SQ(FP32, FLAT refine) search performance

When `refine_k=1`, it means that refine has not yet taken effect. At this point, the recall rate is 0.9532, slightly lower than the recall rate of 0.9562 at `ef=128` in the previous figure. This is due to the data precision loss introduced by SQ8. However, as `refine_k` is increased, the recall rate quickly improves. When `refine_k=4`, the recall rate reaches 0.9962, which is already close to the recall rate of the `FLAT` index.

Figure 10.14 shows the performance data of HNSW with PQ quantization and FLAT refine:

```
HNSW Refine: FLAT
Build index HNSW_PQ time: 128.335s

sift-128-euclidean | HNSW_PQ(FP32) | hnsw_M=16, efc=200, ef=128, nbits=8, pq_m=8
================================================================================
  refine_k =  1, nq = 10000, k =  100, elapse =  0.268s, R@ = 0.4407
  refine_k =  2, nq = 10000, k =  100, elapse =  0.389s, R@ = 0.6184
  refine_k =  4, nq = 10000, k =  100, elapse =  0.709s, R@ = 0.7766
  refine_k =  8, nq = 10000, k =  100, elapse =  1.396s, R@ = 0.8917
  refine_k = 16, nq = 10000, k =  100, elapse =  2.648s, R@ = 0.9576
================================================================================
```

Figure 10.14: HNSW_PQ(FP32, FLAT refine) search performance

Still remember from the `IVF_PQ` test data, *Figure 10.7*, that when `m=8`, the recall rate could not be improved beyond 0.4757. Here, by increasing the `refine_k` parameter, the recall rate can be further enhanced to over 0.95. Moreover, the query time at this point is only half of the query time required by `IVF_FLAT` to achieve the same recall rate.

Let's now move our focus to **disk-based approximate nearest neighbor** (**DiskANN**).

DiskANN

The IVF series indexes and `HNSW` indexes introduced earlier are all **in-memory indexes**, which require loading all index data into memory for querying. This limits the ability of a single machine to handle large-scale data. To address this limitation, researchers have explored a new **disk-based indexing** solution – DiskANN – which stores the index on the disk to reduce dependence on memory and optimizes the number of random disk accesses to reduce query latency.

As of now, Milvus is the only vector database that supports a disk-based indexing solution. Since disks are much cheaper than memory, especially in the cloud, DiskANN indexing is the most cost-effective solution for users who wish to save on cloud resource costs.

DiskANN indexing requires multiple disk I/O operations during querying, so the read/write performance of the disk has a significant impact on the query performance of DiskANN. The query efficiency of DiskANN running on **non-volatile memory** (**NVMe**) disks is about twice that of **solid-state drive** (**SSD**) disks. Therefore, for users who choose DiskANN indexing, it is recommended to use NVMe disks.

DiskANN indexing has many parameters, which makes it somewhat difficult to configure and use correctly. This can also be considered a minor drawback of DiskANN indexing.

An example of creating a DISKANN index with an L2 metric type using the Python SDK is shown in the following code snippet. An empty "`params`" means use all default configurations:

```
index_param = {
    "index_type": "DISKANN",
    "metric_type": "L2",
    "params": {}
}
collection.create_index("vector_field", index_param)
```

Figure 10.15 shows the build and query performance of the DiskANN index:

```
Build index DISKANN time: 312.717s

[313.185 s] sift-128-euclidean | DISKANN(FP32)
================================================================================
  search_list_size =  100, nq = 10000, k =  100, elapse =  3.726s, R@ = 0.9214
  search_list_size =  200, nq = 10000, k =  100, elapse =  4.634s, R@ = 0.9975
  search_list_size =  400, nq = 10000, k =  100, elapse =  8.374s, R@ = 0.9996
================================================================================
```

Due to the complexity of the DiskANN parameters, they are not listed here. The building time of the DiskANN index is even longer than that of HNSW, but the recall rate and query time are comparable to IVF_FLAT.

Milvus also supports GPU indexes, which are the **reusable accelerated functions and tools** (**RAFT**) series for vector search and more. Let's talk about them.

RAFT is an open source code repository on GitHub by NVIDIA (`https://github.com/rapidsai/raft`).

RAFT series indexes

Milvus had already implemented support for GPU indexing in its early versions (v1.x), utilizing the GPU index types provided by the Faiss library. However, when Milvus evolved toward the v2.x distributed architecture, GPU indexing was temporarily removed. Now, thanks to the industry-leading RAFT algorithm library contributed by NVIDIA engineers to the Milvus community, Milvus has reintroduced support for GPU indexing.

Knowhere now supports four types of GPU indexes, namely, `GPU_RAFT_BRUTE_FORCE`, `GPU_RAFT_IVF_FLAT`, `GPU_RAFT_IVF_PQ`, and `GPU_RAFT_CAGRA`.

The following test data was obtained using a GeForce1660 GPU card.

`GPU_RAFT_BRUTE_FORCE` is the implementation of the brute-force search algorithm in the GPU RAFT library. Its basic principle is the same as the brute-force search algorithm executed on the

CPU. However, since GPUs are particularly adept at large-scale parallel computing, the `GPU_RAFT_BRUTE_FORCE` index offers performance improvements of several tens of times compared to the `BRUTE_FORCE` algorithm.

An example of creating a GPU_BRUTE_FORCE index with a metric type of L2 using the Python SDK is shown in the following code snippets:

```
    index_param = {
        "index_type": "GPU_BRUTE_FORCE",
        "metric_type": "L2",
        "params": {}
    }
collection.create_index("vector_field", index_param)
```

Figure 10.16 shows the query performance of the `GPU_RAFT_BRUTE_FORCE` index:

```
Build index GPU_RAFT_BRUTE_FORCE time: 0.111s

[2.959 s] sift-128-euclidean | GPU_RAFT_BRUTE_FORCE
================================================================================
  nq = 10000, k =  100, elapse =  1.869s, R@ = 0.9999
================================================================================
```

Figure 10.16: GPU_RAFT_BRUTE_FORCE search performance

Compared to the query time of the CPU `BRUTE_FORCE` algorithm (*Figure 10.3*, 52.313 seconds), the performance is nearly 30 times faster.

`GPU_RAFT_IVF_FLAT` is the implementation of the `IVF_FLAT` index in the GPU RAFT library.

Figure 10.17 shows the query performance of the `GPU_RAFT_IVF_FLAT` index:

```
Build index GPU_RAFT_IVF_FLAT time: 0.983s

[3.660 s] sift-128-euclidean | GPU_RAFT_IVF_FLAT | nlist=1024
================================================================================
  nprobe =    1, nq = 10000, k =  100, elapse =  0.106s, R@ = 0.2881
  nprobe =    2, nq = 10000, k =  100, elapse =  0.072s, R@ = 0.4369
  nprobe =    4, nq = 10000, k =  100, elapse =  0.134s, R@ = 0.6028
  nprobe =    8, nq = 10000, k =  100, elapse =  0.251s, R@ = 0.7588
  nprobe =   16, nq = 10000, k =  100, elapse =  0.492s, R@ = 0.8816
  nprobe =   32, nq = 10000, k =  100, elapse =  0.969s, R@ = 0.9578
  nprobe =   64, nq = 10000, k =  100, elapse =  1.917s, R@ = 0.9904
  nprobe =  128, nq = 10000, k =  100, elapse =  3.857s, R@ = 0.9988
  nprobe =  256, nq = 10000, k =  100, elapse =  7.490s, R@ = 0.9999
  nprobe =  512, nq = 10000, k =  100, elapse = 14.488s, R@ = 0.9999
================================================================================
```

Figure 10.17: GPU_RAFT_IVF_FLAT search performance

Compared to CPU `IVF_FLAT` (*Figure 10.5*), the index building time is improved by 10 times, and the query time is improved by 5 times.

`GPU_RAFT_IVF_PQ` is the implementation of the `IVF_PQ` indexing algorithm in the GPU RAFT library. Its performance is similar to that of the `IVF_PQ` index. After `nprobe` reaches 32, further increasing `nprobe` can no longer effectively improve recall.

```
Build index GPU_RAFT_IVF_PQ time: 2.320s

[2.774 s] sift-128-euclidean | GPU_RAFT_IVF_PQ | nlist=1024, nbits=8, m=8
================================================================================
  nprobe =    1, nq = 10000, k =  100, elapse =  0.095s, R@ = 0.2492
  nprobe =    2, nq = 10000, k =  100, elapse =  0.011s, R@ = 0.3364
  nprobe =    4, nq = 10000, k =  100, elapse =  0.017s, R@ = 0.4052
  nprobe =    8, nq = 10000, k =  100, elapse =  0.028s, R@ = 0.4481
  nprobe =   16, nq = 10000, k =  100, elapse =  0.050s, R@ = 0.4698
  nprobe =   32, nq = 10000, k =  100, elapse =  0.085s, R@ = 0.4779
  nprobe =   64, nq = 10000, k =  100, elapse =  0.157s, R@ = 0.4798
  nprobe =  128, nq = 10000, k =  100, elapse =  0.299s, R@ = 0.4801
  nprobe =  256, nq = 10000, k =  100, elapse =  0.592s, R@ = 0.4801
  nprobe =  512, nq = 10000, k =  100, elapse =  1.188s, R@ = 0.4801
================================================================================
```

Figure 10.18: GPU_RAFT_IVF_PQ (m=8) search performance

Increasing the `m` parameter from 8 to 16 can improve recall to some extent, but it also increases index construction time, as shown:

```
Build index GPU_RAFT_IVF_PQ time: 3.061s

[9.196 s] sift-128-euclidean | GPU_RAFT_IVF_PQ | nlist=1024, nbits=8, m=16
================================================================================
  nprobe =    1, nq = 10000, k =  100, elapse =  0.009s, R@ = 0.2738
  nprobe =    2, nq = 10000, k =  100, elapse =  0.013s, R@ = 0.3949
  nprobe =    4, nq = 10000, k =  100, elapse =  0.021s, R@ = 0.5035
  nprobe =    8, nq = 10000, k =  100, elapse =  0.035s, R@ = 0.5809
  nprobe =   16, nq = 10000, k =  100, elapse =  0.060s, R@ = 0.6239
  nprobe =   32, nq = 10000, k =  100, elapse =  0.106s, R@ = 0.6428
  nprobe =   64, nq = 10000, k =  100, elapse =  0.198s, R@ = 0.6486
  nprobe =  128, nq = 10000, k =  100, elapse =  0.405s, R@ = 0.6496
  nprobe =  256, nq = 10000, k =  100, elapse =  0.754s, R@ = 0.6496
  nprobe =  512, nq = 10000, k =  100, elapse =  1.491s, R@ = 0.6496
================================================================================
```

Figure 10.19: GPU_RAFT_IVF_PQ (m=16) search performance

Further increasing the `m` parameter from 16 to 32 can continue to improve recall, but it also leads to a corresponding increase in index construction time, as shown in the following figure.

The behavior described previously is almost identical to that of the `IVF_PQ` index.

```
Build index GPU_RAFT_IVF_PQ time: 6.017s

[19.254 s] sift-128-euclidean | GPU_RAFT_IVF_PQ | nlist=1024, nbits=8, m=32
================================================================================
  nprobe =    1, nq = 10000, k =  100, elapse =  0.013s, R@ = 0.2865
  nprobe =    2, nq = 10000, k =  100, elapse =  0.025s, R@ = 0.4248
  nprobe =    4, nq = 10000, k =  100, elapse =  0.044s, R@ = 0.5641
  nprobe =    8, nq = 10000, k =  100, elapse =  0.076s, R@ = 0.6750
  nprobe =   16, nq = 10000, k =  100, elapse =  0.136s, R@ = 0.7422
  nprobe =   32, nq = 10000, k =  100, elapse =  0.251s, R@ = 0.7735
  nprobe =   64, nq = 10000, k =  100, elapse =  0.475s, R@ = 0.7839
  nprobe =  128, nq = 10000, k =  100, elapse =  0.908s, R@ = 0.7862
  nprobe =  256, nq = 10000, k =  100, elapse =  1.751s, R@ = 0.7864
  nprobe =  512, nq = 10000, k =  100, elapse =  3.386s, R@ = 0.7864
================================================================================
```

Figure 10.20: GPU_RAFT_IVF_PQ (m=32) search performance

Figures 10.18, *10.19*, and *10.20* show the building time and query performance of the `GPU_RAFT_IVF_PQ` index under different parameters. You can compare it with the CPU `IVF_PQ` index (*Figures 10.7*, *10.8*, and *10.9*) to understand the performance improvement brought by the GPU. Similar to the `IVF_PQ` index, the recall rate hardly increases with the increase of `nprobe` (after we set `nprobe=32`).

`GPU_RAFT_CAGRA` is the most advanced graph-based GPU vector index in the NVIDIA RAFT library. Unlike previous GPU indexes that only had performance advantages in large batch sizes, CAGRA demonstrates overwhelming advantages even in small batch queries, which is traditionally the domain where CPU indexes excel. Moreover, **Cuda Anns Graph** (**CAGRA**)-based performance in large batch queries and index building speed is indeed incomparable.

Take a look at *Figures 10.21*, *10.22*, and *10.23*:

```
Build index GPU_RAFT_CAGRA time: 77.655s

[80.762 s] sift-128-euclidean | GPU_RAFT_CAGRA | graph_degree=8
================================================================================
  itopk_size =  128, nq = 10000, k =  100, elapse =  0.086s, R@ = 0.7157
  itopk_size =  192, nq = 10000, k =  100, elapse =  0.091s, R@ = 0.8048
  itopk_size =  256, nq = 10000, k =  100, elapse =  0.095s, R@ = 0.8554
================================================================================
```

Figure 10.21: GPU_RAFT_CAGRA (graph_degree=8) search performance

`graph_degree` is a core parameter for CAGRA graph index construction, which defines the number of neighbor nodes connected to each vector node in the graph. Increasing this parameter improves the connectivity of the graph, thereby boosting recall:

```
Build index GPU_RAFT_CAGRA time: 77.966s

[162.113 s] sift-128-euclidean | GPU_RAFT_CAGRA | graph_degree=16
================================================================================
  itopk_size =  128, nq = 10000, k =  100, elapse =  0.104s, R@ = 0.8938
  itopk_size =  192, nq = 10000, k =  100, elapse =  0.123s, R@ = 0.9400
  itopk_size =  256, nq = 10000, k =  100, elapse =  0.143s, R@ = 0.9618
================================================================================
```

Figure 10.22: GPU_RAFT_CAGRA (graph_degree=16) search performance

Further increasing the `graph_degree` parameter can further improve recall:

```
Build index GPU_RAFT_CAGRA time: 71.453s

[237.291 s] sift-128-euclidean | GPU_RAFT_CAGRA | graph_degree=32
================================================================================
  itopk_size =  128, nq = 10000, k =  100, elapse =  0.154s, R@ = 0.9680
  itopk_size =  192, nq = 10000, k =  100, elapse =  0.201s, R@ = 0.9857
  itopk_size =  256, nq = 10000, k =  100, elapse =  0.244s, R@ = 0.9924
================================================================================
```

Figure 10.23: GPU_RAFT_CAGRA (graph_degree=32) search performance

As shown in these figures, the `GPU_RAFT_CAGRA` index can improve recall by adjusting the `graph_degree` parameter. Compared to the HNSW index, the `GPU_RAFT_CAGRA` index offers nearly a 10x improvement in query performance.

From the performance test data of the aforementioned GPU indexes, we can appreciate the performance advantages of GPUs in vector queries. Due to the GPU's suitability for large-scale operations, the larger the `nq` (number of queries) value and the higher the data dimension, the more significant the performance improvement brought by GPU indexes.

However, this performance enhancement does not come without costs. Firstly, when using GPU indexes for queries, all index data must be loaded into the GPU memory, and after the query, the result data must also be copied back to the CPU memory. Compared to in-memory indexes, using GPU indexes involves two additional data copies between CPU memory and GPU memory, which requires extra CPU time and resources. Secondly, the cost of GPU memory is one to two orders of magnitude more expensive than that of CPU memory, which means that users considering the use of GPU indexes need to carefully weigh whether their business needs justify such an expensive expenditure.

Now, let's see how SPARSE indexes work.

SPARSE series indexes

The **SPARSE series indexes** were introduced by Milvus to support semantic search and must be used in conjunction with `SparseFloatVector`. The SPARSE series indexes currently supported by Milvus include `SPARSE_INVERTED_INDEX` and `SPARSE_WAND`.

`SPARSE_INVERTED_INDEX` is an inverted index structure that maps each dimension to its non-zero vectors, facilitating direct access to relevant data during search. This structure allows Milvus to efficiently retrieve vectors with non-zero values in specific dimensions, enabling fast similarity searches. `SPARSE_INVERTED_INDEX` provides 100% recall rate and is suitable for relatively small datasets.

`SPARSE_WAND` (**Weighted AND**) is an efficient multi-constraint vector retrieval method optimized for sparse vector search performance. By calculating the maximum possible score for each dimension, `SPARSE_WAND` can effectively prune a large number of irrelevant documents, thereby improving retrieval efficiency. `SPARSE_WAND` is particularly effective in scenarios requiring high-efficiency retrieval, especially when dealing with large-scale sparse vector data, such as in information retrieval and recommendation systems. When the data volume is large, the WAND algorithm can significantly reduce computational costs while maintaining reasonable search accuracy. When 100% recall rate is not required, both indexing algorithms can adjust the `drop_ratio_search` parameter during search to trade off some accuracy for substantial performance gains, balancing efficiency and accuracy.

These two indexes are specifically designed for sparse vectors and are not applicable to dense vectors, unlike the indexes discussed earlier. Therefore, they are not suitable for the `sift` dataset used in this chapter. As a result, performance data for these indexes is not included here.

For more detailed information on these indexes, it is recommended to visit the Milvus official website (`https://milvus.io/`). If you need some dataset for testing these sparse index types, it can be obtained from this URL: `https://github.com/harsha-simhadri/big-ann-benchmarks/blob/main/dataset_preparation/sparse_dataset.md`.

Recommendations for index selection

As a developer, you might want to experiment with different indexes. However, not all indexes are applicable to all use cases. Therefore, here, we provide some index selection recommendations and guidelines based on different application scenarios:

- **Text search or semantic search**: If your application involves text or semantic search, the `SPARSE` series indexes will be your ideal choice.
- **High VPS demand with moderate data volume**: If your application has extremely high VPS requirements (e.g., VPS > 10,000) and the data volume is moderate, fitting entirely

into GPU memory, then GPU indexes are undoubtedly your best choice. GPU indexes can fully utilize the parallel processing capabilities of GPUs to provide extremely high query throughput.

- **Cloud-based big data business**: If your business is deployed in the cloud, dealing with large volumes of data, but the VPS requirements are not particularly high, and you want to minimize cloud resource costs, then the DiskANN index will be your best choice. DiskANN indexes are cost-effective when handling large-scale data, balancing performance and cost.
- **Business with moderate performance requirements**: If your business does not have particularly stringent performance requirements, you can consider using the HNSW index. HNSW indexes perform well across various performance metrics and can meet the needs of most scenarios.
- **Individual developers**: If you are an individual developer with no particularly high requirements for index performance, the IVF index is a good choice. IVF indexes are fast to build, easy to implement and maintain, and are suitable for rapid personal development.

By following these guidelines, you can choose the most suitable index type based on your business needs and resource constraints. The correct index choice can significantly enhance application performance, reduce costs, and improve user experience. Hopefully, these recommendations will help you make wise decisions in practical applications.

Summary

This chapter has helped you understand that vector indexing is essentially a set of efficient data structures and algorithms, with no particularly advanced or obscure techniques involved. Its core methods mainly fall into two categories: one is to reduce the vector space that needs to be computed through efficient algorithms, and the other is to lower the computational complexity of single vector distance calculations through various quantization techniques.

Additionally, we have tested the performance of different vector indexes using the same dataset, helping you gain a more intuitive understanding of the performance of various indexes, thereby enabling you to make more informed choices when selecting the appropriate index type for different application scenarios.

In the next chapter, we will explore how a complex query request is decomposed and executed by Milvus. You will also gain insight into the role that vector indexing plays within the complete query pipeline.

Subscribe for a free eBook

New frameworks, evolving architectures, research drops, production breakdowns – *AI_Distilled* filters the noise into a weekly briefing for engineers and researchers working hands-on with LLMs and generative AI systems. Subscribe now and receive a free eBook, along with weekly insights that help you stay focused and informed.

Subscribe at `https://packt.link/8Oz6Y` or scan the QR code below.

11

Handling Complicated Search Requests

In the previous chapter, we explored the principles behind various indexes and gained an understanding of their performance. However, performing **approximate nearest neighbor search** (**ANNS**) via vector indexes is only part of executing a complete search request. In real-world user scenarios, the user requirements that Milvus has to deal with are much more complicated than this. This chapter helps you understand how Milvus processes and executes a complex query request.

This chapter is relatively advanced because these operations are all processed and executed by Milvus in the background after a search request, without requiring user involvement. If you are a developer new to Milvus, you can choose to skip this chapter for now, as it will not affect your understanding of other chapters.

However, if you aspire to advance from a beginner to a Milvus expert, this chapter will open a new window for you. For instance, you will gain insights into why seemingly identical query statements can have vastly different execution efficiencies.

In this chapter, we will delve deeper into how a complex search request is actually executed and introduce you to several key techniques for handling search requests.

This chapter covers the following key topics:

- Handling attribute filtering
- Using bitsets to soft delete vectors
- Using SIMD to accelerate distance calculations

Handling attribute filtering

In this section, we will see how Milvus deals with the adhered scalar query conditions.

From *Chapter 3*, you should already know that when creating a collection, you need to use a schema to declare the data types of each field item. A collection must contain at least one vector column; it can include multiple scalar columns or none at all. For Milvus, the core of a search request is the similarity search operation for vectors. Scalars exist to assist vector queries. Search results can be filtered based on scalar data associated with vectors. This enables users to combine scalar field conditions with vector similarity searches, further narrowing down the results to more accurately retrieve data that meets specific criteria. This operation is known as **scalar attribute filtering** or simply **attribute filtering**.

Let's look at a concrete example to facilitate understanding. Suppose there is an online shopping platform that uses the Milvus vector database in its backend to manage information about all shoe products. The names and data types of the fields are defined as follows:

Field name	Field type	Comments
id	`int64`	unique ID
time	`int64`	launched year
style	`Bool`	**True** for men, **False** for women
color	`Varchar`	Color
category	`Varchar`	"sneakers", "sandal", "leather shoes", ...
price	`Float`	Price
photo	`float_vector`	embeddings for shoes' photos

Table 11.1: Schema definitions for shoe products

Now, let's consider a scenario where a female user spots a pair of beautiful new shoes in her friend's social media post and wants to search for similar shoes on an online shopping platform. Modern e-commerce platforms typically offer image-based search functionality, where users can upload a product image. The platform then converts the image into an embedding and performs similarity searches to find the most similar items from its database.

However, if the user can provide additional scalar information along with the image, such as "women's sandals launched in 2024, priced below 500 dollars," the platform can leverage this information to filter results more precisely. By combining scalar filtering with vector similarity search, the platform can return more accurate and relevant results that better meet the user's needs. This hybrid search approach is a powerful feature of vector databases such as Milvus, which supports both vector and scalar data types to enhance search capabilities.

Each of the terms "launched in 2024", "priced below 500 dollars", "women's", and "sandals" represents a separate filtering condition, each corresponding to a scalar expression.

The filter conditions described correspond to the expression filtering syntax in Milvus, as shown in the following table:

Condition	**Expression**
Women's	`Filter = 'style == false'`
Sandal	`Filter = 'category in ["sandal"]'`
Launched in 2024	`Filter = 'time >= 2024'`
Priced below 500 dollars	`Filter = 'price <= 500'`

Table 11.2: Scalar expression

The following sections will provide a detailed explanation of how Milvus parses these expressions and ultimately applies them to the queries. We will first begin with the Boolean expressions.

Note

It should be clarified in advance that in Milvus, "*search*" and "*query*" are two distinct operations. "*Search*" refers to ANNS, which is the similarity comparison of vectors. "*Query*", on the other hand, refers to retrieving the original vector data or scalar data. However, in this chapter, whenever we mention "*search*" or "*query*," we are both specifically referring to ANNS.

Boolean or logical expression

The expression is essentially a string that is passed into the query via the filter parameter of the SDK.

We use various operators to declare the filtering conditions for a query, and these conditions declared using operators are collectively referred to as Boolean expressions:

```
res = client.search(
    collection_name="my_collection",
    data=[query_vector],limit=5,
    filter='color like "red%" and price <= 500',
    output_fields=["color", "likes"]
)
```

Take the expression `price <= 500` as an example. `price` is the column name on the left side, and `500` is a constant expression, a very basic type of expression, on the right side. The <= in the middle is the operator.

A Boolean expression will always evaluate to either `True` or `False`, as shown in the following figure:

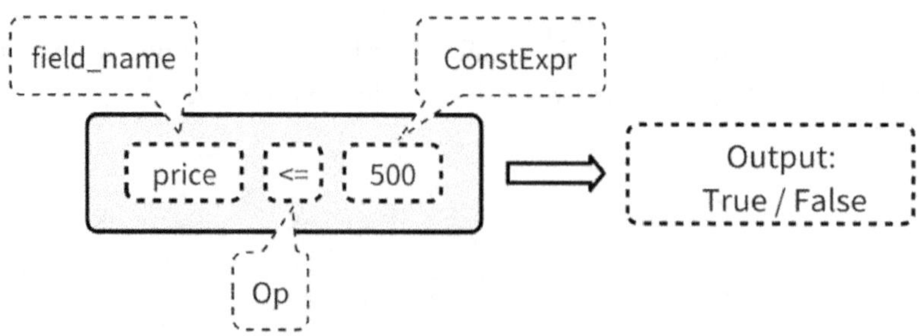

Figure 11.1: Boolean expression

For a specific row of data in the collection, the `price` in the expression is substituted with the actual data from that row for evaluation, resulting in a Boolean value of either `True` or `False`. `True` indicates that the row of data meets the filtering condition and can be included in the query results; `False` indicates that the row does not meet the condition and will not appear in the query results. Since the output of an expression is always a Boolean value of `True` or `False`, it is also known as a Boolean expression or a logical expression.

Just as different human languages have different grammatical rules, Boolean expressions also have their own syntax rules. The Boolean expressions in Milvus adopt the **Extended Backus-Naur Form** (**EBNF**) syntax rules, as shown in the following figure:

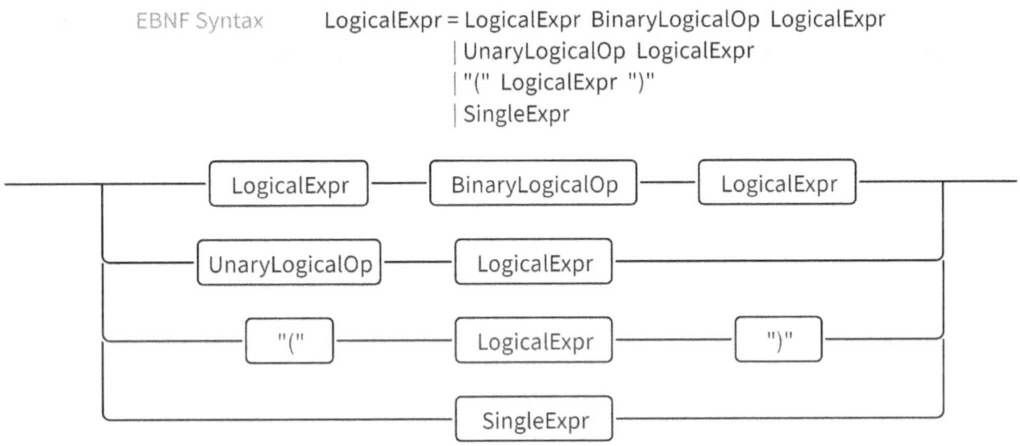

Figure 11.2: An overview of the logical expression syntax

Figure 11.2 illustrates the syntax of the logical expression. As shown in the figure, `LogicalExpr` can be the following:

- Two `LogicalExpr` connected by a binary logical operator.
  For example: `(price <= 500) && (category in ["sandal"])`
- A `LogicalExpr` preceded by a unary logical operator.
  For example: `! (price <= 500)`
- An indivisible `SingleExpr`.
  For example: `(price <= 500)`
- Be defined recursively.
  For example: `(! style) && (category in ["sandal"])&&(price<= 500)`

It can be one of these four cases, or any combination of these four cases, and they can be nested within each other. With this recursively nestable expression syntax, Milvus can express very complex filtering conditions.

Let's now talk about various logical operations in Milvus. There are three types of logical operations:

- **UnaryLogicalOp**: There is only one unary logical operator, which is `not`. It is placed before an expression to indicate negation of the result of that expression.

BinaryLogicalOp: There are two sets of binary logical operators: `&&` and `and`, which represent logical `AND`, and `||` and `or`, which represent logical `OR`.

- **SingleExpr**: `SingleExpr` is an expression that cannot be further decomposed. The currently supported `SingleExpr` are shown in the following figure:

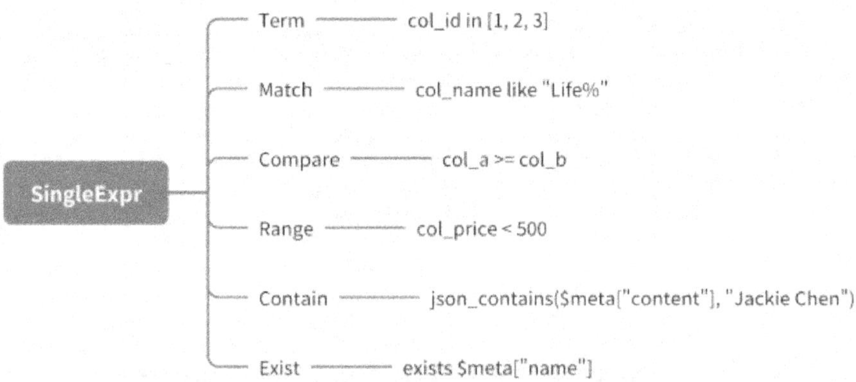

Figure 11.3: An overview of the single expression

Milvus currently supports dozens of `SingleExpr`, including constant expressions, unary arithmetic expressions, binary arithmetic expressions, comparison expressions, array expressions, and more. For specific details, you can refer to `https://milvus.io/docs/boolean.md`.

Expressions in Milvus, as a kind of declarative language that resembles natural language, are easy for humans to understand, but Milvus cannot directly interpret them. Just as programs written in C++ or Go need to be compiled into bytecode before they can be executed by a computer, expressions must also be "compiled" into a data structure that Milvus can recognize before they can be executed.

This data structure in Milvus is called a **Plan**. A Plan is an **abstract syntax tree** (**AST**) that represents all the information of the expression and can be interpreted and executed by Milvus.

Next, let's take a look at what AST actually looks like.

AST

Continuing with the example mentioned at the beginning of this chapter, suppose a user is searching for pictures of shoes on the e-commerce website and includes a query filter condition "women's sandals priced below 500 dollars". The textual string representation of this query filter condition would look like this:

```
(! style) && (category in ["sandal"])&&(price<= 500)
```

For users with some programming background, it's easy to recognize that this AST is a binary tree. The leaf nodes of the AST are `SingleExpr`, such as `!style` (this can be a leaf node of the AST), `category in ["sandal"]`, and `price <= 500`. These `SingleExpr` are combined using the logical operator &&.

Figure 11.4 shows what the typical AST corresponding to the preceding Boolean expression looks like:

Figure 11.4: An overview of AST

Milvus interprets and executes the Boolean expression by performing a post-order traversal of this AST.

Next, we will explore how Milvus generates Plan ASTs.

Plan AST generation

There are many existing open source tools for compiling an expression from a string into an AST. Milvus has chosen the open source tool **Another Tool for Language Recognition** (**ANTLR**). ANTLR is a powerful parser generator that can produce a parser capable of constructing and traversing an AST based on predefined grammar and rules.

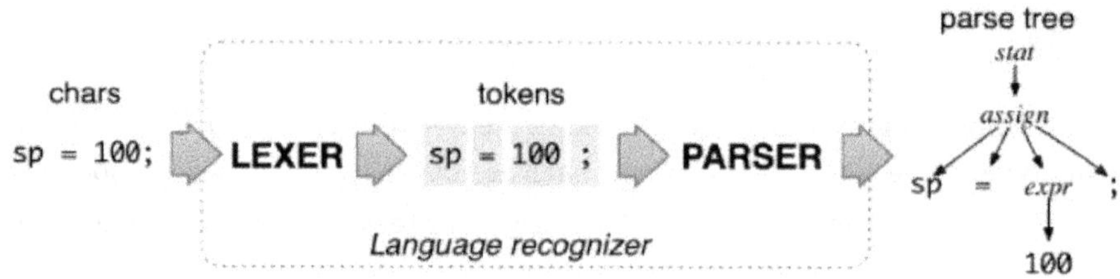

Figure 11.5: Another Tool for Language Recognition

Figure 11.5 illustrates the process of ANTLR parsing the simplest expression, `sp = 100;`, into an AST. The lexer in ANTLR breaks down the expression into four tokens: `sp`, `=`, `100`, and `;`. Then, the parser constructs an AST from these tokens. ANTLR provides a built-in walker mechanism that can be used to traverse the entire AST to check whether each node complies with the grammar rules or to inspect certain sensitive words.

Now that the expression string has been parsed into an AST, where should this AST be executed in a query pipeline? There are two possible solutions that were considered (see *Figure 11.6*).

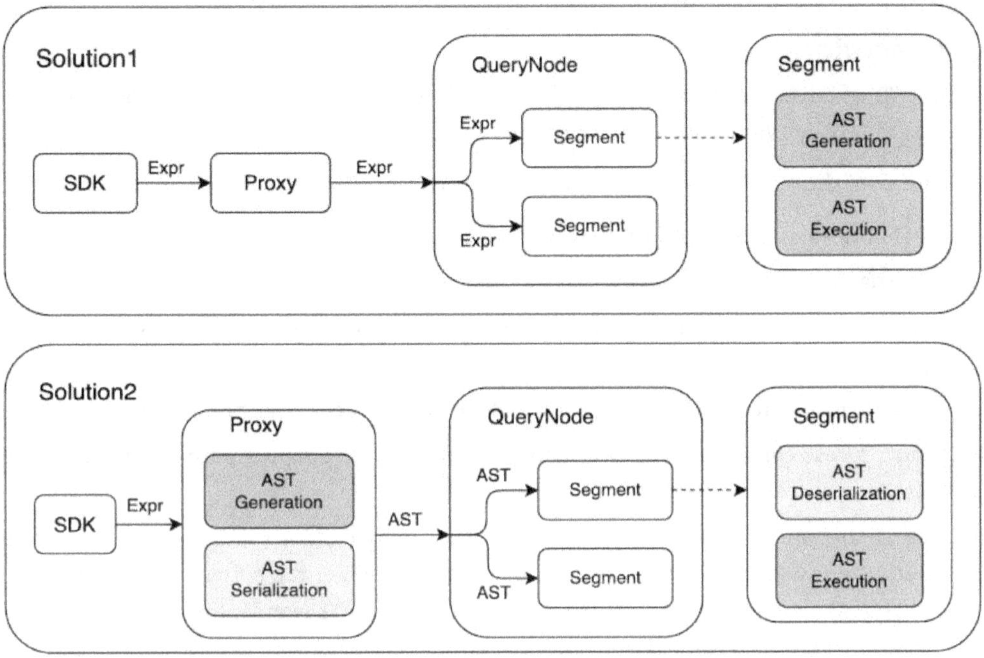

Figure 11.6: AST generation solution

For solution 1, after the Expr is input from the SDK, it is passed downstream in plain text until it reaches the segment. Each segment generates an AST and executes it. The advantage of this approach is that Expr is in plain text, which has a lower cost for transmission. However, the downside is that each segment needs to repeatedly generate the same AST, which is time-consuming and wastes computational resources.

For solution 2, the AST is generated at the Proxy node, serialized, and then passed downstream until it reaches the segment. Each segment deserializes the AST and executes it. The advantage of this approach is that if there is a syntax error in Expr, it can be detected early, reducing the burden on the backend. Additionally, each segment only needs to perform AST deserialization, which is a lighter operation compared to generating the AST. The downside is that the transmission cost is higher than solution 1, and the segment layer lacks an Expr parser, making it less convenient to write unit tests.

Considering the overall system stability, query efficiency, and resource utilization, the benefits of early error detection and reduced repeated computation far outweigh the slightly higher transmission overhead. This trade-off makes solution 2 more suitable for Milvus' distributed, high-throughput query architecture. Milvus has chosen solution 2, generating the AST at the Proxy node and performing AST deserialization on the segment side.

Let's now see how this AST execution works.

AST execution

Once the AST, which is the execution plan for scalar filtering, is constructed, each segment begins to execute the AST by evaluating it against actual data.

The execution of the AST follows a bottom-up, recursive evaluation pattern:

- Leaf nodes represent column data, constants, or attribute values
- Internal nodes represent operators (comparison, logical, arithmetic)
- Starting from the leaf nodes, the node loads the corresponding column data or literal value
- It then propagates upward to compute the result of each parent operator
- This process continues recursively until the root node outputs a final boolean result for each row

By evaluating the entire AST row by row across the segment, the system produces a bitset: a compact bitstream where each bit maps to one row in the segment. A bit value of 1 means the row satisfies the filter condition (the AST evaluates to `True`), while 0 means it does not.

After necessary processing and transformation, this bitset is passed as a filtering parameter to the search interface of Knowhere, so that vector similarity search is only performed on rows that pass the scalar filter.

Next, we will talk about the deletion of vectors.

Using bitsets to soft delete vectors

In Milvus, several features or operations can affect the query results, including **multi-version concurrency control** (**MVCC**), attribute filtering, and deletion operations.

As introduced in the previous section, the Bool expression is used for attribute filtering; only entities that meet the filtering conditions will appear in the query results. These features or operations are interrelated because they all utilize a common data structure: **bitset**.

What's a bitset?

Consider a scenario where a user inserts data and then deletes some of it. Can Milvus ensure that the deleted data will not appear in the query results? For another example, if a user includes additional query conditions when searching, such as `red color` or `price less than 100`, can Milvus handle such kinds of query requests?

The answer is, of course, *yes*. Milvus employs a data structure known as a **bitset** to handle these more complex query requests.

A bitset is essentially a binary bitstream, with the number of bits matching the row number of entities in the segment on a one-to-one basis. Bitsets provide built-in bitwise operation functions, such as bitwise AND, bitwise OR, and bit flipping. BitsetView, mentioned in *Chapter 9*, is a read-only snapshot of a bitset.

Starting with Milvus version 0.7, to support the *delete* functionality, the data structure bitset was introduced. It is used to mark whether an entity in a segment has been deleted or not. This method of marking deletions is also known as **soft deletion**, a common practice in the database industry.

Additionally, other threads in Milvus periodically monitor the proportion of entities marked for deletion in each segment. When the ratio of deleted data reaches a predefined threshold, multiple segments are merged into one segment through a process called **compaction**. During this merge, entities marked for deletion are *hard deleted*, meaning they are truly removed from memory and disk.

In Milvus, if the corresponding bit in a bitset is set to 1, it indicates that the entity has been deleted and that row of data does not participate in computations during queries. As Milvus has expanded its functionalities, both MVCC and attribute filtering also impact the computation of the bitset. However, to maintain backward compatibility, the semantics of the bitset have remained unchanged, meaning that data corresponding to bits marked as 1 in the bitset will not participate in query computations.

Next, we will illustrate through three examples how a bitset is computed.

How to calculate a bitset

Now, assume we have one segment, and we perform two *insert* operations, one *delete* operation, and three *search* operations on this segment sequentially:

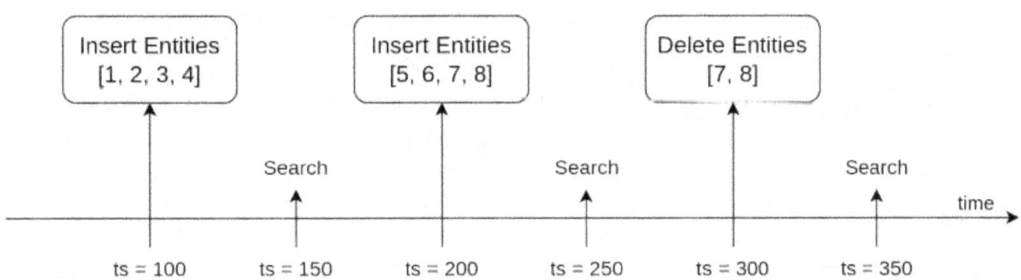

Figure 11.7: Order of operations

Let's discuss *Figure 11.7* in more detail:

1. At `ts = 100`, the first insert operation is performed, adding four entities with IDs `[1, 2, 3, 4]`.
2. At `ts = 200`, the second insert operation is performed, adding another four entities with IDs `[5, 6, 7, 8]`.
3. At `ts = 300`, a delete operation is performed, removing two entities with IDs `[7, 8]`.

Search operations are executed at `ts = 150`, `ts = 250`, and `ts = 350`.

Assume that the IDs that meet the attribute filtering conditions are `[1, 3, 5, 7]`. At `ts = 150`, the user performs the first query operation.

The bitset calculation process is as shown in *Figure 11.8*:

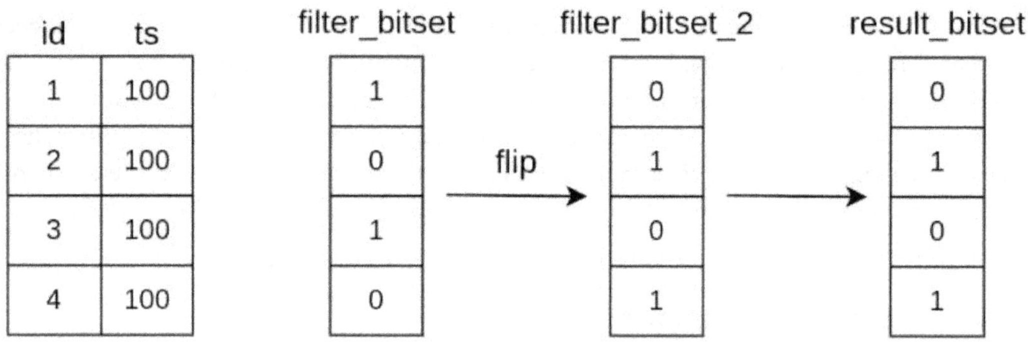

Figure 11.8: Search with ts=150

Since only four entities were inserted by `ts = 150`, the initial state of `filter_bitset` is `[1, 0, 1, 0]` (where a bit value of `1` indicates that the corresponding row of data meets the attribute filtering conditions and is valid). Because in the final result bitset, a value of `1` should indicate that the row of the entity is invalid, which is opposite to the semantics of each bit in the `filter_bitset`, it is necessary to flip all bits in `filter_bitset` to obtain `filter_bitset_2 = [0, 1, 0, 1]`.

You might be slightly confused here, so let me try to explain it more clearly. Attribute filtering and deletion operations each generate a bitset. In the bitset generated by attribute filtering, `1` indicates that the row meets the conditions and is valid. However, in the bitset generated by the deletion operation, `1` indicates that the row has been deleted and is invalid. The semantics of the bitsets generated by these two operations are opposite. Therefore, before combining these two bitsets, one of them must be bitwise flipped. Since Milvus initially introduced a bitset to support the deletion operation, at that time, `1` in the bitset indicated that the row was deleted and invalid. To maintain backward compatibility, Milvus has to keep the semantics of the bitset unchanged, that is, `1` in the bitset indicates that the row is invalid. Therefore, here we can only bitwise flip the bitset generated by attribute filtering to align its semantics with that of the bitset generated by the deletion operation.

In this simplest case, `filter_bitset_2` becomes the final `result_bitset = [0, 1, 0, 1]`. Therefore, only the vectors `[1, 3]` will participate in the query computation.

> Note
>
> **Bit-wise flip**
>
> Bit-wise flip means changing each bit from 0 to 1 or from 1 to 0. For example, if a bitset has a value of 1100, after a bit-wise flip, it becomes 0011.

At `ts = 250`, the user performs the second query operation:

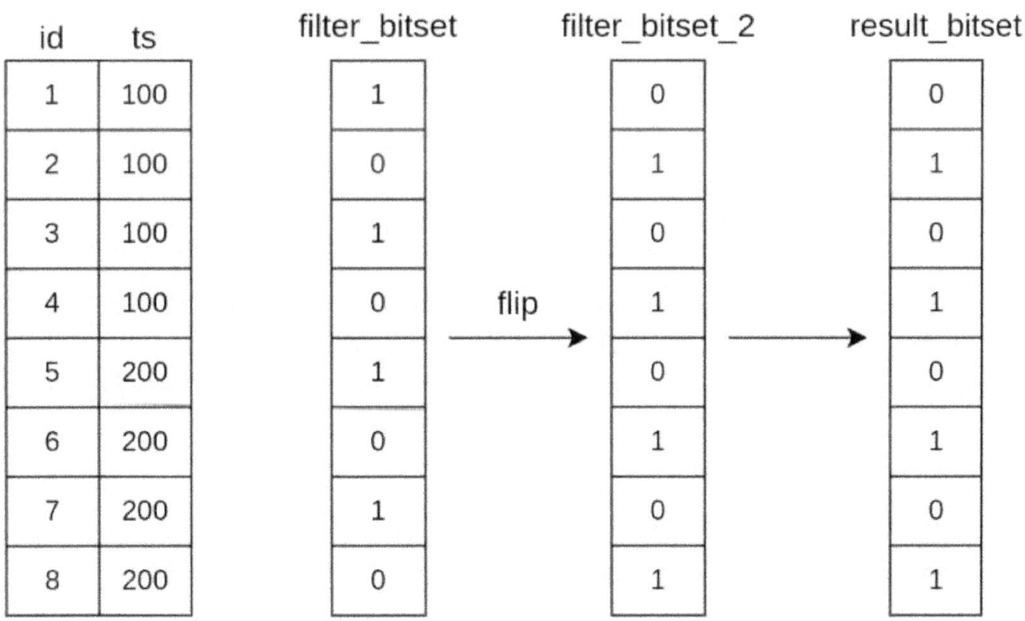

Figure 11.9: Search with ts=250

The bitset calculation process is as shown in *Figure 11.9*. Since a total of eight entities have been inserted by `ts = 250`, the initial state of the `filter_bitset` is `[1, 0, 1, 0, 1, 0, 1, 0]`. Similarly, we need to flip all bits to obtain `filter_bitset_2 = [0, 1, 0, 1, 0, 1, 0, 1]`.

The final `result_bitset` is `[0, 1, 0, 1, 0, 1, 0, 1]`. Therefore, only the entities `[1, 3, 5, 7]` will participate in the query computation.

At `ts = 350`, the user performs the third query operation. The bitset calculation process is shown in *Figure 11.10*:

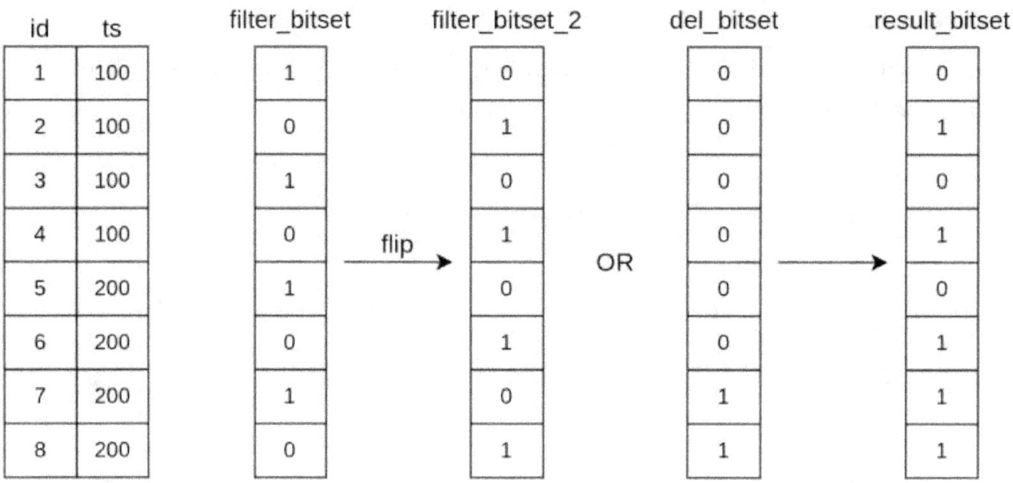

Figure 11.10: Search with ts=350

The previous calculations are the same as in scenario 2, resulting in `filter_bitset_2 = [0, 1, 0, 1, 0, 1, 0, 1]`. However, in scenario 3, we need to consider the delete operation. An OR operation must be performed between `filter_bitset_2` and `del_bitset`, yielding the final `result_bitset = [0, 1, 0, 1, 0, 1, 1, 1]`. Therefore, only the entities `[1, 3, 5]` will participate in the query computation.

Do you still remember the two questions asked at the beginning of this section?

- Can Milvus ensure that deleted data does not appear in the query results?
- Can Milvus handle query requests with additional filtering conditions?

After reading through these examples, you should no longer worry about these two questions.

All the bitset calculations described in this section are automatically handled and executed by Milvus in the background, requiring no user intervention. However, it is hoped that readers, through this understanding of the underlying mechanisms, can gain deeper insights into how Milvus processes query requests.

Now it's time to consider the calculation of distances between vectors. One of the most effective ways to accelerate vector computations is through **single instruction multiple data** (**SIMD**), which we will discuss next.

Using SIMD to accelerate distance calculations

This section talks about how Milvus leverages dynamically loaded instruction set functions to fully utilize the CPU's computing power to accelerate vector distance calculations.

As introduced in the previous chapter, no matter which type of index is used, ANNS ultimately requires the computation of distances between vectors, using methods such as L2, IP, or COSINE. Calculating distances between vectors is a quintessential compute-intensive task. Take the simplest calculation of IP distance as an example: for two vectors of dimension N, it requires performing N floating-point multiplications and N floating-point additions.

Single instruction multiple data (**SIMD**) is a parallel computing technique that enables the execution of the same operation on multiple data elements simultaneously within a single instruction, thereby achieving efficient data parallelism and significantly improving computational efficiency.

Intel introduced the **Streaming SIMD Extensions** (**SSE**) instruction set in 1999, capable of processing 4 x 32-bit floating-point numbers simultaneously. In 2011, Intel launched the **Advanced Vector Extensions** (**AVX**) instruction set, which can handle 8 x 32-bit floating-point numbers at once. In 2013, Intel further introduced the AVX512 instruction set, capable of processing 16 x 32-bit floating-point numbers simultaneously.

In native third-party vector indexing libraries, SIMD has already been adopted to accelerate vector computations. For example, both FAISS and HNSWlib support calculating vector distances using SIMD instruction sets such as SSE, AVX, and AVX512. However, as third-party indexing libraries, Faiss and HNSWlib implement SIMD support by wrapping different instruction set implementations of the distance calculation functions with predefined macros. During compilation, corresponding macro switches need to be enabled to select the desired instruction set implementation. For instance, in HNSWlib, if the macro switch `USE_SSE` is enabled during compilation, the distance calculation function is implemented using the SSE instruction set; if the macro switch `USE_AVX` is enabled, the function is implemented using the AVX instruction set. For third-party indexing libraries, this approach of selecting different instruction set implementations is understandable. However, for Milvus, this method of selecting instruction sets through compilation is inconvenient.

As a vector database, Milvus typically releases new versions in the form of Docker images, which contain precompiled Milvus binaries. If Milvus were to follow the approach of using compile-time macro switches to control the selection of instruction sets, then which switch should be enabled when releasing a new version: `USE_SSE` or `USE_AVX`?

Computer A	Computer B
CPU core (Nehalem 2008)	CPU core (Haswell 2013)
Support SSE4.2	Support SSE4.2 / AVX / AVX2

Table 11.3: Two computers with different CPU cores

As shown in *Table 11.3*, suppose we now need to deploy Milvus onto two different computers. Computer A is an old machine with a CPU based on the Nehalem architecture, which only supports the SSE4.2 instruction set and does not support the AVX2 instruction set. Computer B is a relatively new machine with a CPU based on the Haswell architecture, which can support the SSE4.2, AVX, and AVX2 instruction sets.

If Milvus binary is built with the macro switch `USE_SSE` enabled, then for a computer like Computer B, its CPU resources would not be fully utilized. Computer B supports AVX2, but we only used SSE4.2.

Conversely, if Milvus binary is built with the macro switch `USE_AVX` enabled, the Docker image would not run properly on Computer A, because Computer A only supports SSE4.2, but we forcibly ran AVX2 on it, which it does not support.

One solution is for Milvus to release a separate Docker image for each instruction set. For example, it could release three Docker images for the SSE, AVX, and AVX512 instruction sets, respectively. However, the drawbacks of this approach are quite evident. First, it increases the workload for releasing new versions. Second, users would need to choose different Docker images based on their specific CPU models. When deploying Milvus Docker images to the cloud environment, where there are countless different CPU models, this solution is clearly impractical.

Knowhere has adopted a very intelligent and convenient solution to address this issue: SIMD APIs' **dynamic hooking**.

SIMD APIs' dynamic hooking

As mentioned earlier, in third-party indexing libraries such as Faiss, multiple versions of distance calculation functions are implemented using different instruction sets. Take the `fvec_L2sqr()` function as an example, which is used to calculate the L2 distance between vectors. Under the `USE_AVX` macro, there is an implementation using the AVX instruction set; under the `USE_SSE` macro, there is an implementation using the SSE instruction set. These multiple implementations of the function share the same function name, `fvec_L2sqr()`.

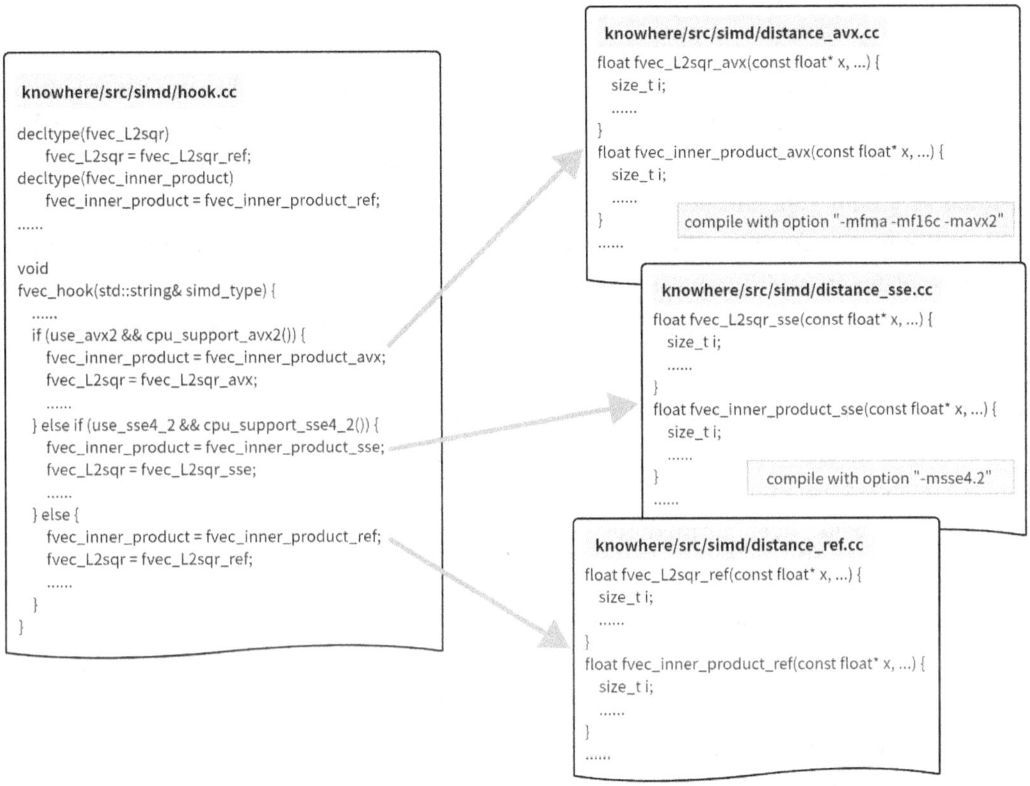

Figure 11.11: An overview of SIMD APIs' dynamic hooking

Now, we rename all functions that calculate distances using specific instruction sets and place them into separate files. For example, the `fvec_L2sqr()` function implemented using the SSE instruction set is renamed to `fvec_L2sqr_sse()` and placed in the file `distance_sse.cc`. The `fvec_L2sqr()` function implemented using the AVX instruction set is renamed to `fvec_L2sqr_avx()` and placed in the `distance_avx.cc` file. We perform the same operation for all functions that calculate distances using specific instruction sets. As a result, we obtain multiple files categorized by instruction set, as shown in the preceding figure.

The reason for separating the distance calculation functions by instruction set is that different instruction sets require different compilation parameters. For instance, functions containing the AVX instruction set need to be compiled with parameters such as `-mfma -mf16c -mavx2`, while functions containing the SSE instruction set need to be compiled with parameters such as -

`msse4.2`. With functions implemented using different instruction sets now placed in separate files, we can add compilation parameters based on the filename. For the `distance_avx.cc` file, we add the compilation parameters `-mfma -mf16c -mavx2`; for the file `distance_sse.cc`, we add the compilation parameters `-msse4.2`.

The automatic selection of the appropriate SIMD APIs at runtime in Knowhere is implemented by the `fvec_hook()` function. In the `hook.cc` file, multiple hook function pointers are defined. For example, `fvec_L2sqr`, which was originally the function name for calculating L2 distance, is now redefined as a hook function pointer. The `cpu_support_avx2()` function is used to determine whether the host machine's CPU supports AVX. If it returns `true`, the distance calculation function implemented with the AVX instruction set is mounted onto the hook function pointer. Subsequently, all calls to `fvec_L2sqr` will execute the implementation using the AVX instruction set.

The `fvec_hook()` function is executed automatically at system startup. By default, `fvec_hook()` always mounts the more advanced SIMD APIs. If the host machine's CPU is too old and does not support any instruction sets, the `fvec_hook()` function will mount the functions that calculate vector distances using algebraic methods.

Currently, the third-party indexing libraries supported by Knowhere, including Faiss, HNSWlib, and Diskann, have had their vector distance calculation functions replaced with the hook function pointers defined in the `hook.cc` file. This means that the selection of the appropriate SIMD API at system startup takes effect for all third-party indexing libraries.

The instruction sets currently supported by Knowhere include AVX512, AVX2, SSE4.2, NEON, and PowerPC. If you need to support a new instruction set, you can add the implementation of the distance calculation functions for the corresponding instruction set in the `knowhere/src/simd` directory and include the mounting logic in `hook.cc`.

Connecting the dots – an overview of Milvus query execution

For beginners, Milvus is like a large machine, and its critical query process is often seen as an abstract black-box operation. Some of you may be wondering: How does this machine work? How is a query request executed?

In simple terms, the core process of Milvus executing a complex query can be broken down into the following steps:

1. **Scalar attribute filtering**: Milvus first parses the scalar filtering conditions in the query (e.g., price < 100), converts the Boolean expression into an AST, and generates an initial bitset to mark data that meets the conditions.
2. **Bitset integration**: The bitset generated from attribute filtering is merged with the bitset marking deleted data to produce the final filtering mask bitset.
3. **Vector calculation acceleration**: The mask bitset and vector data are passed together to the underlying vector computation engine, **Knowhere**. At this stage, Milvus leverages dynamic instruction set optimization (e.g., SIMD instructions) to fully utilize CPU computing power, significantly improving the efficiency of vector similarity calculations.
4. **Result return**: After multi-level optimization and parallel computation, the system finally returns the query results that meet the filtering conditions and have the highest similarity.

Through these steps, we can clearly see how Milvus organically combines scalar filtering and vector retrieval to efficiently complete end-to-end query tasks.

This layered and modular design also makes Milvus both highly efficient and strongly extensible in real-world production environments.

Summary

In this chapter, we learned the complete process that Milvus employs to execute a complex query request. As a complex query request, it definitely comes with scalar attribute filtering conditions, expressed using Boolean expressions. Milvus parses and processes these scalar attribute filtering conditions to generate a bitset. It then passes the bitset along with the vector data to the vector computing engine, Knowhere, to obtain the query results. During the vector computation in Knowhere, Milvus also employs the method of dynamically loading instruction set functions to fully utilize the CPU's computing power to accelerate vector calculations.

With this chapter, we attempted to unveil the inner workings of Milvus' query black box, helping you understand its underlying design philosophy and engineering implementation details. Understanding the internal query execution mechanism lays a solid foundation for analyzing and optimizing system performance. Against this background, we will proceed to explore Milvus performance benchmarking in the next chapter.

Get this book's PDF version and more

Scan the QR code (or go to `packtpub.com/unlock`). Search for this book by name, confirm the edition, and then follow the steps on the page.

UNLOCK NOW

Note: Keep your invoice handy. Purchases made directly from the Packt website don't require an invoice.

Part 4

System Evaluation, Tuning, and Ecosystem Application

This final practical part centers on enterprise-grade production deployment and ecosystem integration, covering performance benchmarking, stability and scalability testing, and targeted system tuning. It also addresses key enterprise requirements, such as multi-tenancy implementation, and explores Milvus' integration with mainstream AI frameworks to familiarize readers with real-world scenarios, such as vector search and RAG. By completing this part, readers will master full-lifecycle operation and maintenance skills and learn to apply Milvus to build scalable, high-performance AI-driven applications.

This part contains the following chapters:

12

Getting Started with Milvus Performance Benchmarking

Vector search has become a core technology in modern AI applications like recommendation systems, fraud detection, and RAG systems. As a popular vector database, Milvus' performance directly impacts the responsiveness, accuracy, and cost-effectiveness of these applications. In this chapter, we'll explore performance benchmarking for the Milvus vector database together. Whether you're just starting with Milvus or looking to optimize an existing application's performance, understanding how to benchmark effectively is crucial.

By the end of this chapter, you will be able to understand why performance is crucial for vector search, measure Milvus performance, and identify factors influencing it. You will also learn about various benchmark tools and use VectorDBBench to run benchmarks.

We will cover the following topics in this chapter:

- Understanding ANN Search and Milvus performance metrics
- Benchmarking tools overview
- Running your benchmark with VectorDBBench and Locust

Technical requirements

Before we dive in, let's quickly cover the technical prerequisites for following along with the examples and concepts in this chapter:

- **Python development environment:** The primary benchmarking tools discussed (VectorDBBench, Locust) are Python-based. You'll need Python `3.12` installed on your system, along with `uv`, a fast Python package installer and resolver, to install the benchmarking tools and their dependencies.

- **Terminal/Command line:** Basic familiarity with using your system's terminal or command-line interface is necessary for installing tools and running commands.
- **Milvus instance:** You need access to a running Milvus instance to benchmark. Please refer to *Chapter 2* for detailed instructions on how to create and set up a Milvus instance. You can choose from:
    - A local instance run via Docker Compose (Milvus Standalone)
    - A distributed cluster deployment via k8s

For VectorDBBench, use the following command:

```
pip install vectordb-bench==1.0.11
```

For Locust, use the following command:

```
pip install 'locust[milvus]==2.42.0'
```

Note

Since a large portion of the subsequent code focuses on how to use Locust to implement a Milvus user, the authors submitted a PR to merge this code into the Locust repo. Readers who install Locust via `pip install 'locust[milvus]==2.42.0'` will have a built-in Milvus user included.

The code used in this chapter can be found on our GitHub repository: `https://github.com/PacktPublishing/The-Architecture-Handbook-for-Milvus-Vector-Database`

Understanding ANN search and Milvus performance metrics

Before diving into performance evaluation, it's crucial to understand how Milvus implements **approximate nearest neighbor** (**ANN**) search and why its performance characteristics matter in real-world applications.

What is ANN search?

ANN search is a fundamental technique in vector databases that finds vectors most similar to a query vector. Unlike exact nearest neighbor search, which guarantees finding the absolute closest matches, ANN algorithms trade a small amount of accuracy for significantly faster search performance.

Think of it this way: if you're looking for restaurants similar to your favorite one in a city with millions of options, you don't need to check every single restaurant. Instead, you might first narrow down by neighborhood, cuisine type, or price range. ANN algorithms work similarly, organizing vectors into efficient structures that allow rapid elimination of unlikely candidates.

How ANN search works in Milvus

Traditional exact nearest neighbor search requires comparing a query vector against every vector in the database, which becomes computationally prohibitive for large datasets. For example, searching through 1 billion 768-dimensional vectors would require roughly 768 billion distance calculations per query. ANN search algorithms solve this scalability challenge by using intelligent indexing structures and search strategies that reduce the search space dramatically.

Recall from *Chapter 10* that Milvus implements various ANN algorithms through different index types:

- **FLAT**: Performs exact search (brute-force), guaranteeing 100% recall but with linear time complexity
- **Inverted file** (**IVF**): Divides vectors into clusters, searching only the most promising clusters
- **Hierarchical navigable small world** (**HNSW**): Creates a multi-layer graph structure for efficient navigation
- **GPU-accelerated indexes**: Create parallel processing for faster search

Each algorithm makes different trade-offs between speed, memory usage, and recall accuracy. Understanding these trade-offs is essential for evaluating Milvus performance effectively.

You can learn more about ANN search algorithms in the *Appendix*.

For this chapter, we will focus on performance considerations for ANN search and tools you can use to evaluate performance. So, let's get started.

Why Milvus performance matters

Performance in the context of vector search has unique characteristics that distinguish it from traditional relational or graph databases. While relational databases focus on transactional consistency and complex joins, and graph databases optimize for traversing relationships, vector databases like Milvus must navigate a different set of trade-offs.

Vector search systems often operate under a Cost–Accuracy–Performance trade-off, where improving one dimension typically affects the others:

- **Cost**: The computational and storage resources required to maintain and query the vector index

- **Accuracy**: The quality of search results, typically measured as recall (the percentage of true nearest neighbors found)
- **Performance**: The speed of search operations, measured in **queries per second** (**QPS**) and latency

Just as traditional databases can't simultaneously maximize consistency, availability, and partition tolerance, vector databases must make trade-offs among these three dimensions. For instance, using a more complex index like HNSW might improve accuracy and performance but increase memory costs. Conversely, simpler indexes might reduce costs but sacrifice either speed or accuracy.

Unlike traditional databases, where queries are exact and deterministic, vector search performance must account for the inherent trade-off between speed and accuracy. You're not just measuring how fast you can retrieve data, but also how relevant and complete your results are. This fundamental difference means that vector database performance benchmarking requires specialized metrics and considerations that go beyond simple query response times.

As your systems go up and running, it is important to evaluate how they are functioning. The performance of ANN search directly impacts your application's success in several ways:

Speed, recall, and effective utilization of resources are the key aspects that are impacted by database performance. Let's talk about them in detail:

- **Speed** (**Latency**): For user-facing applications (like search engines, chatbots), users expect near-instantaneous responses. Vector search speed directly determines the user experience. Slow searches lead to user dissatisfaction and potential abandonment. Furthermore, as datasets grow, fast search is essential to maintain application performance.
- **Recall:** Recall measures the search algorithm's ability to retrieve relevant results. In recommendation systems, low recall means potentially missing items a user might be interested in; in fraud detection, it could mean overlooking anomalous transactions. High recall is crucial for ensuring the quality of search results but often involves a trade-off between speed and accuracy.
- **Resource efficiency:** Vector databases often handle massive datasets containing billions of high-dimensional vectors, posing significant challenges for storage (memory, disk) and computation (CPU, GPU) resources. Efficient resource utilization not only reduces operational costs but also ensures system scalability.

The performance of your database is impacted for several reasons.

Common performance challenges in vector search

Vector databases face unique performance challenges that require careful consideration during benchmarking and optimization. Let's explore these challenges and strategies to mitigate their impact:

1. **Dealing with large datasets:**
   - **Why it occurs:** As datasets grow from millions to billions of vectors, the search space grows dramatically. Memory requirements increase, index structures become more complex, and maintaining consistent performance becomes challenging.
   - **Mitigation strategies:** Implement data partitioning to divide large collections into manageable segments, use distributed deployments to scale horizontally (*Chapter 14*). Milvus' segment-based architecture and automatic data management help address these challenges (refer to *Chapter 6* for a quick refresher)
2. **Balancing speed and recall**:
   - **Why it occurs:** ANN algorithms inherently trade accuracy for speed. Aggressive pruning of the search space improves query times but may miss relevant results. This trade-off becomes more pronounced with larger datasets and higher-dimensional vectors.
   - **Mitigation strategies:** Choose appropriate index types based on your use case (HNSW for high recall requirements, IVF for balanced performance), tune search parameters dynamically based on query patterns, and implement query result caching for frequently accessed data. Consider using Milvus' `AUTOINDEX` feature to automatically optimize this balance:

     ```
     index_params = client.prepare_index_params()
     index_params.add_index(
         field_name="my_vector",
         index_type="AUTOINDEX",
         metric_type="COSINE"
     )
     ```
3. **Storage and compute resource management:**
   - **Why it occurs:** Vector indexes can consume significant memory (often 2-3x the raw data size), and search operations are computationally intensive. Resource

contention between indexing, searching, and data loading operations can create bottlenecks.

  - **Mitigation strategies:** Use disk-based indexes like DiskANN for cost-sensitive applications, implement ***mmap*** (*Chapter 15*), and leverage GPU acceleration for compute-intensive operations. Monitor resource utilization patterns to identify and address bottlenecks proactively.

4. **Real-time data updates:**
   - **Why it occurs:** Many applications require continuous data ingestion while maintaining search performance. Index updates can be expensive, and ensuring data consistency while handling concurrent reads and writes presents challenges.
   - **Mitigation strategies:** Leverage Milvus' streaming architecture, which separates growing and sealed segments. Implement batch insertions to reduce overhead and configure consistency levels based on your requirements. If needed, use separate collections for real-time and historical data.
5. **High-dimensional data (curse of dimensionality):**
   - **Why it occurs:** In high-dimensional spaces, the concept of "nearest" becomes less meaningful as distances between points converge. This phenomenon makes it harder for indexing algorithms to effectively prune the search space and maintain good recall.
   - **Mitigation strategies:**
     - Apply techniques like PCA or embedding model compression when appropriate (though this may impact accuracy) for dimensionality reduction
     - For **product quantization** (**PQ**), decompose high-dimensional vectors into sub vectors and quantize each independently.

Understanding these challenges helps us conduct more targeted benchmarking and optimization. To measure how well your Milvus deployment handles these challenges, you need to track several core performance metrics that provide insight into your vector database's behavior.

Measuring Milvus performance

When evaluating Milvus performance, several metrics reveal how well your vector database meets your application's needs. Understanding these metrics, how they're calculated, and what constitutes good versus poor performance is essential for effective benchmarking and optimization.

Some of these metrics—QPS, latency, and Recall—we have already discussed in *Chapter 10*. Let's talk about how these and some other metrics help us measure and improve Milvus' performance:

- **QPS** measures the throughput of your Milvus instance, that is, how many query requests the system can process in one second. QPS is calculated by dividing the total number of queries executed by the total time taken. For example, if you execute 1,000 queries in 10 seconds, your QPS is 100. To get accurate measurements, it's important to use concurrent queries that simulate real-world load patterns, as single-threaded sequential queries won't reveal the system's true throughput capacity.

  For a recommendation system serving millions of users, good performance might mean sustaining 200-300 QPS with stable response times, while poor performance would be struggling to maintain 50 QPS with frequent timeouts.

- **Latency metrics** capture the time taken for individual queries to complete, from request initiation to receiving results. Calculating latency percentiles requires collecting individual query response times and sorting them. Average latency is the arithmetic mean of all response times, while P95 and P99 represent the values below which 95% and 99% of queries complete, respectively. For instance, if you have 1,000 query times sorted from fastest to slowest, the 950th query time value is your P95 latency.

  These percentile metrics are more informative than averages because they reveal the consistency of your system's performance. In a chatbot application, good performance means average latency under 50ms with P99 latency below 200ms, ensuring conversations feel natural. Poor performance would show average latency exceeding 500ms with P99 spikes above 2 seconds.

```
import numpy as np
# Simulate latency data for 1000 requests (unit: milliseconds)
latencies = [10, 15, 12, 200, 18, 25, 30, 500, ...] # 1000 values
p95 = np.percentile(latencies, 95)
p99 = np.percentile(latencies, 99)
```

- **Recall** measures the accuracy of your ANN search results, which is the proportion of true nearest neighbors retrieved compared to what an exact search would find. Recall calculation requires comparing ANN search results against ground truth from an exact search.

  For each query, you count how many returned results appear in the true top-k nearest neighbors, then divide by k. If an ANN search returns 8 correct results out of the top 10 true nearest neighbors, the recall for that query is 0.8 or 80%. Average recall across multiple queries provides an overall accuracy measure. In a facial recognition system for security, good performance requires 99%+ recall to ensure no authorized individuals are denied access. Conversely, a music recommendation system might operate well with 85% recall if it delivers results quickly.

- **Indexing time** affects both initial deployment and ongoing operations when new data is added. This metric is straightforward to measure; record timestamps before and after index building operations. However, it's important to distinguish between data insertion time and actual index construction time, as these are separate phases in Milvus.
  Total indexing time includes insertion, segment flushing, and index construction, including data flushing and persistence overhead. A news aggregation service adding thousands of articles hourly needs indexing times under 5 minutes to keep content fresh, representing good performance. Poor performance would be indexing times exceeding 30 minutes, causing significant delays in content availability.

```
index_params = milvus_client.prepare_index_params()
index_params.add_index(field_name = "embeddings", metric_type="L2")
t0 = time.time()
milvus_client.create_index(collection_name, index_params)
tt=time.time() - t0
print(f"index time {tt}")
```

- **Resource utilization** encompasses CPU, memory, and disk I/O consumption during various operations. These metrics are typically sampled at regular intervals during operations. CPU and memory usage percentages are collected using system monitoring tools, then aggregated to show average and peak values. It's crucial to monitor these metrics throughout the entire operation duration to capture resource usage patterns and identify potential bottlenecks.
  Good performance shows CPU utilization staying below 70% during peak query loads with predictable memory usage patterns, allowing headroom for traffic spikes. Poor performance manifests as CPU regularly hitting 95%+ with memory exhaustion, causing frequent garbage collection pauses.

The following table summarizes these key metrics:

Metric	Definition	Relevance	How to improve these metrics
QPS	Number of queries processed per second	Measures throughput and capacity to handle query loads	Scale horizontally with distributed deployment, use connection pooling, optimize index parameters, and implement query result caching
Average latency	Mean response time for a query	Provides a general overview of query performance	Use faster index types (HNSW), reduce search scope with partitions, ensure data is loaded in memory, and optimize search parameters
P95 Latency	Response time below which 95% of queries complete	Indicates performance for most users; helps identify outliers	Implement request prioritization, avoid resource contention, use dedicated query nodes, monitor and eliminate slow queries
P99 Latency	Response time below which 99% of queries complete	Highlights the worst-case performance for almost all users	Increase system resources, implement circuit breakers, use separate collections for different workload types
Recall	Ratio of correctly identified neighbors to total true neighbors	Measures the accuracy and quality of search results	Adjust index parameters (increase *nprobe* for IVF, *ef* for HNSW), use more precise index types, consider FLAT index for critical queries
Indexing Time	Duration to build the vector index	Indicates initial setup cost and time for index updates	Use GPU acceleration, increase indexing parallelism, choose appropriate index types for your data size, and batch insertions

Metric	Definition	Relevance	How to improve these metrics
CPU Utilization	Percentage of CPU time used by Milvus	Reflects computational load; high usage during queries might indicate bottlenecks	Optimize search parameters, use GPU indexes for compute-intensive operations, upgrade to CPUs with better SIMD support
Memory Utilization	Amount of RAM used by Milvus	Crucial for in-memory operations and caching; insufficient memory can degrade performance	Use disk-based indexes, implement data tiering, optimize collection schemas, regularly release unused collections
Disk I/O	Rate of data read from/written to disk	Important for data loading, indexing, and persistence; high I/O might indicate bottlenecks	Use SSDs (preferably NVMe), implement proper caching strategies, optimize flush intervals, use memory-mapped files

Table 12.1: A summary of metrics to measure and improve Milvus' performance

These performance metrics work together to paint a complete picture of your Milvus deployment's health and efficiency. While it's tempting to optimize for a single metric like QPS or latency, remember that vector database performance is multidimensional as improvements in one area often come with trade-offs in others. Regular monitoring and benchmarking of all these metrics will help you maintain the delicate balance between speed, accuracy, and resource efficiency that your application demands. With this understanding of what to measure and how to improve each metric, let's explore the various factors that influence these performance characteristics.

Next, we will discuss various factors that impact Milvus' performance.

Factors influencing Milvus' performance

Milvus' performance isn't static; it's influenced by various factors. Understanding these helps us optimize effectively.

1. **Hardware specifications**: The foundation of any high-performance Milvus deployment begins with hardware. Just as a race car needs a powerful engine and precision components to achieve peak performance, Milvus requires carefully selected hardware to handle the computational demands of vector search. The right hardware configuration can mean the difference between a system that struggles with thousands of vectors and one that effortlessly handles billions. Let's examine the critical hardware components that directly impact your Milvus performance:
    - **CPU:** Multi-core processors (recommend at least 8 cores) and SIMD instruction sets (like AVX2, AVX-512) are crucial for parallel processing and vector computations. In particular, vector instructions such as AVX2 and AVX-512 significantly accelerate similarity computations. Insufficient CPU resources lead to query bottlenecks and slow index building. A system with 4 cores might handle 50 QPS while struggling with latency spikes, whereas 16 cores with AVX-512 support can sustain 200+ QPS with consistent sub-50ms latency.
    - **Memory (RAM):** Sufficient RAM (recommend at least 32GB, clusters might need 128GB+) for caching data and indexes significantly speeds up queries. Memory shortage forces frequent disk I/O, degrading performance by 10-100x. A deployment with 16GB RAM serving 100 million vectors might show 500ms+ latencies due to constant swapping, while 64GB RAM enables sub-20ms searches with everything cached. Monitor memory usage patterns and implement data tiering strategies for cost-effective scaling.
    - **Storage (Disk)**: SSDs (especially NVMe SSDs) are recommended for faster read/write speeds, particularly for large datasets and disk-based indexes. Traditional HDDs create severe bottlenecks during data loading and index persistence. HDD-based systems might take hours to load a billion-vector dataset that NVMe SSDs handle in minutes. Index building on HDDs can be 5-10x slower. Invest in NVMe SSDs for production workloads and use proper I/O scheduling.
    - **Network:** Stable, high-speed networking (recommend at least 1Gbps) is vital for distributed deployments. Network latency and bandwidth limitations create coordination overhead between nodes. A distributed cluster on 100Mbps network might add 50-100ms latency per query compared to 10Gbps networking that adds

only 1-2ms. Use dedicated network interfaces for Milvus traffic and implement proper network topology design.

- **GPU:** Can be used to accelerate index building and search, significantly improving throughput and recall, especially under high load. Without GPU acceleration, CPU-based systems might struggle with real-time requirements. A CPU-only system building HNSW indexes for 100 million vectors might take 6 hours, while a single A100 GPU reduces this to 30 minutes. GPU-accelerated search can improve QPS by 5-10x for certain workloads. Consider GPU instances for high-throughput applications.

2. **Dataset characteristics:** Your data's nature fundamentally shapes how Milvus performs. Different datasets present unique challenges. For instance, a collection of product images behaves very differently from text embeddings or genomic sequences. Understanding your dataset's characteristics is crucial because the same Milvus configuration that excels with one type of data might struggle with another. The following characteristics determine not only which optimizations will be most effective but also set the theoretical limits of what performance you can achieve:

    - **Size:** The number of vectors directly impacts search time and resource requirements. As datasets grow from millions to billions of vectors, linear search becomes impossible and memory requirements explode. A facial recognition system with 10 million faces might achieve 20ms searches using HNSW, but scaling to 1 billion faces often requires switching to IVF_PQ to fit in memory, accepting 50-100ms latency as a trade-off. Mitigation strategies include using hierarchical indexes like IVF to partition data and leveraging disk-based indexes for extremely large datasets.
    - **Dimensionality:** Vector dimension affects computational cost and memory footprint. In high-dimensional spaces like 1536-dimensional text embeddings, distances between points converge, making nearest neighbor search less meaningful while doubling computational requirements. Many applications find that reducing dimensions provides 95% of the quality at half the cost—for instance, using OpenAI's 1536-dim embeddings instead of their 3072-dim version for semantic search. See `https://huggingface.co/spaces/mteb/leaderboard`. This leaderboard demonstrates that embedding models with smaller dimensions can outperform those with higher dimensions.

3. **Milvus configuration parameters**: While hardware provides the raw capability and your dataset defines the challenge, Milvus configuration parameters determine how effectively these resources are utilized. Think of these parameters as the tuning knobs of

your vector database; small adjustments can lead to dramatic performance improvements or degradations. The art of Milvus optimization lies in finding the right combination of settings that balance your specific requirements for speed, accuracy, and resource usage.

- **Index type:** Milvus supports various indexes (e.g., `FLAT`, `IVF_FLAT`, HNSW, GPU indexes). Each offers different trade-offs between build time, memory usage, query speed, and recall. Wrong index choice can degrade performance by orders of magnitude. Using `FLAT` index on 100 million vectors might result in 10-second queries, while HNSW reduces this to 10ms with 95% recall. However, HNSW might consume 2-3x more memory. Use `AUTOINDEX` for automatic selection or benchmark different indexes for your specific use case.
- **Search parameters:** Each index type has tunable parameters (e.g., `nprobe` for IVF, `efSearch` for HNSW) to balance search speed and recall. Suboptimal parameters can waste resources or miss relevant results. Setting `nprobe = 1` for IVF might achieve 5ms latency but only 70% recall, while `nprobe = 32` improves recall to 95% at 20ms latency. Dynamic parameter tuning based on query importance can optimize the speed-accuracy trade-off.
- **Other parameters:** Consistency Level, Batch Operations, memory management settings, etc., also impact performance. Strong consistency might add 10-50ms latency compared to eventual consistency. Single-record operations versus batch operations can differ by 100x in throughput; for example, inserting 1 million vectors individually might take hours, while batch insertion completes in minutes. Configure these based on your application's consistency and throughput requirements.

4. **Deployment mode:** The way you deploy Milvus fundamentally affects its performance characteristics and scalability potential. Each deployment mode offers distinct advantages and trade-offs, from the simplicity of standalone installations to the power and complexity of distributed clusters. Your choice of deployment mode should align with your current needs while providing a path for future growth, as migrating between deployment modes can require significant operational effort.

   - **Standalone:** Suitable for smaller workloads, development, and prototyping. Simple setup but limited scalability and high availability. Performance degrades rapidly beyond hardware limits. A standalone instance might handle 10 million vectors with 100 QPS effectively but struggles with 100 million vectors, showing a

10x latency increase. Consider distributed deployment when approaching standalone capacity limits.

   - **Distributed:** Deployed via Kubernetes cluster (refer to *Chapter 2*), suitable for large datasets and high query loads, offering scalability and redundancy but potentially introducing network latency. Coordination overhead can impact performance. A 3-node cluster might show 5-10ms additional latency compared to a standalone, but can scale to billions of vectors and 1000+ QPS. Proper resource allocation and network optimization are crucial for distributed performance (see `https://milvus.io/tools/sizing` for the guidelines).

5. **Concurrency levels:** Real-world applications rarely process queries one at a time. Concurrency introduces complexity as configurations optimized for sequential queries may degrade under high concurrency. The challenge lies in finding the sweet spot where you maximize throughput. Beyond a certain concurrency level, further increases lead to resource contention that actually reduces overall throughput rather than improving it.

   - **Definition:** The number of simultaneous query or insert operations performed on Milvus. Too little concurrency underutilizes resources while too much causes contention. A system handling 10 concurrent queries might achieve 100 QPS with 50ms latency, but 100 concurrent queries could degrade to 80 QPS with 1000ms latency due to resource contention. Find the optimal concurrency through load testing (refer to *Chapter 13*).
   - **Impact:** Increasing concurrency can boost QPS, but beyond a certain threshold, resource contention can lead to increased latency and performance degradation. Implement connection pooling, request queuing, and circuit breakers. Monitor thread pool sizes and adjust based on workload patterns. Use dedicated resources for different operation types to prevent interference.

The following table summarizes these factors and their impact on performance metrics:

Factor	Impact on performance metrics
CPU (Cores, SIMD)	Higher core count and SIMD support improve QPS, reduce indexing time, and query latency
Memory (RAM)	SufficientRAMreducesquerylatencyviain-memoryoperationsandcaching; larger datasets & complex indexes need more memory

Factor	Impact on performance metrics
Storage (SSD, IOPS)	SSDs with high IOPS improve data loading speed, indexing time (disk indexes), and query latency
Network (Bandwidth, Latency)	High bandwidth and low latency are crucial for distributed deployments, impacting QPS and latency
GPU	Can significantly accelerate indexing and search, improving QPS, potentially reducing latency for certain workloads
Dataset size	Larger datasets generally lead to higher query latency and resource consumption; ANN algorithms help mitigate
Dataset dimensionality	Higher dimensionality increases computational cost and memory footprint, potentially increasing query latency
Dataset distribution	Affects the efficiency of different index algorithms and the effectiveness of search params, impacting recall & latency
Index type (e.g., IVF, HNSW)	Different types offer varying trade-offs between indexing time, memory usage, query speed, and recall
Search params (e.g., *nprobe*, *efSearch*)	Allows fine-grained control over the latency-recall trade-off
Consistency level	Strong consistency ensures immediate visibility but might increase latency; weaker levels offer faster writes
Deployment mode (Standalone, Distributed)	Distributedoffersbetterscalability&HA,butmightaddnetworklatency; Standalone is simpler but limited
Concurrency levels	Increasing concurrency can improve QPS up to a point, after which resource contention might increase latency & failure rates

Table 12.2: A summary of factors affecting Milvus' performance

Understanding these performance factors is essential for optimizing your Milvus deployment. While each factor presents its own challenges, the real complexity lies in their interactions. Insufficient memory might amplify the impact of suboptimal index choices, while network latency in distributed deployments could mask CPU bottlenecks. Successful performance optimization requires a holistic approach: start with adequate hardware, understand your data characteristics, carefully tune configuration parameters, choose the appropriate deployment mode, and manage concurrency effectively. Remember that performance tuning is an iterative process as what works for one dataset or workload may not be optimal for another, making continuous monitoring and adjustment crucial for maintaining peak performance.

Now that we understand performance metrics and influencing factors, let's look at the tools available for benchmarking.

Benchmarking tools overview

Benchmarking is the systematic process of measuring and comparing the performance of your Milvus deployment under controlled conditions. Think of it as a health checkup for your vector database; just as medical tests reveal hidden issues before they become critical, benchmarks expose performance bottlenecks, capacity limits, and optimization opportunities that might not be apparent during normal operations.

Why are benchmarks crucial for vector databases? Unlike traditional databases, where performance characteristics are well understood, vector search presents unique challenges with its multidimensional trade-offs between speed, accuracy, and resource usage.

Benchmarks provide objective data to answer critical questions: Can your system handle expected traffic? How will it perform as data grows? What's the optimal configuration for your specific use case? Without benchmarking, you're essentially flying blind, making architectural decisions based on assumptions rather than evidence.

Effective benchmarking goes beyond running a few queries and measuring response times. It requires understanding different types of benchmarks, choosing appropriate tools, designing representative workloads, and interpreting results in context.

The tools and methodologies we'll explore in this section will equip you to make data-driven decisions about your Milvus deployment, ensuring it meets both current needs and future growth.

Standardized benchmarks vs. real-world workloads

Before choosing a tool, it's important to understand the difference between standardized benchmarks and real-world workloads.

- **Standardized benchmarks** use industry-standard datasets and methodologies to create a level playing field for comparing different vector databases and configurations. These benchmarks employ predefined datasets like SIFT or GLoVe and established metrics, providing an objective framework that makes cross-system comparison straightforward and results easily reproducible. Tools like ann-benchmarks exemplify this approach, offering consistent testing conditions that help you understand how Milvus performs relative to other vector databases. However, standardized benchmarks have limitations.

They may not fully capture your specific application's data characteristics, which are often dynamic and domain-specific. They also tend to focus on pure search performance, missing the complexity of real applications that mix searches with inserts, deletes, and filtering operations under varying concurrency patterns. Over-optimizing for standardized benchmarks can sometimes lead to poor performance in actual production scenarios.

- **Real-world workload benchmarks** take a different approach by attempting to replicate the actual usage patterns, data characteristics, and operational conditions your application will face in production. These benchmarks work with dynamic, domain-specific data that mirrors your actual use case, incorporating mixed operations that reflect how your application truly behaves—combining searches with inserts, updates, and deletes under fluctuating concurrency levels. They measure end-to-end latency, including all system components, not just the vector database in isolation.

  Creating these benchmarks typically requires custom tools like Locust to simulate your application's specific behavior patterns, making them more complex to design and implement but ultimately more representative of actual performance.

Both approaches have their place in a comprehensive benchmarking strategy. Standardized benchmarks provide valuable baseline comparisons and help you understand fundamental performance characteristics, while real-world workload testing ensures your Milvus deployment will meet actual production requirements.

The most effective approach combines both, using standardized benchmarks for initial evaluation and comparison, then validating with custom benchmarks that simulate your specific use case.

Now that we understand the distinction between standardized and real-world benchmarks, let's explore the specific tools available for benchmarking Milvus performance. Each tool serves different purposes and offers unique capabilities for measuring various aspects of your vector database deployment.

Common benchmarking tools

The vector database ecosystem has evolved a rich set of benchmarking tools, each designed to address specific aspects of performance evaluation. From comprehensive suites that test entire database systems to specialized tools that focus on algorithm-level performance, choosing the right tool depends on your benchmarking goals.

Some tools excel at providing standardized comparisons across different vector databases, while others give you the flexibility to simulate your exact production workloads. Understanding the strengths and limitations of each tool will help you build a benchmarking strategy that provides actionable insights for your Milvus deployment.

Let's examine the most popular and effective tools available today:

- **VectorDBBench** (`https://github.com/zilliztech/VectorDBBench`) is an open-source tool sponsored by Zilliz (the company behind Milvus), designed to provide standardized, reproducible performance and cost-effectiveness evaluations for various vector databases. This comprehensive benchmarking suite offers predefined test scenarios covering capacity, search performance, and filtering capabilities, while supporting multiple standard datasets including SIFT, GIST, LAION, and Cohere. VectorDBBench stands out with its GUI mode, making it easy for users to set up tests.
  The tool generates detailed reports and leaderboards featuring metrics like QPS, latency, recall, and notably, cost-effectiveness measures such as **queries per dollar** (**QP$**). Its flexible index configuration and built-in concurrency testing capabilities make it ideal for standardized comparisons across different vector databases and understanding the cost-performance trade-offs of various configurations.
- **Locust** (`https://locust.io/`) takes a different approach as a popular open-source load testing framework written in Python. Rather than focusing solely on vector search, Locust enables you to simulate complex, real-world application behaviors with large numbers of concurrent users. You define user behaviors directly in Python code, giving you complete flexibility to model your specific workload patterns by mixing searches with inserts, updates, deletes, and filters in **Approximate Nearest Neighbor** (**ANN** proportions that match your production environment.
  The framework can simulate millions of concurrent users while providing a real-time web UI that displays key metrics like requests per second, latency distributions, and failure rates. Its event system allows custom reporting and integration with monitoring tools. Locust excels at testing system performance under realistic concurrent pressure and measuring end-to-end latency, making it invaluable for understanding how your Milvus deployment will perform as part of your complete application stack.

- **ANN-Benchmarks** (`http://ann-benchmarks.com/`) focuses on a different layer of the stack, evaluating the performance of isolated **Approximate Nearest Neighbor** (**ANN**) search algorithms independent of any database system. This specialized tool uses standard datasets to measure fundamental algorithm characteristics, including recall rates, query speed, memory usage, and index build time. While valuable for deep research into core ANN algorithm performance, it operates at a lower level than complete database systems.

  For most Milvus users looking to evaluate their complete system performance, VectorDBBench or Locust will provide more relevant insights, though ANN-Benchmarks remains useful for understanding the theoretical limits of different indexing approaches.

- **Big ANN Benchmark** (`https://big-ann-benchmarks.com/`) pushes the boundaries by evaluating ANN algorithms and systems on billion-scale datasets. Using massive datasets like Deep1B, this benchmark focuses on extreme scale performance, measuring not just traditional metrics like QPS and recall, but also practical considerations like power consumption and hardware costs. Results are typically accessed through official leaderboards that showcase how different systems perform at the cutting edge of scale.

  While most end-users won't run these benchmarks directly, the results provide valuable insights into the scalability potential of Milvus' underlying algorithms and help inform decisions about future growth capacity.

Selecting the right benchmarking tool, or combination of tools, depends on your specific goals and stage of deployment. Start with VectorDBBench for initial comparisons and standardized testing, especially if you're evaluating Milvus against other vector databases. Move to Locust when you need to simulate your actual application workload with its unique mix of operations and concurrency patterns.

Reference ANN-Benchmarks and Big ANN Benchmark results to understand the theoretical capabilities and limits of different approaches. Remember that no single tool tells the complete story. Effective performance evaluation combines multiple perspectives to build a comprehensive understanding of how your Milvus deployment will perform in production.

As readers, you are perhaps now eager to test out Milvus' performance.

Without further ado, let's get started.

Running your benchmark with VectorDBBench and Locust

After all the theory, let's get practical. First, we'll use **VectorDBBench** as an example to show how to run a basic search performance test.

Why start with VectorDBBench? For users new to benchmarking Milvus, this tool offers the ideal balance of simplicity and comprehensiveness. Unlike Locust, which requires writing custom Python code, VectorDBBench provides pre-configured test scenarios that work out of the box. Its standardized datasets and metrics make it easy to compare your results with published benchmarks, helping you quickly understand if your deployment is performing as expected.

Let's get started with the example. Here are the steps:

1. **Install VectorDBBench**: First, let's set up the benchmarking environment. We'll use uv for faster Python package management:

```
# Install uv (Python package manager)
curl -LsSf https://astral.sh/uv/install.sh | sh # Note: You need to restart
the terminal after installing uv

# Create a virtual environment with Python 3.12
uv venv -p 3.12
source .venv/bin/activate

# Install VectorDBBench
uv pip install vectordb-bench

# Initialize the benchmark environment
init_bench # Note: This command takes some time to load and install
dependencies
```

The frontend page of VectorDBBench is based on Streamlit. After executing the `init_bench` command, a welcome page will automatically open in the browser:

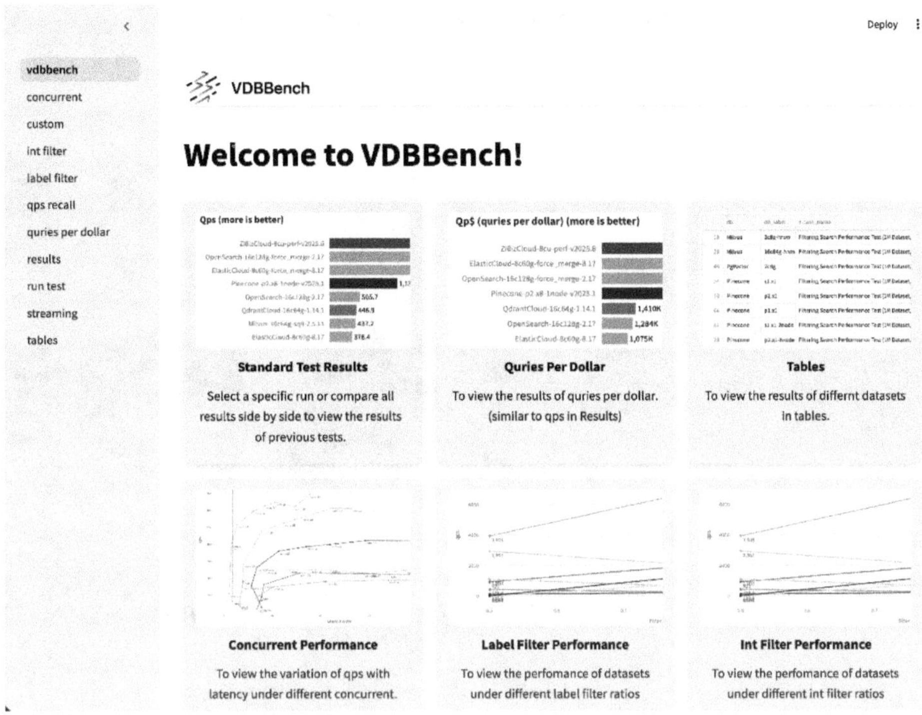

Figure 12.1: An overview of the welcome page of VectorDBBench

2. **Run the Benchmark**: Use VectorDBBench GUI mode to run the test. The GUI mode provides an intuitive interface where you can:

    1. Go to the **run test** page and select your database (**Milvus**)

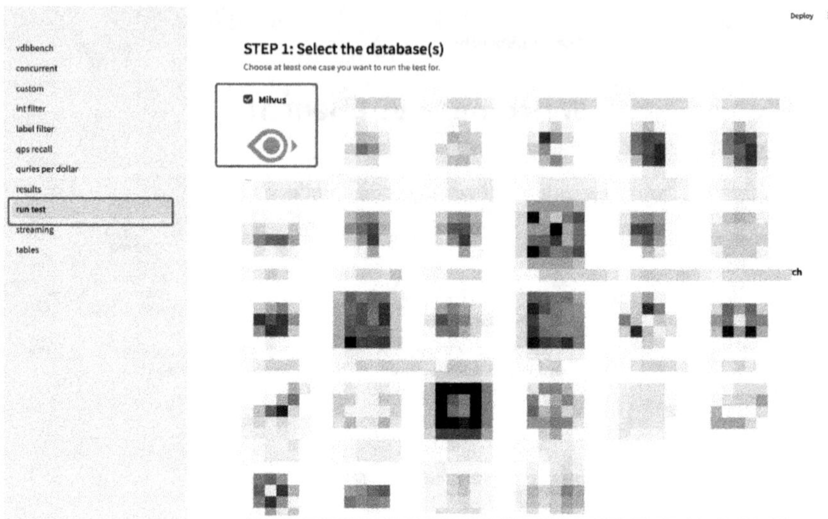

Figure 12.2: An overview of the run test page

2. Select test cases:

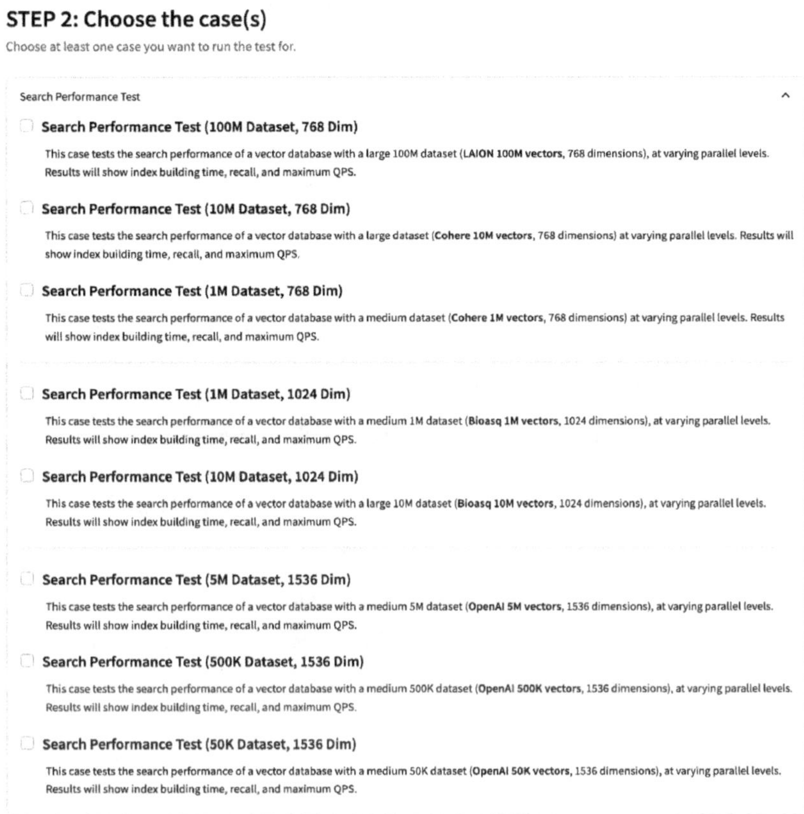

Figure 12.3: Choosing the cases

This test suite evaluates search performance across different **data scales** (50K to 100M vectors) and **vector dimensions** (768, 1024, 1536 dims). You can select the case that best fits your data scale and vector dimensions based on your own usage.

3. Configure index parameters: This is a search performance test using HNSW index on a 100M dataset with 768 dimensions.

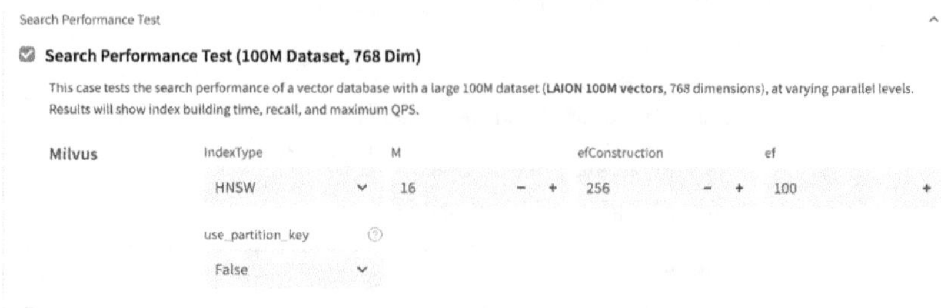

Figure 12.4: Configuring parameters

Here are the selected parameters:

- Build Parameters: **M** = **16**: Maximum number of connections per node in the graph (affects recall and index size); **efConstruction** = **256**; search depth during index building (higher = better quality but slower build)
- Search Parameters: **ef** = **100**: Size of the candidate list during search (higher = better recall but slower search)
- Others: **use_partition_key** = **False**; partition key feature is disabled

In addition to HNSW, there are also indexes such as IVF and DISKANN available for selection.

4. View real-time results and visualizations:

Figure 12.5: Real-time results page

3. **Interpret the results**: After the test completes, VectorDBBench will generate reports in the results/directory and output summary information to the console and result page. Focus on key metrics in the report:
    - **QPS:** queries per second
    - **Latency (p99):** 99th percentile and average latency
    - **Recall:** Recall rate of the search results
    - **Index Build Time:** Time taken to build the index
    - **QP$:** Queries Per Dollar (only for cloud services)

The following figures show these key metrics:

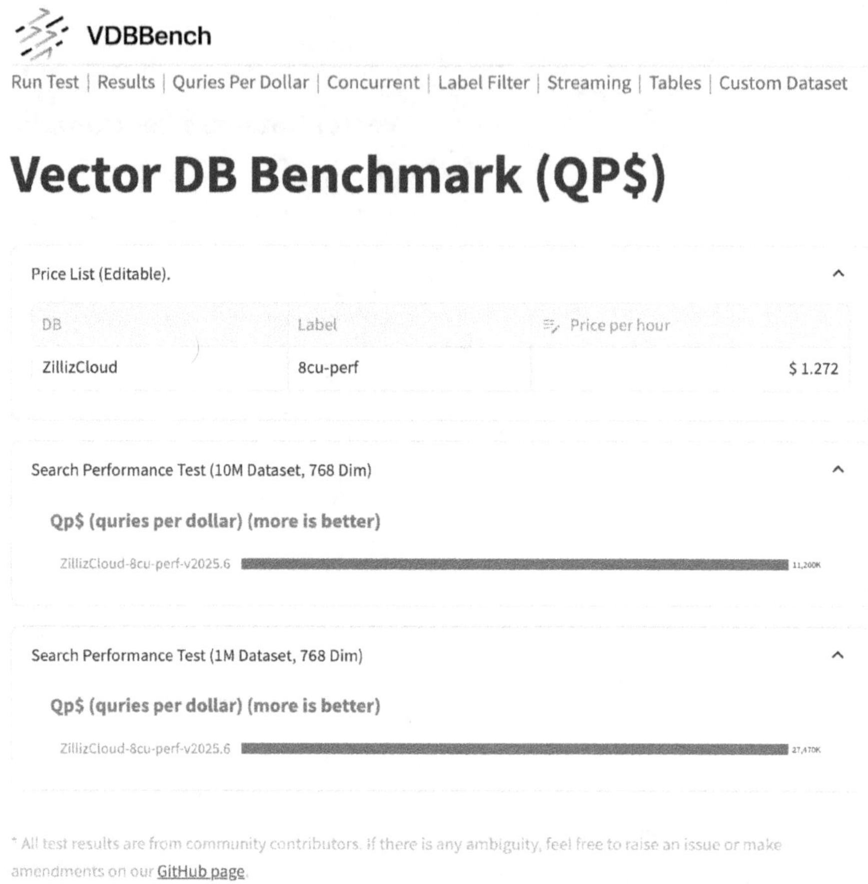

Figure 12.6: Key metrics of the report

When analyzing your results, consider the following:

- **Hardware**: Results vary significantly between CPU models, memory capacity, and storage types
- **Index configuration**: Different index types and parameters create different trade-offs between speed and accuracy

You can refer to the section in *Chapter 15* on how to optimize search performance.

While VectorDBBench excels at standardized testing, real-world applications rarely follow standard patterns. This is where Locust becomes invaluable. Let's take a look at Locust to customize performance testing.

Using Locust for custom performance testing

Unlike VectorDBBench's predefined scenarios, Locust lets you script exactly how your application interacts with Milvus. Perhaps you search for products, immediately insert user interactions, then update recommendation vectors, all while handling spiky traffic patterns throughout the day. Where VectorDBBench measures isolated vector search performance, Locust captures the full complexity of your production workload, including the interplay between different operations and realistic user behavior patterns. Its Python-based scripting might require more initial effort than VectorDBBench's configuration files, but this investment pays off when you need to answer questions such as "How will our system handle Black Friday traffic?" or "What happens when we mix real-time updates with heavy search loads?" By simulating thousands of concurrent users with authentic behavior patterns, Locust helps you discover performance issues that standardized benchmarks might miss, making it the go-to choice when you need confidence that your Milvus deployment can handle your specific production challenges.

If you need to simulate more complex, application-specific loads, follow these steps:

1. Install `Locust` and `PyMilvus`:

```
pip install locust pymilvus # Note: If you face an issue installing this,
run: # python3 -m pip install ipykernel -U --user --force-reinstall
```

2. Write your test scenarios (`locustfile.py`):

```
from locust import between, task
from locust.contrib.milvus import MilvusUser
import random
from pymilvus import CollectionSchema, DataType, FieldSchema
from pymilvus.milvus_client import IndexParams

class SimpleMilvusUser(MilvusUser):
    wait_time = between(1, 3)

    def on_start(self):
        """Generate test vectors."""

        self.dimension = 128
        self.test_vectors = [
            [random.random() for _ in range(self.dimension)]
            for _ in range(10)]
```

```
    def __init__(self, environment):

        # Define collection schema
        schema = CollectionSchema(
            fields=[
                FieldSchema(
                    name="id", dtype=DataType.INT64,
                    is_primary=True),
                FieldSchema(
                    name="vector", dtype=DataType.FLOAT_VECTOR,
                    dim=128),
                FieldSchema(
                    name="name", dtype=DataType.VARCHAR,
                    max_length=50),
            ],
            description="Test collection",
        )

        # Define index parameters
        index_params = IndexParams()
        index_params.add_index(
            field_name="vector",
            index_type="HNSW",
            metric_type="COSINE",
        )

        super().__init__(
            environment,
            uri=environment.host,
            collection_name="perf_test_collection",
            schema=schema,
            index_params=index_params,
        )

    @task(3)
    def insert_data(self):
        """Insert data into Milvus."""

        data = [
            {
                "id": random.randint(1, 10000),
```

```
                "vector": random.choice(self.test_vectors),
                "name": f"item_{random.randint(1, 1000)}",
            }
        ]

        self.insert(data)

    @task(5)
    def search_vectors(self):

        """Search for similar vectors."""
        search_vector = random.choice(self.test_vectors)

        self.search(
            data=[search_vector], anns_field="vector", limit=5)
```

This script simulates multiple concurrent users interacting with a Milvus collection, allowing you to measure performance. The example defines a simple collection schema with a 128-dimensional vector field and configures an HNSW index with COSINE similarity. It implements two primary operations: data insertion (weighted at 3) and vector search (weighted at 5), simulating a read-heavy workload typical of vector search applications. The `wait_time = between(1, 3)` configuration introduces realistic delays between operations, mimicking actual user behavior.

3. This example uses randomly generated data for demonstration purposes only. For meaningful performance testing that accurately reflects your production environment, you should customize both the schema and data sources to match your actual use case.
4. Next, run Locust:

```
# Run with web UI
locust -f locustfile.py --host=http://localhost:19530

# Run headless with specific parameters
locust -f locustfile.py --headless \
        --users 100 \
        --spawn-rate 10 \
        --run-time 5m \
        --host=http://localhost:19530
```

5. Access Web UI (`http://localhost:8089`): Set the number of concurrent users and spawn rate, and start the test:

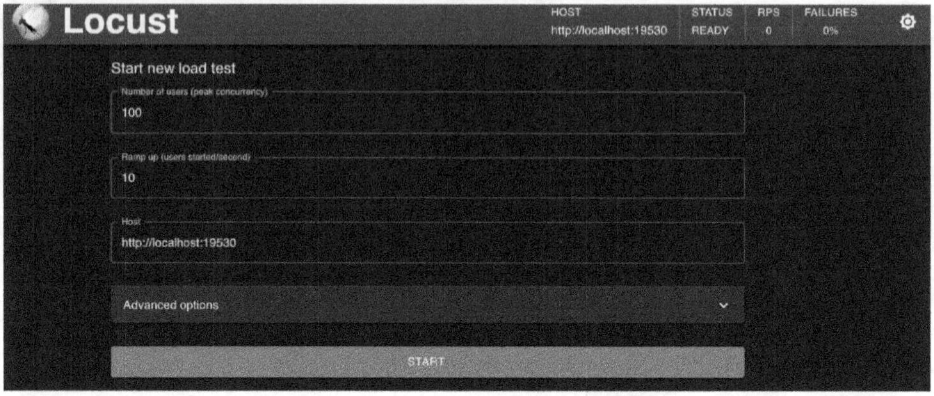

Figure 12.7: An overview of the web UI of Locust

6. Finally, monitor real-time metrics such as **requests per second** (**RPS**), response time distribution, and failure rate:

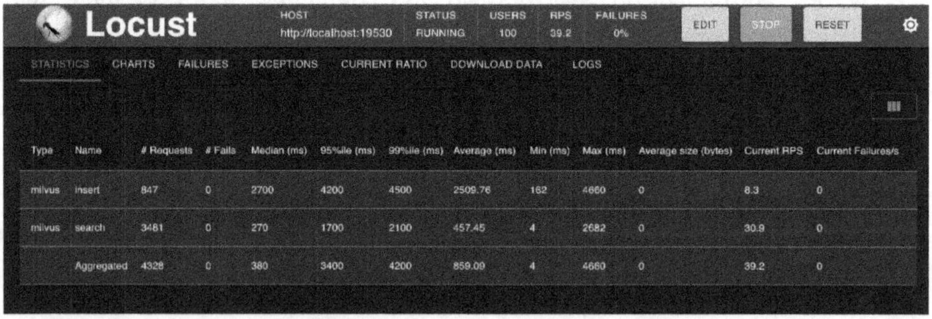

Figure 12.8: Monitoring real-time metrics

As shown in the results above, VectorDBBench provides a comprehensive view of how your Milvus deployment performs across different scenarios, helping you identify optimization opportunities and validate configuration changes.

Summary

Congratulations on completing this introduction to Milvus performance benchmarking! In this chapter, we explored the importance of performance for Milvus applications, mastered the key metrics for measurement (QPS, latency, recall, resource utilization, etc.), and learned about the main influencing factors (hardware, dataset, configuration, deployment mode, concurrency).

We also introduced different benchmarking tools, understanding the pros and cons of standardized benchmarks (like VectorDBBench) and custom load testing (like Locust), and their use cases. Through the hands-on section, you learned how to run a basic search performance test using VectorDBBench and how Locust can be used to simulate more realistic workloads that resemble production environments.

Remember, benchmarking is an ongoing process rather than a one-time task. By regularly measuring performance under different configurations and workloads, you can identify bottlenecks, optimize resource utilization, and ensure your Milvus deployment continues to meet the evolving demands of your applications. Regular benchmarking transforms performance management from reactive troubleshooting into proactive optimization, giving you greater confidence in the scalability and reliability of your vector search infrastructure.

In the next chapter, we'll explore how to ensure your Milvus deployment is stable and reliable under real-world conditions.

Subscribe for a free eBook

13

Stability and Reliability Evaluation for the Milvus Vector Database

Welcome to this chapter, where we will explore practical methods for stability/reliability testing of the Milvus vector database. Vector databases have become core infrastructure supporting intelligent applications in the world of GenAI applications. Milvus, a popular open source vector database, is widely used due to its ability to efficiently process and search massive vector data. However, any distributed system faces challenges in stability and reliability. Ensuring Milvus operates stably under various conditions, without data loss and with continuous service availability, is crucial for building reliable AI applications.

Vector search workloads introduce unique reliability challenges compared to traditional databases. Unlike relational databases, where consistency is primarily about transactions, vector databases must maintain index consistency across distributed segments, handle segment loading and balancing during node failures, and coordinate distributed search operations across replicas. These factors require specialized stability testing approaches that go beyond conventional database testing methodologies.

This chapter aims to provide a quick-start guide to Milvus stability/reliability testing. We will focus on the following practical methods and steps:

- Understanding Milvus stability and reliability
- Setting up the Milvus reliability testing environment (based on Kubernetes)
- Load testing for Milvus reliability
- Simulating Milvus component failures and verifying recovery

Technical requirements

As a reference, the Milvus architecture diagram in *Chapter 5* illustrates the roles of each component (Proxy, QueryNode, DataNode, and MixCoord) that we will be testing.

Before we begin exploring Milvus' stability and reliability testing, let's review the technical prerequisites to follow along with the examples in this chapter:

- **Kubernetes environment**: Since we'll be deploying Milvus in a distributed manner for reliability testing, you'll need access to a Kubernetes cluster. This can be any of the following:
    - A local Kubernetes setup using Minikube, Kind, or Docker Desktop
    - A managed Kubernetes service from cloud providers (GKE, EKS, or AKS)
    - An on-premises Kubernetes cluster with sufficient resources
- **kubectl CLI**: The Kubernetes command-line tool is essential for interacting with your cluster, checking Pod statuses, and troubleshooting issues.
- **System resources**: For meaningful reliability testing, ensure your Kubernetes cluster has the following:
    - At least three worker nodes (for simulating node failures)
    - Minimum 16 GB RAM per node
    - 100 GB+ storage available for persistent volumes
    - Network connectivity between nodes for distributed testing
- **Testing tools**: We'll be using several tools for load generation and fault injection:
    - Python 3.10+ for running test scripts
    - The pymilvus SDK (v2.5.0+) for interacting with Milvus
    - Locust (v2.17.0+) for load testing; Locust now includes official Milvus integration via `locust.contrib.milvus`
    - The Faker library for generating realistic test data
    - NumPy and `pandas` for data processing

  You will need basic familiarity with YAML for Kubernetes configurations.
- **Chaos Mesh (v2.6.0+)**: Required for fault injection testing. This cloud-native chaos engineering platform will be used to simulate component failures. Installation

instructions are provided in the *Simulating Milvus component failures and verifying recovery* section.

- **Monitoring stack (required)**: Prometheus and Grafana are essential for this chapter as we'll use Grafana dashboards to observe system behavior during fault recovery. Please refer to the Milvus documentation for monitoring setup instructions.

The examples and configurations in this chapter are designed to work with Milvus 2.5.x or later. If you're using an earlier version, some features or configurations may differ. All code examples are available in the book's GitHub repository:

`https://github.com/PacktPublishing/The-Architecture-Handbook-for-Milvus-Vector-Database/tree/main/ch13`

Understanding Milvus stability and reliability

In the world of AI-powered applications, vector databases serve as the backbone for critical functionalities such as semantic search, recommendation engines, and **retrieval-augmented generation** (**RAG**) systems. When these systems fail or perform unpredictably, the consequences can range from poor user experiences to significant business losses. For instance, an e-commerce recommendation system that crashes during peak shopping hours could result in millions of dollars worth of lost revenue, while an unreliable fraud detection system might miss critical security threats. This is why stability and reliability are fundamental to the trust users place in AI applications. As organizations increasingly rely on Milvus to power mission-critical vector search capabilities, ensuring the database can handle real-world pressures, recover from failures, and maintain data integrity becomes paramount. This chapter will equip you with the knowledge and tools to thoroughly test these aspects before deploying Milvus in production environments.

Stability refers to Milvus' ability to maintain consistent and predictable performance under continuous operation and various pressures. To quantify stability, we measure the following:

- **Performance consistency**: The variance in response times compared to baseline performance under normal operating conditions. *Baseline performance* refers to the standard performance metrics (QPS, latency, and error rate) measured during stable operation without any failures or unusual load conditions, similar to the benchmark results you may have observed in *Chapter 12* using VectorDBBench. *Normal operating conditions* represent the typical production state: moderate load (100–300 QPS), stable resource utilization (CPU 40–60%, memory below 70%), and minimal error rates (below 0.1%).
- **Error rate**: The percentage of failed operations relative to total operations, tracked separately for read and write operations. For detailed information on measuring error

rates and resource utilization metrics, refer to *Chapter 12*, where these concepts are covered in the context of performance benchmarking.

- **Resource utilization**: The consumption patterns of CPU, memory, and disk I/O relative to available capacity.

These metrics help distinguish between a stable system and one experiencing degradation, allowing teams to set clear SLAs and monitoring thresholds based on their specific requirements.

Reliability refers to the probability that Milvus will perform its function correctly under specified conditions for a specified period. For a vector database, reliability is primarily reflected in the following:

- **Data durability**: Ensuring that successfully written data is not lost
- **Availability**: The system's uptime is measured as a percentage (e.g., 99.9% availability means less than 8.76 hours of downtime per year, while 99.99% means less than 52.56 minutes of downtime per year)
- **Fault tolerance**: The system can continue to run or recover quickly when some components or dependent services fail
- **Correctness of results**: Search and query results are accurate, and data remains consistent

To compute Milvus' reliability, we combine these metrics using the following formula:

$$\textit{Overall reliability} = \textit{Data durability} \times \textit{Availability} \times \textit{Fault recovery rate} \times \textit{Query accuracy}$$

Here is an example:

- Data durability = 99.999% (five nines)
- Availability = 99.9% (three nines)
- Fault recovery rate = 99.5% (successful recoveries/total failures)
- Query accuracy = 99.99% (correct results/total queries)

Thus, overall reliability = $0.99999 \times 0.999 \times 0.995 \times 0.9999 \approx 99.39\%$.

This means the system has a 99.39% probability of performing all its functions correctly over the measurement period. Each component metric is measured through continuous monitoring and testing, which we'll explore in the following sections.

Understanding the relationship between stability and reliability

While stability and reliability are related concepts, they focus on different aspects of system behavior:

- **Stability** is about consistent performance under varying conditions. A stable system maintains predictable response times and resource usage even when load increases or conditions change.
- **Reliability** is about correctness and availability over time. A reliable system performs its intended functions accurately and remains accessible when needed.

A system can be stable but unreliable (performs consistently but produces incorrect results), or reliable but unstable (functions correctly but with highly variable performance). For production deployments, Milvus must achieve both: maintaining stable performance characteristics while reliably storing and retrieving vector data. The testing methods in this chapter will help you evaluate both aspects comprehensively.

Setting up the Milvus reliability testing environment

Having established a solid understanding of stability and reliability concepts, let's now turn our attention to the practical aspects of setting up a proper testing environment. The foundation of effective reliability testing lies in creating an environment that closely mirrors production conditions while remaining isolated from actual production systems.

It is essential to conduct reliability testing in an independent environment, never directly in a production environment. We'll use Kubernetes for deployment as it provides the best platform for simulating real-world failure scenarios.

Configuring Milvus for high-availability testing

If you haven't already deployed Milvus in Kubernetes, please refer to *Chapter 3* for detailed deployment instructions using the Milvus Operator.

For reliability testing, you'll need to modify the standard deployment configuration to enable **high-availability** (**HA**) features. The key configuration is `enableActiveStandby: true`, which enables the Active-Standby HA mode for Milvus coordinators. When enabled, multiple coordinator instances run simultaneously, one as the active node handling all requests, while others remain in standby mode ready to take over if the active node fails. This ensures automatic failover with minimal service disruption. Additionally, setting replicas greater than 1 for each component provides redundancy for worker nodes.

Let's now operationalize these concepts by setting up a Kubernetes-based HA test environment.

Take a look at the following YAML file, where we configure the HA deployment. These are key points to note:

- `enableActiveStandby:true` enables the coordinator failover capability
- `mixCoord.replicas:2` ensures one active and one standby coordinator
- `queryNode.replicas:3` and `dataNode.replicas:3` provide redundancy for data processing
- `msgStreamType:pulsar` configures Pulsar as the message queue for **write-ahead logging** (**WAL**)

Here is the code:

```
apiVersion: milvus.io/v1beta1
kind: Milvus
metadata:
  name: milvus-ha-demo
  namespace: milvus-ha-test
  labels:
    app: milvus
spec:
  mode: cluster
  config:
    mixCoord:
      enableActiveStandby: true
  components:
    image: milvusdb/milvus:v2.5.14
    mixCoord:
      replicas: 2
    proxy:
      replicas: 2
    dataNode:
      replicas: 3
    indexNode:
      replicas: 2
    queryNode:
      replicas: 3
  dependencies:
    msgStreamType: pulsar
```

The replica counts shown in the preceding code (2 for coordinators and proxies, 3 for data and query nodes) are recommended values for testing purposes. Production deployments may require higher replica counts based on data volume, query throughput, and availability requirements.

Deploy the cluster for reliability testing:

```
kubectl create namespace milvus-ha-test
kubectl apply -f milvus-ha.yaml
```

Wait for all Pods to start and run. Use `kubectl get pods -n milvus-ha-test` to check the status:

```
# kubectl get pods -n milvus-ha-test
NAME                                              READY   STATUS    RESTARTS   AGE
milvus-ha-demo-etcd-0                             1/1     Running   0
4m42s
milvus-ha-demo-milvus-mixcoord-756759f9d6-65qgl   1/1     Running   0
102s
milvus-ha-demo-milvus-mixcoord-756759f9d6-t4ltb   1/1     Running   0
102s
milvus-ha-demo-milvus-proxy-79f456cdfd-87qpp      1/1     Running   0
102s
milvus-ha-demo-milvus-querynode-0-59b755956c-846vq 1/1    Running   0
101s
milvus-ha-demo-milvus-datanode-699c7685d-m4cjr    1/1     Running   0
102s
# ... (additional etcd, minio, pulsar pods omitted for brevity)
```

The output shows key Milvus components running with multiple replicas. You should see two `mixcoord` Pods (Active-Standby), at least two `proxy` Pods, three `querynode` Pods, and three `datanode` Pods, along with the dependency services (`etcd`, `minio`, and `pulsar`).

To verify the cluster health status, run the following:

```
# kubectl get milvus
NAME             MODE      STATUS    UPDATED   AGE
milvus-ha-demo   cluster   Healthy   True      6m29s
```

The `Healthy` status confirms that all components are properly initialized and the cluster is ready for reliability testing.

The preceding configuration ensures that all dependent services (`etcd`, `minio`, and `pulsar`) are deployed in HA mode with multiple replicas and persistent storage, providing a robust foundation for reliability testing.

During reliability testing, focus on these specific metrics that indicate system health:

- **Error rates**: The failure rate of various operations (search, insert, etc.)
- **Component status**: The running status of each Milvus component
- **Message queue lag**: The consumption delay of Milvus' internal message queues (DML channel)
- **Data consistency**: Verification that inserted data is queryable and accurate
- **Recovery time**: How quickly the system recovers from component failures

For performance and resource utilization metrics, please refer to *Chapter 12*, where these are covered in detail.

Key Grafana monitoring panels for reliability testing

During reliability testing, focus on monitoring the following pre-configured Grafana panels to effectively observe the Milvus cluster health and failure recovery processes.

Some of the essential monitoring panels are shown in the following figure:

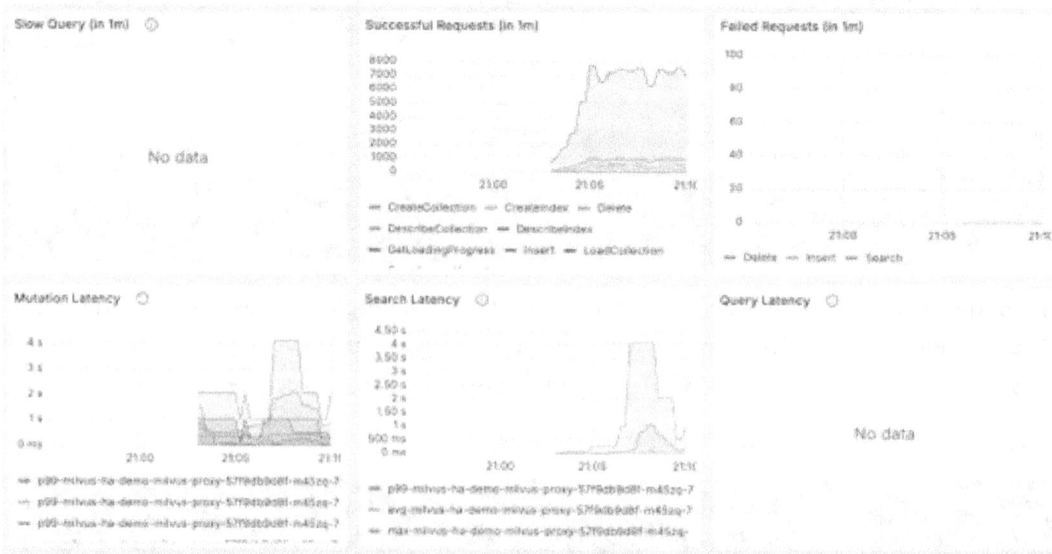

Figure 13.1: An overview of the Grafana dashboard showing the Successful Requests, Failed Requests, and various latency panels for Milvus reliability monitoring

The essential monitoring panels of the Grafana dashboard are as follows:

- **Successful Requests**: Displays successful request counts per minute for various operations, including `CreateCollection`, `CreateIndex`, `Insert`, `Search`, and `Query`
- **Failed Requests**: Shows failed request counts for different operations, helping identify when failures occur and their scope
- **Mutation Latency**: Displays `insert/delete/upsert` operation latency distribution (P99, average, and maximum) across different Proxy instances
- **Search Latency**: Displays search operation latency distribution (P99, average, and maximum) across different Proxy instances
- **Query Latency**: Monitors query operation latency metrics, providing key insights into system performance during various conditions

These metrics are especially critical during fault injection and failover testing, as they reveal exactly when and how failures propagate through the system, helping you distinguish between expected transient errors during recovery and actual system degradation.

Beyond request-level metrics, monitoring resource utilization across Milvus components is essential for identifying infrastructure bottlenecks and capacity issues:

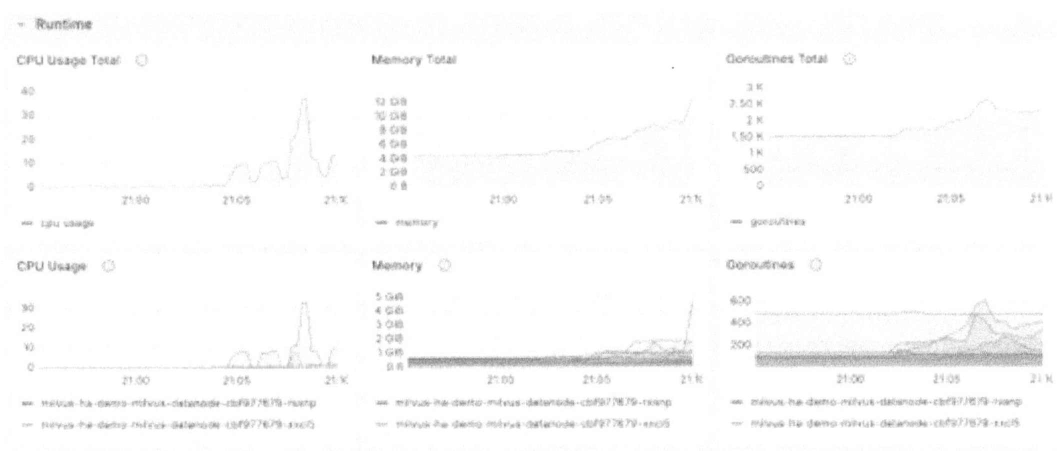

Figure 13.2: An overview of the resource utilization panels showing CPU and memory usage across Milvus components

The following are the resource utilization panels:

- **CPU Usage panel**: Shows CPU consumption across DataNode instances, helping identify computational resource utilization patterns
- **Memory Usage panel**: Tracks memory consumption patterns across components, which is important for detecting memory leaks and resource management issues

In addition to compute resources, understanding how data segments are distributed across nodes provides critical insight into cluster balance and recovery behavior:

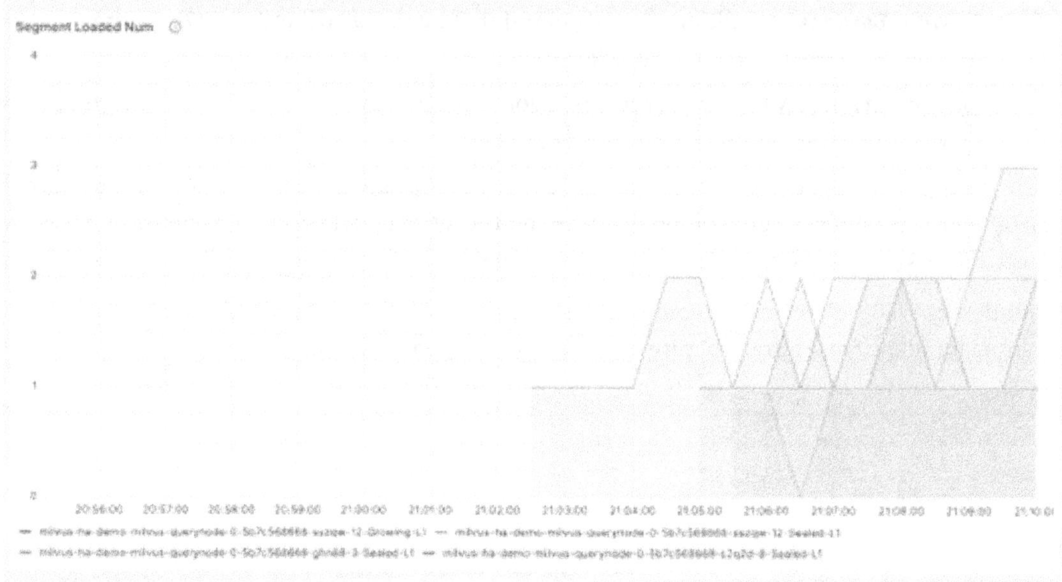

Figure 13.3: An overview of the Segment Loaded panel showing data segment distribution across QueryNodes

This panel displays the number of data segments loaded on QueryNodes, which is critical for understanding segment rebalancing.

Together, these three dashboards provide a comprehensive view of your Milvus cluster's health during reliability testing. By monitoring request patterns, resource utilization, and segment distribution simultaneously, you can quickly identify and diagnose issues as they arise.

How to interpret Grafana metrics for cluster health

Understanding what these metrics indicate about cluster health is essential for effective reliability testing. Here's a guide to interpreting key indicators:

Metric	Normal range	Warning signs	Possible causes
Successful requests	Stable, consistent rate	Sudden drops to zero	Component failure, network issues
Failed requests	Near zero (<0.1%)	Sustained failures >1%	Resource exhaustion, configuration errors
Search latency (P99)	<100 ms (typical)	>500 ms or increasing trend	Insufficient QueryNodes, large segments
Insert latency (P99)	<200 ms (typical)	>1,000 ms	DataNode bottleneck, storage issues
CPU usage	40–70%	>90% sustained	Need horizontal scaling
Memory usage	<80%	>90% or continuous growth	Memory leak, need more resources

Table 13.1: Key Grafana metrics and their normal ranges for Milvus cluster health monitoring

Here's a guide to interpreting the panels and other patterns and signs.

Reading the Successful/Failed Requests panel:

- A healthy cluster shows consistent "sawtooth" patterns in successful requests
- During fault injection tests, expect brief dips followed by recovery
- If search requests drop while insert continues normally, suspect QueryNode issues
- If both drop simultaneously, check Proxy or network connectivity

Detecting memory leaks:

- **Healthy pattern**: Stepwise increases followed by plateaus after garbage collection
- **Warning sign**: Continuous linear growth over 24+ hours without stabilization
- **Action**: Enable heap profiling and check for unreleased segments

By combining these panel-reading techniques with the metric thresholds defined previously, you can systematically assess cluster health and take proactive action before issues escalate. With this monitoring foundation in place, let's proceed to actively test the system under load.

Load testing for Milvus reliability

With our HA testing environment now configured and operational, we can proceed to the next crucial phase: subjecting Milvus to realistic load conditions. While the previous section focused on infrastructure setup, this section will guide you through actively stressing the system to uncover performance boundaries and potential weaknesses.

> **Note**
>
> The performance metrics, test results, and numerical data presented in this section are illustrative examples only. Actual results will vary based on your hardware configuration, data characteristics, index parameters, and workload patterns. Use these examples as a reference for designing your own tests rather than as expected benchmarks.

Load testing simulates real-world traffic to identify performance bottlenecks, memory leaks, and scalability limits before they impact production. For Milvus, this is especially important given the computational intensity of vector similarity searches. Beyond basic load testing, long-term running (soak tests), complex mixed workloads, and high-concurrency scenarios are essential for comprehensive reliability evaluation.

For load testing Milvus, we'll use **Locust**, an open source load-testing tool based on Python. For detailed installation and basic usage instructions of Locust, please refer to *Chapter 12*.

Locust allows you to define user behavior using Python code, making it very suitable for testing PyMilvus applications. We'll demonstrate how to use Locust for Milvus reliability testing in the upcoming sections.

First, let's learn how to design load scenarios.

Designing load scenarios

Effective load testing requires carefully designed scenarios that mirror real-world usage patterns. Let's explore how to design comprehensive load scenarios using a practical example.

Example scenario: e-commerce product recommendation system

Consider an e-commerce platform that uses Milvus to power product recommendations. The system stores product embeddings and performs similarity searches to suggest relevant items to users.

The first step is to determine the correct operation mix.

Operation mix refers to the proportional distribution of different operation types (search, insert, update, and delete) that your load test should simulate. A well-designed operation mix accurately reflects your application's real-world usage patterns, ensuring that test results are representative of actual production behavior.

To determine the appropriate operation mix, analyze your application's typical usage patterns through production logs, monitoring data, or business requirements. The following are key factors to consider:

- **Peak versus off-peak hours**: During sales events, search queries might increase 10x while product insertions remain constant
- **User behavior patterns**: E-commerce platforms typically see 90–95% read operations (searches) and 5–10% write operations (new product insertions)
- **Business operations**: Product catalog updates happen in batches, usually during low-traffic periods

For our e-commerce example, a representative load scenario might include the following:

- 80% similarity searches (users browsing products)
- 10% batch insertions (new products being added)
- 5% metadata updates (product information changes)
- 5% deletion of products

Next is designing search complexity.

Search design involves planning the variety and complexity of search operations that your load test should include. This ensures your tests cover the full range of queries that your application will face in production. Key design considerations include the following:

- **Filter complexity**: Simple equality filters are faster than range queries or complex Boolean expressions
- **Result set size**: Larger `limit` values increase memory and network overhead
- **Batch queries**: Multiple vectors in a single search (`nq > 1`) test throughput differently than single-vector queries
- **Index utilization**: Different filter patterns may bypass or utilize indexes differently

Design searches that reflect real-world complexity. The following code snippets illustrate a few examples:

- **Simple searches**:

```
# Basic similarity search - most common operation
client.search(
    collection_name="ecommerce_products",
    data=[search_vector],
    anns_field="embedding",
    search_params={"metric_type": "COSINE"},
    limit=10
)
```

- **Filtered searches**:

```
# Price range filter - common in e-commerce
client.search(
    collection_name="ecommerce_products",
    data=[search_vector],
    anns_field="embedding",
    search_params={"metric_type": "COSINE"},
    limit=10,
    filter="price >= 50 and price <= 200"
)
```

- **Complex filtered searches**:

```
# Multi-attribute filter - high complexity
client.search(
    collection_name="ecommerce_products",
    data=[search_vector],
    anns_field="embedding",
    search_params={"metric_type": "COSINE"},
    limit=20,
    filter="category in ['electronics', 'home'] and price < 500 and rating
> 4.0 and in_stock == true"
)
```

Next up is simulating data scale. Plan your data scale progression:

- **Phase 1: Baseline (1M vectors)**: Start with 1 million product vectors to establish baseline performance metrics. At this scale, you should measure the QPS, P99 latency, and resource utilization under normal operating conditions. For our e-commerce example, this represents a small catalog with essential products. Document these baseline metrics as they will serve as reference points for later phases.
- **Phase 2: Growth simulation (10M vectors)**: Increase the data volume to 10 million vectors to test how index performance scales with data growth. Monitor memory usage patterns closely—HNSW indexes grow linearly with data size. For the e-commerce scenario, this simulates a mid-sized catalog including all product variants. Observe whether search latency increases proportionally or whether there are sudden performance cliffs.
- **Phase 3: Production scale (100M+ vectors)**: Scale to your target production volume (100M+ vectors) to validate performance at full scale and identify system limits. For our e-commerce platform, this represents a comprehensive product catalog including historical items. Test beyond your expected peak to find the breaking point where performance degrades unacceptably.

Then comes simulating concurrent clients. Design concurrency patterns that match real usage:

- **Gradual ramp-up**:
  - Start with 10 concurrent users
  - Increase by 10 users every 30 seconds
  - Monitor system response and identify breaking points
- **Burst traffic simulation**:
  - Simulate flash sales or viral events
  - Look out for sudden spikes from 50 to 500 concurrent users
  - Test system resilience
- **Sustained load**:
  - Maintain a steady rate of 200–300 concurrent users
  - Run for 2–4 hours to identify memory leaks
  - Monitor long-term stability

By following this systematic approach, you can design load scenarios that accurately reflect your application's requirements and identify potential issues before they impact production systems.

Executing load tests

Once you have designed your load scenarios, the next step is to execute them systematically. Proper execution involves careful preparation, monitoring during the test, and thorough analysis of the results. This section will guide you through implementing a comprehensive load test using Locust, from initial setup to interpreting the results. We'll build upon the e-commerce example from the previous section to create a complete, runnable load test that demonstrates how to validate Milvus' performance under realistic conditions.

Step 1: preparing test data

Create a script to generate representative test data that matches your production data characteristics. For our e-commerce scenario, this would include product vectors with realistic metadata such as categories, prices, ratings, and stock status. Use tools such as the Faker library for generating realistic test data, or extract a representative sample from your actual dataset if available.

Step 2: writing load scripts with Locust

Create a comprehensive load-testing script using Locust. First, install the required dependencies:

```
pip install locust>=2.17.0 pymilvus>=2.5.0 faker numpy pandas
```

Starting from Locust `2.17.0`, there's official Milvus integration available via `locust.contrib.milvus`. This eliminates the need to write custom client wrappers. The `MilvusUser` class handles connection management, response time tracking, and Locust event firing automatically.

The key classes provided by `locust.contrib.milvus` are the following:

- `MilvusUser`: Base class for Milvus load tests. Automatically tracks performance metrics for all operations (`insert`, `search`, `query`, `delete`, and `upsert`).
- `MilvusV2Client`: Internal client wrapper that measures response times and reports them to Locust.

Create a file, `milvus_load_test.py`, with the following structure:

```
from locust import task, between, events, LoadTestShape
from locust.contrib.milvus import MilvusUser  # Official Locust Milvus integration
from pymilvus import MilvusClient
import numpy as np
import random
```

```
class EcommerceUser(MilvusUser):
    """E-commerce user simulating realistic product recommendation workload.

    Operation mix: 80% searches, 10% inserts, 5% upserts, 5% deletes
    Task weights control frequency: @task(80) = 8x more likely than @task(10)
    """
    wait_time = between(0.1, 1.0)

    def __init__(self, environment):
        super().__init__(
            environment=environment,
            uri=environment.host or "http://localhost:19530",
            collection_name="ecommerce_products",
            token="root:Milvus"
        )
        self.dim = 768

    @task(80)  # 80% - Similarity searches
    def search_similar_products(self):
        query_vector = np.random.rand(self.dim).astype(np.float32).tolist()
        self.search(data=[query_vector], anns_field="embedding", limit=10)

    @task(10)  # 10% - Batch insertions
    def batch_insert_products(self):
        products = self._generate_product_data(random.choice([10, 50, 100]))
        self.insert(products)

    @task(5)  # 5% - Product updates
    def upsert_products(self):
        # Implementation in GitHub repository
        pass

    @task(5)  # 5% - Delete products
    def delete_out_of_stock(self):
        self.delete(filter="in_stock == false and rating < 3.5")
```

Note

The full implementation, including collection setup, data generation helpers, and filtered search examples, is available in this book's GitHub repository.

Step 3: writing your own custom load shape

Execute the load test with a gradual ramp-up starting from a low user count and gradually increasing to identify breaking points. Monitor key Milvus metrics during testing using a Grafana dashboard, track system resource utilization and response times, and observe how the system behaves under increasing load:

```
class StagesLoadShape(LoadTestShape):
    """Custom load shape simulating different traffic patterns."""

    stages = [
        # Phase 1: Gradual ramp-up (0-3 min)
        {"duration": 60, "users": 20, "spawn_rate": 2},
        {"duration": 180, "users": 100, "spawn_rate": 5},
        # Phase 2: Sustained load (3-10 min)
        {"duration": 600, "users": 200, "spawn_rate": 10},
        # Phase 3: Burst traffic simulation (10-12 min)
        {"duration": 630, "users": 500, "spawn_rate": 50},
        # Phase 4: Cool down (12-15 min)
        {"duration": 900, "users": 10, "spawn_rate": 5},
    ]

    def tick(self):
        run_time = self.get_run_time()
        for stage in self.stages:
            if run_time < stage["duration"]:
                return (stage["users"], stage["spawn_rate"])
        return None
```

To execute comprehensive load testing, run the following:

```
# Run the load test
locust -f milvus_load_test.py --host=http://localhost:19530 -headless
```

Next, we will analyze the results.

Analyzing the results and deriving action items

After running the load test, systematically analyze the results by examining response time patterns, identifying performance bottlenecks, calculating error rates and their causes, comparing results against your performance targets, and generating specific recommendations for improvement.

The following is a sample analysis from our e-commerce scenario test:

Load level	QPS	P99 latency	Error rate	CPU	Memory	Observation
50 users	285	48 ms	0.01%	45%	62%	Baseline: stable
100 users	310	52 ms	0.02%	55%	65%	Slight increase: normal
200 users	295	78 ms	0.05%	72%	71%	Latency increasing
300 users	245	156 ms	0.8%	89%	78%	Performance degradation
400 users	180	420 ms	3.2%	95%	85%	Critical – bottleneck

Table 13.2: A tabular representation of the analysis from our e-commerce scenario test

Next, we will do a bottleneck analysis:

- **Performance degradation point**: At 300 concurrent users, QPS dropped 16% while P99 latency tripled. This indicates that the system is reaching its capacity.
- **Root cause identification**: CPU usage at 89% suggests a compute-bound bottleneck. QueryNode is likely the constraint, as complex filtered searches are CPU-intensive.
- **Error rate spike**: The jump from 0.05% to 0.8% at 300 users indicates timeout-related failures, not data errors.

Based on the analysis, the recommended action items, prioritized using severity levels, are P0 (critical, immediate action required), P1 (important, address in current cycle), and P2 (monitor, address if confirmed). Let's take a closer look:

- **P0: CPU bottleneck at QueryNode**: Add two QueryNode replicas to support 400+ users
- **P1: Latency spike with complex filters**: Optimize filter field indexing for 30% latency reduction
- **P2: Memory growth trend**: Monitor with 24-hour soak tests to identify potential leaks

Let's now shift our focus to the soak test.

Long-term running (soak) test

While our previous load tests focused on immediate performance under varying conditions, we must also consider how Milvus behaves over extended periods. Many reliability issues only manifest after hours or days of continuous operation, making long-term testing an essential complement to our short-duration load tests.

Long-term running tests aim to evaluate Milvus' performance under sustained operation and stable load for an extended period. These tests help uncover issues that are difficult to expose in short-term tests, such as memory leaks, gradual resource exhaustion, or performance degradation after long-term operation.

Methods and goals

Long-term running tests require careful planning to simulate realistic production conditions over extended periods. The following elements are essential for conducting effective soak tests:

- **Workload profile**: Define a continuous workload that simulates typical production environment usage patterns, including data ingestion (insert or update), search, query, and periodic data deletion or index management operations. Ensure the proportion of various operations matches reality.
- **Test duration**: The test should last for a considerable time, typically at least 24–72 hours. To detect potential issues more comprehensively, it may need to run for several days or even weeks. The extended duration is critical because many reliability issues only manifest after prolonged operation—for example, small memory leaks that accumulate over time, cache inefficiencies that worsen with data growth, or connection pool exhaustion that occurs after thousands of connection cycles. Some race conditions or deadlock scenarios may only appear after specific sequences of operations that take hours or days to occur naturally.

The key goals of the soak test include the following:

- **Memory leak detection**: Identify whether the memory usage of any Milvus component or dependent service continuously grows over time and is unstable
- **Resource exhaustion**: Determine whether the system experiences exhaustion of resources such as CPU, disk space, file descriptors, or network bandwidth under long-term operation
- **Performance degradation**: Observe whether key performance metrics (QPS, query latency, or ingestion rate) gradually worsen over time

- **Stability issues**: Discover crashes, hangs, or increased error rates that only appear after long-term operation
- **Race conditions/deadlocks**: Identify subtle concurrency issues that may arise after long-term operation and the accumulation of a large number of operations

E-commerce soak test scenario

For our e-commerce recommendation system, the soak test simulates 24–72 hours of continuous operation with realistic traffic patterns:

- **0–6 h (night, low traffic)**: 50 users with 90% search, 10% batch insert
- **6–12 h (morning ramp-up)**: 100 to 200 users with 85% search, 10% insert, 5% update
- **12–18 h (peak hours)**: 200 users with 80% search, 15% insert, 5% delete
- **18–24 h (evening decline)**: 200 down to 50 users with 85% search, 10% insert, 5% update

For monitoring checkpoints, record metrics at regular intervals to track trends. For example, in a typical 24-hour soak test, you might observe memory growing from 8.2 GB (baseline) to 9.5 GB (+16%) while QPS slightly decreases from 250 to 235 and P99 latency increases from 52 ms to 72 ms. If memory grows more than 20% over 24 hours without stabilization, investigate potential memory leaks in QueryNode segment management.

Let's now look at the soak test implementation example. Create a comprehensive soak test script, `milvus_soak_test.py`:

```
class SoakTestLoadShape(LoadTestShape):
    """
    Long running soak test - adjust duration as needed:
    - 24 hours: 60*60*24 (for basic soak testing)
    - 7 days: 60*60*24*7 (for comprehensive testing)
    """

    stages = [
        {"duration": 60*60*24, "users": 200, "spawn_rate": 10},  # 24 hours
    ]

    def tick(self):
        run_time = self.get_run_time()
        for stage in self.stages:
            if run_time < stage["duration"]:
                return (stage["users"], stage["spawn_rate"])
        return None
```

To execute the soak test, run the following command:

```
locust -f milvus_soak_test.py --host=http://localhost:19530 --headless
```

Soak testing reveals issues invisible in short-duration tests. Watch for gradual memory growth indicating leaks, increasing P99 latency suggesting resource exhaustion, and rising error rates that may signal connection pool depletion or segment management issues over time.

Having examined Milvus' behavior under sustained load through soak testing, we now need to evaluate its performance under more diverse and complex operational patterns.

Complex workload testing simulating real-world scenarios

Real-world applications rarely generate uniform workloads; instead, they present a mix of operations with varying complexity and resource demands.

In addition to continuous load, it is also very important to test Milvus' behavior under diverse and complex operations that simulate real application scenarios.

Design test cases to stress test different Milvus functionalities simultaneously:

- **Concurrent data operations**:
  - **Batch insert**: Simulate adding a large number of vectors at once.
  - **Streaming insert**: Continuously ingest small batches or individual vectors.
  - **Upserts**: Modify existing vectors or insert new ones if they do not exist.
  - **Delete**: Delete vectors by ID or using metadata filter expressions. Test the impact of large-scale deletions on subsequent search performance and accuracy and observe the behavior of compaction.
- **Diverse search and query operations**:
  - Execute searches with or without metadata filtering. The complexity of filter conditions should be varied, from simple equality checks to complex Boolean expressions involving multiple fields and range queries.
  - Change the `limit` (number of results returned) and `nq` (number of query vectors in batch search) parameters to evaluate performance under different retrieval requirements.
  - Perform search tests on collections using different index types (`HNSW`, `IVF_FLAT`, and `DiskANN`) and different index parameters (such as `efConstruction`, `M` for `HNSW`, and `nlist` for `IVF_FLAT`).

- **Dynamic collection and index management**:
    - Perform operations to create and delete collections or partitions while performing regular read and write operations
    - Build or delete indexes on collections that are currently being queried and updated
    - Load and release collections/partitions to/from memory and observe the impact on query availability and latency
- **Flush and compaction**: Although these are automatic background processes in Milvus, there are manual trigger APIs or configurations to adjust their frequency. You can test the system's behavior under frontend load while these potentially resource-intensive background tasks are running. Observe whether flush or compaction operations significantly reduce query performance or ingestion rate.

Another important aspect of a reliable system is its ability to recover from failures. Let's talk about this next.

Simulating Milvus component failures and verifying recovery

Up to this point, we've tested Milvus under various load conditions while all components remained healthy. However, true reliability testing must go beyond normal operations to examine how the system responds when things go wrong. This section focuses on deliberately introducing failures to validate Milvus' resilience and recovery mechanisms.

Testing Milvus' fault tolerance is a key part of reliability testing. We will simulate failures of various Milvus components using Chaos Mesh. PodChaos experiments and observes how the system automatically recovers.

Prerequisites: installing Chaos Mesh

Chaos Mesh is an open source cloud-native chaos engineering platform for Kubernetes. It enables you to simulate various types of faults, such as Pod failures, network delays, and I/O errors, in a controlled and declarative manner, making it ideal for testing distributed system resilience.

Before proceeding with component failure simulation, install Chaos Mesh in your Kubernetes testing environment:

```
# Add Chaos Mesh Helm repository
helm repo add chaos-mesh https://charts.chaos-mesh.org
helm repo update
```

```
# Create namespace for Chaos Mesh
kubectl create namespace chaos-testing

# Install Chaos Mesh (adjust socketPath according to your container runtime)
helm install chaos-mesh chaos-mesh/chaos-mesh -n chaos-testing \
  --set chaosDaemon.runtime=containerd \
  --set chaosDaemon.socketPath=/run/containerd/containerd.sock

# For Docker runtime, use:
# helm install chaos-mesh chaos-mesh/chaos-mesh -n chaos-testing \
#   --set chaosDaemon.runtime=docker \
#   --set chaosDaemon.socketPath=/var/run/docker.sock

# Verify installation
kubectl get pods -n chaos-testing
```

Wait for all Chaos Mesh components to be running before proceeding with the experiments.

Simulating active MixCoord failure

Active-Standby is the HA deployment mode for Milvus coordinators. The `MixCoord` component (which consolidates `RootCoord`, `QueryCoord`, `DataCoord`, and `IndexCoord`) uses the Active-Standby pattern described next for automatic failover.

In this section, we will deliberately kill the Active `MixCoord` Pod and verify that a Standby node automatically takes over coordination responsibilities, ensuring continuous service availability.

The HA of `MixCoord` is based on the Active-Standby mode, with the following workflow:

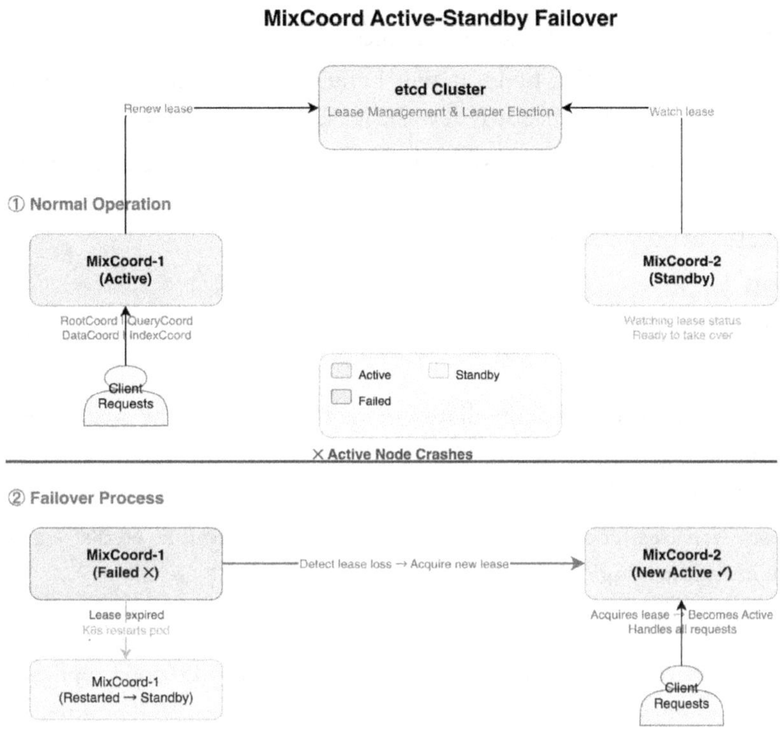

Figure 13.4: MixCoord Active-Standby failover mechanism showing normal operation and automatic recovery process

Let's look at the workflow in detail:

1. **Startup and registration**: When multiple `MixCoord` instances are deployed, they start simultaneously. Each instance registers its server ID with etcd (a distributed key-value store system used for service discovery and state synchronization).
2. **Leader competition**: After registration, these `MixCoord` instances compete for the Active role by attempting to write a specific key (lease) to etcd. This is an atomic operation where only one instance can succeed.

3. **Role assignment**:
   - **Active node**: The `MixCoord` instance that successfully acquires the etcd lease becomes the Active node. It will handle all coordination tasks, serve external requests, and periodically renew the lease to maintain its Active status.
   - **Standby nodes**: Other instances that fail to acquire the lease enter the Standby state. They do not process business requests but continuously watch the lease status of the Active node.
4. **Failover**:
   - If the Active node crashes or loses connection to etcd, its lease will expire or be released.
   - The standby nodes immediately detect the loss of the Active lease and begin competing again. The first Standby node to acquire the new lease becomes the new Active node and takes over service.

This mechanism ensures coordinator service continuity through etcd's lease and watch functionality, eliminating single points of failure.

Test steps

Ensure your testing environment is configured with multiple `MixCoord` replicas (refer to the `milvus-ha.yaml` configuration in the *Configuring Milvus for high-availability testing* section):

```
spec:
  mode: cluster
  config:
    mixCoord:
      enableActiveStandby: true
```

Before running the chaos experiment, find an active `MixCoord`. You need to identify which `mixcoord` instance is currently active. Check the logs of both `MixCoord` Pods to determine their current roles:

```
# Check logs of all mixcoord pods to identify active/standby status
kubectl logs -f -l app.kubernetes.io/component=mixcoord -n milvus-ha-test | grep -
E "(STANDBY|ACTIVE)"
```

You should see log entries similar to the following:

```
[2025/07/14 14:49:15.725 +00:00] [INFO] [sessionutil/session_util.go:1098]
["serverName: rootcoord enter STANDBY mode"]
```

```
[2025/07/14 14:49:15.725 +00:00] [INFO] [sessionutil/session_util.go:1098]
["serverName: querycoord enter STANDBY mode"]
[2025/07/16 15:39:52.843 +00:00] [INFO] [sessionutil/session_util.go:1143]
["serverName: rootcoord quit STANDBY mode, this node will become ACTIVE, ID: 10"]
[2025/07/16 15:39:52.926 +00:00] [INFO] [sessionutil/session_util.go:1143]
["serverName: datacoord quit STANDBY mode, this node will become ACTIVE, ID: 10"]
```

To identify the specific active `MixCoord` Pod, check individual Pod logs:

```
# Get all mixcoord pod names
kubectl get pods -n milvus-ha-test -l app.kubernetes.io/component=mixcoord

# Check individual pod logs for active status
kubectl logs milvus-ha-demo-milvus-mixcoord-756759f9d6-65qgl -n milvus-ha-test |
grep -E "(STANDBY|ACTIVE|quit.*mode)" | tail -5
kubectl logs milvus-ha-demo-milvus-mixcoord-756759f9d6-t4ltb -n milvus-ha-test |
grep -E "(STANDBY|ACTIVE|quit.*mode)" | tail -5
```

The Pod showing `"quit STANDBY mode, this node will become ACTIVE"` messages for all coordinator services (`rootcoord`, `querycoord`, `datacoord`, and `indexcoord`) is the current active `MixCoord` instance. Update the `mixcoord_pod_kill.yaml` file with the active Pod's name before applying the chaos experiment.

Run continuous load testing and simulate active `MixCoord` Pod failure using Chaos Mesh `PodChaos`:

```
apiVersion: chaos-mesh.org/v1alpha1
kind: PodChaos
metadata:
  name: active-mixcoord-pod-kill
  namespace: milvus-ha-test
spec:
  action: pod-kill
  mode: one
  selector:
    pods:
      milvus-ha-test:
        - milvus-ha-demo-milvus-mixcoord-756759f9d6-5xzgw  # replace with active
mixcoord pod name
  gracePeriod: 0
```

Apply the chaos experiment:

```
kubectl apply -f mixcoord_pod_kill.yaml
```

Observe failover, that is, the standby-to-active transition, Pod restart, and new standby registration, by monitoring the logs:

```
# Monitor which mixcoord becomes active after the failure
kubectl logs -f -l app.kubernetes.io/component=mixcoord -n milvus-ha-test | grep
STANDBY
```

Finally, monitor errors/latency changes in load testing during the experiment.

Verification points

Monitor these key metrics during coordinator failure tests:

- **Recovery time objective (RTO)**: Expected <10 seconds; if >20 seconds, this indicates system defects
- **Service disruption**: Expected near-zero errors; watch for significant error rates or latency spikes
- **Automatic recovery**: Expected seamless HA restoration; warning signs include manual intervention required or split-brain scenarios

If issues occur, investigate the etcd lease mechanism, leader election logic, coordinator state synchronization, and service discovery mechanisms.

Simulating worker node failure

Worker nodes (QueryNode, DataNode, and IndexNode) are responsible for actual data processing. They are usually deployed with multiple replicas to share the load and provide redundancy.

> **Note**
>
> In this section, we will primarily use QueryNode as an example to demonstrate worker node failure simulation and recovery testing. QueryNode is responsible for executing vector searches and queries, making it a critical component for read operations. We'll also test Milvus' WAL mechanism to ensure data durability during node failures.

Understanding the Milvus WAL mechanism

WAL is a fundamental technique used by databases to ensure data durability and consistency. In Milvus, the WAL mechanism leverages message queues (Pulsar or Kafka) to create a persistent, ordered log of all data modifications. When you insert or delete vectors, Milvus first writes these operations to the message queue before processing them, ensuring that even if a node crashes immediately after accepting the write, the operation is already safely persisted.

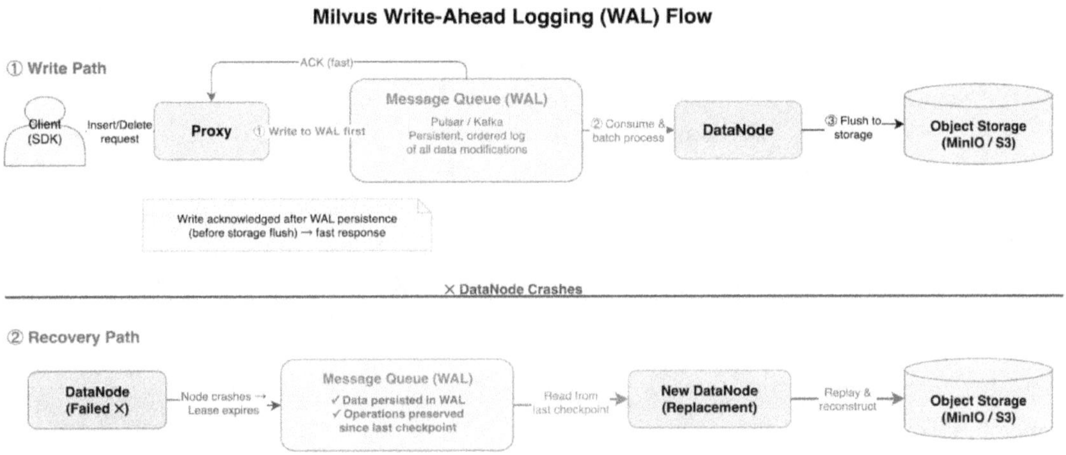

Figure 13.5: Milvus WAL flow showing the write path and recovery mechanism

This approach decouples the acknowledgment of write operations from the actual data storage, allowing Milvus to respond quickly to clients while data nodes asynchronously consume messages from the queue and batch-write them to object storage (MinIO/S3).

The sequential nature of the WAL provides powerful recovery capabilities. If a data node fails, a new node can read the WAL from the last checkpoint and replay all subsequent operations to reconstruct the exact state, ensuring no committed data is lost.

Test steps

Ensure your testing environment is configured with multiple QueryNode replicas (minimum of three replicas recommended for meaningful failure testing)

Simulate QueryNode failure using Chaos Mesh `PodChaos`

The following is example code:

```
apiVersion: chaos-mesh.org/v1alpha1
kind: PodChaos
metadata:
```

```
  name: one-querynode-pod-kill
  namespace: milvus-ha-test
spec:
  action: pod-kill
  mode: fixed
  value: "1"  # Kill 1 QueryNode
  selector:
    namespaces:
      - milvus-ha-test
    labelSelectors:
      app.kubernetes.io/instance: milvus-ha-demo
      app.kubernetes.io/component: querynode
  gracePeriod: 0
```

Note

To test multiple QueryNode failures simultaneously, change `value: "1"` to `value: "2"` or higher in the preceding YAML.

Apply the chaos experiment:

```
kubectl apply -f one_querynode_pod_kill.yaml
```

Observe how Milvus detects the QueryNode failure and reallocates the workload:

```
# Monitor QueryNode pods status
kubectl get pods -n milvus-ha-test -l app.kubernetes.io/component=querynode -w
```

During the failure and after recovery, continuously run insertion and search loads and observe the changes in QPS, latency, and error rate.

Next up, we will test the data durability.

Testing WAL data durability

To verify WAL durability, follow this three-phase test:

- **Setup**: Insert 100K records, delete 10K, and upsert 10K. Save the expected state locally.
- **Trigger failure**: Run `kubectl apply -f one_querynode_pod_kill.yaml` during operations.
- **Verify**: After recovery, compare the Milvus data against the saved state.

Here is an example code snippet:

```
from pymilvus import MilvusClient
import pandas as pd

client = MilvusClient(uri="http://localhost:19530", token="root:Milvus")

# After recovery, verify data integrity
df = pd.read_parquet("milvus_wal_test_data.parquet")  # Saved during setup
res = client.query(
    "ecommerce_products", filter="", output_fields=["count(*)"])
assert res[0]["count(*)"] == len(df), "Record count mismatch - WAL failure!"
print("WAL durability test passed!")
```

With WAL durability validated, let's examine the key verification points to monitor during QueryNode failure scenarios.

Verification points for QueryNode failure

Monitor these key metrics during QueryNode failure tests:

- **Failure detection**: Expected <30 seconds; delayed detection indicates `QueryCoord` issues
- **Segment reallocation**: Expected 2–3 minutes; prolonged reallocation suggests capacity issues
- **Search performance**: Expected 50–100% latency increase during recovery; >300% increase or complete failures is a warning sign
- **Service availability**: Expected <10 seconds interruption; a complete service outage is a warning sign
- **Data consistency**: Expected identical results before/after; missing data indicates WAL issues
- **WAL durability**: Expected 100% data recovery (RPO ≈ 0); data loss suggests WAL mechanism failures

Example test output

Here's what a successful QueryNode failure test looks like for an e-commerce recommendation system:

```
=== QueryNode Failure Test Results ===
Test Environment: 3 QueryNode replicas, 100K product embeddings
```

```
Timeline:
14:23:45 - Pod killed: milvus-ha-demo-milvus-querynode-0-59b755956c-846vq
14:23:47 - Error rate spike: 12% (search requests failing)
14:23:52 - Segment reallocation started by QueryCoord
14:24:10 - Service restored (25 seconds RTO)
14:24:15 - Error rate normalized to 0.01%

Metrics Summary:
- Search QPS: 285 -> 245 (-14%) -> 282
- P99 Latency: 48ms -> 89ms (+85%) -> 51ms
- Error Rate: 0.01% -> 12% -> 0.01%
- Segment Distribution: 33/33/34 -> 0/50/50 -> 33/34/33

WAL Durability Check:
- Records before failure: 100,000
- Records after recovery: 100,000
- Data integrity check: PASSED

Verdict: PASSED
- RTO (25s) < target (30s)
- Zero data loss
- Service remained available
```

Having validated both component resilience and data durability through WAL testing, we have comprehensively tested Milvus' fault tolerance capabilities.

Summary

In this chapter, we explored comprehensive stability and reliability testing for Milvus vector databases. We learned how to quantify stability through performance consistency, error rates, and resource utilization metrics, while measuring reliability through data durability, availability percentages, and fault recovery rates. We covered setting up HA deployments using Milvus Operator, designing realistic load scenarios that mirror production workloads, and systematically testing component failures using Chaos Mesh PodChaos experiments to validate automatic recovery mechanisms. We also examined and tested Milvus' WAL mechanism to ensure data persistence during node failures. These testing practices provide a foundation for validating that your Milvus deployment can maintain both stable performance under pressure and reliable operation in the face of failures.

Remember that reliability testing should be an ongoing practice integrated into your deployment pipeline, not a one-time exercise; as your data grows and workloads evolve, continuous validation ensures your system remains resilient.

In the next chapter, we'll explore how to scale Milvus to handle growing data volumes and increasing query loads through vertical and horizontal scaling strategies, ensuring your system can grow seamlessly with your application's demands.

Get this book's PDF version and more

Scan the QR code (or go to `packtpub.com/unlock`). Search for this book by name, confirm the edition, and then follow the steps on the page.

UNLOCK NOW

Note: Have your invoice handy. Purchases made directly from the Packt website don't require an invoice.

14

Scalability Evaluation for the Milvus Vector Database

In today's data-driven world, AI applications often start with manageable datasets but can quickly grow to handle millions, or even billions, of vectors. Scalability is not just a feature; it's a fundamental requirement. A scalable Milvus deployment ensures that as your data volume and user traffic increase, your system can adapt without performance degradation. This means maintaining fast search responses, low latency, and high throughput, which are crucial for a positive user experience and the overall effectiveness of your AI application. Without effective scalability, applications can become slow, unresponsive, and ultimately fail to meet business or user needs as they grow. Furthermore, a scalable system allows for better resource planning and cost management, as you can incrementally add resources only when needed. We will start by understanding its design philosophy and gradually master the principles and applicable scenarios of its two core strategies: vertical and horizontal scaling. More importantly, through detailed hands-on labs combined with fundamental testing methodologies, we will demonstrate how to effectively scale your Milvus cluster in a Kubernetes environment using the Milvus Operator. This will ensure that your Milvus system can continue to operate efficiently as your data volume grows and search pressure increases.

This chapter will serve as your practical guide to exploring the scalability features of Milvus. In this chapter, we will cover the following main topics:

- Scaling strategies in Milvus
- Introducing scalability testing methodology
- Hands-on lab: vertical scaling with testing methodology
- Hands-on lab: horizontal scaling (performance improvement type)

- Hands-on lab: capacity improvement testing with methodology
- Using scaling to resolve Milvus performance bottlenecks

Technical requirements

To better understand and practice the content of this chapter, it is recommended that you have the following foundational knowledge and environmental preparations:

- **Kubernetes (K8s) basics**: Familiarity with core Kubernetes concepts like Pods, Deployments, Services, Namespaces, and basic kubectl operational skills.
- **Preliminary understanding of Milvus**: A basic understanding of Milvus' fundamental functions, core components (e.g., Proxy, QueryNode, DataNode, IndexNode), and their purposes. Knowledge of what vectors and vector indexes are, and Milvus' main application scenarios.
- **Experimental environment**: Access to a functional Kubernetes cluster with Milvus Operator installed. If you plan to conduct actual performance tests, you will also need the appropriate testing tools and datasets.

The code used in this chapter can be found in our GitHub repository: `https://github.com/PacktPublishing/The-Architecture-Handbook-for-Milvus-Vector-Database`

Scaling strategies in Milvus

When your Milvus cluster needs to handle a growing volume of data or higher concurrent search requests, enhancing the system's overall processing capability becomes crucial. Milvus primarily supports two scaling strategies:

- **Vertical scaling (scale-up)**: Think of this as making a single worker stronger, such as upgrading from a regular computer to a more powerful one.
- **Horizontal scaling (scale-out)**: Think of this as hiring more workers, such as in adding more computers to share the workload.

The following figure makes the concepts of scaling clearer:

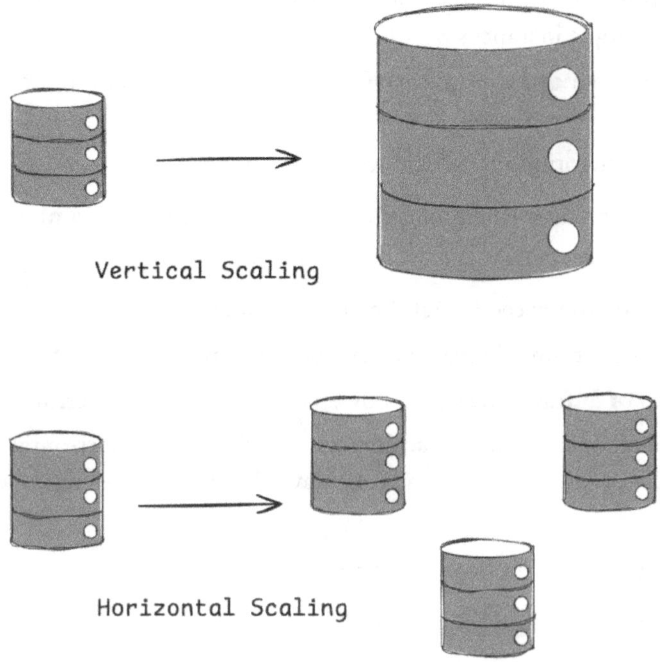

Figure 14.1: Scaling strategies in Milvus

Let's explore each approach with practical examples.

Vertical scaling (scale-up)

Vertical scaling is like upgrading your computer's RAM from 8GB to 16GB or replacing a dual-core processor with a quad-core one. In Milvus terms, it means giving more resources to a single component.

What does this mean in practice?

- Increasing CPU cores: From 2 cores to 4 cores → Faster search processing
- Adding memory: From 8GB to 16GB → Can load more data in memory
- Upgrading storage: To faster SSDs → Load data more quickly in memory

When should we use vertical scaling?

Vertical scaling is typically considered in the following situations:

- **Resource bottleneck**: Your monitoring shows a component (e.g., QueryNode) is using 90%+ of its CPU or memory

- **Quick fix needed**: You need a modest performance boost without the complexity of managing multiple instances
- **Latency-sensitive apps**: Applications where every millisecond counts, and the host machine has spare resources

The following are the limitations of vertical scaling:

1. **The hardware ceiling**: Every machine has limits. In cloud environments:
   - AWS EC2: Largest instance has 448 vCPUs and 12 TB of memory
   - Your Pod can't exceed what the host machine offers
   - Once you hit these limits, vertical scaling stops being an option
2. **Single point of failure**: One super-powered component = one critical failure point

These inherent limitations of vertical scaling are precisely why horizontal scaling is Milvus' preferred strategy for production workloads, as it avoids hardware ceilings and provides built-in redundancy.

Let's now turn our attention to horizontal scaling.

Horizontal scaling (scale-out)

Horizontal scaling is like hiring more employees to handle an increased workload. Instead of making one worker do everything faster, you distribute the work among multiple workers.

Real-world analogy: If one cashier can serve 20 customers per hour, adding three more cashiers allows you to serve 80 customers per hour (assuming ideal conditions).

In Milvus:

- 2 QueryNodes → 4 QueryNodes = Double the search processing capacity
- Each node handles a portion of the total workload
- Built-in load balancing ensures even distribution

This is Milvus' **primary scaling strategy** for handling large-scale workloads. The architecture is specifically designed for this approach.

> Note
>
> Coordinator services (RootCoord, QueryCoord) use active-standby for high availability, not horizontal scaling for load distribution.

Worker nodes and their scaling benefits

Milvus' modular design lets you scale specific components based on your bottlenecks:

Component	What it does	Scaling benefit
Proxy	Entry point for client requests	More concurrent connections, better request distribution
DataNode	Handles data writes and deletions	Higher write throughput, faster data ingestion
IndexNode	Builds vector indexes	Faster index creation, improved search performance on indexed segments
QueryNode	Executes searches and queries	Most common scaling target: Higher QPS, lower latency

Table 14.1: Scaling benefits of worker nodes

As an example, for a recommendation system with 1,000 QPS, scaling QueryNodes from 2 to 4 can potentially double your search capacity.

Making the right scaling decision

Here's a practical decision framework to help you choose the right scaling approach.

Choose vertical scaling in the following scenarios:

- **Single component maxed out**: CPU or Memory at 80-90% on one component
- **Quick wins needed**: Need a 20-50% performance boost quickly
- **Low latency critical**: Every millisecond matters for your use case
- **Budget constraints**: Adding new nodes is expensive
- **Diagnostic phase**: Testing if resources are the actual bottleneck

Key requirement for this scaling: The host machine must have spare resources available!

Choose horizontal scaling in the following scenarios:

- **High concurrency**: Need to handle 1000+ QPS or millions of vectors
- **Hit vertical limits**: Already using the largest available instance
- **Need fault tolerance**: Can't afford single points of failure
- **Large datasets**: Data exceeds what a single node can handle
- **Variable workload**: Traffic spikes during certain hours or days
- **Cloud-native approach**: Desire to leverage Kubernetes autoscaling

Here is a quick decision flowchart:

```
1. Check Metrics → Is one component at >80% CPU/Memory?
   ├─ YES → Can the host provide more resources?
   │   ├─ YES → Try Vertical Scaling first
   │   └─ NO → Use Horizontal Scaling
   └─ NO → Is overall system load high?
       ├─ YES → Use Horizontal Scaling
       └─ NO → Check other bottlenecks (network, disk, etc.)
```

Often, you'll use both strategies together. **Example**: Scale QueryNodes vertically to 4 CPU/16 GB each, then scale horizontally to 6 replicas for optimal performance.

Introduction to scalability testing methodology

Performance testing doesn't have to be complex. Here's a simple framework to validate your scaling decisions.

The 5-step testing framework:

1. **Define your goal**: What are you trying to prove?
2. **Prepare your environment**: Consistent setup for reliable results
3. **Design your workload**: Simulate real usage patterns
4. **Measure key metrics**: Focus on what matters
5. **Use the right tools**: Leverage existing solutions

Let's explore each of these steps in detail.

Define clear test objectives

Start with a specific question you want to answer. Common objectives include:

- **Baseline testing**: "What's my current performance?"
  Example: "My system handles 500 QPS with 100 ms P99 latency"
- **Performance scaling**: "Can I handle more requests faster?"
  Example: "If I double QueryNode CPU, will QPS increase by 80%"
- **Capacity scaling**: "Can I handle more data"
  Example: "Can I scale from 10M to 20M vectors while maintaining less than 150ms latency?"
- **Bottleneck identification**: "What's limiting my performance?"
  Example: "Is it CPU, memory, or network that's maxing out first?"

Prepare test environment and data

Here's your environment checklist

- Same Milvus version across all tests
- Identical hardware/cloud instance types
- Network conditions remain constant
- Test in a production-like environment when possible

Dataset requirements

The following table shows the dataset requirements:

Aspect	What to consider	Example
Volume	Match your scaling goals	10M vectors for baseline, 20M for capacity test
Dimensions	Match your business embedding model output	128-dim for image features, 768-dim for text embeddings
Distribution	Realistic patterns	Clustered data for recommendation systems
Scalar fields	Include if used in queries	`category_id`, `timestamp`, `user_region`

Table 14.2: Dataset requirements before scaling

Here are your data generation options:

1. **Quick synthetic data generation**:

```
import numpy as np

# Generate 1M 128 dimensional vectors
vectors = np.random.randn(1000000, 128).astype('float32')
# Add scalar fields
categories = np.random.randint(0, 100, 1000000)  # 100 categories
timestamps = np.random.randint(1600000000, 1700000000, 1000000)
```

2. **Public vector datasets**: For standardized benchmarking, you can use these well-known public datasets:

Dataset	Size	Dimensions	Use Case	Download link
SIFT1M	1M vectors	128-dim	Computer vision features	`http://corpus-texmex.irisa.fr/`
GIST1M	1M vectors	960-dim	Image descriptors	`http://corpus-texmex.irisa.fr/`
Deep1B	1B vectors	96-dim	Large-scale testing	`https://research.yandex.com/datasets/deep`
GloVe	1.2M vectors	50-300 dim	Text embeddings	`https://nlp.stanford.edu/projects/glove/`

Table 14.3: Public datasets

Note that public datasets are ideal for comparing results with other systems but may lack the scalar fields and data distribution patterns of your specific use case.

Design basic test workloads

Your test workload should mirror real-world usage patterns. Here are three essential test types:

1. **Search performance test**
   Goal: Measure how many searches your system can handle

```
# Example test pattern
for qps in [100, 200, 500, 1000, 2000]:
    run_queries(target_qps=qps, duration="5m")
    measure_latency_and_errors()
```

What to test:

- Simple k-NN search (k = 10, 50, 100)
- Filtered search (with scalar conditions)
- Range search (find all vectors within distance X)

> **Note**
>
> vector search parameters such as `topK`, `nprobe` (for IVF indexes), and `efSearch` (for HNSW indexes) significantly affect search performance. When designing your test workloads, vary these parameters to understand their impact on latency and throughput.

2. **Data ingestion test**
   Goal: Measure write throughput

Test type	Description	Typical metric
Batch insert	Large chunks (100K vectors)	Vectors/second
Stream insert	Small continuous batches (1K)	Latency per batch
Mixed load	Queries + Inserts together	Both metrics

Table 14.4: Data ingestion test types and metrics

3. **Capacity test**
   Goal: Find your system's data limits
   1. Start with baseline (e.g., 10M vectors)
   2. Keep adding data in increments (e.g., +5M each time)
   3. Monitor search latency at each step
   4. Stop when latency exceeds your SLA (e.g., >200 ms)

With these test types established, the next step is identifying the right metrics to track during testing.

Focusing on key performance indicators

During the testing process, you need to focus on monitoring and recording a series of **key performance indicators (KPIs)** to quantitatively assess the system's performance and the effects of scaling. These indicators primarily include:

- **Query throughput (QPS)**: The number of search requests the system can successfully process per second, a core metric for measuring search processing capability.
- **Search latency**: The time required to process a single search request, usually measured by average latency, P95 latency (i.e., 95% of searches are completed within this time),

and P99 latency; high percentile latencies better reflect the system's worst-case performance.

- **Data ingestion rate**: The number of vectors or amount of data (e.g., MB/s) successfully inserted per second, used to measure write performance.
- **Maximum processable data capacity**: The maximum number of vectors or total data volume the system can stably handle under specific performance standards (e.g., acceptable latency)
- **Resource utilization**: This includes several aspects:
    - **CPU utilization**: CPU usage of various Milvus component Pods (especially compute-intensive QueryNodes, IndexNodes, and coordinator services like RootCoord and etcd), as well as host Kubernetes nodes.
    - **Memory usage**: Memory consumption of various Milvus component Pods (especially QueryNodes, which need to load indexes and data into memory), as well as monitoring whether it's approaching the Pod's memory limits.
    - **Disk I/O**: Mainly focus on DataNode disk flushing operations, IndexNode index building (especially for disk-based index types like DiskANN), and the read/write performance of object storage.
    - **Network bandwidth**: Network traffic for inter-component communication and with external dependencies (like object storage and message queues)
    - **Error rate**: The proportion of failed search requests or data operations, an important indicator of system stability.
    - **Recall**: For **approximate nearest neighbor** (**ANN**) search, recall is an important metric for measuring the accuracy of search results (usually requires a ground truth set for comparison)
- **Scalability-specific metrics**: Some metrics that help you measure the scalability of a system are listed as follows:
    - **Linear scalability ratio**: This metric measures how much performance improves when you increase resources by a certain proportion. The formula is typically: `Performance Improvement Percentage / Resource Increase Percentage`

      For example, if QueryNode's CPU resources increase from 2 cores to 4 cores (a 100% resource increase), and QPS increases from 500 to 900 (a performance improvement of `(900-500)/500 = 80%`), then the linear scalability ratio, for example, `80%/100% = 0.8`.

The closer this value is to 1, the closer the system's scalability is to ideal linear growth, meaning each additional unit of resource brings nearly a unit of performance improvement.

- **Scalability efficiency**: This metric assesses the ratio of actual performance improvement achieved to the theoretically (ideally) achievable performance improvement. The formula is typically:

  ```
  Actual Performance Improvement / Theoretical Performance Improvement
  ```

  Theoretical performance improvement usually assumes proportionality with the resource increase. In the example above, with resources doubled, QPS should theoretically double to 1000. If the actual QPS increases to 900, then the scalability efficiency is:

  ```
  (Actual QPS - Baseline QPS) / (Theoretical QPS - Baseline QPS)
  = (900 - 500) / (1000 - 500) = 400 / 500 = 0.8 or 80%
  ```

  This indicator helps us understand how much of the system's potential is actually converted into performance during scaling, reflecting the effectiveness of the scaling operation.

Before conducting tests and analyzing results, it is important to establish a structured testing process supported by reliable testing and monitoring tools. Let's explore that in the next section.

Utilizing basic testing and monitoring tools

Throughout the testing process, utilizing appropriate testing and monitoring tools is fundamental to obtaining accurate data and in-depth analysis. Here are some tools to keep track of:

- **VectorDBBench**: As introduced in *Chapter 12*, this is a powerful open-source tool that can help you perform standardized vector database performance tests, including data import and various types of search loads. It can output key metrics like QPS, latency, and recall, facilitating horizontal comparisons and performance evaluations.
- **Custom scripts**: For more specific or complex test scenarios (e.g., simulating specific business logic), you can use Python (with the PyMilvus SDK) or other programming languages you are familiar with to write custom test scripts to generate and control the load. For advanced load testing scenarios, refer to *Chapter 12*, which covers Locust-based testing scripts that combine PyMilvus with Locust for sophisticated load generation and user behavior simulation.
- **Prometheus and Grafana**: This pair is the gold standard for system monitoring and performance analysis (detailed setup and configuration covered in *Chapter 4*).

Throughout the testing process, you should continuously use Prometheus to collect various performance metrics from Milvus components and the underlying infrastructure (like Kubernetes nodes), and use Grafana to create intuitive visual dashboards for real-time display and subsequent analysis. Chapter 13 provides a comprehensive guide to the essential Grafana monitoring panels for reliability testing, including Successful Requests, Failed Requests, Search Latency, Query Latency, CPU Usage, Memory Usage, and Segment Loaded panels. These pre-configured panels help you understand the system status in real-time, quickly locate bottlenecks, and review and deeply analyze performance data after the test.

Conducting scalability testing is an iterative process. You may need to adjust Milvus' configuration or scaling strategy based on initial test results, then test again, repeating this cycle until satisfactory performance goals are met or you fully understand the system's capability limits and behavioral characteristics.

For beginners, it's not necessary to aim for a perfect, all-encompassing test; rather, it's more important to gain experience through hands-on practice and master basic testing methods and analytical thinking. Let's get started with our first hands-on exercise for vertical scaling.

Hands-on lab: vertical scaling with testing methodologies

Vertical scaling primarily involves allocating more computational resources, mainly CPU and memory, to specific components within a Milvus cluster. We will use the basic testing methodology described earlier to observe and verify the effects of vertical scaling.

Consider a scenario in which we encounter insufficient CPU resources on the QueryNode, leading to high search latency (performance improvement test).

Assume we have a Milvus cluster where basic performance testing reveals that when search concurrency reaches a certain level, the QueryNode component's CPU utilization remains high, nearing its resource limit, and a significant increase in P99 search latency is observed. Our goal is to improve the system's QPS and reduce search latency by vertically scaling the QueryNode's resources, while keeping the dataset and index unchanged.

Let's define a hypothetical current state as follows:

- **Milvus cluster name**: my-milvus-cluster

- **Namespace**: milvus-ns
- **QueryNode current configuration** (1 base unit: 2c8g, meaning 2 CPU cores and 8 GB memory) as follows:
  - Replicas: 1
  - CPU Requests (`requests.cpu`): "2"
  - CPU Limits (`limits.cpu`): "2"
  - Memory Requests (`requests.memory`): "8Gi"
  - Memory Limits (`limits.memory`): "8Gi"

We can then define the test dataset. A collection `test_collection` with 1 million 128-dimensional vectors has been imported, and an HNSW index has been built. We can use a simple Python script using the PyMilvus SDK to simulate 10 concurrent users, each continuously sending ***k*-NN** (`k=10`) queries. For more advanced load testing scenarios, refer to *Chapter 12*, Locust-based testing frameworks.

Let's now look at the detailed steps for conducting testing.

The first test includes two parts: defining the test objective and executing the baseline.

You may define the *test objective* like this: To verify if increasing the CPU and memory resources of the QueryNode reduces P99 search latency and increases QPS under high concurrent search scenarios, and if the QueryNode's CPU utilization becomes more manageable. Also, to preliminarily assess its linear scalability ratio and efficiency.

To execute the baseline test, you need to do the following:

1. Run the prepared Python search script for a period (e.g., 5-10 minutes). For more sophisticated load testing, see *Chapter 12* for Locust + PyMilvus implementations.
2. Monitor and record baseline KPIs using the tools and metrics described in the "Focusing on key performance indicators" section earlier in this chapter.
3. Use the following command to observe and record the average CPU and memory usage of the QueryNode:

   ```
   kubectl top pod -n milvus-ns -l app.kubernetes.io/instance=my-milvus-
   cluster,app.kubernetes.io/component=querynode --containers
   ```

   - If Prometheus and Grafana are configured (refer to *Chapter 4* for setup), check the QueryNode's CPU utilization chart, memory usage chart, and search latency (especially P99) chart, recording peak and average values. Focus on whether CPU or memory usage is approaching the pod's limits, the absolute value and trend of search latency (P99 Latency), and the QPS the system can stably handle with this resource configuration.

- Record the average QPS and P99 latency output by the test script. Assume baseline QPS (with 2c8g configuration: 2 CPU cores, 8GB memory) is 200, P99 latency is 180 ms, and peak CPU utilization reaches 95% of its 2-core limit.

4. Determine target vertical scaling configuration; based on the observation that CPU was the bottleneck in the baseline test, we decide to increase the QueryNode's resources from 1 base unit (2c8g: 2 cores, 8GB) to 2 base units (4c16g: 4 cores, 16GB). This means doubling both CPU and memory.

   - Target CPU requests: "4"
   - Target CPU limits: "4"
   - Target memory requests: "16Gi"
   - Target memory limits: "16Gi"

   The following snippet shows only the key fields relevant to vertical scaling. For the complete Milvus CR configuration file, refer to the chapter GitHub repository.

5. Modify the Milvus CR file. Create `milvus-cr-vertical-scale.yaml`:

```
apiVersion: milvus.io/v1beta1
kind: Milvus
metadata:
  name: my-milvus-cluster
  namespace: milvus-ns
spec:
  components:
    queryNode:
      replicas: 1
      resources:
        requests:
          cpu: "4"          # 2x increase
          memory: "16Gi"    # 2x increase
        limits:
          cpu: "4"
          memory: "16Gi"
    # ... (other components unchanged)
```

6. Apply changes:

```
kubectl apply -f milvus-cr-vertical-scale.yaml -n milvus-ns
```

   Wait for the Milvus Operator to complete the rolling update of the QueryNode. The Operator (as introduced in *Chapter 2*) will ensure that the old pod is smoothly replaced by a new one with higher resource allocation.

7. Verify pod update:

```
# Watch pod replacement
kubectl get pods -n milvus-ns \
  -l app.kubernetes.io/instance=my-milvus-cluster,app.kubernetes.io/
component=querynode -w

# Verify new resource allocation
kubectl describe pod <new-querynode-pod-name> -n milvus-ns
```

Now, to execute a comparative test and analyze results, you need to undertake the following steps:

1. **Rerun test load**: Use the exact same Python search script from *Step 1* under the same test conditions. For advanced testing scenarios, refer to Chapter 12, Locust-based script examples.
2. **Monitor and record new KPIs**:
   - Again, use kubectl top pod or Prometheus/Grafana to monitor the QueryNode's CPU and memory usage.
   - Record the new average QPS and P99 search latency. Assume the new QPS (with 4c16g configuration: 4 CPU cores, 16GB memory) reaches 380, and P99 latency drops to 90ms.
3. **Comparative analysis and scalability metrics calculation**:
   - **P99 latency**: Dropped from 180ms to 90ms, a significant improvement in search response speed.

- **CPU utilization**: Expect peak CPU utilization to decrease or remain more stable at the same or higher QPS, no longer easily hitting the new resource limits.
- **QPS improvement**: Increased from 200 QPS to 380 QPS, enhancing the system's overall processing capacity.

4. **Calculate scalability metrics (using QPS as an example)**:
   - **Resource increase percentage (CPU and memory limit, both increased by 100%)**: `100%`
   - **Performance improvement percentage (QPS)**: `(380 QPS - 200 QPS) / 200 QPS = 180 / 200 = 90%`
   - **Linear scalability ratio**: Performance Improvement Percentage / Resource Increase Percentage = `90% / 100% = 0.9`
   - **Theoretical performance improvement (QPS)**: Baseline QPS * (1 + Resource Increase Percentage) = `200 * (1 + 1.0) = 400 QPS`
   - **Actual performance improvement (QPS)**: `380 QPS - 200 QPS = 180 QPS`
   - **Scalability efficiency**: (Actual QPS Improvement) / (Theoretical QPS Improvement - Baseline QPS) = `180 / (400 - 200) = 180 / 200 = 0.9 or 90%`

We need to keep in mind some important considerations. For example, we must maintain test consistency by ensuring all relevant conditions (dataset, index, search type, concurrency, test duration, etc.) are identical for baseline and comparative tests to assess the scaling effect accurately. The adjustments to your test plan should be gradual and observed carefully. If a single vertical scaling operation does not yield significant results or introduces new problems, make small adjustments and repeat the tests to gradually find the optimal resource allocation. Also, remember that vertical scaling is limited by the physical resources of the Kubernetes nodes hosting the pods.

Let's now move our testing focus to horizontal scaling.

Hands-on lab: horizontal scaling (performance improvement type)

Horizontal scaling, by increasing the number of component replicas, is a key strategy for enhancing overall system throughput. We will continue to use basic testing methodology to verify the effect of horizontal scaling on search QPS.

Here, we will consider a scenario to enhance QueryNode's concurrent search processing capacity (QPS)

Assume our QueryNode component has been appropriately vertically scaled, and a single instance's resource configuration is relatively optimized at 2 base units (i.e., 4c CPU, 16Gi Memory). Now, the throughput of a single instance has reached its limit, and we need to further increase the cluster's overall QPS by increasing the number of QueryNode instances.

The *test objective* is to significantly increase QPS by adding replicas while maintaining acceptable search latency on the same dataset. The hypothetical current state (hypothetical) can be defined as follows:

- **Milvus cluster name**: my-milvus-cluster
- **Namespace**: milvus-ns
- We will assume the **QueryNode current configuration** (single optimized replica, 2 base units: 4c16g, meaning 4 CPU cores and 16GB memory) configuration as follows:
    - Replicas: 1
    - CPU requests (`requests.cpu`): "4"
    - CPU limits (`limits.cpu`): "4"
    - Memory requests (`requests.memory`): "16Gi"
    - Memory limits (`limits.memory`): "16Gi"

The test dataset and tools will be defined, the same as in the vertical scaling lab (`test_collection` with 1 million vectors, HNSW index built), or you can use `VectorDBBench` (detailed usage in *Chapter 12*) to configure a test scenario with gradually increasing target QPS.

Let's now look at the detailed steps for conducting the test.

You can define the **test objective** as follows: To verify if increasing the QueryNode replica count from 1 to 3 significantly boosts the maximum QPS the system can support while maintaining acceptable search latency (e.g., P99 < 100 ms). Also, to assess its linear scalability ratio and efficiency.

To **execute a baseline test for a single replica**, you can perform the following steps:

- Using VectorDBBench (refer to Chapter 12 for configuration details) or a custom script (see Chapter 12 for Locust + PyMilvus examples), gradually increase the search request rate on test_collection until P99 latency starts to exceed 100 ms or the error rate rises noticeably.

To **monitor and record baseline KPIs**:

1. Record the maximum QPS that a single QueryNode (4c16g: 4 cores, 16GB memory) can stably handle under the P99 < 100ms condition that P99 < 100 ms (e.g., baseline `QPS_1 = 380 QPS`, continuing from the previous lab's result).

2. Record the CPU and memory utilization of the QueryNode at this point. Observe whether the load is evenly distributed (only one instance in this baseline) and note the total QPS contributed by the cluster (all QueryNode replicas).
3. Record the P99 latency when the bottleneck is reached.
4. Determine target horizontal scaling configuration. We plan to scale the QueryNode replica count from 1 to 3, with each replica maintaining the 2 base unit (4c16g: 4 cores, 16GB memory) resource configuration.
5. Modify the Milvus CR file. Create a file named `milvus-cr-horizontal-scale.yaml` (ensure you provide the complete Milvus CR configuration in a real application)

```
apiVersion: milvus.io/v1beta1
kind: Milvus
metadata:
  name: my-milvus-cluster
  namespace: milvus-ns
spec:
  components:
    queryNode:
      replicas: 3  # Core change: increase replicas to 3
      resources:   # Keep individual replica resource configuration
unchanged
        requests:
          cpu: "4"
          memory: "16Gi"
        limits:
          cpu: "4"
          memory: "16Gi"
    # ... (Retain full configuration for other components) ...
```

6. Apply the changes using the following command:

```
kubectl apply -f milvus-cr-horizontal-scale.yaml -n milvus-ns
```

Wait for the Milvus Operator to create the new QueryNode pods and ensure all replicas are ready. The Operator will gradually start the new pod instances.

7. To verify pod scaling status, run the following commands:

   a. To observe and ensure all 3 QueryNode pods are created and enter the running state, use the command:

   ```
   kubectl get pods -n milvus-ns -l app.kubernetes.io/instance=my-milvus-cluster,app.kubernetes.io/component=querynode -w
   ```

   b. Use this command to confirm that the desired and ready replica counts for the Deployment are both equal

   ```
   kubectl get deployment my-milvus-cluster-querynode -n milvus-ns
   ```

After increasing the QueryNode replica count to 3, we will execute two comparative tests and analyze the results for the two scenarios. Let's take a look at them next.

Scenario – single in-memory replica test (verify basic horizontal scaling effects)

In this scenario, we do not specifically configure multiple in-memory replicas. The primary goal is to observe the performance improvement from adding more QueryNode compute instances. Milvus' default behavior might distribute data segments across different QueryNodes, or this might be managed by QueryCoord.

You would need to **rerun the test load**. For this, use the exact same VectorDBBench configuration (as covered in *Chapter 12*) or custom script (see *Chapter 12* for Locust-based implementations) from *Step 1*, again gradually increasing the search request rate.

Next, **monitor and record new KPIs**:

- Record the maximum QPS that 3 QueryNode replicas (in single in-memory replica mode) can collectively handle stably under the P99 < 100ms condition (e.g., assume new `QPS_3_single_replica = 950 QPS`).
- Observe the CPU/memory utilization of each QueryNode instance in `Prometheus/Grafana` to confirm that the load is roughly balanced.
- Record the P99 latency when the new bottleneck is reached.

For a **comparative analysis and scalability metrics calculation**, evaluate the following metrics:

- **QPS improvement**: From 380 QPS (single replica) to 950 QPS (three replicas, single in-memory replica mode)

Calculate scalability metrics (using QPS and replica count as an example)

- **Resource increase percentage** (QueryNode instances): `(3 replicas - 1 replica) / 1 replica = 200%`
- **Performance improvement percentage** (QPS): `(950 QPS - 380 QPS) / 380 QPS = 570 / 380 ≈ 150%`
- **Linear scalability ratio**: `150% / 200% = 0.75`
- **Theoretical performance improvement** (QPS): `Baseline QPS_1 * (New Replica Count / Old Replica Count) = 380 * (3 / 1) = 1140 QPS`
- **Actual performance improvement** (QPS): `950 QPS - 380 QPS = 570 QPS`
- **Scalability efficiency**: `570 / (1140 - 380) = 570 / 760 ≈ 0.75 or 75%`

Let's now talk about a scenario in which you can configure multiple replicas based on QueryNode count.

Scenario – multiple in-memory replicas test

In this scenario, we will configure a number of in-memory replicas equal to (or close to) the number of QueryNode instances. If QueryNodes are increased from 1 to 3, we will attempt to configure 3 in-memory replicas. This means each data segment (or its shard) will be loaded onto all 3 QueryNodes.

Here are the steps:

1. **Configure in-memory replicas**: When loading a collection (`collection.load()`), you can specify the `replica_number` parameter. For instance, if QueryNodes are scaled to 3, you can set `replica_number=3`:

```
# Example Python code snippet (assuming PyMilvus)
client = MilvusClient(uri=MILVUS_URI, token=TOKEN)
collection_name = "test_collection"
client.load_collection(collection_name=collection_name, replica_number=3)
# Set in-memory replicas to 3
```

   Alternatively, if your Milvus version and deployment method (e.g., via Milvus Operator CRD) support more granular configuration of Replica Groups or Shard Replicas, refer to the respective documentation to set them up. Aim to have multiple queryable copies of data across all QueryNodes.

2. **Execute test**: After ensuring the collection is loaded with the new in-memory replica count, use the exact same test load (VectorDBBench configuration or custom script from *Chapter 12*)
3. **Monitor and record KPIs**: For this, you will need to record the following:
    - Record the maximum QPS that 3 QueryNode replicas (configured with 3 in-memory replicas) can collectively handle stably under the P99 < 100ms condition (e.g., assume new `QPS_3_multi_replica = 1050 QPS` or higher).
    - Pay close attention to the CPU and memory usage of each QueryNode replica. Since each node loads the data, memory usage will increase accordingly, but CPU load should be more evenly distributed.
    - Record P99 latency to see whether it remains within an acceptable range.
4. **Analyze results**: To understand if the system is scaling well, you can:
    - **Compare QPS**: Compare the QPS from Scenario 6.2 (e.g., 1050 QPS) with that from Scenario 6.1 (e.g., 950 QPS) to determine if in-memory replicas provided additional performance gains?
    - Analyze **Resource utilization**: Analyze if the multiple in-memory replicas scenario more fully utilizes the compute resources of all QueryNodes, especially under high concurrent searches or when data hotspots exist.

In summary, here's how in-memory replicas work. By loading the same data segment onto multiple QueryNodes, in-memory replicas allow searches for that segment to be distributed to more nodes for parallel processing, thereby further boosting QPS in high-concurrency scenarios. They also enhance system availability. For more details on replica concepts and best practices, see `https://milvus.io/docs/replica.md#In-Memory-Replica`.

Some important considerations are load balancing, gradual load increase, monitoring performance bottlenecks, and monitoring memory consumption.

You would need to ensure that the Milvus Proxy frontend (if clients connect directly to Proxies) or your application layer has an appropriate load balancing mechanism to evenly distribute requests to all available QueryNodes. this is usually achieved indirectly through Proxies; the Proxy Service deployed by Milvus Operator typically acts as a load balancer for backend Proxy instances, and Proxies internally distribute searches to appropriate QueryNodes.

When testing, it's advisable to gradually increase the request pressure rather than hitting very high QPS suddenly, as this makes it easier to observe system behavior and pinpoint bottlenecks.

After horizontally scaling QueryNodes, performance bottlenecks might shift to other components, such as Proxy processing capacity, coordinator service (e.g., QueryCoord) scheduling capability, or even external dependencies (e.g., etcd response speed, message queue throughput). Therefore, continuous monitoring of all parts of the system is crucial.

Enabling multiple in-memory replicas increases the overall memory consumption of QueryNodes, as the same data is stored in multiple QueryNodes. Ensure that each QueryNode has sufficient memory to accommodate the data replicas assigned to it.

Next up, we will look at how to improve the capacity of your system.

Hands-on lab: capacity improvement testing with methodology

Besides improving QPS and reducing latency, another common scaling objective is to enhance the system's ability to handle larger datasets, i.e., capacity improvement. We will demonstrate through a hands-on lab how to test whether Milvus, after resource expansion, can stably process a larger volume of data while maintaining acceptable performance metrics. The goal is to achieve a linear relationship between resource and data volume growth for easier analysis.

Scenario – verifying the cluster's ability to linearly handle larger datasets after scaling

Assume we already have a cluster with multiple QueryNode replicas through horizontal scaling, and this configuration can handle a certain dataset size with good performance. The current goal is to further increase the number of QueryNode replicas and proportionally increase the data volume, then verify whether the system can stably load and search this larger dataset while keeping key performance indicators like search latency within acceptable limits.

Here is a hypothetical current state:

- **Milvus cluster name**: my-milvus-cluster
- **Namespace**: milvus-ns
- **QueryNode current configuration**: 3 replicas, each configured with 2 base units (4c16g: 4 CPU cores, 16GB memory).
- **Current dataset**: `test_collection_capacity` contains **10 million** 128-dimensional vectors, with an HNSW index built.
- **Baseline performance**: With this configuration and a 10 million-entry dataset, P99 search latency is 100ms, and the system handles searches stably.

The details of the target scaling and data volume (linear growth) are as follows:

- **Scaling operation**: We will increase the QueryNode replica count from 3 to **6** (a 100% increase), with each replica still maintaining the 2 base unit (4c16g: 4 cores, 16GB memory) resource configuration.
- **Target dataset**: Correspondingly, we will also increase the data volume by 100% by importing an additional 10 million vector entries into `test_collection_capacity`, bringing the total to **20 million entries**.

Here is the list of detailed steps:

1. **Define test objectives and establish a baseline** for the current data volume
    - **Test objective**: To verify if the Milvus cluster, after doubling both QueryNode replicas and data volume, can still maintain P99 search latency within an acceptable range (e.g., close to or slightly above the original 100ms)
    - **Execute baseline test** (for the current 10 million data volume and 3 QueryNode replicas): Do this using a search script or VectorDBBench (performance testing techniques detailed in *Chapter 12*), similar to previous performance tests, search the `test_collection_capacity` containing 10 million entries.
2. **Monitor and record baseline KPIs**: Record P99 search latency, QPS, and resource utilization of each QueryNode. Confirm that the system runs stably under this data volume and resource configuration.
3. **Perform scaling operation** (expand QueryNode replicas): Modify the Milvus CR file to increase QueryNode replicas from 3 to 6.

```
apiVersion: milvus.io/v1beta1
kind: Milvus
metadata:
  name: my-milvus-cluster
  namespace: milvus-ns
spec:
  components:
    queryNode:
      replicas: 6  # Increase replicas to 6
      resources:
        requests:
          cpu: "4"
          memory: "16Gi"
        limits:
          cpu: "4"
```

```
          memory: "16Gi"
    # ... (Retain full configuration for other components) ...
```

4. **Apply changes**:

```
kubectl apply -f <your-milvus-cr-file>.yaml -n milvus-ns
```

   Verify pod status to ensure that all 6 QueryNode pods are running correctly.

5. **Import incremental data and ensure loading and indexing**:
   - Using your data import script or tool, import an additional 10 million vector entries into `test_collection_capacity`, bringing the total to 20 million. For detailed data insertion operations, refer to *Chapter 3*.
   - Ensure the collection is loaded (`load_collection`). For collection loading and management operations, refer to *Chapter 3*.
   - Ensure index building is complete for the newly imported data segments. For index creation and monitoring techniques, refer to *Chapter 3*. This process might take some time, depending on data volume and IndexNode configuration.
6. **Execute comparative test (20M data volume, 6 QueryNode replicas)**: After data import and index building are complete, use the exact same search script or VectorDBBench configuration from *Step 1* to search the `test_collection_capacity` containing 20 million entries.
7. **Monitor and record new KPIs**:
   - Record the P99 search latency when 6 QueryNode replicas are collectively handling searches on the 20 million entry dataset.
   - Record the QPS the system can stably handle.
   - Observe the CPU and memory utilization of each QueryNode instance to confirm if the load is roughly balanced and resources are sufficient.
8. **Analyze results:**
   - **Compare P99 search latency**: Is the new P99 search latency still within an acceptable range? For example, if the target is to stay below 120ms (a slight increase in latency might be expected given the doubled data volume and request load) and the actual test result is 115ms, it is considered acceptable.
   - **Observe QPS**: Can the system maintain a reasonable search throughput with the new data volume? Ideally, if the search pattern remains unchanged, QPS should be

roughly similar to or slightly lower than the baseline test (as each request involves more data)

  - **Resource utilization**: Check the resource utilization of all QueryNode replicas. Do the newly added replicas effectively share the increased memory and computational load due to the larger data volume? Is the load per replica roughly comparable to the baseline test?

If the system, after doubling both QueryNode replicas and data volume, can stably handle the new data volume with acceptable performance metrics (primarily search latency), then this linear capacity improvement test can be considered successful. This indicates that proportionally scaling QueryNode resources can effectively enhance the data handling capacity of the Milvus cluster.

Some important considerations that you need to keep in mind are:

- **Data loading and indexing time**: When conducting capacity tests, importing large amounts of data and waiting for it to be fully loaded and indexed can take a significant amount of time. Always ensure data is ready before starting performance tests.
- **Memory is key**: Ensuring QueryNodes have sufficient memory to load data segments and indexes is essential. While increasing data volume, always verify that the total memory capacity of QueryNodes (memory per replica * number of replicas) can accommodate the increased data and indexes. Insufficient memory, even with more replicas, can lead to loading failures or frequent data swapping, severely impacting performance.
- **Capacity of other components**: Besides QueryNodes, the write capacity of DataNodes, throughput of the message queue, capacity, and I/O performance of object storage, etc., can become potential bottlenecks at larger data scales. Capacity improvement is a systemic effort.
- **Iterative nature of testing**: If one scaling attempt does not achieve the desired capacity improvement target (e.g., latency is too high), further analysis of the bottleneck is needed. This might involve adding more QueryNode replicas, vertically scaling individual replica resources, or optimizing other related components.

By incorporating these testing methodology steps into your scaling exercises, you can more scientifically evaluate the effectiveness of scaling operations and provide solid data to support for subsequent performance optimizations.

Using scaling to resolve Milvus performance bottlenecks

When your Milvus cluster experiences performance issues, scaling is often the most effective solution. Think of this like solving traffic congestion; you can either make the roads wider (vertical scaling) or add more roads (horizontal scaling).

First, let's identify common performance symptoms and their scaling solutions in the following table:

Performance issue	Symptom	Scaling solution
High search latency	Search requests > 200ms	Scale QueryNode (vertical/ horizontal)
Low search throughput	Cannot handle expected QPS	Add more QueryNode replicas
Memory pressure	OOM errors during searches	Increase QueryNode memory or add replicas
Slow data insertion	Insert operations are slow	Scale DataNode resources or add replicas
Slow index building	Index tasks take too long, affecting search performance	Scale IndexNode resources or add replicas

Table 14.5: Performance issues and their scaling solutions

Use Grafana monitoring (detailed in *Chapter 4*) to identify which component needs scaling, then apply the appropriate solution. Refer to *Chapter 13* for specific monitoring panels like CPU usage, memory usage, and search/query latency panels that help identify performance bottlenecks. Let's now review the step-by-step scaling solutions.

1. First are the QueryNode scaling solutions.

   Problem 1: High CPU usage (>85 percent) with slow search responses

   Solution: Vertical scaling; increase individual QueryNode resources

   ```
   # Increase QueryNode CPU and memory (2c8g → 4c16g)
   queryNode:
     resources:
   ```

```
    requests:
      cpu: "4"         # Increased from 2 cores
      memory: "16Gi"  # Increased from 8GB
    limits:
      cpu: "4"
      memory: "16Gi"
```

Problem 2: Memory exhaustion with large datasets

Solution: Horizontal scaling - add more QueryNode replicas

```
# Add more QueryNode replicas to distribute memory load
queryNode:
  replicas: 4  # Increased from 2 replicas
  resources:
    requests:
      cpu: "2"
      memory: "8Gi"
```

2. Next comes the DataNode scaling solutions.
   Problem: Slow data insertion rates affecting real-time applications

   Solution: Scale DataNode resources and replicas

```
# Scale DataNode for better insert performance
dataNode:
  replicas: 3     # Increased from 1 for parallel processing
  resources:
    requests:
      cpu: "4"    # Increased from 2c8g to 4c16g
      memory: "16Gi"
```

3. Now, let's turn to IndexNode scaling solutions.
   Problem: Index building tasks are slow, causing searches to run on growing segments instead of optimized indexes

   Solution: Add more IndexNode resources for faster index building

```
# Scale IndexNode for faster index creation
indexNode:
  replicas: 2     # Add additional IndexNode
  resources:
```

```
    requests:
      cpu: "4"    # Increase CPU for faster index building
      memory: "8Gi"
```

Use this simple decision tree to choose the right scaling approach:

```
Performance Issue Detected
├── Single Component Overloaded?
│   ├── Yes → Vertical Scaling (increase resources)
│   └── No → Check if distributed load
├── Need Higher Throughput?
│   ├── Yes → Horizontal Scaling (add replicas)
│   └── No → Optimize current configuration
└── Memory Issues?
    ├── Per-node limit → Vertical scaling (more memory per node)
    └── Total capacity → Horizontal scaling (more nodes)
```

With this framework in mind, we will look at some practical scaling examples.

- **Example 1: E-commerce search performance**
  Scenario: Online store experiencing slow product searches during peak hours

  Symptoms: Search latency increased from 50 ms to 300 ms

  Monitoring shows: QueryNode CPU at 95%, memory at 80%

  Solution: Combine vertical and horizontal scaling

  ```
  queryNode:
    replicas: 6          # Increased from 3 (horizontal scaling)
    resources:
      requests:
        cpu: "4"         # Increased from 2c8g to 4c16g (vertical scaling)
        memory: "16Gi"
  ```

- **Example 2: Real-time recommendation system**
  Scenario: ML pipeline cannot keep up with data ingestion

  Symptoms: Data insertion backlog, delayed model updates

  Monitoring shows: DataNode CPU at 90%, insert queue growing

Solution: Scale DataNode horizontally

```
dataNode:
  replicas: 4          # Increased from 2
  resources:
    requests:
      cpu: "4"         # Maintain 4c16g per replica
      memory: "16Gi"
```

Monitoring scaling effectiveness

After implementing scaling changes, monitor these key metrics using *Chapter 4*'s Grafana dashboards. *Chapter 13* provides detailed descriptions of the essential monitoring panels (successful requests, failed requests, search latency, query latency) that are particularly useful for tracking scaling effectiveness:

Before vs after scaling:

- **Search latency** (P99): Should decrease
- **System QPS**: Should increase
- **Resource utilization**: Should be more balanced
- **Error rates**: Should remain low or decrease

Validation checklist:

1. Apply scaling configuration using Milvus Operator (see *Chapter 2*)
2. Wait for all pods to be running and ready
3. Run performance tests using the testing framework from *Chapter 12*
4. Compare metrics before and after scaling
5. Adjust further if needed

It is important to remember when NOT to scale. Scaling isn't always the answer. Avoid unnecessary scaling when:

- Resource utilization is below 60% (may indicate configuration issues)
- Only brief spikes occur (consider auto-scaling instead)
- Single searches are extremely slow (may indicate index optimization needed)
- Storage I/O is the bottleneck (scaling compute won't help)

Effective scaling requires understanding your workload patterns and monitoring the right metrics. Always validate scaling decisions with actual performance testing, using the methodologies described in this chapter.

Summary

Congratulations! You have now completed the introductory phase of learning about Milvus' scalability features. In this chapter, we have delved into how Milvus, through its flexible architectural design and diverse scaling strategies, addresses the challenges of ever-growing data and search pressures. We have covered the principles, applicable scenarios, and respective pros and cons of the two core strategies: **vertical scaling** (by enhancing the resources of individual components) and **horizontal scaling** (by increasing the number of worker node replicas), clarifying that horizontal scaling is Milvus' primary approach for handling large-scale demands. We also learned how to conveniently perform these scaling operations on a Milvus cluster in a Kubernetes environment by modifying **custom resource** (**CR**) files, emphasizing the importance of combining this with basic testing methodologies to validate the effects of scaling. Furthermore, we explored a structured 5-step testing framework that includes defining clear objectives, preparing consistent environments, designing realistic workloads, monitoring key metrics like QPS and latency, and utilizing proper testing and monitoring tools. Through hands-on labs, you gained practical experience in both vertical and horizontal scaling scenarios, learning to calculate scalability ratios and efficiency metrics to measure the effectiveness of your scaling operations. It is crucial to remember that scaling and performance optimization in Milvus are not one-time tasks but rather dynamic processes that require continuous monitoring, analysis, iteration, and adjustment based on evolving business needs, data volume growth, and changing search patterns. We sincerely hope that the content of this chapter has provided you with a solid and clear starting point on your journey to explore and practice Milvus scalability.

In the next chapter, we will explore performance tuning for Milvus, focusing on how to effectively boost Milvus' data ingestion and search efficiency, explore how to maximize data capacity and resource utilization, and learn how to prioritize tuning goals based on specific application scenarios such as real-time recommendations or large-scale archiving.

Subscribe for a free eBook

New frameworks, evolving architectures, research drops, production breakdowns – *AI_Distilled* filters the noise into a weekly briefing for engineers and researchers working hands-on with LLMs and generative AI systems. Subscribe now and receive a free eBook, along with weekly insights that help you stay focused and informed.

Subscribe at `https://packt.link/8Oz6Y` or scan the QR code below.

15

Getting Started with Milvus Performance Tuning

Imagine an enterprise knowledge base powering AI-driven customer support for a global company. Users expect instant answers when they search for product documentation or troubleshooting guides. Meanwhile, your content team continuously publishes hundreds of new articles, FAQs, and policy updates throughout the day. At the same time, you need to store years of historical knowledge, millions of document embeddings without exceeding your infrastructure budget. Here's the challenge: optimizing for faster search typically consumes more memory, faster ingestion can slow down searches, and maximizing load capacity often sacrifices both speed and accuracy. These are fundamental trade-offs in vector database performance. You can't optimize everything simultaneously. The key question isn't "how do I make everything faster?" but rather "which performance dimension matters most for my specific use case, and what am I willing to trade off?"

This is where Milvus performance tuning becomes essential. In this chapter, you'll discover how to transform your knowledge base from a slow, resource-hungry system into a responsive search platform that serves thousands of concurrent users while continuously ingesting fresh content. We'll explore practical optimization techniques that balance the critical trade-offs among search speed, ingestion throughput, and load capacity, which are the three pillars of vector database performance.

At a high level, most Milvus performance tuning targets three areas: QueryNode configuration for search optimization, DataNode configuration for ingestion throughput, and index settings that govern the trade-off among accuracy, speed, and resource usage.

Specifically, we will focus on the following topics:

- Understanding performance trade-offs

- Making your searches faster
- Speeding up your data ingestion
- Maximizing queryable data capacity

Technical requirements

Before diving into performance optimization, let's ensure your environment is properly configured.

For environment setup, you need:

1. **Milvus instance**: A running Milvus instance (v2.5.x or later)
2. **Python environment**: Python 3.10 or later

Verify your Python version

```
python -version
```

You should see output like:

```
Python 3.10.x or higher
```

All code examples and datasets used in this chapter are available in the book's GitHub repository: `https://github.com/PacktPublishing/The-Architecture-Handbook-for-Milvus-Vector-Database`

Understanding performance trade-offs

No optimization technique improves all performance dimensions simultaneously. When you optimize one metric, you inevitably trade off others. The sections below explain the specific trade-offs that arise when prioritizing search speed, ingestion throughput, or load capacity.

Goal 1: making searches faster

Search speed directly impacts user experience and system responsiveness. In vector search, you're primarily dealing with **Approximate Nearest Neighbor** (**ANN**) algorithms, which introduce a fundamental trade-off between speed and accuracy that doesn't exist in traditional exact-match databases.

Search speed vs. accuracy

This trade-off becomes critical when choosing your optimization strategy. Let's consider two different scenarios: a Wikipedia search interface needs very fast responses to feel natural, while a scientific research platform cannot afford to miss relevant papers due to approximation errors.

ANN algorithms trade accuracy for speed by approximating distances rather than computing exact matches. The key business question becomes: what level of accuracy loss can you accept for significant speed gains?

When you prioritize speed, you're typically building real-time applications that require sub-100ms responses—think knowledge search systems, autocomplete features, or live recommendation engines where users expect instant results. On the other hand, if your use case demands prioritizing accuracy, you're likely working on research-critical systems where missing relevant results could have serious consequences, such as scientific literature search platforms, fact-checking systems, or academic research tools where comprehensive recall matters more than response time.

```
# Speed-optimized configuration
search_params = {
    "metric_type": "L2",
    "params": {"ef": 64}  # Lower ef = faster but less accurate
}

# Accuracy-optimized configuration
search_params = {
    "metric_type": "L2",
    "params": {"ef": 512}  # Higher ef = slower but more accurate
}
```

Search speed vs. memory usage

Memory is often your most expensive and limited resource. The choice between in-memory and disk-based storage directly impacts both your infrastructure costs and search performance.

Different index types represent different points on the speed-memory spectrum. Your choice depends on your dataset size, budget constraints, and latency requirements. Among the available options, HNSW delivers the fastest search performance but requires significantly more memory—roughly 3-5 times your raw data size. This makes it ideal for premium deployments where query speed is critical and memory costs are acceptable. If you're working with tighter budget constraints, IVF_SQ8 offers a balanced middle ground, using substantially less memory (about 75% reduction compared to uncompressed data) while maintaining moderate search latency that suffices for most production applications. For scenarios where you need to handle massive datasets that simply won't fit in available RAM, DiskANN provides a disk-based alternative that minimizes memory usage at the cost of higher search latency, making it a cost-effective choice for billion-scale vector collections where queries per second requirements are moderate.

Goal 2: speeding up data ingestion

Data ingestion performance becomes critical in applications with real-time data streams or large batch migrations. Unlike traditional databases, where writes are relatively simple row insertions, vector databases must process high-dimensional data and maintain complex spatial indexes.

Write throughput vs. search performance

Fast insertion leads to delayed index building. Unindexed data requires brute-force searching, dramatically increasing search latency from fast indexed searches to much slower sequential scans. The system must fall back to scanning raw vectors, destroying the very performance advantages that led you to choose a vector database.

Ingesting 1 million vectors per second sounds impressive, but if those vectors remain unindexed for hours, every search against recent data becomes a costly full scan.

Write throughput vs. memory usage

High-speed ingestion generates numerous unsealed segments that consume substantial memory. These segments remain in RAM until reaching the threshold for sealing and flushing to disk. In production, this can trigger out-of-memory errors or force expensive hardware upgrades.

A typical scenario: Your system handles a high volume of vectors per second comfortably with adequate RAM, but pushing to significantly higher throughput causes memory exhaustion as unsealed segments accumulate faster than they can be processed.

Write throughput vs. search freshness

During high-speed ingestion with strong consistency, a critical bottleneck emerges: when massive amounts of data accumulate in the message queue without being consumed, search operations become blocked. The system must wait for all pending insertions to be processed before executing searches, creating a cascading failure.

Consider this scenario: You're ingesting a very high volume of vectors per second with strong consistency. The message queue fills faster than workers can process the data. Now every search request must wait for the queue to clear, creating a severe bottleneck for real-time search. Users may see timeouts because searches wait for pending inserts to be processed.

This blocking behavior forces you to make a critical architectural decision. You can choose strong consistency with throttled ingestion, where you deliberately limit write speed to prevent queue buildup and ensure searches remain responsive at all times. Alternatively, you might opt for eventual consistency with high throughput, accepting brief visibility delays (newly inserted data won't appear immediately in searches) but maintaining excellent search availability and maximum ingestion speed. Many production systems find that bounded consistency offers the best compromise, balancing data freshness requirements against system responsiveness by guaranteeing that searches see data within a specific time window rather than requiring immediate visibility.

Goal 3: maximizing load capacity

QueryNode's loading capacity determines how much data your vector database can actively search. When your dataset exceeds available memory, you face a critical decision: sacrifice accuracy through quantization or trade speed for disk-based storage.

Capacity vs. search accuracy

Quantization techniques compress vectors by reducing their precision, allowing QueryNodes to load significantly more data into memory. However, this compression inherently introduces approximation errors that degrade search quality.

IVF_SQ8, a popular quantization index, reduces each dimension from 32-bit floats to 8-bit integers. This significant compression enables loading substantially more data into memory, but introduces accuracy loss. The accuracy impact varies dramatically by use case: face recognition requiring very high precision cannot tolerate even minor degradation, while product recommendations with good accuracy find quantization perfectly acceptable.

Capacity vs. search speed

When quantization's accuracy loss is unacceptable, disk-based solutions offer an alternative: trade memory for storage, accepting slower search speeds to maintain full precision.

Two primary approaches enable this tradeoff. DiskANN, a disk-native index designed for massive datasets, can handle billions of vectors but operates significantly slower than memory-based indexes. It provides predictable performance by explicitly managing disk access patterns, making it suitable for production systems.

Files with **memory mapping** (**mmap**) offer a simpler alternative through **operating system** (**OS**)-managed paging. While easier to implement, mmap creates unpredictable latency spikes when the operating system pages data to disk under memory pressure.

Making the right trade-off decisions

Not all performance goals are equal. This section provides a decision framework to help you identify your critical bottleneck and choose the appropriate optimization strategy.

The following table helps you identify your primary goal:

Scenario	Primary goal	Key metrics	Optimization focus
User-facing search	Search Speed	Low latency	`HNSW` index, replicas, batch searches
Real-time streaming	Write Throughput	High ingestion rate	Multi-shard, batch insert, eventual consistency
Large archives	Load Capacity	Cost per vector	`IVF_SQ8`, `DiskANN`, memory mapping

Table 15.1: Identifying your primary goal

Your application's characteristics and constraints determine which optimization goal must take precedence.

When search speed is your primary goal

You should prioritize search performance when you're building user-facing real-time applications like e-commerce search systems, conversational chatbots, or recommendation engines, where users expect sub-second responses and any delay directly impacts satisfaction. Search speed also becomes critical when you're serving thousands of concurrent searches, because even small latency improvements, say, reducing response time from 100ms to 50ms, multiply into significant capacity gains that allow you to handle more traffic with the same infrastructure. Additionally, prioritize speed optimization when faster responses provide competitive differentiation that directly translates to user retention and revenue growth.

Consider financial services platforms detecting fraudulent transactions in real-time, or emergency response systems coordinating disaster relief; in these scenarios, you simply cannot compromise on speed because every millisecond counts toward preventing losses or saving lives.

When data ingestion is your primary goal

You should focus on maximizing write throughput when you're operating streaming data pipelines from IoT sensors, social media feeds, or log aggregation systems that generate continuous high-volume data streams requiring immediate processing. Ingestion performance also becomes critical when you're working with time-sensitive data like news aggregation or financial market data, where information value decays rapidly, and delays mean missed opportunities or stale insights. Additionally, prioritize write optimization when you're facing limited batch migration windows that require ingesting large historical datasets during constrained time frames, such as overnight maintenance windows or system cutover periods.

Consider a social media monitoring platform that processes millions of posts, comments, and interactions daily. This system must prioritize ingestion speed to maintain data freshness and deliver timely insights to users tracking trending topics or brand mentions.

When load capacity is your primary goal

You should maximize load capacity when you're operating under tight budget constraints, which is common in startups or proof-of-concept projects where hardware costs dominate operational expenses, and you need to demonstrate value before securing additional funding. Capacity optimization also becomes essential when you're building massive archival systems like digital libraries or compliance platforms that store billions of rarely-accessed vectors, where the cost of keeping everything in premium memory would be prohibitive. Additionally, prioritize capacity when you're targeting edge deployments on mobile devices or embedded systems with strict memory limitations that simply cannot accommodate memory-intensive index structures.

Consider a regulatory compliance document archive storing 10 billion historical document embeddings. This system might readily accept slower search speeds (perhaps 500ms instead of 50ms) to avoid million-dollar infrastructure investments in high-memory servers, since compliance queries are infrequent and users understand that searching decades of archives takes time.

Making your searches faster

In this section, you'll discover three powerful techniques to dramatically improve search performance. We'll start with the most impactful optimization, choosing the right index, then explore batch processing and replica scaling. The key insight is that these techniques work best in combination: proper index selection provides the foundation, while batching and replicas multiply that baseline performance.

Let's begin by understanding what makes vector search slow, then systematically address each bottleneck.

Before diving into optimizations, let's understand how Milvus executes vector search queries and where performance bottlenecks occur. Understanding the execution path is crucial for identifying which optimizations will have the most impact on your specific workload.

The vector search execution path

When you send a search request to Milvus, it flows through multiple components in a carefully orchestrated pipeline:

1. **Proxy receives request**: The Proxy node receives your search query and validates the request parameters
2. **QueryNode ANNS execution**: Each QueryNode performs **approximate nearest neighbor search (ANNS)** on its assigned segments in parallel. This is where the actual vector distance calculations happen using the index you've configured
3. **Result aggregation**: The Proxy collects results from all QueryNodes, merges them, and selects the global top-K most similar vectors
4. **Return results**: The final ranked results are returned to the client

This execution path reveals two critical bottleneck categories:

1. **Single-search bottlenecks**:
    - **ANNS search performance**: The speed of distance calculations within each segment depends directly on your index type and search parameters. Complex indexes like HNSW are fast, while brute-force FLAT indexes are slow
2. **Concurrent-search bottlenecks**:
    - **QueryNode resource contention**: When multiple searches arrive simultaneously, they compete for the same QueryNode resources (CPU, memory bandwidth, cache). A single replica can only process a limited number of concurrent searches before request queuing occurs
    - **Request queuing**: As search volume increases beyond a QueryNode's capacity, requests queue up waiting for processing, dramatically increasing end-to-end latency

Understanding these bottlenecks helps explain why the optimization techniques in this section are so effective:

- Choosing faster indexes reduces ANNS execution time
- Batch processing amortizes overhead across multiple searches
- Multiple replicas eliminate QueryNode resource contention

Now let's explore how to address each bottleneck systematically.

Optimization technique 1: choosing and tuning the right index

Your index choice is the single most impactful decision for search performance—it can mean the difference between very fast and very slow search latency. Let's explore how to make the right choice and tune it for optimal performance.

Each index type represents a different point on the speed-memory-accuracy spectrum. Here's a comprehensive comparison to guide your selection:

Index type	Search speed	Memory usage	Recall quality	Best for
`FLAT`	Slowest	Baseline	Exact (100%)	Small datasets
`HNSW`	Fastest	Higher	Excellent	General purpose, speed critical
`IVF_SQ8`	Moderate	Much lower	Acceptable	Memory-constrained systems
`DISKANN`	Slow	Minimal	Very good	Billion-scale datasets

Table 15.2: Index comparison

Recall quality measures how many of the true nearest neighbors are found by the approximate search. These are typical performance characteristics; your actual results depend on data distribution and parameter tuning.

Implementing an index selection strategy

Here's how to implement the HNSW index strategies for your Wikipedia search system.

The following code creates an HNSW index for fast search:

```
# ch15/code/hnsw_index.py

from pymilvus import MilvusClient, DataType

client = MilvusClient(uri="http://localhost:19530")

# Create collection with schema
```

```
schema = client.create_schema(auto_id=True, enable_dynamic_field=False)
schema.add_field(field_name="id", datatype=DataType.INT64, is_primary=True)
schema.add_field(field_name="emb", datatype=DataType.FLOAT_VECTOR, dim=768)
schema.add_field(field_name="title", datatype=DataType.VARCHAR, max_length=100)
schema.add_field(field_name="text", datatype=DataType.VARCHAR, max_length=5000)
schema.add_field(field_name="wiki_id", datatype=DataType.INT64)
schema.add_field(field_name="views", datatype=DataType.FLOAT)

collection_name = "wiki_hnsw"
client.create_collection(collection_name=collection_name, schema=schema)

# Create HNSW index
index_params = client.prepare_index_params()
index_params.add_index(
    field_name="emb",
    index_type="HNSW",
    metric_type="COSINE",
    params={"M": 16, "efConstruction": 200}
)
client.create_index(
    collection_name=collection_name, index_params=index_params)

# Load collection
client.load_collection(collection_name)

# Search with HNSW
search_params = {"metric_type": "COSINE", "params": {"ef": 128}}
client.search(
    collection_name=collection_name,
    data=[search_vector],
    anns_field="emb",
    search_params=search_params,
    limit=10
)
```

You should see output similar to the following:

```
✓ Index creation completed successfully
Index type: HNSW
Build time: under one minute
Ready for Wikipedia search queries!
```

After selecting your index, fine-tuning search parameters can deliver significant additional performance improvements. Each index has specific parameters that control the speed-accuracy trade-off:

```
# HNSW search optimization for Wikipedia article similarity search
# ef parameter controls search thoroughness vs speed - it's easy to tune!
search_params = {
    "metric_type": "L2",
    "params": {
        "ef": 128  # Start with 128 for balanced performance, increase for higher
accuracy
    }
}

# IVF search optimization for topic-based searches
# nprobe controls how many clusters to search
search_params = {
    "metric_type": "L2",
    "params": {
        "nprobe": 10  # Search 10 out of 1024 clusters for speed
    }
}

# Let's search for similar Wikipedia articles using query embedding
def generate_query_embedding(text):
    # Simple placeholder for embedding generation
    return np.random.random(768).tolist()

query_embedding = generate_query_embedding("quantum computing applications")
results = client.search(
    collection_name="wiki_hnsw",
    data=[query_embedding],  # User's search query as vector
    anns_field="emb",
    search_params=search_params,
    limit=10,  # Return top 10 similar articles
)
```

Index selection and tuning should be your **first optimization step** for any Milvus deployment, as it provides the most significant performance impact with relatively simple configuration changes.

Choose this optimization when index optimization becomes essential when you're experiencing search latencies that exceed your SLA requirements. This is often your first sign that the default index configuration isn't suitable for your workload. You should also prioritize index tuning when you need to carefully balance search speed with memory usage for cost optimization, especially if infrastructure costs are becoming a significant concern. Additionally, consider index optimization when your accuracy requirements vary significantly by use case, such as needing fast approximate results for real-time user searches but higher accuracy for offline analytics. Finally, if you're building a new collection from scratch, choosing the right index from the start prevents costly re-indexing operations later.

Index selection priority must include the following:

1. **Start with HNSW** if memory is enough; it provides the best balance of speed and accuracy for most use cases
2. **Switch to IVF_SQ8** when memory costs become prohibitive (75% memory reduction)
3. **Consider DiskANN** when your dataset exceeds available RAM entirely (covered in the capacity optimization section)

Now, let's turn our attention to batch processing.

Optimization technique 2: leveraging batch search processing

Batch processing can deliver substantial throughput improvements by amortizing overhead costs and enabling SIMD vectorization. Let's explore how to implement this powerful optimization effectively.

Single search processing creates inefficiencies at multiple levels that dramatically impact overall system throughput. Understanding these bottlenecks helps explain why batch processing can deliver 10-50x performance improvements. Here are the bottlenecks:

- **Network inefficiency: the round-trip bottleneck**: Every single search requires a complete network round-trip between client and server. Consider what happens when you process 100 searches individually: you incur 100 TCP connection setups (or reuses from the connection pool), 100 separate request serialization operations, 100 distinct network transmissions each carrying latency overhead, and 100 response deserializations. Even on a high-speed local network with just 1ms latency, these 100 round-trips add 100ms of pure network overhead before any actual vector computation begins. This overhead multiplies dramatically in cloud environments where network latency can be 5-10ms or higher
- With batch processing, all 100 searches travel in a single request, reducing the 100ms network overhead to just 1ms, which is a 100x improvement in network efficiency alone.

- **Computational waste: missing SIMD opportunities**: Modern CPUs feature Single Instruction Multiple Data (SIMD) capabilities through instruction sets like AVX-512, which can process 16 floating-point operations simultaneously. However, processing vectors one at a time creates a fundamental mismatch with how modern hardware works. When Milvus processes a single search vector against an index segment, it computes distances sequentially

  ```
  search_vector[0] compared with index_vectors[0], then [1], then [2]...
  ```

  This sequential processing leaves most of the CPU's parallel execution units idle. With batch processing, Milvus can leverage SIMD instructions to compute multiple distance calculations in parallel:

  ```
  search_vectors[0-15] all compared with index_vectors[0] simultaneously
  ```

  This parallel execution can deliver 8-16x speedup on modern processors, transforming what would be 16 separate operations into a single SIMD instruction.

- **Request processing overhead**: Beyond network and computation, each request incurs fixed overhead for request validation and authentication, parameter parsing and type checking, result serialization and response formatting, and Proxy coordination and routing. These overheads are constant per request, not per search vector. A single request with 100 search vectors pays these costs once. 100 individual requests pay them 100 times

Batch processing transforms these bottlenecks into optimization opportunities. By grouping searches, Milvus can apply SIMD instructions to compute distances for multiple search vectors against the same index segment simultaneously while minimizing network overhead and maximizing cache efficiency.

Implementing effective batch searches

The implementation difference between single and batch searches is straightforward, but the performance impact is dramatic. Here's how to implement batch processing effectively:

```
# ch15/code/batch_search.py

from pymilvus import MilvusClient
from datasets import load_dataset

client = MilvusClient(uri="http://localhost:19530")
collection_name = "wiki_articles"
```

```
# Get search vectors from Wikipedia dataset
def get_search_vectors(num_searches=100):
    docs = load_dataset("Cohere/wikipedia-22-12-simple-embeddings", split="train")
    search_vectors = []
    for i, doc in enumerate(docs):
        if i >= num_searches:
            break
        search_vectors.append(doc["emb"])
    return search_vectors

search_vectors = get_search_vectors(num_searches=100)
search_params = {"metric_type": "COSINE", "params": {"ef": 128}}

# Example 1: Single Search (Sequential)
for i, search_vector in enumerate(search_vectors):
    client.search(
        collection_name=collection_name,
        data=[search_vector],
        anns_field="emb",
        search_params=search_params,
        limit=10
    )

# Example 2: Batch Search (All at Once)
results = client.search(
    collection_name=collection_name,
    data=search_vectors,
    anns_field="emb",
    search_params=search_params,
    limit=10
)
```

Test different batch sizes systematically to find the sweet spot for your system (the optimal batch size)

```
def find_optimal_batch_size(client, collection_name, max_batch_size=1000):
    """Find the optimal batch size for searches"""
    batch_sizes = [1, 10, 50, 100, 200, 500, 1000]

    for batch_size in batch_sizes:
```

```
        search_vectors = np.random.random((batch_size, 768)).tolist()

        start = time.time()
        client.search(
            collection_name=collection_name,
            data=search_vectors,
            anns_field="emb",
            search_params={"metric_type": "L2", "params": {"ef": 128}},
            limit=10
        )
        elapsed = time.time() - start

        throughput = batch_size / elapsed
        avg_latency = (elapsed / batch_size) * 1000

        print(f"Batch size {batch_size:4d}: {avg_latency:6.2f}ms per search,
{throughput:7.1f} QPS")

# Test your system
find_optimal_batch_size(client, "wikipedia_articles")
```

The following are the batch size guidelines:

- **Real-time serving**: Small batches (10-50) for low latency
- **Batch analytics**: Medium batches (100-500) for maximum throughput
- **Offline processing**: Large batches (1000+) when latency doesn't matter

> **Note**
>
> Batch size affects memory usage proportionally. Monitor your QueryNode memory when processing large batches. The optimal size typically plateaus at moderate batch sizes for most systems.

Let's now discuss when to use this technique. Batch processing is one of the easiest optimizations to implement with substantial gains, making it a high-priority optimization for most applications. You should choose this approach when you can accumulate multiple searches before processing, such as in web applications where users submit searches within milliseconds of each other, or periodic analytics workloads. It also makes sense when throughput matters more than individual search latency; recommendation systems scoring thousands of items or batch scoring applications prioritize overall capacity over per-query speed. Additionally, batch processing excels when you're processing multiple user requests concurrently through microservices with connection pooling, or when system utilization remains low despite high search load, indicating that CPU and network resources are underutilized. Remember the following:

- **Implementation complexity:** Low (single line of code change from single to batch searches)
- **Performance impact:** Substantial (10-50x throughput improvement typical)
- **Best combined with:** Index optimization (provides baseline), replica scaling (distributes batches)

Optimization technique 3: scaling with multiple replicas

When your Wikipedia search system needs to handle thousands of concurrent users, replicas provide the most straightforward path to horizontal scaling. Let's explore how to implement and optimize replica deployment.

Replicas work by loading identical copies of your collection's segments across multiple QueryNodes in memory. When you set `replica_number=3`, Milvus creates three complete copies of your data, each managed by a different QueryNode. The proxy layer maintains a real-time mapping of which segments are available on which QueryNodes and intelligently distributes incoming search requests across these replicas. If QueryNode 1 is processing a search on a particular segment, the next search request can immediately go to QueryNode 2 or 3, which hold identical copies of that segment. This parallel processing capability means your throughput scales nearly linearly with the number of replicas—three replicas can theoretically handle three times as many concurrent searches as a single replica. The beauty of this approach lies in its simplicity: unlike sharding, which requires data redistribution, or index tuning which demands careful parameter selection, adding replicas is a single configuration change that delivers immediate and predictable performance gains.

Implementing and managing replicas

Here's a code example that shows multi-replica concurrent search:

```
# ch15/code/multi_replicas.py

from pymilvus import MilvusClient
from multiprocessing import Pool

client = MilvusClient(uri="http://localhost:19530")
collection_name = "wiki_multi_replica"

# Worker function for concurrent search
```

```
def search_worker(args):
    collection_name, search_vector, milvus_uri = args
    client = MilvusClient(uri=milvus_uri)
    search_params = {"metric_type": "COSINE", "params": {"ef": 128}}
    client.search(
        collection_name=collection_name,
        data=[search_vector],
        anns_field="emb",
        search_params=search_params,
        limit=10
    )

# Example 1: Single Replica
client.load_collection(collection_name=collection_name, replica_number=1)

# Example 2: Multi-Replica (2 replicas)
client.release_collection(collection_name)
client.load_collection(collection_name=collection_name, replica_number=2)

# Run concurrent searches with multiprocessing
args_list = [
    (collection_name, search_vector, milvus_uri)
    for search_vector in search_vectors]
with Pool(processes=8) as pool:
    search_times = pool.map(search_worker, args_list)
```

Each replica requires a complete copy of the collection data in memory. With 3 replicas of a 100GB collection, you need 300GB of total RAM across your QueryNodes. Additionally, you must have at least as many QueryNodes as replicas.

Combining techniques for maximum performance

The real power comes from combining multiple optimization techniques. While each technique delivers significant gains independently, their effects multiply when used together. Index optimization establishes your baseline performance by making individual searches fast. Replicas scale this performance horizontally by allowing many searches to execute in parallel across multiple QueryNodes. Batch processing maximizes efficiency by grouping requests together, reducing network overhead, and enabling better resource utilization across all your replicas.

Think of it as a three-layer performance multiplier: a well-tuned HNSW index might give you 50x faster searches, three replicas can handle 3x more concurrent users, and batching 20 queries together adds another 10x throughput improvement. Combined, these optimizations can transform a system handling tens of searches per second into one serving thousands of concurrent users with consistent sub-100ms latency. The key is applying them systematically; start with index optimization for baseline speed, add replicas when concurrency grows, and implement batching whenever you can accumulate multiple requests.

Speeding up your data ingestion

In this section, you'll discover three powerful techniques to dramatically improve write throughput. We'll start with batch insertion, the simplest optimization with the biggest impact, then explore multi-shard parallelization and bulk import for massive datasets. The progression is intentional: batch insertion is your first optimization (easy to implement, substantial gains), multi-shard configuration scales throughput linearly with hardware, and bulk import handles special cases like initial data migrations.

Let's begin by understanding the Milvus write pipeline and identifying where bottlenecks occur.

Understanding data ingestion performance challenges

Vector database ingestion differs fundamentally from traditional databases. Each write operation triggers a complex pipeline involving multiple components, creating unique optimization opportunities and challenges.

Data flows through multiple stages in Milvus. The Milvus write pipeline includes:

1. Client sends writes to Proxy.
2. Proxy validates and enqueues to the Message Queue (Pulsar/Kafka)
3. DataNode consumes messages and writes sealed segments
4. If the collection is loaded, QueryNode maintains growing segments for immediate visibility.

Three critical bottlenecks limit write throughput in vector databases:

1. **Request processing overhead**: Processing individual insert requests creates excessive overhead throughout the entire ingestion pipeline. Each request requires the Proxy to perform validation, authentication, schema verification, and routing operations. Every single vector insert incurs TCP overhead and network latency from client to Proxy communication. The message queue layer must serialize individual messages, select partition routing, and handle acknowledgments for each operation. At the DataNode level, per-record operations process vectors one at a time instead of leveraging batch optimizations. Sending single vectors wastes system resources on protocol overhead rather than actual data processing. This overhead multiplies with volume, and at scale, network round-trips and protocol processing can consume the majority of insertion time rather than actual data handling.

2. **Single-consumer bottleneck**: The default single-shard configuration creates a fundamental throughput limitation that prevents horizontal scaling. With a single shard, only one DataNode processes inserts for the collection, regardless of how many DataNodes exist in your cluster. Other DataNodes sit idle with wasted capacity because Milvus assigns each shard to exactly one consumer. All inserts must flow through this single consumption pipeline sequentially, creating a processing bottleneck. When the insert production speed exceeds the single DataNode's consumption capacity, messages accumulate in the queue, and end-to-end latency grows. This bottleneck prevents horizontal scaling; adding more DataNodes doesn't improve throughput because only one actively processes the collection's inserts.
3. **Online pipeline overhead for massive datasets**: For billion-scale data migrations, the online ingestion pipeline becomes inefficient because it optimizes for real-time streaming rather than batch loading. Every record must flow through the complete multi-hop processing path: ***Client* → *Proxy* → *Message Queue* → *DataNode* → *Segment building***. DataNodes build segments incrementally as they consume streaming inserts, which creates more overhead than batch segment construction. This incremental approach processes data through multiple system components when massive datasets could be loaded more directly.

The standard pipeline optimizes for real-time ingestion but wastes resources when loading massive pre-existing datasets that could be processed more efficiently in batch.

Optimization technique 1: batch insertion for immediate impact

Batch insertion is your first and most impactful optimization. It's straightforward to implement and can deliver substantial throughput improvements immediately. Understanding why batch insertion works is key to optimizing your ingestion pipeline.

Single-record insertion suffers from the same overhead issues we saw with single searches, but the impact on write performance is even more pronounced. Every insert request, regardless of size, triggers a complete processing pipeline through the proxy layer, message queue serialization, and DataNode operations. When you insert 1000 vectors individually, you pay network round-trip costs 1000 times, each DataNode must lock and update segments 1000 times, and the message queue must process 1000 separate messages. With batching, these operations happen just once for all 1000 vectors, eliminating nearly all the per-record overhead.

Implementing efficient batch insertion

Here's a code example illustrating batch insertion for maximum throughput:

```
# ch15/code/batch_insert.py

from pymilvus import MilvusClient
from datasets import load_dataset

client = MilvusClient(uri="http://localhost:19530")
collection_name = "wiki_insert_test"

# Get Wikipedia records
def get_wikipedia_records(limit=5000):
    docs = load_dataset("Cohere/wikipedia-22-12-simple-embeddings",
                        split="train", streaming=True)
    records = []
    for i, doc in enumerate(docs):
        if i >= limit:
            break
        records.append({
            "emb": doc["emb"],
            "title": doc["title"][:100],
            "text": doc["text"][:5000],
            "wiki_id": doc["wiki_id"],
            "views": float(doc["views"])
        })
    return records

# Example 1: Single Record Insert (Inefficient)
records = get_wikipedia_records(limit=1000)
for i, record in enumerate(records):
    client.insert(collection_name=collection_name, data=[record])

# Example 2: Batch Insert (Efficient)
records = get_wikipedia_records(limit=1000)
client.insert(collection_name=collection_name, data=records)

# Example 3: Streaming Micro-batch Pattern
total_records = 5000
micro_batch_size = 500
```

```
docs = load_dataset("Cohere/wikipedia-22-12-simple-embeddings",
                    split="train", streaming=True)

batch_buffer = []
for i, doc in enumerate(docs):
    if i >= total_records:
        break

    record = {
        "emb": doc["emb"],
        "title": doc["title"][:100],
        "text": doc["text"][:5000],
        "wiki_id": doc["wiki_id"],
        "views": float(doc["views"])
    }
    batch_buffer.append(record)

    if len(batch_buffer) >= micro_batch_size or i == total_records - 1:
        client.insert(collection_name=collection_name, data=batch_buffer)
        batch_buffer = []
```

So, when should you use batch insertion? Batch insertion should be your **first optimization step** for any data ingestion workload. It's the easiest to implement with the most substantial immediate impact. This technique delivers 10-100x throughput improvements over single-record insertion with a single line of code change, making it the default approach for virtually all write operations.

You should implement batch insertion whenever you have continuous streaming data where brief accumulation is acceptable, such as real-time data pipelines from IoT sensors, user activity streams, or ML inference services generating embeddings. It's equally essential for ETL and data migration scenarios where you're loading pre-existing data from external databases, file systems, or data lakes. The technique excels in microservices architectures where application servers can buffer multiple user-generated requests before database writes, and in any high-throughput environment requiring thousands to millions of vectors per second.

Optimization technique 2: multi-shard parallelization

When batch insertion alone isn't enough, a multi-shard configuration multiplies your ingestion capacity through parallel processing. Sharding is the key to achieving linear scaling of write throughput as you add more hardware resources.

Sharding transforms Milvus' write path from a single-bottleneck pipeline into a parallel processing system. Understanding how sharding works reveals why it can deliver near-linear throughput scaling with additional DataNodes.

By default, Milvus collections use a single shard, which creates a fundamental throughput limitation. In a single-shard configuration, the Proxy receives insert requests and routes them to the message queue, where a single message queue vchannel stores all inserts sequentially. A single DataNode then consumes messages from that vchannel, and its processing becomes the bottleneck; one DataNode must process all inserts alone.

Even with multiple DataNodes in your cluster, only one DataNode actively processes inserts for a single-shard collection. The other DataNodes sit idle, representing wasted capacity. This is analogous to having a 10-lane highway that merges into a single lane; all traffic must pass through that one bottleneck.

When you configure a collection with multiple shards, Milvus transforms the architecture into a parallel processing system. The Proxy hashes each insert's primary key to determine the target shard, distributing the workload across multiple vchannels. Each of these vchannels stores inserts in parallel, and multiple DataNodes consume from different vchannels simultaneously. This parallel processing allows multiple DataNodes to work concurrently, breaking the single-DataNode bottleneck.

Implementing multi-shard configuration

Here's a code example illustrating multi-shard parallel ingestion:

```
# ch15/code/multi_shard_insert.py

from pymilvus import MilvusClient, DataType
from datasets import load_dataset

client = MilvusClient(uri="http://localhost:19530")

# Create collection schema
schema = client.create_schema(auto_id=True, enable_dynamic_field=False)
schema.add_field(
    field_name="id", datatype=DataType.INT64, is_primary=True)
schema.add_field(
```

```
    field_name="emb", datatype=DataType.FLOAT_VECTOR, dim=768)
schema.add_field(field_name="title", datatype=DataType.VARCHAR, max_length=100)
schema.add_field(field_name="text", datatype=DataType.VARCHAR, max_length=5000)
schema.add_field(field_name="wiki_id", datatype=DataType.INT64)
schema.add_field(field_name="views", datatype=DataType.FLOAT)

# Example 1: Single Shard Collection
collection_name = "wiki_single_shard"
client.create_collection(
    collection_name=collection_name,
    schema=schema,
    num_shards=1
)

# Create index
index_params = client.prepare_index_params()
index_params.add_index(
    field_name="emb",
    index_type="HNSW",
    metric_type="COSINE",
    params={"M": 16, "efConstruction": 200}
)
client.create_index(
    collection_name=collection_name, index_params=index_params)

# Example 2: Multi-Shard Collection (4 Shards)
collection_name = "wiki_4_shards"
client.create_collection(
    collection_name=collection_name,
    schema=schema,
    num_shards=4
)
client.create_index(
    collection_name=collection_name, index_params=index_params)
```

The following table shows the best practices for shard configuration

Write throughput	Dataset size	Recommended shards	Infrastructure required
Low	Small	1	1 DataNode
Moderate	Medium	2	2+ DataNodes
High	Large	4	4+ DataNodes
Very High	Very Large	8	8+ DataNodes
Extreme	Massive	16	16+ DataNodes

Table 15.3: overview of shard configuration best practices

So, when should you use multi-shard parallelization? Multi-shard configuration is your **horizontal scaling strategy** when batch insertion alone cannot meet throughput requirements. It transforms single-DataNode write bottlenecks into parallel processing that scales linearly with hardware additions.

Deploy multi-shard parallelization when you need sustained high-throughput ingestion, such as real-time data pipelines from IoT sensor networks, clickstream analytics systems, or massive log processing workloads generating continuous vector streams. It becomes essential for multi-producer architectures where multiple application servers or services simultaneously write to the same collection, and their combined write volume overwhelms a single DataNode's consumption capacity. Large-scale ETL operations benefit significantly when parallel data migration from multiple sources requires maximizing ingestion speed. This technique is also critical for capacity planning when monitoring shows your single-shard DataNode consistently approaching 80-90% CPU or memory utilization during writes, adding shards preemptively prevents future bottlenecks. Systems designed for horizontal scalability should configure multiple shards from the start, as the shard count cannot be changed after collection creation without rebuilding.

> **Note**
>
> Sharding involves trade-offs. While it dramatically improves write throughput, queries must aggregate results from all shards, adding latency. Choose shard count based on actual write requirements; excessive sharding wastes resources without benefits.

Optimization technique 3: bulk import for massive datasets

When you need to load billions of vectors, bulk import bypasses the entire online ingestion pipeline for dramatic throughput improvements. Let's explore how to leverage this powerful technique for large-scale data migrations.

The standard path processes each batch through multiple components: the Proxy validates and forwards data, the message queue buffers writes, and DataNodes gradually build segments that undergo multiple flushes and compactions. Each hop adds latency and resource overhead, limiting maximum throughput to hundreds of thousands of vectors per second in typical deployments.

Bulk import takes a fundamentally different approach by preparing data offline and loading it directly into sealed segments. You prepare Parquet or JSON files containing millions of vectors using tools that can fully utilize your data preparation infrastructure—whether that's Spark clusters, Python scripts on powerful machines, or ETL pipelines. Once files are uploaded to object storage (MinIO, S3, or Azure Blob), Milvus reads them directly and creates sealed segments without involving the Proxy, message queue, or standard DataNode write path. This architecture eliminates the bottlenecks inherent in online systems: no network round-trip between components, no message queue throughput limits.

Implementing high-performance bulk import

Here's a code example illustrating bulk import for massive datasets:

```
# ch15/code/bulk_import.py

from pymilvus import MilvusClient
from pymilvus.bulk_writer import (
    RemoteBulkWriter, BulkFileType, bulk_import, get_import_progress)
from datasets import load_dataset

client = MilvusClient(uri="http://localhost:19530")

# MinIO configuration
MINIO_ENDPOINT = "localhost:9000"
ACCESS_KEY = "minioadmin"
SECRET_KEY = "minioadmin"
BUCKET_NAME = "a-bucket"

collection_name = "wiki_bulk_import"
num_vectors = 100000
```

```
# Step 1: Prepare Data Files with RemoteBulkWriter
connect_param = RemoteBulkWriter.S3ConnectParam(
    endpoint=MINIO_ENDPOINT,
    access_key=ACCESS_KEY,
    secret_key=SECRET_KEY,
    bucket_name=BUCKET_NAME,
    secure=False
)

writer = RemoteBulkWriter(
    schema=schema,
    remote_path="/wiki_bulk/",
    connect_param=connect_param,
    file_type=BulkFileType.PARQUET
)

# Load Wikipedia dataset and write to Parquet files
docs = load_dataset("Cohere/wikipedia-22-12-simple-embeddings",
                    split="train", streaming=True)

batch_size = 10000
for i, doc in enumerate(docs):
    if i >= num_vectors:
        break

    row = {
        "emb": doc["emb"],
        "title": doc["title"][:100],
        "text": doc["text"][:5000],
        "wiki_id": doc["wiki_id"],
        "views": float(doc["views"])
    }
    writer.append_row(row)

    if (i + 1) % batch_size == 0:
        writer.commit()

batch_files = writer.batch_files

# Step 2: Execute Bulk Import Job
resp = bulk_import(
```

```
    url="http://localhost:19530",
    collection_name=collection_name,
    files=batch_files
)

job_id = resp.json()["data"]["jobId"]

# Step 3: Monitor Import Progress
while True:
    progress_resp = get_import_progress(
        url="http://localhost:19530",
        job_id=job_id
    )

    data = progress_resp.json()["data"]
    state = data["state"]

    if state == "Completed":
        break
    elif state == "Failed":
        break
    elif state in ["Pending", "Importing"]:
        time.sleep(2)
```

When to use bulk import? Bulk import is your specialized tool for massive one-time data loading. It bypasses the entire online ingestion pipeline to achieve 10-100x throughput improvements over standard batch insertion, making it essential for large-scale migrations and periodic rebuilds.

Use bulk import for initial data migrations when moving existing embeddings from another vector database, traditional database, or file-based storage into Milvus, in scenarios where you have millions to billions of pre-computed vectors requiring rapid initial loading. It excels for massive dataset onboarding of 100M+ vectors, where loading speed is critical and temporary unavailability is acceptable. Use it for periodic batch updates involving complete dataset refreshes, such as monthly reindexing of a product catalog or quarterly historical data updates where downtime windows align with maintenance schedules. Bulk import is ideal for data lake integration when importing large Parquet or JSON files directly from object storage systems (S3, MinIO, GCS) without requiring intermediate processing.

Combining ingestion techniques for maximum throughput

The real power comes from combining multiple techniques strategically to maximize DataNode utilization. While each technique delivers substantial improvements individually, combining batch insertion with multi-shard configurations or pairing bulk import with multi-shard design enables 100-1000x throughput improvements by fully exploiting parallel processing across multiple DataNodes.

Batch insertion combined with multi-shard configuration multiplies throughput by reducing per-vector overhead while parallelizing processing across DataNodes. Batching minimizes network round-trip costs, serialization costs, and coordination overhead for each vector, while multi-shard distribution spreads these efficient batch operations across multiple DataNodes that process independently in parallel. Each DataNode handles batches for its assigned shard at full speed, making total throughput scale proportionally with shard count. Similarly, bulk import paired with multi-shard configuration enables parallel import jobs that fully utilize multiple DataNodes concurrently.

Maximizing queryable data capacity

This section focuses on expanding your queryable data capacity, the amount of vector data you can load and search. We'll explore three complementary strategies that work within Milvus' memory-centric architecture to maximize the data you can keep searchable while managing costs and performance trade-offs. These strategies form a progression: IVF_SQ8 quantization provides immediate capacity gains with minimal complexity, mmap extends capacity through intelligent OS management, and DiskANN breaks the RAM barrier entirely for billion-scale datasets.

Let's start by understanding how Milvus uses memory and then explore each capacity expansion strategy.

Understanding queryable capacity bottlenecks

Milvus' memory-centric architecture creates specific capacity constraints that differ fundamentally from traditional databases. Understanding these constraints is essential for maximizing your searchable data capacity.

Unlike traditional databases that can search data directly from disk, Milvus requires loading collections into the QueryNode memory before they become searchable. This design choice enables blazing-fast vector search but creates a hard capacity constraint.

When a collection is loaded, QueryNodes store multiple data components in memory, each contributing to the total memory footprint. Three critical bottlenecks limit your queryable data capacity in Milvus:

- **Raw vector volume**: Your vectors simply exceed available RAM. Large vector collections with hundreds of millions of embeddings can require hundreds of GB just for raw data storage before even considering index overhead. This bottleneck emerges when your dataset size fundamentally outgrows your infrastructure's memory capacity.

- **Index amplification**: Complex indexes like HNSW can nearly double memory requirements with their graph structures and connection metadata. While these indexes deliver excellent search performance, they multiply your baseline memory requirements by turning a 100GB dataset into a 200GB+ memory footprint. This bottleneck forces you to choose between search speed and capacity.
- **Scalar field accumulation**: VARCHAR and JSON fields gradually consume more memory as your application evolves. Adding product descriptions (*VARCHAR*), user tags (`JSON`), categories (`VARCHAR`), and dynamic fields increases per-vector overhead. Over time, what started as a small scalar field footprint grows to represent a substantial portion of total memory usage, especially with millions of vectors.

Now let's explore three strategies to maximize your queryable capacity within these constraints.

Optimization technique 1: IVF_SQ8 quantization for substantial capacity expansion

`IVF_SQ8` is Milvus' most practical capacity optimization technique, combining inverted file clustering with scalar quantization to achieve substantial memory reduction while maintaining reasonable search accuracy. You may ask how `IVF_SQ8` dramatically expands capacity.

`IVF_SQ8` achieves 4x capacity expansion by compressing vector data from 32-bit floats to 8-bit integers—reducing each dimension from 4 bytes to 1 byte. This Scalar Quantization (SQ8) works because vector search tolerates small approximations when ranking results: finding the top-10 most similar items from millions of candidates rarely changes when values are compressed to 256 discrete levels. The IVF (Inverted File) component divides vectors into clusters and applies separate quantization mappings to each cluster, which dramatically improves compression accuracy since vectors within a cluster have similar value distributions. During search, you only examine vectors in a few relevant clusters rather than the entire dataset.

Together, these techniques deliver 4x capacity expansion with typically just 1-5% recall reduction. For example, an e-commerce platform with 50 million product embeddings requiring 150 GB with HNSW indexing can compress to approximately 38 GB with `IVF_SQ8`—fitting on a 64GB QueryNode instead of requiring a costly 256GB upgrade. This makes `IVF_SQ8` the first optimization choice for capacity-constrained deployments.

Here's how to create a memory-optimized collection with `IVF_SQ8` for maximum capacity (4x memory compression)

```
# ch15/code/ivf_sq8_quantization.py

from pymilvus import MilvusClient, DataType

client = MilvusClient(uri="http://localhost:19530")
dim = 768

# Create collection schema
schema = client.create_schema(auto_id=True, enable_dynamic_field=False)
schema.add_field(
    field_name="id", datatype=DataType.INT64, is_primary=True)
schema.add_field(field_name="emb", datatype=DataType.FLOAT_VECTOR, dim=dim)
schema.add_field(field_name="title", datatype=DataType.VARCHAR, max_length=100)
schema.add_field(field_name="text", datatype=DataType.VARCHAR, max_length=5000)
schema.add_field(field_name="wiki_id", datatype=DataType.INT64)
schema.add_field(field_name="views", datatype=DataType.FLOAT)

# Example 1: IVF_FLAT Index (No Quantization)
collection_name = "wiki_ivf_flat"
client.create_collection(collection_name=collection_name, schema=schema)

index_params = client.prepare_index_params()
index_params.add_index(
    field_name="emb",
    index_type="IVF_FLAT",
    metric_type="COSINE",
    params={"nlist": 4096}
)
client.create_index(
    collection_name=collection_name, index_params=index_params)

# Example 2: IVF_SQ8 Index (With Quantization - 4x memory reduction)
collection_name = "wiki_ivf_sq8"
client.create_collection(collection_name=collection_name, schema=schema)

index_params = client.prepare_index_params()
index_params.add_index(
    field_name="emb",
```

```
    index_type="IVF_SQ8",
    metric_type="L2",
    params={"nlist": 4096}
)
client.create_index(collection_name=collection_name, index_params=index_params)

# Load and search
client.load_collection(collection_name)
search_params = {"metric_type": "COSINE", "params": {"nprobe": 32}}
results = client.search(
    collection_name=collection_name,
    data=[search_vector],
    anns_field="emb",
    search_params=search_params,
    limit=10
)

# Tune nprobe parameter
for nprobe in [8, 16, 32, 64, 128]:
    search_params = {"metric_type": "COSINE", "params": {"nprobe": nprobe}}
    client.search(
        collection_name=collection_name,
        data=[search_vector],
        anns_field="emb",
        search_params=search_params,
        limit=10
    )
```

The following are the tuning guidelines:

- `nlist`: Set during index creation (typically 1024-8192). More clusters equal better accuracy, but more memory consumption
- `nprobe`: Set during search (typically 8-128). More probes equal better accuracy, but a slower search
- Start with `nprobe=16` for balanced performance, then increase for higher accuracy requirements
- For most production workloads: `nlist=4096` and `nprobe=32` provide a good balance

The next question is *when you should choose* `IVF_SQ8`. `IVF_SQ8` works best for scenarios sharing three characteristics: large-scale datasets (millions to billions of vectors), tolerance for approximate results (1-5% recall reduction), and memory cost sensitivity. This pattern fits most production applications where search quality matters less than scalability and cost. Common scenarios include large-scale recommendation systems with billions of product or content embeddings, e-commerce platforms searching millions of products, log analysis pipelines processing massive time-series vector data, and development environments that need to fit production-scale datasets on limited hardware. The key insight is that users rarely notice the difference between 98% and 99.5% recall when browsing search results, but they immediately notice when infrastructure costs double.

Avoid `IVF_SQ8` for high-precision applications requiring >99% recall (medical diagnosis, scientific research), small datasets that already fit comfortably in RAM with uncompressed indexes, or ultra-low-latency scenarios where decompression overhead matters (sub-millisecond trading systems).

Optimization technique 2: mmap for intelligent hot/cold data management

Memory mapping (**mmap**) enables Milvus to exceed physical RAM limitations by letting the operating system intelligently manage which data stays in memory versus disk. This technique is particularly effective for collections with uneven access patterns. Mmap breaks the hard RAM constraint by leveraging the operating system's virtual memory management, enabling Milvus to work with datasets that far exceed physical RAM. Unlike data compression techniques, mmap expands effective capacity by intelligently managing what stays in RAM versus what lives on disk, delivering 5-10x capacity gains for workloads with skewed access patterns.

Traditional vector databases face a hard wall: if your collection requires 500GB but you have 128GB RAM, loading fails. Mmap sidesteps this by creating an illusion; Milvus "sees" the entire 500GB as if it's in memory, but the OS keeps only actively accessed portions (perhaps 100GB) in physical RAM while the rest stays on disk. When accessing a memory page, the OS delivers it from RAM in ~100 nanoseconds if cached, or loads it from NVMe SSD in ~5-10 milliseconds if not. The key insight is that real-world workloads rarely access all data equally.

Capacity expansion directly correlates with access skew. Consider a content platform with 100 million article embeddings (300GB). Recent articles get 80% of the traffic, while historical archives see 20%. On a 64GB QueryNode with mmap, the OS keeps hot recent content (~50GB) in RAM while the 250GB archive stays on disk. Without mmap, you'd need a 300GB server. With mmap, the 64GB server handles the same load; recent content at RAM speed, historical content at acceptable disk latency (50ms vs 5ms).

Time-series data, multi-tenant systems, and e-commerce catalogs naturally exhibit this skew. The OS's **least recently used** (**LRU**) page cache adapts automatically without configuration; for example, frequently accessed pages remain in RAM while cold pages migrate to disk. This automatic management means you can load a 300GB dataset on a 64GB machine and achieve near-RAM performance for hot data while cold data accepts disk latency. The smaller working set in RAM also improves cache hit rates, reducing disk I/O overhead.

However, mmap provides little benefit for uniform access patterns where every vector gets equal traffic. In these cases, add more RAM or use DiskANN's explicit disk management instead.

Implementing mmap for maximum effectiveness

Milvus provides fine-grained mmap control through a hierarchical configuration system with four levels of precedence. Understanding these levels enables you to optimize memory usage by applying mmap selectively to large fields while keeping frequently accessed data in RAM.

Here's the mmap configuration hierarchy (highest to lowest precedence):

1. **Field-level**: Configure mmap for individual scalar/vector fields
2. **Index-level**: Configure mmap for specific indexes
3. **Collection-level**: Configure mmap for entire collections
4. **Global-level**: System-wide default settings in `milvus.yaml`

The key strategy is to enable mmap on large, infrequently accessed fields (like long text content or historical embeddings) while keeping hot data (such as recent vectors or small metadata) in RAM.

Strategy 1: collection-level mmap (simplest approach)

Enable mmap for the entire collection when most of your data is cold or when you want the OS to automatically manage all data placement

Here's a code example of collection-level mmap

```
from pymilvus import MilvusClient, DataType

# Connect to Milvus
client = MilvusClient(uri="http://localhost:19530")

dim = 768

# Define schema for a document collection
schema = client.create_schema(auto_id=True, enable_dynamic_field=False)
schema.add_field(field_name="id", datatype=DataType.INT64, is_primary=True)
schema.add_field(field_name="embedding", datatype=DataType.FLOAT_VECTOR, dim=dim)
schema.add_field(field_name="title", datatype=DataType.VARCHAR, max_length=500)
schema.add_field(field_name="content", datatype=DataType.VARCHAR, max_length=5000)
```

```
# Create collection with mmap enabled at collection level
collection_name = "articles_collection_mmap"
client.create_collection(
    collection_name=collection_name,
    schema=schema,
    properties={"mmap.enabled": "true"} # All fields and indexes use mmap
)

# Create index - automatically inherits collection-level mmap setting
index_params = client.prepare_index_params()
index_params.add_index(
    field_name="embedding",
    index_type="IVF_FLAT",  # IVF_FLAT and HNSW support mmap
    metric_type="L2",
    params={"nlist": 2048}
)
client.create_index(
    collection_name=collection_name, index_params=index_params)

print("Collection created with mmap enabled - can load datasets exceeding physical 
RAM")
```

Strategy 2: field-level mmap (granular control)

Apply mmap selectively to specific fields for optimal performance. Keep hot fields in RAM while using mmap only for cold or large fields.

Here's a code example of field-level mmap:

```
# Define schema with selective mmap settings per field
schema_selective = client.create_schema(
    auto_id=True, enable_dynamic_field=False)
schema_selective.add_field(
    field_name="id", datatype=DataType.INT64, is_primary=True)

# Hot field: Embeddings frequently searched - keep in RAM
schema_selective.add_field(
    field_name="embedding",
    datatype=DataType.FLOAT_VECTOR,
    dim=dim,
    mmap_enabled=False  # Keep in RAM for fast search
)
```

```
# Hot field: Category used for filtering - keep in RAM
schema_selective.add_field(
    field_name="category",
    datatype=DataType.VARCHAR,
    max_length=100,
    mmap_enabled=False  # Keep in RAM for fast filtering
)

# Cold field: Large text content rarely accessed - use mmap
schema_selective.add_field(
    field_name="full_text",
    datatype=DataType.VARCHAR,
    max_length=10000,
    mmap_enabled=True  # Use disk to save RAM
)

collection_name_selective = "articles_selective_mmap"
client.create_collection(
    collection_name=collection_name_selective,
    schema=schema_selective
)

print("Selective mmap: hot embeddings in RAM, cold text on disk")
```

This approach provides the best balance as frequently accessed vectors remain in RAM for fast search, while large text fields use mmap to save memory.

Strategy 3: index-level mmap (index-specific control)

Configure mmap settings per index, allowing different indexes on the same collection to use different memory management strategies.

Here's a code example of index-level mmap:

```
# Define schema
schema_index = client.create_schema(
    auto_id=True, enable_dynamic_field=False)
schema_index.add_field(
    field_name="id", datatype=DataType.INT64, is_primary=True)
schema_index.add_field(
    field_name="title", datatype=DataType.VARCHAR, max_length=500)
schema_index.add_field(
```

```
    field_name="embedding", datatype=DataType.FLOAT_VECTOR, dim=dim)

collection_name_index = "articles_index_mmap"
client.create_collection(
    collection_name=collection_name_index, schema=schema_index)

# Create indexes with different mmap settings
index_params_index = client.prepare_index_params()

# Vector index: Large size, use mmap
index_params_index.add_index(
    field_name="embedding",
    index_type="IVF_FLAT",
    metric_type="L2",
    params={"nlist": 2048, "mmap.enabled": "true"}  # Vector index uses mmap
)

# Scalar index: Small size, keep in RAM for fast filtering
index_params_index.add_index(
    field_name="title",
    index_type="AUTOINDEX",
    params={"mmap.enabled": "false"}  # Scalar index stays in RAM
)

client.create_index(
    collection_name = collection_name_index,
    index_params = index_params_index)

print("Index-level mmap: vector index on disk, scalar index in RAM")
```

You can also dynamically adjust mmap settings for existing collections. Changes require releasing and reloading the collection to take effect.

Here's a code example that shows modifying mmap settings:

```
# Change collection-level mmap setting
client.alter_collection_properties(
    collection_name="articles_collection_mmap",
    properties={"mmap.enabled": False}  # Disable mmap for entire collection
)
```

```
# Change field-level mmap setting
client.alter_collection_field(
    collection_name="articles_selective_mmap",
    field_name="full_text",
    field_params={"mmap.enabled": False}  # Move field from disk to RAM
)

# Change index-level mmap setting
client.alter_index_properties(
    collection_name="articles_index_mmap",
    index_name="embedding",
    properties={"mmap.enabled": False}  # Move index from disk to RAM
)

# IMPORTANT: Release and reload collection for changes to take effect
client.release_collection("articles_collection_mmap")
client.load_collection("articles_collection_mmap")

print("mmap settings modified - collection reloaded to apply changes")
```

So, *when should you choose* mmap? Mmap works best for scenarios sharing three characteristics: natural access skew (some data queried frequently, most rarely), dataset size exceeding available RAM, and fast SSD storage. This pattern perfectly fits time-series workloads where recent data dominates traffic; for e.g., a content platform where 80%+ queries hit recent articles while historical archives sit idle, or multi-tenant systems where active tenants stay in RAM while inactive ones migrate to disk automatically. E-commerce catalogs with seasonal patterns, development environments needing production-scale data on limited hardware, and tiered applications separating premium/active users from free/inactive users all benefit from mmap's automatic hot/cold management.

Avoid mmap when access patterns are uniform (all vectors accessed equally means no caching benefit), latency requirements are strict (sub-10ms queries can't tolerate disk access), storage is traditional HDD (100ms+ access makes mmap unusable), or datasets already fit comfortably in RAM. High write workloads also cause excessive disk I/O with mmap enabled.

> **Note**
>
> Mmap's effectiveness depends on access skew. With 80/20 patterns (80% queries hit 20% of data), mmap enables 5-10x capacity expansion with minimal performance impact—loading datasets that far exceed physical RAM by intelligently caching hot data while keeping cold data on disk.

Optimization technique 3: DiskANN for breaking the billion-vector barrier

DiskANN represents Milvus' most advanced capacity solution, designed specifically for datasets that dwarf available RAM. By keeping only essential navigation data in memory and storing vectors on high-speed SSDs, DiskANN enables querying billion-scale datasets with a minimal memory footprint.

DiskANN achieves 20-30x capacity expansion by separating navigation from storage. It keeps only product quantization compressed codes in RAM (32x compression: 3,072 bytes to 96 bytes per vector) for graph navigation, while storing full-precision vectors on NVMe SSD. For 1 billion 768-dimensional vectors, traditional HNSW needs approximately 3TB of RAM, but DiskANN needs only approximately 100GB in memory, which is manageable on a standard 256GB server. During search, DiskANN performs graph navigation entirely in RAM using compressed codes to identify 100-200 candidates, then reads only those finalists from disk for exact distance computation. With NVMe SSDs, reading 200 vectors (~600KB) takes 1-2ms, keeping total query latency in the 10-50ms range.

This transforms economics for billion-scale deployments. A 5 billion photo search platform needs approximately 15TB RAM with HNSW (around $500K annually in cloud costs), but only approximately 500GB RAM plus 15TB NVMe SSD with DiskANN; NVMe costs roughly 10x less than RAM. The trade-off is accepting 10-50ms latency instead of sub-millisecond latency, and requiring high-performance NVMe storage with excellent IOPS.

Implementing DiskANN for ultra-scale datasets

DiskANN is Milvus' solution for billion-scale vector search. Before implementing DiskANN, ensure your Milvus deployment has `queryNode.enableDisk: true` configured, as this index requires explicit disk support.

DiskANN uses three key parameters to control memory usage and build performance.

Here's a code example that shows DiskANN for billion-scale search:

```
# ch15/code/diskann_index.py

from pymilvus import MilvusClient, DataType

client = MilvusClient(uri="http://localhost:19530")
dim = 768

# Create collection schema
schema = client.create_schema(auto_id=True, enable_dynamic_field=False)
```

```
schema.add_field(
    field_name="id", datatype=DataType.INT64, is_primary=True)
schema.add_field(field_name="emb", datatype=DataType.FLOAT_VECTOR, dim=dim)
schema.add_field(
    field_name="title", datatype=DataType.VARCHAR, max_length=100)
schema.add_field(
    field_name="text", datatype=DataType.VARCHAR, max_length=5000)
schema.add_field(field_name="wiki_id", datatype=DataType.INT64)
schema.add_field(field_name="views", datatype=DataType.FLOAT)

collection_name = "wiki_diskann"
client.create_collection(collection_name=collection_name, schema=schema)

# Create DiskANN index
try:
    index_params = client.prepare_index_params()
    index_params.add_index(
        field_name="emb",
        index_type="DISKANN",
        metric_type="COSINE",
        params={
            "search_list": 100,
            "pq_code_budget_gb": 0.125,
            "build_dram_budget_gb": 2.0
        }
    )
    client.create_index(
        collection_name=collection_name, index_params=index_params)
except Exception as e:
    print(f"DiskANN creation failed: {e}")

# Load and search
client.load_collection(collection_name)
search_params = {"metric_type": "COSINE", "params": {"search_list": 100}}
results = client.search(
    collection_name=collection_name,
    data=[search_vector],
    anns_field="emb",
    search_params=search_params,
    limit=10
)
```

```
# Tune search_list parameter
for search_list in [50, 100, 200, 300]:
    search_params = {"metric_type": "COSINE",
                    "params": {"search_list": search_list}
                    }
    client.search(
        collection_name=collection_name,
        data=[search_vector],
        anns_field="emb",
        search_params=search_params,
        limit=10
    )
```

Let's now understand the DiskANN parameters:

- `search_list`: Controls the candidate list size during search. Higher values improve accuracy but increase latency. Typical range: 50-300
- `pq_code_budget_gb`: RAM allocated to store compressed vector codes. For 1 billion 768-dim vectors, 0.125GB per million vectors is typical
- `build_dram_budget_gb`: Temporary RAM used during index construction. More RAM speeds up building but doesn't affect query performance

DiskANN search behavior is controlled primarily by the `search_list` parameter, which determines the accuracy-latency trade-off:

```
import numpy as np

# Load collection
client.load_collection("images_billion_scale")

# Configure search parameters
search_params = {
    "metric_type": "L2",
    "params": {
        "search_list": 100  # Balance between accuracy and speed
    }
}

# Perform search
search_vector = np.random.random(768).tolist()
```

```
results = client.search(
    collection_name="images_billion_scale",
    data=[search_vector],
    anns_field="embedding",
    search_params=search_params,
    limit=10
)

print(f"Found {len(results[0])} similar images from billion-scale collection")
```

To tune `search_list` for your use case, test different `search_list` values to find the optimal balance for your application:

```
# Test different accuracy/speed trade-offs
for search_list in [50, 100, 200, 300]:
    search_params = {
        "metric_type": "L2",
        "params": {"search_list": search_list}
    }

    results = client.search(
        collection_name="images_billion_scale",
        data=[search_vector],
        anns_field="embedding",
        search_params=search_params,
        limit=10
    )
    print(f"search_list={search_list}: Retrieved {len(results[0])} results")
```

The next question to answer is when to choose DiskANN. DiskANN works best for scenarios sharing three characteristics: billion-scale datasets (1B+ vectors) where even compressed indexes exceed available RAM, tolerance for 100ms+ latency, and high-performance NVMe storage. This pattern fits massive embedding archives where RAM costs dominate infrastructure budgets: historical data collections, large-scale image search platforms, or any deployment where traditional in-memory indexes become economically infeasible (multi-TB RAM requirements). The key insight is that NVMe costs roughly 10x less than RAM, transforming billion-scale search from impossible to practical on standard hardware.

HNSW, real-time applications requiring sub-10ms latency, systems without high-performance NVMe (DiskANN needs 50K+ IOPS), high write throughput workloads where DiskANN rebuilding becomes expensive, or deployments with traditional HDDs (200ms+ latencies make DiskANN unusable).

Combining capacity techniques for maximum efficiency

The real power of capacity optimization comes from combining techniques strategically. `IVF_SQ8` and DiskANN both work synergistically with mmap to further reduce memory footprint and extend capacity.

IVF_SQ8 + mmap delivers the most practical combination for medium-scale deployments. `IVF_SQ8` compresses vectors by 4x, then mmap extends effective capacity further by keeping hot data in RAM while cold data lives on disk. For example, a content platform with hundreds of millions of article embeddings might exceed available RAM with `IVF_SQ8` alone but enabling mmap allows the OS to automatically cache frequently accessed recent articles in RAM while historical archives stay on NVMe. This combination works best when you have access to skew patterns; enable `IVF_SQ8` for compression, then add collection-level mmap (`properties={"mmap.enabled": "true"}`) to let the OS manage hot/cold data placement automatically.

DiskANN + mmap optimizes for billion-scale deployments by applying mmap to scalar fields while DiskANN handles vector storage. DiskANN already stores vectors on disk efficiently, but large collections often have substantial scalar metadata (JSON fields, long text, timestamps). Use field-level mmap to offload these scalar fields to disk while keeping DiskANN's compressed navigation codes in RAM. For instance, a massive image collection with rich metadata might need significant RAM for metadata alone; applying mmap to metadata fields (`mmap_enabled=True` on scalar fields) keeps only DiskANN's navigation structures in memory. This selective mmap usage is more effective than collection-level mmap because DiskANN's access patterns don't benefit from OS caching.

Summary

In this chapter, we explored comprehensive strategies for optimizing Milvus performance across three critical dimensions: search speed, ingestion throughput, and load capacity. You discovered how to transform a basic vector database into a high-performance system capable of handling production workloads. For search optimization, we examined index selection (HNSW for speed, `IVF_SQ8` for efficiency), batch processing for multiplying throughput, and replicas for horizontal scaling. For ingestion optimization, we implemented batch insertion, multi-shard parallelization, and bulk import for massive data migrations. For capacity optimization, we explored `IVF_SQ8` quantization for 4x compression, mmap for hot/cold data management, and DiskANN for billion-scale datasets.

Most importantly, you learned that real performance gains come from combining techniques strategically. A production system might use HNSW indexing with batch searches and replicas for search optimization, multi-shard configuration with batching for ingestion, and IVF_SQ8 with mmap for capacity, achieving substantial improvements in throughput, capacity, and cost efficiency.

In the next chapter, we'll explore multi-tenancy and resource isolation strategies, building on these performance optimizations to support multiple applications and teams on shared Milvus infrastructure while maintaining quality of service guarantees for each tenant.

Get this book's PDF version and more

16

Implementing Multi-Tenancy in Milvus

Consider the following scenario: Your vector search application started serving a single organization, but now you need to support multiple independent customers. A healthcare company requires strict data isolation for HIPAA compliance, a university needs different schemas across 50 departments, and an e-commerce platform must serve 5,000 retailers with shared structures but isolated data.

This is where Milvus' multi-tenancy capabilities become essential. Multi-tenancy allows you to serve multiple independent customers from a single Milvus cluster while maintaining appropriate isolation for each use case. Choosing the correct approach determines whether your platform can scale from dozens to millions of users while maintaining security and performance.

In this chapter, we'll explore four multi-tenancy strategies: database-level isolation for maximum security, collection-level isolation for schema flexibility, partition-based approaches for resource efficiency, and resource groups for performance guarantees. We'll also provide a decision framework to help you choose the optimal strategy for your specific requirements.

We will cover the following key topics:

- How Milvus enables multi-tenancy
- Multi-tenancy strategy comparison

Technical requirements

Before diving into the examples, ensure you have the following environment set up:

1. **Milvus instance**: A running Milvus instance (e.g., v2.5.27)
    - For database and partition strategies: Standalone deployment is sufficient
    - For resource group examples: Distributed cluster with multiple Query Nodes required
2. **Python environment**: Python 3.11 or later. Verify your Python version:

```
python -version
```

3. **PyMilvus SDK**: Install the official Python SDK for Milvus:

```
pip install pymilvus==2.5.18
```

The code used in this chapter can be found in our GitHub repository: `https://github.com/PacktPublishing/The-Architecture-Handbook-for-Milvus-Vector-Database`

How Milvus enables multi-tenancy

Milvus is designed from the ground up to support multi-tenancy, which is the ability to serve multiple users or clients (tenants) from a single cluster. We explored basic Milvus architecture and deployment patterns in *Chapter 3*, and now you'll build on that foundation to implement sophisticated isolation strategies. You'll discover that understanding how Milvus achieves multi-tenancy helps you choose the right strategy for your use case.

A multi-tenant architecture in Milvus needs to address four key areas. First, data isolation ensures that Tenant A cannot see or access Tenant B's data under any circumstances. Second, resource management provides fair performance for all tenants while avoiding the "noisy neighbor" problem where one tenant's heavy usage degrades service for others. Third, scalability allows you to easily add new tenants without major architectural changes or system redesigns. Finally, security protects both the system and tenant data through proper access controls, authentication, and authorization mechanisms.

Available multi-tenancy strategies

Milvus provides four primary mechanisms to achieve multi-tenancy, each optimized for different scenarios. Understanding these options helps you choose the right approach for your specific needs:

- **Database-level isolation**: Provides the strongest isolation with complete data separation, suitable for organizations with strict compliance policies (supports up to 64 tenants).
- **Collection-level isolation**: Enables flexible schema management by assigning a dedicated collection to each tenant, ideal for medium-scale deployments (supports up to 10,000 tenants).
- **Partition-based isolation**: A resource-efficient approach that uses partitions within shared collections to provide logical multi-tenancy while also improving query performance. By scoping queries to specific partitions, Milvus only searches segments belonging to those partitions, effectively reducing the overall search scope and enhancing QPS and latency. This makes it ideal for SaaS applications (supports up to 10,000 tenants).
- **Resource group isolation**: A performance-centric isolation strategy that allocates dedicated compute resources, making it essential for premium service tiers.

> Note
>
> These strategies can be combined. For example, you might use database-level isolation for enterprise customers while serving standard customers through partition-based isolation. This hybrid approach balances security, performance, and cost efficiency.

Strategy 1: Database-level isolation

Consider this scenario: You're building a healthcare document management system where three different hospitals need to store and search through their patient records using vector embeddings. Hospital A handles cancer research documents, Hospital B manages cardiac care records, and Hospital C stores pediatric medical files. Due to HIPAA compliance requirements, each hospital's data must be completely isolated from the others, with no possibility of accidental data leakage or cross-tenant access.

This is where database-level isolation comes in. At the highest level, Milvus uses databases to provide the strongest form of tenant isolation. Each tenant gets their own dedicated database, creating complete logical separation as shown in *Figure 16.1*:

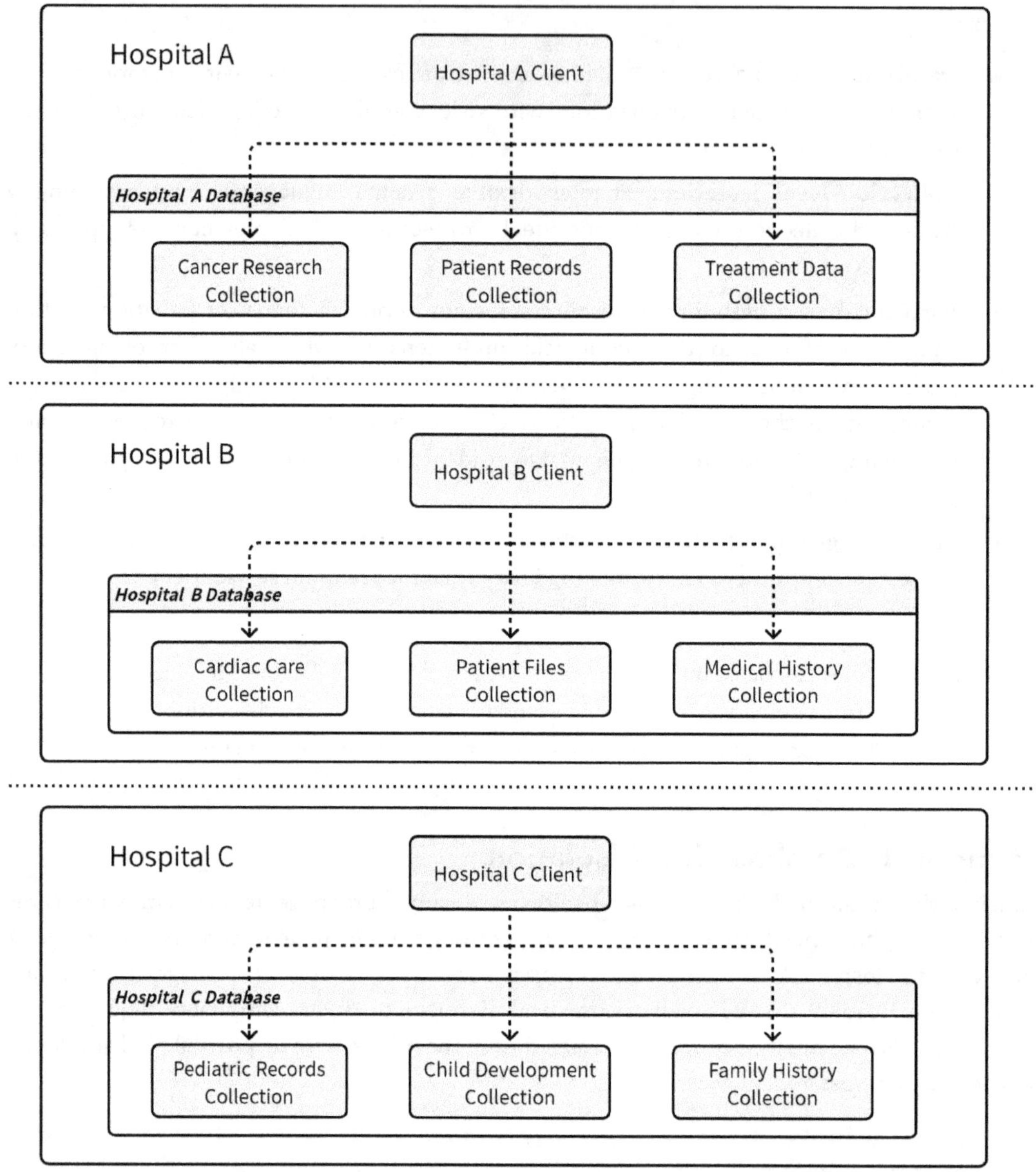

Figure 16.1: Database-level multi-tenancy

The **benefits** of database-level isolation include complete data separation at the database level, ensuring maximum security for sensitive data. The approach offers simple tenant lifecycle management through straightforward database operations like create, drop, and backup. It supports granular **role-based access control** (**RBAC**) per database, meeting enterprise compliance requirements for regulated industries . The clear separation between databases significantly reduces the risk of accidental data leakage or cross-tenant access.

Limitations: The resource overhead of maintaining separate databases limits scalability to approximately 64 tenants, which is a hard limit in current Milvus versions. Administrative complexity increases significantly with tenant count, requiring more operational tasks per tenant compared to other strategies. The approach also incurs higher operational costs due to resource duplication, with higher memory usage per tenant compared to partition-based approaches.

> Note
>
> **Important**
>
> Database-level isolation is designed for scenarios requiring the highest level of data separation. If you're serving more than 50--60 tenants or need to optimize costs, consider partition-based strategies. The 64-database limit is a hard constraint in current Milvus versions and cannot be exceeded regardless of hardware resources.

Implementing database-level multi-tenancy

Let's implement database-level isolation for healthcare organizations; it's straightforward!

```
from pymilvus import MilvusClient, DataType
import numpy as np

MILVUS_URI = "http://localhost:19530"
client = MilvusClient(uri=MILVUS_URI)

# Hospital tenant configurations
HOSPITALS = {
    "hospital_a": {"db_name": "tenant_hospital_a", "specialty": "oncology"},
    "hospital_b": {"db_name": "tenant_hospital_b", "specialty": "cardiology"},
    "hospital_c": {"db_name": "tenant_hospital_c", "specialty": "pediatrics"}
}

def setup_hospital_database(hospital_id, config):
    """Create dedicated database for each hospital"""
    db_name = config["db_name"]
```

```
    # Create isolated database
    client.create_database(db_name)
    print(f"Created secure database '{db_name}' for {hospital_id}")

    # Switch to hospital database
    client.using_database(db_name)

    # Create patient records collection
    schema = client.create_schema(auto_id=True)
    schema.add_field("id", DataType.INT64, is_primary=True)
    schema.add_field("patient_id", DataType.VARCHAR, max_length=50)
    schema.add_field("record_type", DataType.VARCHAR, max_length=100)
    schema.add_field("content", DataType.VARCHAR, max_length=5000)
    schema.add_field("vector", DataType.FLOAT_VECTOR, dim=768)

    client.create_collection("patient_records", schema)
    print(f"Created collection for {config['specialty']} records")

def search_hospital_records(hospital_id, query_vector):
    """Search within specific hospital's database only"""
    db_name = HOSPITALS[hospital_id]["db_name"]

    # Switch to hospital's isolated database
    client.using_database(db_name)

    # Search is completely isolated to this hospital
    results = client.search(
        collection_name="patient_records",
        data=[query_vector],
        limit=3,
        output_fields=["patient_id", "record_type"]
    )
    return results
```

```
# Setup databases for all hospitals
for hospital_id, config in HOSPITALS.items():
    setup_hospital_database(hospital_id, config)

# Verify complete isolation
databases = client.list_databases()
print(f"\nIsolated hospital databases: {databases}")
```

You should see output similar to:

```
Created secure database 'tenant_hospital_a' for hospital_a
Created collection for oncology records
Created secure database 'tenant_hospital_b' for hospital_b
Created collection for cardiology records
Created secure database 'tenant_hospital_c' for hospital_c
Created collection for pediatrics records

Isolated hospital databases: ['default', 'tenant_hospital_a', 'tenant_hospital_b',
'tenant_hospital_c']
```

This approach provides the strongest isolation guarantees but comes with resource overhead. Each tenant operates in a completely separate namespace.

Strategy 2: Collection-level isolation

Consider this scenario: You're managing a knowledge base system for a large corporation with 50 different departments. The Legal department stores contract templates and case precedents with complex metadata fields, the R&D department manages technical specifications with version histories, and the HR department maintains employee handbooks with access control requirements. Each department needs a completely different data structure: different fields, different vector dimensions, even different indexing strategies. Creating 50 separate databases would be excessive, but forcing all departments into the same schema would be impossible.

This is where collection-level isolation provides the perfect balance. See the following figure:

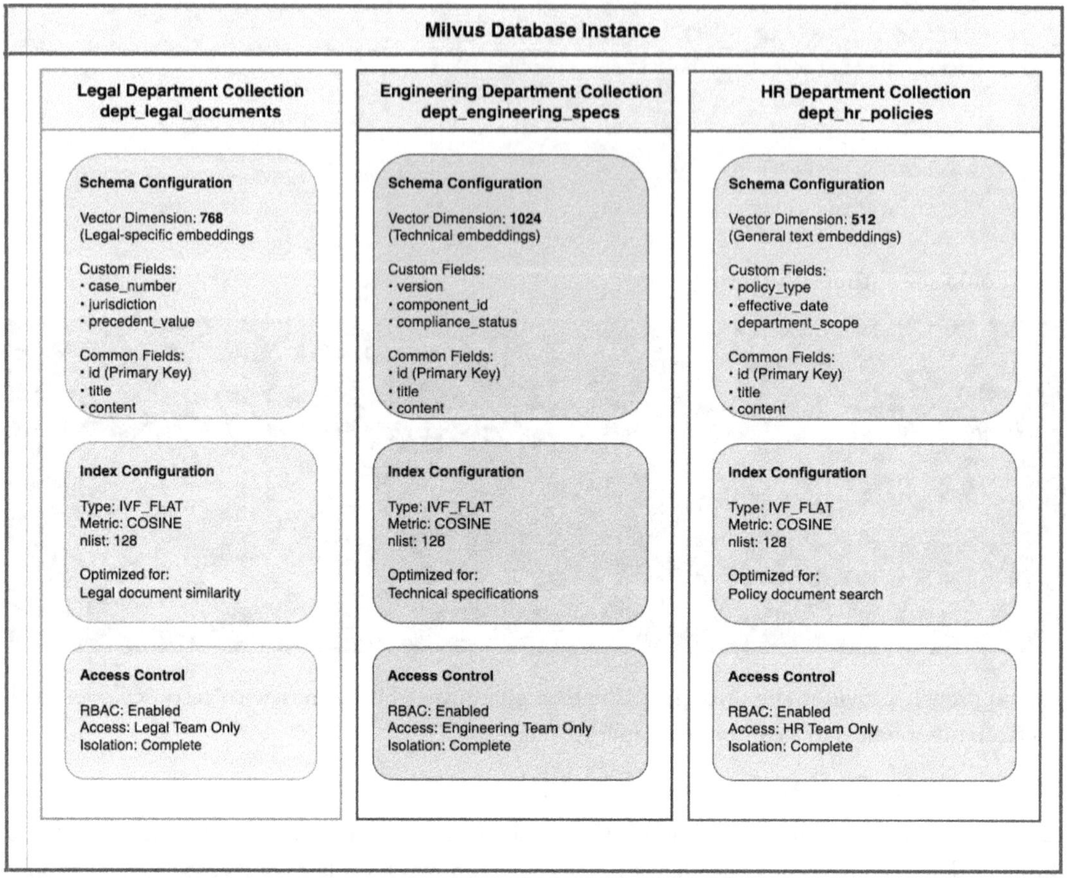

Figure 16.2: Collection-level multi-tenancy

Each tenant gets their own collection within a shared database, allowing complete schema flexibility while maintaining efficient resource utilization. This approach supports up to 10,000 tenants and also provides strong isolation with full RBAC support:

- **Collection strategy benefits:** Collection-level isolation offers exceptional schema flexibility, allowing each tenant to have completely different data structures, vector dimensions, and field types. This makes it ideal for scenarios where departments or customers have diverse data requirements. Collections provide strong physical separation with full RBAC support, ensuring proper access control and security. The strategy supports moderate scale efficiently, handling up to 10,000 tenants while maintaining performance. Each collection can be independently indexed, backed up, and managed, providing operational flexibility for different tenant requirements.

- **Collection strategy limitations:** The management overhead increases as each collection requires separate index management and maintenance operations. Resource consumption is higher than partition-based approaches, typically requiring 20-30% more memory due to the overhead of maintaining separate collection metadata and indexes. The hard limit of 10,000 collections per Milvus instance cannot be exceeded, regardless of available hardware resources, which may constrain very large deployments.

Note

Important

Collection-level isolation is ideal when tenants have different data structures or require different vector dimensions. If all your tenants share the same schema, consider partition-based isolation for better resource efficiency. The collection limit of 10,000 is a hard constraint that cannot be exceeded regardless of hardware resources.

Implementing collection-level multi-tenancy

Let's implement collection-level isolation for a multi-department knowledge base system:

```
from pymilvus import MilvusClient, DataType
import numpy as np

MILVUS_URI = "http://localhost:19530"
client = MilvusClient(uri=MILVUS_URI)

# Department configurations with different schemas
DEPARTMENTS = {
    "legal": {
        "collection": "dept_legal_documents",
        "vector_dim": 768,  # Using Legal-specific embedding model
        "fields": ["case_number", "jurisdiction", "precedent_value"]
    },
    "engineering": {
        "collection": "dept_engineering_specs",
        "vector_dim": 1024,  # Using technical embedding model
        "fields": ["version", "component_id", "compliance_status"]
    },
```

```
    "hr": {
        "collection": "dept_hr_policies",
        "vector_dim": 512,  # Using general text embedding model
        "fields": ["policy_type", "effective_date", "department_scope"]
    }
}

def setup_department_collection(dept_name, config):
    """Create a collection with department-specific schema"""
    collection_name = config["collection"]

    # Create custom schema for each department
    schema = client.create_schema(
        auto_id=True, enable_dynamic_fields=True)

    # Common fields
    schema.add_field("id", DataType.INT64, is_primary=True)
    schema.add_field("title", DataType.VARCHAR, max_length=500)
    schema.add_field("content", DataType.VARCHAR, max_length=5000)

    # Department-specific vector dimension
    schema.add_field(
        "vector",
        DataType.FLOAT_VECTOR,
        dim=config["vector_dim"]
    )

    # Create collection with department-specific configuration
    client.create_collection(
        collection_name=collection_name,
        schema=schema
    )
    print(f"Created collection '{collection_name}' for {dept_name}")

    # Create optimized index for department's use case
    index_params = {
        "index_type": "IVF_FLAT",
        "metric_type": "COSINE",
        "params": {"nlist": 128}
    }
    client.create_index(collection_name, "vector", index_params)
```

```
    return collection_name

def insert_department_data(dept_name, collection_name, documents):
    """Insert data into department-specific collection"""
    config = DEPARTMENTS[dept_name]

    # Prepare data with department-specific vector dimensions
    data = []
    for doc in documents:
        data.append({
            "title": doc["title"],
            "content": doc["content"],
            "vector": np.random.random(config["vector_dim"]).tolist()
        })

    client.insert(collection_name, data)
    print(f"Inserted {len(data)} documents for {dept_name}")

# Setup collections for all departments
for dept_name, config in DEPARTMENTS.items():
    setup_department_collection(dept_name, config)

    # Sample data insertion
    sample_docs = [
        {"title": f"{dept_name} Document 1", "content": f"Content for
{dept_name}"},
        {"title": f"{dept_name} Document 2", "content": f"More content for
{dept_name}"}
    ]
    insert_department_data(dept_name, config["collection"], sample_docs)

# Verify isolation - each department has its own collection
collections = client.list_collections()
print(f"\nDepartment collections: {collections}")
```

You should see output similar to:

```
Created collection 'dept_legal_documents' for legal
Inserted 2 documents for legal
Created collection 'dept_engineering_specs' for engineering
```

```
Inserted 2 documents for engineering
Created collection 'dept_hr_policies' for hr
Inserted 2 documents for hr

Department collections: ['dept_legal_documents', 'dept_engineering_specs',
'dept_hr_policies']
```

Collection-level isolation works well for medium-scale deployments that value independent schema design. When you need higher resource efficiency while retaining scalability, consider the partition-based isolation approach described next.

Strategy 3: Partition-based multi-tenancy

Consider this scenario: You're running an e-commerce recommendation platform that serves 2,000 different online retailers. Each retailer has their own product catalog with embeddings for recommendation purposes. While the data structure is identical across all retailers (product name, category, price, vector embedding), each retailer needs their search results to show only their own products. Creating 2,000 separate databases would be prohibitively expensive and operationally complex.

This is where partition-based multi-tenancy becomes essential. See the following figure:

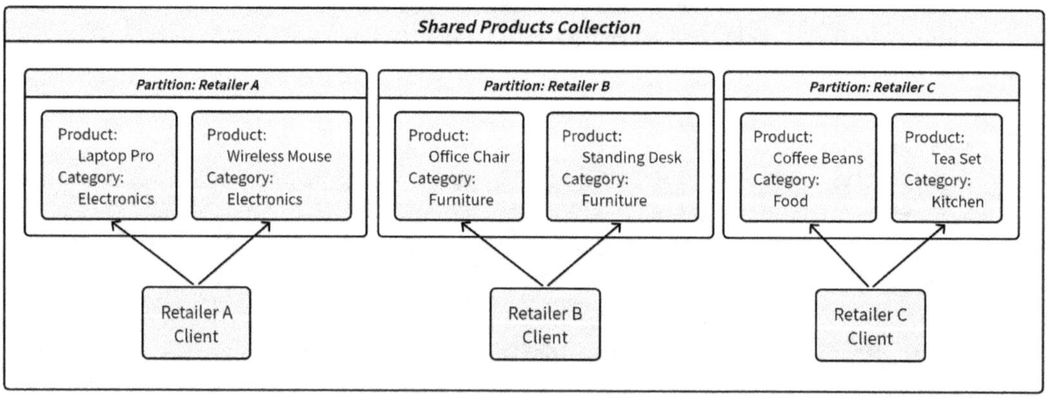

Figure 16.3: Partition-level multi-tenancy

For applications serving many tenants where resource efficiency is critical, partition-based isolation provides an optimal balance. This approach uses partitions within a shared collection, where all tenants share the same collection schema while their data remains logically separated in dedicated partitions.

Implementing partition-based multi-tenancy

Here's how to implement tenant isolation using partitions within a shared collection:

```
from pymilvus import MilvusClient, DataType
import numpy as np

MILVUS_URI = "http://localhost:19530"
client = MilvusClient(uri=MILVUS_URI)

SHARED_COLLECTION = "shared_products"
RETAILERS = ["retailer_a", "retailer_b", "retailer_c"]

def setup_shared_collection_with_partitions():
    """Create shared collection with retailer-specific partitions"""

    # Create schema - same for all retailers
    schema = client.create_schema(auto_id=True)
    schema.add_field("id", DataType.INT64, is_primary=True)
    schema.add_field("product_name", DataType.VARCHAR, max_length=200)
    schema.add_field("category", DataType.VARCHAR, max_length=50)
    schema.add_field("price", DataType.FLOAT)
    schema.add_field("vector", DataType.FLOAT_VECTOR, dim=768)

    # Create collection
    client.create_collection(SHARED_COLLECTION, schema)
    print(f"Created shared collection '{SHARED_COLLECTION}'")

    # Create partition for each retailer
    for retailer_id in RETAILERS:
        partition_name = f"partition_{retailer_id}"
        client.create_partition(SHARED_COLLECTION, partition_name)
        print(f"Created partition for {retailer_id}")

def insert_retailer_products(retailer_id, products):
    """Insert products into retailer's partition"""
    partition_name = f"partition_{retailer_id}"

    # Insert into specific partition
    client.insert(
        collection_name=SHARED_COLLECTION,
```

```
        data=products,
        partition_name=partition_name
    )
    print(f"Inserted {len(products)} products for {retailer_id}")

def search_retailer_products(retailer_id, query_vector):
    """Search only within retailer's partition"""
    partition_name = f"partition_{retailer_id}"

    # Critical: Specify partition_names for isolation
    results = client.search(
        collection_name=SHARED_COLLECTION,
        data=[query_vector],
        partition_names=[partition_name],  # Only search this retailer's data
        limit=3,
        output_fields=["product_name", "price"]
    )
    return results

# Setup and use
setup_shared_collection_with_partitions()

# Sample product data
products = [
    {"product_name": "Laptop", "category": "Electronics", "price": 999.99,
     "vector": np.random.random(768).tolist()},
    {"product_name": "Mouse", "category": "Electronics", "price": 29.99,
     "vector": np.random.random(768).tolist()}
]

insert_retailer_products("retailer_a", products)

# Verify partitions
partitions = client.list_partitions(SHARED_COLLECTION)
print(f"\nAll partitions: {partitions}")
```

You should see output similar to:

```
Created shared collection 'shared_products'
Created partition for retailer_a
Created partition for retailer_b
Created partition for retailer_c
Inserted 2 products for retailer_a

All partitions: ['_default', 'partition_retailer_a', 'partition_retailer_b',
'partition_retailer_c']
```

This code implements multi-tenancy isolation by explicitly creating three dedicated partitions for `retailer_a/b/c`, and the corresponding partition names must also be manually specified when inserting data. However, this manual partition management approach can be automated using Milvus' partition key mechanism, which will be covered in detail in the next section as a more efficient management solution.

Automatic partition key management

The manual partition management approach (creating partitions explicitly and specifying them during data insertion) works well for small-scale deployments but becomes cumbersome as tenant numbers scale. Milvus' automatic partition key management solves this challenge by automating the entire partition lifecycle, from creation to data routing, using a dedicated partition key. You specify the number of partitions for the partition key during collection creation, and a consistent hashing function maps tenant data to these partitions in a fixed manner; during queries, the same hashing function is used to quickly locate the specific partition(s) associated with the target tenant. See the following figure:

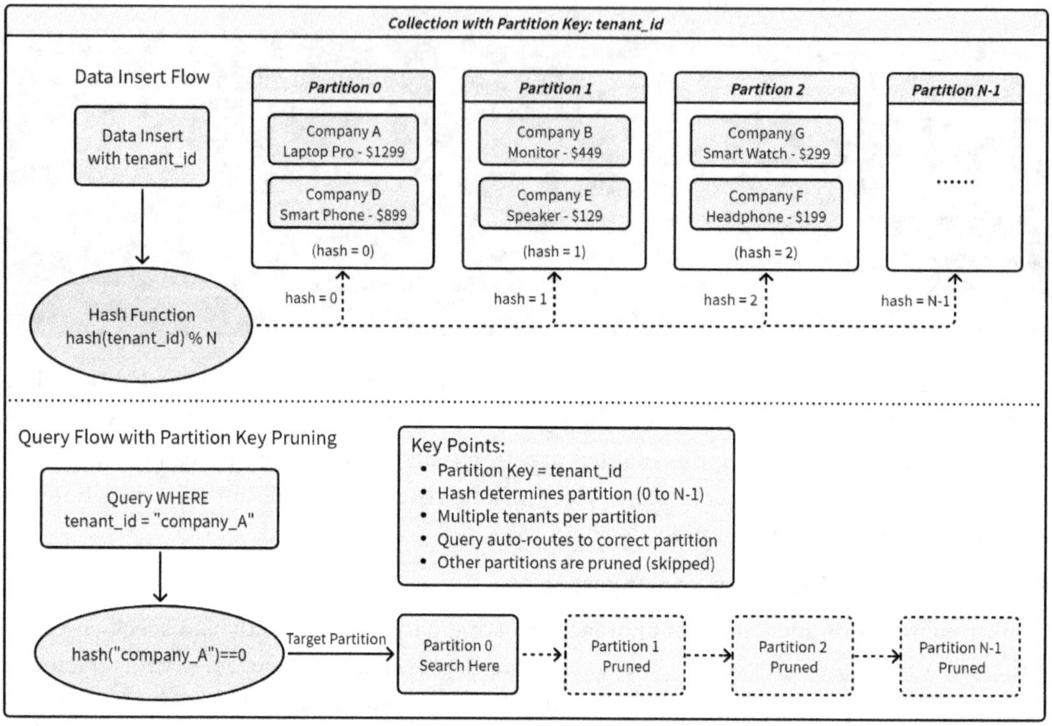

Figure 16.4: Partition key level multi-tenancy

This diagram illustrates the core workflow of the automatic partition key mechanism: during data insertion, the `tenant_id` (as the partition key) is processed through a hash function to route data to the corresponding partition; during query execution, the same `tenant_id` is hashed to directly target the specific partition(s) containing the tenant's data, ensuring isolation and performance efficiency.

Implementing partition key-based multi-tenancy

Partition keys provide automatic tenant isolation by using a field value to determine partition placement:

```
from pymilvus import MilvusClient, DataType
import numpy as np

MILVUS_URI = "http://localhost:19530"
client = MilvusClient(uri=MILVUS_URI)

def setup_collection_with_partition_key():
```

```
    """Create collection with automatic partition key routing"""

    schema = client.create_schema(auto_id=True)

    # tenant_id as partition key for automatic routing
    schema.add_field("id", DataType.INT64, is_primary=True)
    schema.add_field(
        "tenant_id",
        DataType.VARCHAR,
        max_length=50,
        is_partition_key=True  # Automatic partition routing
    )
    schema.add_field("product_name", DataType.VARCHAR, max_length=200)
    schema.add_field("price", DataType.FLOAT)
    schema.add_field("vector", DataType.FLOAT_VECTOR, dim=768)

    # Create collection
    client.create_collection(
        collection_name="auto_partitioned_products",
        schema=schema,
        num_partitions=64  # total partitions number
    )
    print("Created collection with partition key 'tenant_id'")

def insert_multi_tenant_data(all_products):
    """Insert - Milvus automatically routes by tenant_id"""

    # Single insert, automatic partition routing
    client.insert("auto_partitioned_products", all_products)
    print(f"Inserted {len(all_products)} products (auto-routed)")

def search_by_tenant(tenant_id, query_vector):
    """Search with automatic partition pruning"""

    results = client.search(
        collection_name="auto_partitioned_products",
        data=[query_vector],
        filter=f'tenant_id == "{tenant_id}"',  # Auto partition pruning
        limit=3,
        output_fields=["product_name", "price", "tenant_id"]
    )
```

```
    return results

# Setup and use
setup_collection_with_partition_key()

# Mixed tenant data
all_products = [
    {"tenant_id": "store_001", "product_name": "Laptop", "price": 999,
     "vector": np.random.random(768).tolist()},
    {"tenant_id": "store_002", "product_name": "Phone", "price": 699,
     "vector": np.random.random(768).tolist()},
    {"tenant_id": "store_001", "product_name": "Tablet", "price": 499,
     "vector": np.random.random(768).tolist()}
]

insert_multi_tenant_data(all_products)
print("\nData automatically distributed across partitions")
```

You should see output similar to:

```
Created collection with partition key 'tenant_id'
Inserted 3 products (auto-routed)

Data automatically distributed across partitions
```

The partition key approach offers automatic data distribution and excellent performance while maintaining logical isolation through filtering.

Note

Important

When using partition keys for multi-tenancy, always include the tenant filter in your search queries. Unlike database-level isolation, where access is automatically restricted, partition-based approaches rely on application-level filtering to ensure tenant isolation. Missing this filter could result in cross-tenant data exposure. Consider implementing a query wrapper that automatically adds tenant filters to prevent accidental data leakage.

Let's now discuss the benefits and limitations of the partition strategy:

- **Benefits**: Partition-based multi-tenancy offers significantly reduced resource overhead, enabling you to serve thousands of tenants with better resource utilization compared to database isolation. The single collection architecture simplifies schema management, reducing maintenance tasks since all tenants share the same schema definition. When using partition keys, automatic data distribution eliminates manual partition management tasks, making operations more efficient. This approach delivers better cost efficiency for SaaS applications.
- **Limitations:** The logical isolation model requires careful application code to prevent data leakage, increasing development complexity due to the need for consistent filtering logic. RBAC granularity is limited within shared collections, placing greater responsibility on the application layer for security enforcement. Shared resources may create performance contention between active tenants, potentially causing query latency variance during peak loads.

Strategy 4: Resource group-based performance isolation

Consider this scenario: You're operating a multi-tier AI search service where your Enterprise customers pay premium prices and expect guaranteed sub-100ms query response times, while your Basic tier customers use a shared resource pool. Your current challenge is that when Basic tier customers run large batch queries, they consume significant compute resources, causing Enterprise customers to experience degraded performance and breach their SLA guarantees.

This is where resource group-based performance isolation solves the problem. Milvus allows creating **resource groups**, which are logical pools used to isolate computational resources, specifically Query Nodes. Think of resource groups as dedicated lanes on a highway for different types of traffic. See the following figure:

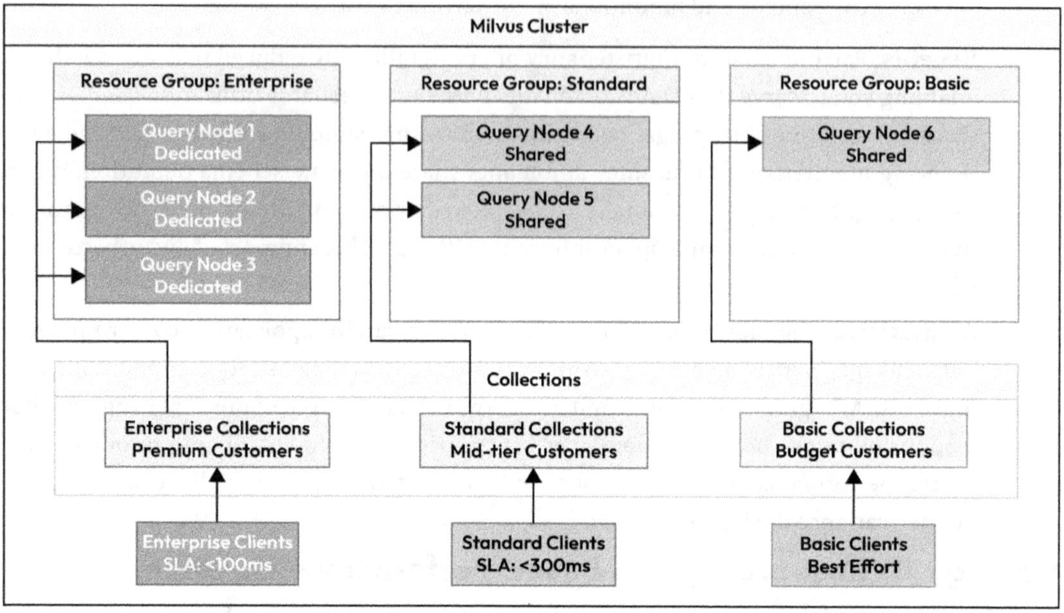

Figure 16.5: Resource group multi-tenancy involves performance isolation through dedicated Query Nodes

Here's how resource groups work:

1. **Default setup**: Initially, all Query Nodes reside in a `DEFAULT_RESOURCE_GROUP`
2. **Group creation**: You can create new resource groups and transfer Query Nodes from the default group
3. **Collection assignment**: Load collections or partitions into specific resource groups
4. **Isolated execution**: All operations on that data use only the assigned Query Nodes

This mechanism ensures complete performance isolation between tenants by dedicating specific compute resources to each tenant tier, effectively eliminating the "noisy neighbor" problem that can degrade service quality in shared environments.

Implementation example

Let's look at how you can implement resource group multi-tenancy for different service tiers:

```
from pymilvus import MilvusClient
from pymilvus.client.constants import DEFAULT_RESOURCE_GROUP
from pymilvus.client.types import ResourceGroupConfig

MILVUS_URI = "http://127.0.0.1:19530"
client = MilvusClient(uri=MILVUS_URI)
```

```
def setup_service_tiers():
    """Create resource groups for Basic, Standard, and Enterprise tiers"""

    # Define service tiers
    tiers = {
        "rg_basic": 1,       # 1 Query Node for basic customers
        "rg_standard": 2,    # 2 Query Nodes for standard customers
        "rg_enterprise": 3   # 3 Query Nodes for enterprise customers
    }

    for tier_name, node_count in tiers.items():
        # Create resource group
        client.create_resource_group(tier_name)

        # Allocate Query Nodes from default group
        client.update_resource_group(
            tier_name,
            ResourceGroupConfig(
                requests={"node_num": node_count},
                limits={"node_num": node_count},
                transfer_from=[{"resource_group": DEFAULT_RESOURCE_GROUP}]
            )
        )
        print(f"Created '{tier_name}' with {node_count} Query Node(s)")

def assign_tenant_to_tier(tenant_collection, tier_name):
    """Load tenant collection to specific resource group"""
    client.load_collection(tenant_collection, [tier_name])
    print(f"Assigned '{tenant_collection}' to '{tier_name}'")

# Setup tiers and assign tenants
setup_service_tiers()
assign_tenant_to_tier("enterprise_search", "rg_enterprise")
assign_tenant_to_tier("standard_search", "rg_standard")
assign_tenant_to_tier("basic_search", "rg_basic")
```

You should see output similar to:

```
Created 'rg_basic' with 1 Query Node(s)
Created 'rg_standard' with 2 Query Node(s)
```

```
Created 'rg_enterprise' with 3 Query Node(s)
Assigned 'enterprise_search' to 'rg_enterprise'
Assigned 'standard_search' to 'rg_standard'
Assigned 'basic_search' to 'rg_basic'
```

The resource group strategy guarantees performance for critical applications/tenants by dedicating specific hardware (Query Nodes) to them, preventing noisy neighbors. Let's now discuss its benefits and limitations:

- **Key benefits**: Resource group isolation provides strong performance isolation through dedicated Query Nodes, eliminating performance variance caused by noisy neighbors. This ensures predictable performance by guaranteeing compute resources for critical tenants, maintaining consistent sub-100ms query latency for premium service tiers. The approach offers flexible assignment options and can be combined with any other isolation strategy, providing both data and performance guarantees. Collections can be dynamically moved between resource groups, enabling real-time tenant tier changes without service downtime.
- **Limitations**: Implementing resource groups requires a distributed Milvus cluster deployment with a minimum of 2 Query Nodes for meaningful resource separation. Careful capacity planning is essential, as you'll need to allocate nodes across groups strategically. While resource groups don't incur additional infrastructure costs, they can lead to resource underutilization as dedicated nodes assigned to one group cannot be shared with other groups during idle periods.

As things stand, we have systematically introduced the four multi-tenancy isolation strategies supported by Milvus: database-level, collection-level, partition-level, and resource group-based. We have clarified their implementation principles, applicable scenarios, isolation strength, and performance characteristics, respectively. Understanding and choosing appropriately among these approaches enables you to meet strict data security and compliance requirements while maximizing resource utilization and ensuring service stability, delivering fit-for-purpose deployment architectures for various business types, especially SaaS platforms and multi-tenant systems.

Multi-tenancy strategy comparison

To help you quickly compare and choose the right solution for your scenario, the following table provides a structured comparison of the four isolation strategies across key dimensions:

Strategy	Tenant scale	Isolation level	Implementation complexity	Typical use case
Database	1-50 tenants	Strongest (Physical)	Simple	Healthcare systems with HIPAA compliance
Collection	50-1,000 tenants	Strong (Physical)	Moderate	Multi-department corporate systems
Partition	1,000-10,000 tenants	Medium (Logical)	Moderate	SaaS e-commerce platforms
Partition key	10,000+ tenants	Medium (Logical)	Simple	Large-scale consumer applications
Resource group	Any scale	Performance isolation	Complex (requires cluster)	Premium/Basic service tiers

Table 16.1: Multi-tenancy isolation strategies comparison

Here's a detailed discussion of the strategy characteristics:

- **Database-level isolation** provides complete data separation with independent schemas for each tenant, allowing maximum customization and security. It offers full RBAC support for enterprise security requirements, but is limited to 64 databases as a hard constraint. This approach incurs the highest resource overhead, typically requiring 40-60% more memory compared to other strategies.
- **Collection-level isolation** enables flexible schemas per tenant, including different vector dimensions and field structures. It maintains strong isolation with full RBAC support and can scale to support up to 10,000 collections. However, it introduces higher management complexity as each collection requires a separate index configuration and maintenance.
- **Partition-based isolation** delivers excellent resource efficiency and enables fast tenant onboarding through simple partition creation. The main constraint is that all tenants

must share the same schema structure, and the approach requires careful application-level filtering to maintain tenant isolation.

- **Partition key isolation** offers automatic data distribution and can scale to millions of tenants with simplified management through Milvus' built-in routing. While highly scalable, it provides the weakest isolation level since all data resides in a single collection, relying entirely on filter expressions for tenant separation.

> Note
>
> These strategies can be combined for hybrid approaches. For example, use database-level isolation for your top-tier enterprise customers while serving mid-tier customers through collection-based isolation, and basic customers through partition-based approaches. This provides appropriate isolation levels for each customer segment while optimizing resource utilization.

Choosing the right multi-tenancy strategy

When implementing multi-tenancy with Milvus, selecting the right strategy determines your application's success. Start by answering these three key questions:

1. How many tenants will you serve? (Determines scalability needs)
2. What isolation level do you require? (Compliance, security, performance)
3. Do tenants share the same data structure? (Schema flexibility needs)

Here's a practical decision framework or guide:

- **Choose database-level when** you're serving fewer than 50 tenants and compliance requirements demand complete data separation for standards like HIPAA, GDPR, or SOX. This strategy is ideal when each tenant needs different schemas or vector dimensions, and security takes precedence over cost considerations. For example, a medical imaging platform serving 20 hospitals would choose this approach because each hospital has strict HIPAA requirements and uses different image processing models with varying vector dimensions.
- **Choose collection-level when** you're serving 50-1,000 tenants who need different data structures or vector dimensions. This strategy works well when you require strong isolation and you have the operational capacity to manage multiple indexes and schemas. A corporate knowledge base serving 200 departments would benefit from this approach, as the Legal department might use 768-dimensional embeddings for contract analysis, while Engineering uses 1024-dimensional vectors for technical specifications.

- **Choose partition-based when** you're serving 1,000-10,000 tenants who all share identical schemas. This strategy excels when cost efficiency is critical, and you can implement robust application-level access control. An e-commerce platform with 5,000 retailers would adopt this approach since all retailers use the same product catalog structure but need their inventory searches isolated.
- **Choose partition key when** you're serving more than 10,000 tenants and need maximum scalability with automatic management. This approach is optimal when all tenants share schemas, and you want Milvus to handle partition distribution automatically. A consumer mobile app with millions of users would use this strategy, as each user needs their own data space, but the app structure remains consistent across all users.
- **Add resource groups when** you have distinct service tiers like Basic and Premium that require different performance guarantees. Resource groups become essential when you must guarantee specific SLAs, prevent noisy neighbor issues, and run a distributed Milvus cluster with sufficient Query Nodes for meaningful resource separation.

> Note
>
> Resource groups can be combined with any other strategy. For example, use database isolation for enterprise customers while adding resource groups to guarantee their performance.

Summary

In this chapter, we explored how to implement multi-tenant vector database architectures using Milvus' four isolation strategies. Database-level isolation provides the strongest separation for compliance-critical scenarios, collection-level offers schema flexibility for diverse data structures, partition-based delivers resource efficiency for large-scale deployments, and resource groups ensure performance guarantees across service tiers. Each strategy balances different trade-offs between isolation strength, scalability, and operational complexity.

In the next chapter, we will explore implementing security in Milvus through authentication and RBAC. You'll learn how to protect your vector database with proper user management, granular permission controls, and security best practices.

Subscribe for a free eBook

New frameworks, evolving architectures, research drops, production breakdowns – *AI_Distilled* filters the noise into a weekly briefing for engineers and researchers working hands-on with LLMs and generative AI systems. Subscribe now and receive a free eBook, along with weekly insights that help you stay focused and informed.

Subscribe at `https://packt.link/8Oz6Y` or scan the QR code below.

17

How Milvus Works in AI

Over the past decade, the rapid development of deep learning has not only reshaped the paradigms of AI technology but also driven the innovation of data infrastructure. From the breakthroughs of **convolutional neural networks** (**CNNs**) in computer vision to the sweeping success of transformer architectures in **natural language processing** (**NLP**), the demand for efficient processing and storage of high-dimensional vector data by AI models has grown exponentially. The need to handle massive amounts of high-dimensional data has propelled the rise of vector databases, making them an indispensable infrastructure in the AI era.

In November 2022, the release of ChatGPT marked the advent of the era of large models. The explosive popularity of large models has further highlighted the value of vector databases. The industry often likens large models to the *brain*, while vector databases play the role of the *hippocampus*; the key brain region responsible for storing long-term memories. Through dynamic data update mechanisms, vector databases enable large models to access the latest industry knowledge in real time, allowing them to regain learning capabilities. In **Retrieval-Augmented Generation** (**RAG**) architectures, vector databases support precise semantic retrieval of everything from legal provisions to medical literature, significantly reducing hallucinations in large models and making their responses more accurate. In dialogue systems, vector databases enable efficient long-context association recall, allowing AI to better understand user needs and deliver more personalized services.

However, the value of vector databases extends far beyond this. They are not designed solely for large models but serve the entire AI field, with a broader range of scenarios and markets. Large language models are merely the first killer application of vector databases. In the field of autonomous driving, vector databases can efficiently manage LiDAR data, enabling real-time perception and decision-making in complex environments. In biomedicine, vector databases accelerate protein structure similarity searches, significantly shortening drug development cycles. In financial risk control, vector databases improve the accuracy and efficiency of risk detection by enabling real-time retrieval of abnormal transaction patterns.

Vector databases have become the *data foundation* of AI infrastructure and a key engine driving the AI wave.

In this chapter, we will cover the following topics:

- Identifying Milvus' role in AI applications
- Image search with Milvus
- Building a chatbot with Milvus and LlamaIndex

Technical requirements

This chapter contains two examples of building AI applications, which require a Python environment to run. It is recommended to use Conda to create a Python virtual environment to isolate dependencies.

For instructions on how to install Conda, please refer to

`https://www.anaconda.com/docs/getting-started/miniconda/install#quickstart-install-instructions`.

For a chatbot application, you will need an OpenAI API key. You can obtain an OpenAI API key by creating an account (`https://auth.openai.com/log-in`).

The code used in this chapter can be found in our GitHub repository: `https://github.com/PacktPublishing/The-Architecture-Handbook-for-Milvus-Vector-Database/tree/main/ch17`.

Identifying Milvus' role in AI applications

According to IDC, over 80% of newly generated data worldwide is unstructured, and the volume of such data continues to grow rapidly each year (`https://my.idc.com/getdoc.jsp?containerId=prCHC52667624`). As mathematical abstraction carriers for unstructured data, vector databases have become an essential infrastructure for processing such data in the AI era. Among the three core elements of AI (computing power, algorithms, and data), Milvus, as a globally leading open source vector database, bridges the gap between human information and machine intelligence by transforming high-dimensional data such as images, text, and audio-video into machine-understandable semantic vectors.

In today's rapidly evolving AI landscape, Milvus, as the world's first cloud-native open source vector database, has become a crucial tool for handling massive amounts of data. It can quickly process queries at the scale of billions of data points, acting as a *data search engine* to provide core support for various AI applications. For example, it helps e-commerce platforms achieve precise product recommendations, enables corporate intelligent customer service systems to quickly understand user questions, assists pharmaceutical companies in analyzing complex molecular data, and supports autonomous driving systems in processing real-time traffic information. Whether it is financial risk control or multi-modal AI training, Milvus is driving the intelligent upgrade of various industries through its flexible and scalable architecture and real-time update capabilities. As large model technology enters deeper waters, the ecosystem value of Milvus continues to expand. Its out-of-the-box API design lowers the barrier to AI engineering, while deep integration with mainstream frameworks such as LangChain and LlamaIndex accelerates technological adoption. With a high recall rate and millisecond-level response capabilities, Milvus provides industrial-grade reliability for AI applications. As one of the most active open source vector databases globally, Milvus has become the preferred tool for AI developers to build intelligent systems.

Milvus with unstructured data

AI applications are flooded with vast amounts of unstructured data, such as natural language text, images, audio, and videos. These data types are diverse in form and rich in content, yet they are difficult to directly store and query using traditional databases. Milvus is a globally leading open source vector database.

It primarily focuses on providing vectorized storage and efficient retrieval capabilities, serving as the core infrastructure that connects unstructured data with upper-layer applications.

As shown in *Figure 17.1*, in the unstructured data processing pipeline, Milvus plays the role of a storage and retrieval hub for vectorized data:

Figure 17.1: Unstructured data process pipeline

This is how Milvus' data processing pipeline works with unstructured data:

- **Upstream data processing**: The upstream processing of unstructured data can generally be divided into three steps: data collection, data cleaning, and data transformation. Data collection involves gathering raw data from various sources, which can be anything from a news article on a web page to a photo on social media. Data cleaning aims to remove useless information from the raw data, such as advertisements and garbled text, and to repair missing or erroneous data. Data transformation is to convert the raw data into numerical representations that computers can process through feature extraction methods, such as transforming text into word vectors (e.g., using **Bidirectional Encoder Representations from Transformers** or **BERT**) or images into feature vectors (e.g., using ResNet).
- **Data storage and retrieval**: Milvus receives and stores these vectors, leveraging distributed architecture, **approximate nearest neighbor** (**ANN**) algorithms, and hybrid search technologies to achieve millisecond-level precision search across billions of vectors.
- **Downstream application empowerment**: The retrieval results are returned to applications such as data visualization, recommendation systems, and driving business decisions.

Taking text processing as an example, when unstructured texts such as news articles or legal clauses are converted into vectors via NLP models, Milvus can efficiently store these semantic vectors. When a user initiates a query, the system first vectorizes the query text, and then Milvus quickly retrieves the most semantically relevant documents. This capability has been validated in fields such as e-commerce recommendations and biomedicine.

Efficiently processing unstructured data is just the basic functionality of Milvus. It is when Milvus serves as the vector engine for a RAG system that its value as an AI infrastructure is truly realized.

Milvus with RAG

Retrieval-augmented generation (**RAG**) is an emerging AI technique that combines vector databases with **large language models** (**LLMs**) to generate more accurate and richer content compared to a standalone LLM.

Figure 17.2 depicts a basic RAG architecture with Milvus:

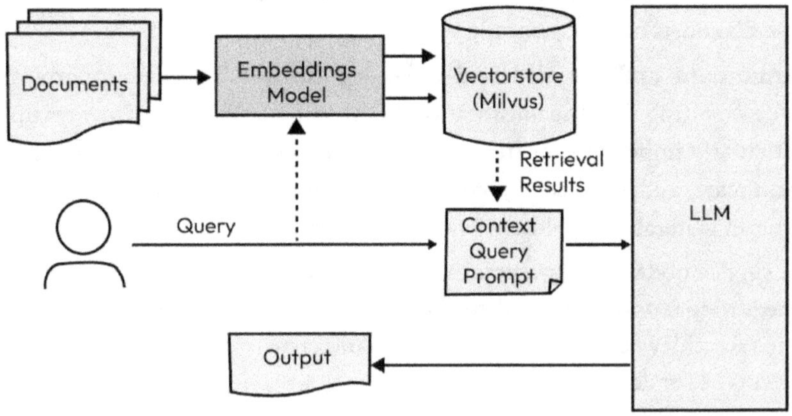

Figure 17.2: Milvus with RAG

The RAG system implements knowledge-enhanced intelligent Q&A through a two-stage workflow. In the knowledge base construction phase, domain-specific information and private data are vectorized and stored in Milvus to form a proprietary knowledge base. In the query response phase, the user's question first undergoes vector similarity search in the knowledge base to retrieve relevant knowledge snippets. These search results are then used as context prompts and fed into the LLM together with the original question, enabling the model to generate precise answers based on factual evidence. This architecture effectively addresses the core issues of large models, such as limitations in knowledge timeliness, insufficient domain specificity, and factual errors, and demonstrates significant advantages in scenarios such as intelligent customer service and professional consulting.

Milvus plays the following key roles in a RAG system:

- **Vectorized storage of knowledge bases**: Milvus is responsible for storing the vectorized representations of documents, which can include books, web pages, and domain-specific materials. Through natural language processing models such as BERT and GPT, documents are transformed into high-dimensional semantic vectors and stored in Milvus. Milvus' distributed architecture and optimized index structures, such as `IVF_FLAT` and **hierarchical navigable small world** (**HNSW**), enable it to efficiently manage billions of vectors, providing a solid data foundation for RAG.
- **Efficient similarity search**: When the RAG model receives a query task, Milvus uses its ANN algorithm to retrieve the most relevant document vectors from the massive knowledge base within milliseconds. This efficient retrieval capability ensures the real-time performance and accuracy of the RAG system. For example, in medical RAG

applications, Milvus can quickly retrieve medical literature and case reports related to disease diagnosis or treatment plans.

- **Dynamic data updates and real-time capabilities**: Milvus supports dynamic data updates, ensuring that the information in the knowledge base is always up to date. This is particularly important for fields that require real-time access to the latest data, such as healthcare and finance. By continuously updating the knowledge base, the RAG system can generate reliable content based on the most recent information.

In traditional single-modal RAG systems, Milvus is typically used for efficient retrieval of text vectors. By integrating cross-modal embedding models, Milvus can be further extended to multi-modal scenarios to achieve unified vector indexing and cross-modal similarity search for images, audio, and other types of data.

Milvus with multi-modal AI

Multimodal AI is another hot topic in current AI research. It integrates multiple types of data, such as text, images, audio, and sensor inputs, to enhance the way models understand and generate responses. Unlike single-modal systems, which process only one type of input (for example, a text-only chatbot), multimodal AI incorporates various data streams. To achieve this, the system first processes each type of input separately using specialized neural networks, such as **convolutional neural networks** (**CNNs**) for images or transformers for text. These individual representations are then combined through cross-modal attention mechanisms to generate joint embeddings, enabling the model to establish semantic mappings between different modalities. **Vector databases**, represented by Milvus, play a crucial role as a core component of the infrastructure layer in multimodal AI systems in the following ways:

- **Multimodal vector management**: Milvus can store and manage vectorized representations of various modalities, such as text, images, and audio. For example, in a multimodal recommendation system, Milvus can store users' text review vectors, product image vectors, and audio feedback vectors. By calculating the similarity between these vectors, the recommendation system can gain a more comprehensive understanding of user preferences and needs, thereby delivering more accurate and personalized recommendations.
- **Cross-modal retrieval capabilities**: Milvus supports cross-modal retrieval tasks, allowing users to query related data across different modalities using one type of data. For instance, in cross-modal image-text retrieval, a user can input a descriptive text, which is then converted into a text vector. Milvus retrieves similar image vectors and returns relevant image results. This cross-modal retrieval capability significantly

expands the boundaries of AI applications, offering users a richer and more convenient interactive experience.

- **Multimodal fusion and reasoning**: Milvus' efficient retrieval capabilities provide a technical foundation for multimodal AI fusion and reasoning. For example, in intelligent customer service scenarios, Milvus can simultaneously process user text inputs and voice inputs, generating more accurate responses through cross-modal retrieval and fusion.

Next, we will use several practical examples to demonstrate how to build AI systems with Milvus. We will discuss image search with Milvus, and then we will build a ChatBot.

Follow the steps in these use cases to experience the important role that Milvus plays in AI systems.

Image search with Milvus

Image search is one of the simplest and most fundamental AI applications. Let's take a look at the basic process of image search with Milvus:

1. Convert the image data in the database into vector embeddings using an embedding model.
2. Extract the image vector embeddings and store them in the vector database Milvus.
3. Use the same embedding model to convert the query image into a vector embedding.
4. Pass the vector embedding of the query image as an input parameter to Milvus.
5. Milvus performs an ANN search, comparing the query vector with the vectors in the database to retrieve the top-K most relevant results.
6. Milvus returns the top-K results to the user.

In this example, we will demonstrate how to implement a simple image search using *Milvus-Lite*. The image data used for the search is from the Impressionist-Classifier dataset, and the embedding model employed is the pre-trained ResNet50 model from Torchvision.

The complete code is available at `https://github.com/PacktPublishing/The-Architecture-Handbook-for-Milvus-Vector-Database/blob/main/ch17/image_search.ipynb`, which can be opened using Jupyter Notebook.

Let's get started:

1. **Install dependencies**: In this example, we will use `pymilvus` to connect to the lightweight Milvus-Lite, `torch` to extract image embeddings, `torchvision` for model

preprocessing, gdown to download the image dataset, tqdm to display the processing progress, and matplotlib to visualize the image search results:

```
pip install pymilvus torch gdown torchvision tqdm matplotlib
```

2. **Obtain test data**: Use gdown to download the dataset file from Google Drive and then decompress it in the current directory using the built-in zipfile library:

```
import zipfile

!wget -c https://github.com/towhee-io/examples/releases/download/data/
reverse_image_search.zip

with zipfile.ZipFile("./reverse_image_search.zip", "r") as zip_ref:
    zip_ref.extractall("./data")
```

The dataset is 128 MB in size, and the download time depends on your network conditions.

3. **Set global params**: Set the collection name to image_search. The dimension of the image embeddings is set to 2048 (which is the default embedding size of ResNet50). This is the dimension of the vectors generated by ResNet50. If another value is specified here, an error will occur when inserting the vectors into Milvus. BATCH_SIZE is used to specify that 128 data entries are inserted in each batch. Batch insertion is much faster than inserting one by one. The TOP_K parameter is used to determine the number of search results to be returned:

```
# Milvus Setup Arguments
COLLECTION_NAME = 'image_search'
DIMENSION = 2048

# Inference Arguments
BATCH_SIZE = 128
TOP_K = 3
```

In this example, we use Milvus-Lite to simplify the operations on the Milvus side. You can also use Milvus Standalone/Cluster or Zilliz Cloud as the service end of the vector database. We created a collection named COLLECTION_NAME, which contains three data columns: an id column as the primary key, a filepath column to store the local path of the images, and an `image_embedding` column to store the feature vector embeddings extracted from the images.

The index type is FLAT, which is the only index type supported by Milvus-Lite. The vector distance measurement method is `COSINE`.

```
from pymilvus import MilvusClient, DataType
client = MilvusClient("./milvus_demo.db")
```

4. **Remove any previous collections with the same name**:

```
if client.has_collection(COLLECTION_NAME):
    client.drop_collection(COLLECTION_NAME)
```

5. **Create schema**:

```
schema = client.create_schema(
    auto_id=False,
    enable_dynamic_field=True,
)
```

6. **Add fields to the schema**:

```
schema.add_field(
    field_name="id", datatype=DataType.INT64,
    is_primary=True, auto_id=True)
schema.add_field(
    field_name="filepath", datatype=DataType.VARCHAR,
    max_length=256)
schema.add_field(
    field_name="image_embedding",
    datatype=DataType.FLOAT_VECTOR, dim=DIMENSION)
```

7. **Prepare index parameters**:

```
index_params = client.prepare_index_params()
index_params.add_index(
    field_name="image_embedding",
    index_type="FLAT",
    index_name="vector_index",
```

```
    metric_type="COSINE"
)
```

8. **Create a collection with the index loaded simultaneously**:

```
client.create_collection(
    collection_name=COLLECTION_NAME,
    schema=schema,
    index_params=index_params
)
res = client.get_load_state(
    collection_name=COLLECTION_NAME
)
print(res)
```

9. **Set model**: The following code is used to load the pre-trained `ResNet50` model, remove its last layer, and set the model to evaluation mode. This process repurposes the pre-trained model as a feature extractor. The `torchvision.transforms` module is used to define the image preprocessing pipeline, which converts images into a format suitable for input to the pre-trained model.

> Note
>
> **Residual Network with 50 layers (ResNet-50)** is a classic deep CNN model that is primarily used for image classification and computer vision tasks. If you want to learn more about the ResNet50 model, refer to this article: `https://wisdomml.in/understanding-resnet-50-in-depth-architecture-skip-connections-and-advantages-over-other-networks/`.

```
import torch
from torchvision import transforms

# Load the embedding model with the last layer removed
model = torch.hub.load(
    'pytorch/vision:v0.10.0', 'resnet50', pretrained=True)
model = torch.nn.Sequential(*(list(model.children())[:-1]))
model.eval()

# Preprocessing for images
```

```
preprocess = transforms.Compose([
    transforms.Resize(256),
    transforms.CenterCrop(224),
    transforms.ToTensor(),
    transforms.Normalize(mean=[0.485, 0.456, 0.406],
        std=[0.229, 0.224, 0.225]),
    ])
```

10. **Extract image embeddings and insert data**: In the previous steps, we downloaded `reverse_image_search.zip` and extracted it into the current directory. Now, we can iterate through all the `.JPEG` files in the `./data/train` directory, use the model set up in the previous step to extract feature vectors, and insert them into Milvus according to the data format defined in the collection schema:

```
import glob from PIL import Image from tqdm import tqdm
```

11. **Embed a function that embeds the batch and inserts it**:

```
def embed(data_array):
    with torch.no_grad():
        output = model(
            torch.stack(data_array[0])).squeeze().tolist()
        data = [
            {"filepath": data_array[1][i],
                "image_embedding": output[i]
            } for i in range(len(data_array[0]))
        ]
        client.insert(collection_name=COLLECTION_NAME, data=data)
data_batch = [[], []]
```

12. **Get the** `filepaths` **of the images**:

```
paths = glob.glob(
    './data/train/**/*.JPEG', recursive=True) len(paths)
```

13. **Read the images into batches for embedding and insertion**:

```
for path in tqdm(paths):
    im = Image.open(path).convert('RGB')
    data_batch[0].append(preprocess(im))
```

```
        data_batch[1].append(path)
        if len(data_batch[0]) % BATCH_SIZE == 0:
            embed(data_batch)
            data_batch = [[], []]
```

14. **Embed and insert the remainder**:

```
    if len(data_batch[0]) != 0:
        embed(data_batch)
```

Extracting feature vectors from images can be time-consuming and may take approximately 1 to 2 minutes.

15. **Execute image search**: After all the image data is inserted into Milvus, you can proceed with the search. In this example, we will search for two sample images. The images to be searched are converted into vector embeddings using the same model and then passed as input to Milvus for the search request. The search results include the image IDs, distances, and storage paths of the images.

16. **Embed the search images**:

```
    def embed(data):
        with torch.no_grad():
            ret = model(torch.stack(data))
            # If more than one image, use squeeze
            if len(ret) > 1:
                return ret.squeeze().tolist()
            # Squeeze would remove batch for single image, so using flatten
            else:
                return torch.flatten(ret, start_dim=1).tolist()
    data_batch = [[], []]
```

17. **Get the file paths of the search images**:

```
    search_paths = glob.glob(
        './data/test/goblet/*.JPEG', recursive=True)
    len(search_paths)
    for path in search_paths:
        im = Image.open(path).convert('RGB')
        data_batch[0].append(preprocess(im))
        data_batch[1].append(path)
    embeds = embed(data_batch[0])
```

```
res = client.search(
    collection_name=COLLECTION_NAME,
    data=embeds,
    anns_field='image_embedding',
    limit=TOP_K,
    output_fields=['filepath']
)
print(res)
```

18. **Show search result**: Use the following code to display the search results:

```
# Show the image results
f, axarr = plt.subplots(
    len(data_batch[1]), TOP_K + 1, figsize=(20, 10), squeeze=False)
for hits_i, hits in enumerate(res):
    axarr[hits_i][0].imshow(Image.open(data_batch[1][hits_i]))
    axarr[hits_i][0].set_axis_off()
    for hit_i, hit in enumerate(hits):
        axarr[hits_i][hit_i + 1].imshow(
            Image.open(hit['entity']['filepath']))
        axarr[hits_i][hit_i + 1].set_axis_off()
        axarr[hits_i][hit_i + 1].set_title(
            'Distance: ' + str(hit['distance']))
```

19. **Save the search results in a separate image file alongside your script**:

```
plt.savefig('search_result.png')
```

The query results are shown in the following figure:

Figure 17.3: Query results for image search

The first image is the queried image, and the following three images are the query results. It is obvious that the last three images are similar to the first one. The vector distance between the query results and the queried image embeddings is displayed above the images. Since the COSINE metric type is used in Milvus, a larger distance value indicates higher similarity. Therefore, you can see that from the second image to the fourth image, the vector distance values gradually decrease, indicating that the similarity also gradually decreases.

As you can see, with Milvus, building an image search system is not difficult at all, is it?

The core principles behind this image search system prototype are **embedding vectorization** and **similarity search**; this is also the basic logic behind all recommendation systems. For example, image-based product search on e-commerce websites, news recommendations in news apps, and even plagiarism detection in academic papers all follow the same core technical process. First, domain-specific models are used to generate feature vectors, then efficient similarity matching is achieved through the nearest-neighbor search capabilities of a vector database, and finally, the results are filtered according to business rules.

Next, let's see how to quickly build a chatbot using Milvus and the popular LlamaIndex framework.

Building a chatbot with Milvus and LlamaIndex

RAG combines retrieval and generation to enhance the accuracy and efficiency of LLMs when handling complex tasks. During the retrieval phase, RAG first searches for the most relevant documents or information snippets from an external knowledge base based on the user's query. It then passes the retrieved information, along with the user's query, as context to the LLM to generate more accurate and relevant responses. This method is particularly suitable for tasks that require precise answers, such as question-and-answer systems, as it can leverage the rich information in the external knowledge base to compensate for the limitations of the language model's own knowledge.

> **Note**
>
> RAG narrows down the scope of generation through retrieval, which reduces the number of generated tokens. It allows large models to expand their knowledge without retraining, thereby shortening the deployment cycle. Therefore, RAG enhances the efficiency of LLMs.

LlamaIndex is currently one of the most popular data frameworks for connecting custom data sources to LLMs. This example demonstrates how to use Milvus as an external knowledge base and build a RAG system together with LlamaIndex.

The complete code is available in `https://github.com/PacktPublishing/The-Architecture-Handbook-for-Milvus-Vector-Database/blob/main/ch17/chatbot.ipynb`, which can be opened using Jupyter Notebook.

Let's build a chatbot:

1. **Prepare data**: Here, two documents are downloaded and placed in the data directory. The first document is a short essay titled "What I Worked On," written by the American computer scientist and writer Paul Graham. The second document consists of some financial agreements and regulatory clauses. These two documents have no content-related connections; they are simply used for demonstration purposes.

```
mkdir -p data
!wget https://raw.githubusercontent.com/run-llama/llama_index/main/docs/
docs/examples/data/paul_graham/paul_graham_essay.txt -O data/
paul_graham_essay.txt
!wget https://raw.githubusercontent.com/run-llama/llama_index/main/docs/
docs/examples/data/10k/uber_2021.pdf -O data/uber_2021.pdf
```

2. **Install dependencies**: `llama-index-vector-stores-milvus` is the vector store based on Milvus used by LlamaIndex:

```
pip install pymilvus llama-index-vector-stores-milvus llama-index
```

3. **Set OpenAI**: Set the OpenAI API key to allow us to access ChatGPT, because we use OpenAI's embedding model in this case:

```
import openai
openai.api_key = "Your Key"
```

4. **Read document**: As the first example, we use `SimpleDirectoryReader` to load the document, `./data/paul_graham_essay.txt`:

```
from llama_index.core import SimpleDirectoryReader
# Load documents
documents = SimpleDirectoryReader( input_files=["./data/
paul_graham_essay.txt"] ).load_data()
print("Document ID:", documents[0].doc_id)
```

We will get an output that is similar to this:

```
Document ID: 618ce01d-676f-45a3-bfd6-45be6c769f1f
```

5. **Create an index on the document data**: Now, we can create an index and insert the document. Here, we use `MilvusVectorStore` as the vector database, setting the vector dimension to `1536`, which is usually consistent with the output dimension of the embedding model:

```
# Create an index over the documents
from llama_index.core import VectorStoreIndex, StorageContext
from llama_index.vector_stores.milvus import MilvusVectorStore
vector_store = MilvusVectorStore(
    uri="./milvus_demo.db", dim=1536, overwrite=True)
storage_context = StorageContext.from_defaults(
    vector_store=vector_store)
index = VectorStoreIndex.from_documents(
    documents, storage_context=storage_context)
```

6. **Run a query**: Now that we have stored the document in the index, we can ask questions based on the index. The index will use its stored data as the knowledge base for ChatGPT to provide precise answers. The following three questions are all specific to the document `paul_graham_essay.txt`, and ChatGPT has provided precise answers based

on the information in the document. Please pay attention to the first question, which will be asked again in the subsequent demonstration:

```
query_engine = index.as_query_engine()
res = query_engine.query("What did the author like most before college?")
print(res)
# (The output looks like this) The author liked writing and programming the
most before college.

res = query_engine.query(" What made the author turn to AI during
college??")
print(res)
# (The output looks like this) The author turned to AI during college after
being inspired by a novel by Heinlein called The Moon is a Harsh Mistress,
which featured an intelligent computer called Mike, and a PBS documentary
that showed Terry Winograd using SHRDLU.
```

In this demonstration, we only loaded a single document. With the following code, we can load all documents in the directory `./data/` at once. Additionally, we specify `overwrite=True` in the parameters of `MilvusVectorStore` to overwrite and generate new data:

```
from llama_index.core.vector_stores import (
    ExactMatchFilter, MetadataFilters)

# Load all the two documents loaded before
documents_all = SimpleDirectoryReader("./data/").load_data()

vector_store = MilvusVectorStore(
    uri="./milvus_demo.db", dim=1536, overwrite=True)
storage_context = StorageContext.from_defaults(vector store=vector_store)
index = VectorStoreIndex.from_documents(documents_all, storage_context)
```

Metadata filtering

LlamaIndex supports generating results by filtering specific data sources. In the previous step, we loaded all the documents in the `./data/` directory. Now, let's intentionally specify an incorrect data source to see how ChatGPT responds.

`uber_2021.pdf` and `paul_graham_essay.txt` are completely unrelated in content. We deliberately specify `uber_2021.pdf` as the data source to test model's response. Since the answers to the questions here are not in the provided PDF files, the model starts to fabricate answers based on its pre-training, which is what we call the *hallucination* of the LLM:

```
filters = MetadataFilters(
    filters=[ExactMatchFilter(key="file_name", value="uber_2021.pdf")]
)
query_engine = index.as_query_engine(filters=filters)
res = query_engine.query("What did the author like most before college??")
print(res)
# (The output looks like this) The author liked participating in, administering,
and performing various financial activities before college.
```

We re-specify the correct data source, `paul_graham_essay.txt`, and ask ChatGPT to answer the question again:

```
filters = MetadataFilters(
    filters=[ExactMatchFilter(
        key="file_name", value="paul_graham_essay.txt")]
)
query_engine = index.as_query_engine(filters=filters)
res = query_engine.query("What did the author like most before college?")
print(res)
```

This time, we obtain the expected result, which is the same as the first time. The output is as follows:

```
The author liked writing and programming the most before college.
```

Let's try again with the next query:

```
res = query_engine.query("What made the author turn to AI during college?")
print(res)
```

Take a look at the output now:

```
The author turned to AI during college after finding philosophy courses boring and
being inspired by a novel featuring an intelligent computer called Mike, as well
as a PBS documentary showing Terry Winograd using SHRDLU.
```

Here, we have built a simple chatbot with just a few lines of Python code. It can analyze the information in the files we provide and answer our questions based on that information. In such a RAG system, Milvus, as the core vector retrieval engine, ensures both the real-time performance and the scalability and accuracy of the system.

Summary

In this chapter, we demonstrated two specific applications of Milvus in the AI field: building an image search system and constructing a question-answering robot with LlamaIndex. These examples showcase Milvus' powerful capabilities in handling unstructured data within AI applications. However, the use cases of Milvus extend far beyond these examples.

Milvus is a versatile vector database that can be applied across various domains. In natural language processing, Milvus enables semantic search by finding documents semantically similar to a query. For recommendation systems, it models user interests to provide personalized recommendations. In bioinformatics, Milvus accelerates biomedical research through gene sequence similarity searches. In the financial sector, Milvus assists in fraud detection systems by analyzing patterns in high-dimensional data vectors to identify suspicious activities.

As AI technologies continue to evolve, the applications of vector databases such as Milvus will become even more widespread and profound. From image and video analysis to speech recognition, and from NLP to complex system modelling, vector databases will play an essential role in driving the advancement of AI.

Get this book's PDF version and more

Scan the QR code (or go to `packtpub.com/unlock`). Search for this book by name, confirm the edition, and then follow the steps on the page.

UNLOCK NOW

Note: Keep your invoice handy. Purchases made directly from Packt don't require an invoice.

18

Unlock Your Exclusive Benefits

Your copy of this book includes the following exclusive benefits:

- Next-gen Packt Reader
- DRM-free PDF/ePub downloads

Follow the guide below to unlock them. The process takes only a few minutes and needs to be completed once.

Unlock this Book's Free Benefits in 3 Easy Steps

Step 1

Keep your purchase invoice ready for *Step 3*. If you have a physical copy, scan it using your phone and save it as a PDF, JPG, or PNG.

For more help on finding your invoice, visit `https://www.packtpub.com/unlock-benefits/help`.

> **Note**
>
> If you bought this book directly from Packt, no invoice is required. After *Step 2*, you can access your exclusive content right away.

Step 2

Scan the QR code or go to `packtpub.com/unlock`.

On the page that opens (similar to *Figure 18.1* on desktop), search for this book by name and select the correct edition.

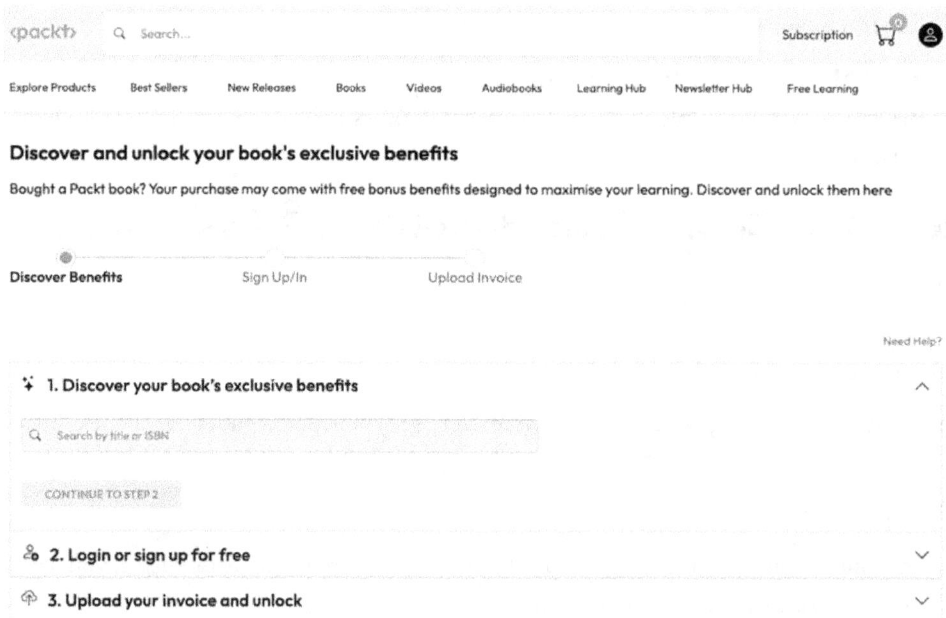

Figure 18.1: Packt unlock landing page on desktop

Step 3

After selecting your book, sign in to your Packt account or create one for free. Then upload your invoice (PDF, PNG, or JPG, up to 10 MB). Follow the on-screen instructions to finish the process.

Need help?

If you get stuck and need help, visit `https://www.packtpub.com/unlock-benefits/help` for a detailed FAQ on how to find your invoices and more. This QR code will take you to the help page.

Note

If you are still facing issues, reach out to `customercare@packt.com`

Stay Sharp in Cloud and DevOps – Join 44,000+ Subscribers of CloudPro

CloudPro is a weekly newsletter for cloud professionals who want to stay current on the fast-evolving world of cloud computing, DevOps, and infrastructure engineering.

Every issue delivers focused, high-signal content on topics like:

- AWS, GCP & multi-cloud architecture
- Containers, Kubernetes & orchestration
- **Infrastructure as Code** (**IaC**) with Terraform, Pulumi, etc.
- Platform engineering & automation workflows
- Observability, performance tuning, and reliability best practices

Whether you're a cloud engineer, SRE, DevOps practitioner, or platform lead, CloudPro helps you stay on top of what matters, without the noise.

Scan the QR code to join for free and get weekly insights straight to your inbox:

`https://packt.link/cloudpro`

Appendix

Throughout this book, we referred to the **K-nearest neighbor search** (**KNNS**) and **approximate nearest neighbor search** (**ANNS**). If you are new to these terms, we have specifically added this appendix to provide a more in-depth explanation of these two concepts to help you gain a deeper understanding of vector search.

This appendix will cover the following main topics:

- Introducing KNNS and ANNS
- Understanding ANNS-based algorithms

Introducing KNNS and ANNS

Let's start with KNNS.

KNNS

KNNS stands for **K-nearest neighbor search**, which is a general similarity search or classification algorithm, not specifically designed for the vector search domain. Its core idea is to "find the K most similar samples," which can be applied to various data types and scenarios with different implementations across different fields. Since this book mainly focuses on Milvus, which is oriented toward vector search, the KNNS and ANNS mentioned in this book specifically refer to the vector search domain.

The essence of KNNS is to use brute-force search to traverse and calculate the distances between the query point and all samples in the dataset, ultimately returning the *K* nearest samples. Here, "*K*" represents the number of nearest neighbors to be returned (for example, when *K*=3, it returns the top 3 most similar results). KNNS does not refer to a specific algorithm but is a general term for a class of methods that retrieve the *K* closest data points to a query. While brute-force KNNS computes full distances without index optimization, many optimized KNNS methods (e.g., KD-Tree and LSH) use advanced indexing to accelerate the search.

For example, consider a vector dataset containing 100 samples labeled $v_0, v_1, \cdots, v_{99}$. To find the three nearest neighbors to a query vector v_q using brute-force KNNS, the method would do the following.

First, it computes all pairwise distances between v_q and each sample:

$$D(v_q, v_0)$$

$$D(v_q, v_1)$$

$$\cdots$$

$$D(v_q, v_{99})$$

This requires 100 full-distance computations, generating 100 distance values.

Then, the system sorts these distances and selects the three closest values, identifying the corresponding vectors as v_q's nearest neighbors.

In *Chapter 10*, in the *Measuring performance of indexes* section, **the FLAT index**, **brute-force series**, and **GPU_RAFT_BRUTE_FORCE** are typical implementations of brute-force search algorithms on different hardware architectures.

The significant advantages of KNNS are its simplicity and accuracy. It requires no data preprocessing or model training, directly computing based on raw data, thus ensuring a 100% recall rate (i.e., completely accurate results). This characteristic makes it the gold standard for generating benchmark datasets' ground truth to evaluate the recall rate of ANNS algorithms, and it is often used in academic research or scenarios with extremely high precision requirements (such as pathological matching in medical diagnosis, which requires domain-specific distance metrics). However, the limitations of KNNS are also very evident. Its time complexity for each query is O(dN), where *d* is the vector dimension and *N* is the data volume. On a typical x86 server configuration, when the data scale reaches the level of millions, and the dimension exceeds hundreds, the computation time may reach minutes or even hours. Therefore, KNNS is usually only suitable for small-scale (less than 1,00,000 data points) and low-dimensional (less than 100 dimensions) scenarios, or as a benchmark tool for verifying the recall rate of other indexing algorithms.

Next, we will talk about ANNS.

ANNS

ANNS stands for **approximate nearest neighbor search**. It does not refer to a specific algorithm but is a general term for a class of techniques that improve search efficiency through controllable precision loss. These techniques mainly include two major categories: indexing algorithms and vector quantization methods. Since exact search (KNNS) of high-dimensional vectors is too costly, the ANNS technology has been most deeply developed and applied in the field of vector retrieval. Therefore, in both academia and industry, "ANNS" is usually closely associated with "vector retrieval."

Unlike KNNS, ANNS does not rely on full computation but reduces search complexity significantly by constructing index structures (such as clustering, graphs, etc.) and using quantization techniques to partition or reduce the dimensionality of high-dimensional spaces. For example, the **hierarchical navigable small world** (**HNSW**) algorithm achieves efficient search by constructing a multi-layer graph structure, while **product quantization** (**PQ**) reduces the computational load through vector compression techniques.

The core value of ANNS lies in balancing efficiency and precision. Typical algorithms can achieve millisecond-level response times for large-scale data while maintaining a recall rate of over 90%. This characteristic enables it to support practical applications such as e-commerce recommendations and image retrieval. However, ANNS requires index construction time, which is proportional to the volume of data. The dynamic data updates also pose challenges for index rebuilding. Additionally, ANNS usually has a false negative rate of 1–10%, so it should still be used with caution in scenarios with absolutely strict precision requirements.

To help you build a basic understanding, the following sections will focus on introducing the most representative IVF and HNSW indexing algorithms, as well as the two most commonly used quantization methods, **scalar quantization** (**SQ**) and PQ.

We will first talk about indexing algorithms.

Understanding ANNS indexing algorithms

The technical solutions for implementing ANNS mainly include two major approaches: indexing algorithms and vector quantization.

After decades of development and evolution, the field of vector search has seen the emergence of a variety of distinctive indexing algorithms, which mainly include the following:

- Clustering-based algorithms (e.g., IVF)
- Graph-based algorithms (e.g., HNSW and NSG)
- Tree-based algorithms (e.g., ANNOY)
- Locality-sensitive hashing-based algorithms (e.g., LSH)

These algorithms have undergone a process of natural selection in industrial practice: some algorithms have been eliminated due to insufficient performance or low recall rates, while others have been restricted in their widespread application due to overly complex parameters. Ultimately, IVF and HNSW have become the mainstream choices in the industry due to their excellent performance and engineering practicability.

Let's first talk about indexing algorithms. First up is the IVF algorithm.

IVF algorithm

The **inverted file index** (**IVF**) algorithm is an efficient clustering-based ANNS algorithm. Its core idea is to divide the high-dimensional vector space into multiple non-overlapping regions through clustering. Each region is called a **cluster**, and each cluster has a corresponding centroid.

You can imagine the entire vector space as a vast music library, where each cluster is like a thematic section in the library, and the centroid is the representative feature of each section. For example, in a music recommendation platform that stores 1 million songs, each song is represented by a 128-dimensional feature vector. During the training phase, the algorithm uses clustering methods such as K-means to divide these feature vectors into `nlist` different groups, resulting in `nlist` centroids. Each centroid represents the common features of the songs in that group, such as "classical," "pop," or "light music."

During the allocation phase, each vector in the dataset is assigned to the cluster whose centroid is closest to it, meaning each vector belongs to only one cluster. This process is similar to strictly categorizing songs into the most matching music style sections.

When querying, the system first calculates the distance between the query vector and all centroids, then selects the *nprobe* nearest clusters (usually `nprobe << nlist`, for example, `nprobe = 8` or `16`, `nlist = 1024`), and then performs a search only within these clusters, calculating the distances between the query vector and all vectors within the clusters. The final result returns the **K** nearest results. This two-stage search strategy reduces the complexity from `O(N)` to `O (nlist + N * nprobe / nlist)`, where `nlist` is the number of clusters and *N* is the total amount of data.

The core parameters of the IVF index are as follows:

- **nlist**: This is the construction parameter that controls the number of clusters and affects the granularity of the index and memory usage.
- **nprobe**: This is the query parameter that controls the number of clusters to search during the query process, directly impacting search speed and recall rate. The larger the `nprobe` value, the slower the query speed but the higher the recall rate. When `nprobe` equals `nlist`, the IVF algorithm degrades to a brute-force search.

Additionally, during querying, the *k* parameter (the number of nearest neighbors to return) must be specified. However, this is a general parameter for ANNS algorithms and not unique to IVF. It is important to note that the performance of IVF depends on the data distribution. If some clusters are too large or too small after clustering, it may lead to unbalanced search efficiency. However, in practical applications, by reasonably setting `nlist` and `nprobe`, IVF can achieve efficient approximate search in large-scale vector retrieval.

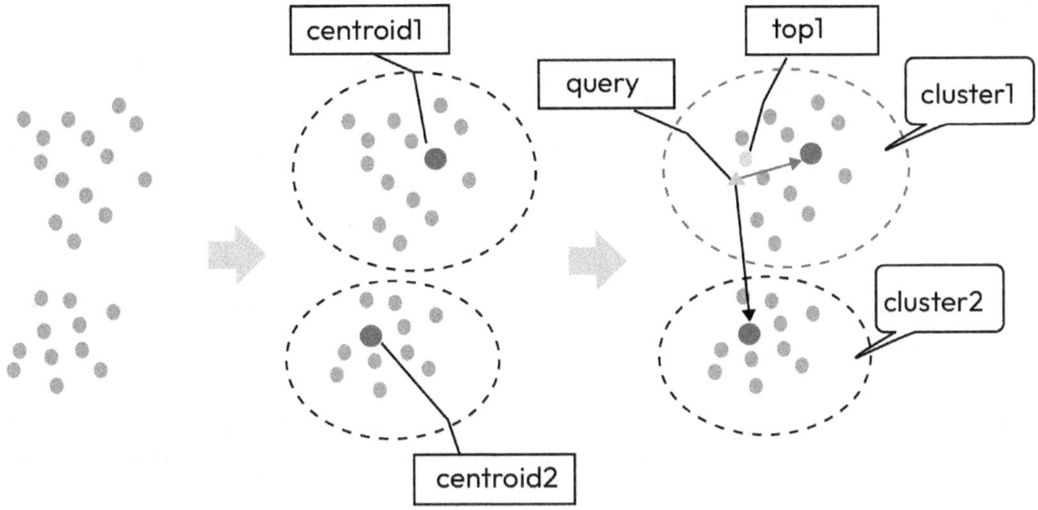

Figure 1: IVF algorithm

This figure should help you better understand the IVF algorithm. In *Figure 1*, each point on the far left represents a vector in a two-dimensional space. These two-dimensional vectors are divided into two clusters (`nlist=2`) through K-means clustering, with centroids labeled as `centroid1` and `centroid2`. Each vector is hard-assigned to the cluster whose centroid is closest (e.g., `cluster1` or `cluster2`).

When executing a query with `nprobe=1`, the IVF algorithm performs in two sequential phases:

- **Coarse search stage**: The distance between the query and the two centroids is calculated, and the closest `centroid1` value is selected
- **Fine search**: The distances between the query and all vectors within `cluster1` are calculated, and the nearest neighbors within the cluster are returned

Since `nprobe=1`, the algorithm may miss the true nearest neighbors (e.g., points near the boundary of `cluster2`). Increasing `nprobe` can improve the recall rate but will increase the computation time.

> **Note**
>
> The choice of `nprobe` depends on the level of recall that you desire.

We will now discuss the HNSW algorithm.

HNSW algorithm

The HNSW algorithm is an efficient graph-based ANNS algorithm that constructs a hierarchical structure to enable fast approximate nearest neighbor searches.

The core principle of HNSW is to build a multi-layered graph where each layer serves a different purpose. The top layers contain fewer nodes with long-range connections, facilitating rapid navigation, while the bottom layers have more nodes with short-range connections, enabling precise searches.

When inserting a new node, HNSW probabilistically determines the highest layer in which the node will appear (e.g., Layer 3). The node is then automatically added to all lower layers (Layer 2, Layer 1, and Layer 0). In each layer, the algorithm finds the M nearest neighbors for the new node and establishes bidirectional connections. This connection strategy not only considers distance but also optimizes the overall network structure to prevent clustering or isolation of nodes, ensuring efficient navigation.

When searching with the HNSW algorithm, the process begins at a single-entry node in the top layer and proceeds as follows:

1. Starting from the current candidate node, the algorithm explores its neighboring nodes and calculates their distances to the query vector.
2. A dynamic priority queue (with a length of `ef`) is maintained, which always keeps the `ef` nearest nodes discovered so far.
3. When no closer nodes than those in the queue can be found in the current layer (i.e., the queue stabilizes), the algorithm moves down to the next lower layer and continues the search.
4. Once the search reaches the bottom layer (Layer 0), the k nearest nodes in the priority queue are returned as the final approximate nearest neighbors.

This hierarchical search strategy allows HNSW to efficiently navigate through the multi-layered graph structure, combining coarse and fine searches to balance speed and accuracy.

The HNSW algorithm has three key parameters:

- `M`: This is the construction parameter that controls the maximum number of connections each node can have in the graph. A higher value of `M` makes the graph denser, which improves search precision by providing more pathways for the search to explore. However, it also increases memory usage and slows down index construction.
- `efConstruction`: This is another construction parameter that determines the number of candidate neighbors explored when inserting a node into the graph. A higher

`efConstruction` value leads to a better-optimized graph structure, improving recall and search efficiency. However, it significantly increases the time required to build the index.

- `ef`: This is the query parameter that controls the size of the candidate queue during search queries. A higher `ef` value increases recall by considering more candidates, but it also slows down query speed due to additional distance computations.

By leveraging this hierarchical navigation mechanism, HNSW achieves near-logarithmic time complexity in high-dimensional vector searches, making it suitable for large-scale similarity search scenarios.

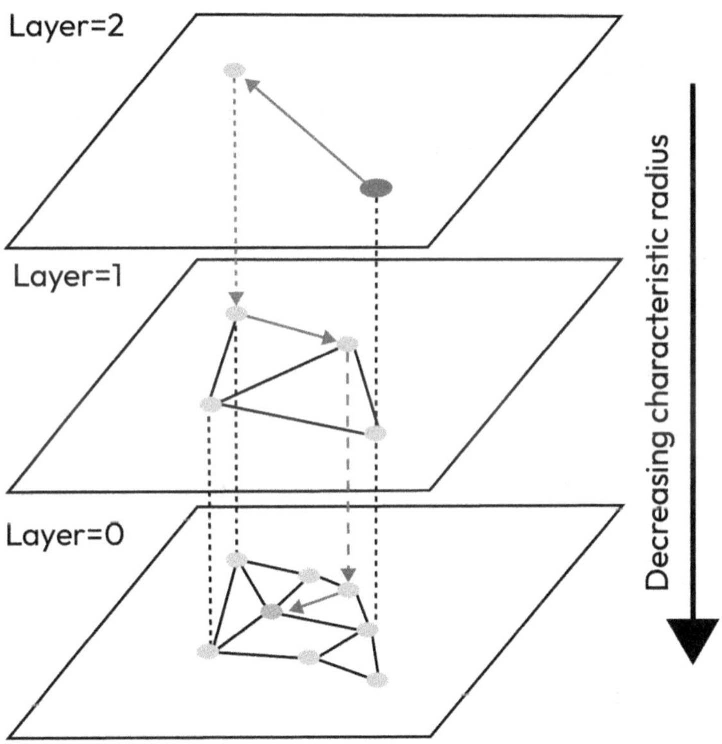

Figure 2: HNSW algorithm

Figure 2 shows a three-layer HNSW network structure diagram, where each layer is an independent small-world network structure. Layer 2 has the fewest nodes with the largest distance span between them. The lower the layer, the more nodes there are, and the shorter the distance between them. The highest layer to which each node belongs is determined by a randomized algorithm. Nodes in the upper layers must also exist in all lower layers (for example, the two nodes in Layer 2 must also be present in Layer 1 and Layer 0, and the four nodes in Layer 1 must also be present in Layer 0).

During querying, the algorithm starts from a random node in the highest Layer 2 (or a fixed entry point), explores its neighboring nodes, and calculates their distances to the query vector. When no closer unvisited nodes than those in the priority queue can be found in the current local region of that layer, the algorithm descends to the next lower layer to continue the search. After completing the search in the bottom layer (Layer 0), the *k* nearest nodes in the priority queue are returned as the final ANN results.

Let's now shift our focus to quantization techniques.

Understanding ANNS quantization techniques

Vector quantization is a data compression technique that maps high-dimensional vectors to a finite discrete codebook, preserving key features of the vectors in a lossy manner. It can improve storage efficiency and reduce computational complexity in similarity calculations. There are many popular approaches to vector quantization, such as SQ, PQ, **product residual quantization** (**PRQ**), and **random bit quantization** (**RaBitQ**).

We will talk about SQ and PQ in this section.

Scalar quantization

SQ is a data compression technique that is particularly suitable for processing vector data. In ANNS algorithms, SQ is often used to reduce storage requirements and improve search speed. Specifically, SQ refers to converting a floating-point number (usually a 32-bit float) into a smaller data type. Here are some examples:

- Quantizing a float to a 4-bit unsigned integer (with a range of 0 to 15), which is typically denoted as SQ4 (or SQ4bit)
- Quantizing a float to an 8-bit unsigned integer (with a range of 0 to 255), which is typically denoted as SQ8 (or SQ8bit)

This process typically involves the following steps:

1. **Defining the quantization range**: Determine the numerical range, usually based on the minimum and maximum values of each dimension of the vectors.
2. **Quantization mapping**: Linearly map the continuous values within the range to discrete quantized values, then round to the nearest integer.
3. **Quantization decoding**: Convert the quantized integer values back to floating-point numbers through an inverse linear transformation (the decoded values are approximations and contain quantization loss).

SQ has only one control parameter, `nbits`, which specifies the number of quantization bits (such as 4 or 8 bits) and determines the precision and storage overhead.

Let's illustrate the process of SQ with a concrete example.

Suppose we have a four-dimensional floating-point vector, for example, `[0.1, 0.2, 0.5, 1.0]`, and we need to scalar quantize it into 4-bit unsigned integers. We would take the following steps:

1. **Define the quantization range**: The minimum value in the vector is `0.1`, and the maximum value is `1.0`. The quantization range is defined as `[0.1, 1.0]`.
2. **SQ**: The offset is the minimum value of the range, which is `0.1`. The step value is calculated using the following formula:

   $$step = \frac{(val_{max} - val_{min})}{(quant_{max} - quant_{min})} = \frac{1.0 - 0.1}{15 - 0} = 0.06$$

   The specific mapping (rounding to the nearest integer) is as follows:

   - $0.1 \rightarrow (0.1 - 0.1)/0.06 \approx 0$
   - $0.2 \rightarrow (0.2 - 0.1)/0.06 \approx 2$
   - $0.5 \rightarrow (0.5 - 0.1)/0.06 \approx 7$
   - $1.0 \rightarrow (1.0 - 0.1)/0.06 \approx 15$

   The corrected quantized result should be `[0, 2, 7, 15]`.
3. **Dequantization**: The decoding formula is as follows:

   $$quant\_val \times step + offset$$

   In *Step 2*, we quantized the floating-point values of each dimension in the original vector into 8-bit integers: `[0, 2, 7, 15]`. Now we can use this formula to dequantize each of these 8-bit integers back to floating-point numbers:

   - $0 \rightarrow 0 \times 0.06 + 0.1 = 0.1$
   - $2 \rightarrow 2 \times 0.06 + 0.1 = 0.22$
   - $7 \rightarrow 7 \times 0.06 + 0.1 = 0.52$
   - $15 \rightarrow 15 \times 0.06 + 0.1 = 1.0$

   The decoded result is `[0.1, 0.22, 0.52, 1.0]`.

The main advantage of SQ is that it is very simple and easy to implement, while significantly reducing storage requirements. Here are some examples:

- Quantizing a 32-bit floating-point number to an 8-bit integer (SQ8) can achieve a compression ratio of 25% (8/32)
- Quantizing a 32-bit floating-point number to a 4-bit integer (SQ4) can achieve a compression ratio of 12.5% (4/32)

Of course, this type of quantization introduces precision loss because the original values are approximated to a limited number of discrete values, which can lead to a decrease in search precision (such as in distance calculations). In some cases (such as building an `IVF_SQ8` index), SQ can effectively balance storage efficiency and search precision. By optimizing the quantization parameters, the loss of precision can be controlled within an acceptable range.

Next up is PQ.

Product quantization

PQ is another efficient vector compression technique, primarily used for vector quantization in high-dimensional spaces. It significantly reduces data storage and search time while maintaining relatively high retrieval accuracy.

The core idea of PQ is to divide the high-dimensional space into multiple low-dimensional subspaces and then perform independent clustering and quantization in each subspace. While SQ quantizes each dimension of a vector independently, PQ segments the vector into multiple subspaces and performs vector quantization on each subspace separately.

Here are the specific steps to follow:

1. **Vector decomposition**: Split the high-dimensional vector into M sub-vectors (e.g., a 128-dimensional vector is divided into M=16 sub-vectors of 8 dimensions each; each such 8-dimensional sub-vector set is referred to as a "subspace"). Typically, M is set to 8, 16, or 32.
2. **Subspace clustering**: Instead of clustering the full high-dimensional vector, we independently cluster each decomposed subspace. This reduces dimensionality and greatly speeds up both indexing and querying.
3. **Codebook generation**: Independently perform k-means clustering on each sub-vector space to generate codebooks (e.g., 256 centroids per subspace; each codeword is 8-bit).
4. **Sub-vector assignment**: Map each sub-vector to the nearest centroid (codeword) in its corresponding subspace.

5. **Quantization encoding**: The original vector is represented as a concatenation of *M* codeword indices (e.g., 16 subspaces × 8-bit indices = 16 bytes total).
6. **Query processing**: The query vector is decomposed and quantized in the same manner. The distance is approximated by table lookup (using precomputed inter-cluster distances) or by dequantization, which introduces some precision loss but is much more efficient than computing the exact distance.

PQ has two control parameters:

- `m`: The number of subspaces the original vector is divided into (must be a divisor of the vector dimension). For example, for a 128-dimensional vector with `m = 16`, each subspace is 8-dimensional.
- `nbits`: Determines the number of cluster centers (codebook size) for each subspace, satisfying *K = 2^nbits*. The following are examples:
    - (`nbits = 4`) ⟶ 16 cluster centers per subspace
    - (`nbits = 8`) ⟶ 256 cluster centers per subspace

In practical applications, `nbits` is usually set to `8` (256 centers per subspace) because it can be directly stored using 1 byte.

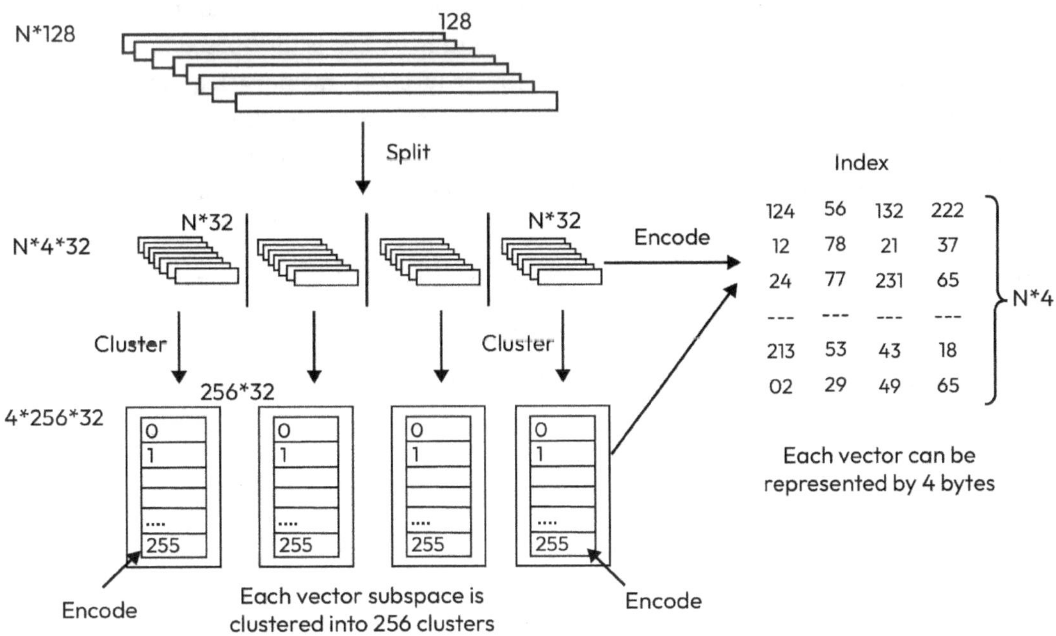

Figure 3: Product quantization

Figure 3 should help you understand the basic principles of PQ.

As shown in *Figure 3*, there are *N* rows of 128-dimensional vectors, which are divided into 4 subspaces (*m = 4*), each with 32 dimensions. K-means clustering is applied to each subspace (illustrated as clustering into 256 classes in the figure), generating a corresponding codebook. At this point, note the following:

- The original values of each sub-vector are replaced with the ID of the nearest cluster center (must satisfy *K = 2^nbits* with *nbits = 8*).
- Each original vector is represented by the IDs of the four subspaces (each ID occupies 1 byte), with a total of 4 bytes (the original 128-dimensional float occupies 512 bytes, resulting in a compression ratio of 4/512 = 0.78%).
- During decoding, for each ID value, the corresponding codeword (cluster center vector) is retrieved from the associated codebook, and the *M* codeword vectors are concatenated to reconstruct the decoded vector.
- The substantial precision loss caused by PQ's aggressive compression makes it unsuitable for standalone use in high-recall scenarios. Therefore, in real-world systems, PQ is primarily deployed as a **coarse retrieval** component, integrated with graph traversal methods (e.g., DiskANN) or exact search for subsequent reranking.

With the rapid development of ANNS technology, new algorithms and quantization methods are constantly emerging. For example, the DiskAnn algorithm, which is disk-based, may not match the performance of HNSW but can significantly reduce the memory requirements of the algorithm. Another recent technology is the RaBitQ quantization method, which can further increase the data compression rate while maintaining a certain level of query precision. For brevity, this appendix will not introduce each of these new algorithms and quantization methods in detail.

You may refer to the following resources if you need to further explore these algorithms:

- **DiskANN**: `https://github.com/microsoft/DiskANN`
- **RaBitQ**: `https://github.com/gaoj0017/RaBitQ`

Subscribe for a free e-book

New frameworks, evolving architectures, research drops, production breakdowns—*AI_Distilled* filters the noise into a weekly briefing for engineers and researchers working hands-on with LLMs and generative AI systems. Subscribe now and receive a free e-book, along with weekly insights that help you stay focused and informed.

Subscribe at `https://packt.link/8Oz6Y` or scan the following QR code.

packtpub.com

Subscribe to our online digital library for full access to over 7,000 books and videos, as well as industry leading tools to help you plan your personal development and advance your career. For more information, please visit our website.

Why subscribe?

- Spend less time learning and more time coding with practical eBooks and Videos from over 4,000 industry professionals
- Improve your learning with Skill Plans built especially for you
- Get a free eBook or video every month
- Fully searchable for easy access to vital information
- Copy and paste, print, and bookmark content

At `www.packtpub.com`, you can also read a collection of free technical articles, sign up for a range of free newsletters, and receive exclusive discounts and offers on Packt books and eBooks.

Other Books You May Enjoy

If you enjoyed this book, you may be interested in these other books by Packt:

Agentic Architectural Patterns for Building Multi-Agent Systems

Dr. Ali Arsanjani, Juan Pablo Bustos

ISBN: 9781806029570

- Apply design patterns to handle instruction drift, improve coordination, and build fault-tolerant AI systems
- Design systems with the three layers of the agentic stack: function calling, tool protocols (MCP), and A2A collaboration
- Develop responsible, ethical, and governable GenAI applications
- Use frameworks such as ADK, LangGraph, and CrewAI with code examples
- Master prompt engineering, LLMOps, and AgentOps best practices
- Build agentic systems using RAG, fine-tuning, and in-context learning

Unlocking Data with Generative AI and RAG

Keith Bourne

ISBN: 9781806381654

- Architect graph-powered RAG agents with ontology-driven knowledge bases
- Build semantic caches to improve response speed and reduce hallucinations
- Code memory pipelines for working, episodic, semantic, and procedural recall
- Implement agentic learning using LangMem and prompt optimization strategies
- Integrate retrieval, generation, and consolidation for self-improving agents
- Design caching and memory schemas for scalable, adaptive AI systems
- Use Neo4j, LangChain, and vector databases in production-ready RAG pipelines

Packt is searching for authors like you

If you're interested in becoming an author for Packt, please visit `authors.packt.com` and apply today. We have worked with thousands of developers and tech professionals, just like you, to help them share their insight with the global tech community. You can make a general application, apply for a specific hot topic that we are recruiting an author for, or submit your own idea.

Share your thoughts

Once you've read *The Architecture Handbook for Milvus Vector Database*, we'd love to hear your thoughts! Scan the QR code below to go straight to the Amazon review page for this book and share your feedback.

https://packt.link/r/1835881718

Your review is important to us and the tech community and will help us make sure we're delivering excellent quality content.

Index

E

F

G

N

www.ingramcontent.com/pod-product-compliance
Lightning Source LLC
LaVergne TN
LVHW060016210926
848481LV00013B/3720
* 9 7 8 1 8 3 5 8 8 1 7 0 5 *